FREE TRADE
UNDER FIRE

D0377225

Princeton University Press   *Princeton and Oxford*

FREE TRADE
UNDER FIRE

FOURTH EDITION

DOUGLAS A. IRWIN

Copyright © 2015 by Princeton University Press

Published by Princeton University Press, 41 William Street, Princeton, New Jersey 08540

In the United Kingdom: Princeton University Press, 6 Oxford Street, Woodstock, Oxfordshire OX20 1TW

press.princeton.edu

Cover photograph: Protestors demonstrate against the World Trade Organization gathering, Seattle, February 22, 2002. © Christopher J. Morris/Corbis.

All Rights Reserved

Library of Congress Control Number 2015936929
ISBN 978-0-691-16625-4

British Library Cataloging-in-Publication Data is available

This book has been composed in ITC Garamond Light and Frutiger

Printed on acid-free paper. ∞

Printed in the United States of America

10 9 8 7 6 5 4 3 2 1

FOR THE DARTMOUTH STUDENTS OF ECONOMICS 39

Contents

Figures

_____Tables

_____Preface

In his 2014 State of the Union address, President Barack Obama asked Congress to give his administration special authority to conclude agreements that would reduce trade barriers with the European Union and Pacific Rim countries. The next day Senate Majority leader Harry Reid, a Democrat from Nevada, announced his opposition to this request. "I think everyone would be well advised just not to push this right now," he stated. A few days later, Nancy Pelosi, the Democratic minority leader in the House of Representatives, agreed, saying that the president's request was "out of the question."

In his 2015 State of the Union address, President Obama repeated his plea. "Look, I'm the first one to admit that past trade deals haven't always lived up to the hype," he said, "but 95 percent of the world's customers live outside our borders, and we can't close ourselves off from those opportunities." Once again, Democrats in Congress demurred. Rep. Peter DeFazio (D-OR) said he couldn't support "another job-killing, job-exporting free trade agreement identical to the ones pushed by [former Presidents Bill] Clinton and [George W.] Bush." "These trade deals make it much easier for corporations to send American jobs overseas," complained Rep. Rosa DeLauro (D-CT). Why have top Democrats in Congress been so dismissive of a request coming from a Democratic president?

This episode was a simple reminder that trade policy always and inevitably generates controversy. Simply put, free trade is always under fire. These congressional leaders were simply warning, correctly, that new efforts to expand world trade would generate significant opposition in the House and Senate. That has always been the case, but the nature of the controversy and the arguments about trade have nevertheless changed over time.

This book aims to introduce the reader to some basic economic principles and empirical evidence regarding international trade and trade policy so that we can better understand this controversy. The first edition of this book was published in 2002, shortly after huge anti-globalization protests rocked Seattle during the 1999 World Trade Organization (WTO) meeting there. Protesters demonstrated against the WTO and its potential impact on national sovereignty and environmental regulations, but the anti-globalization movement all but disappeared after the terrorist attacks of September 11, 2001. Then, in the mid-2000s, the American public began to fear the offshoring of service-sector jobs to India and the loss of manufacturing jobs to China. Just as these fears were peaking, the global financial crisis of 2008 struck and the volume of world trade plummeted 12 percent in 2009. Economists and policymakers worried that the Great Recession could lead to a protectionist response like that seen during the Great Depression of the 1930s, but were surprised when trade policies remained relatively open. As world trade recovered, the issue of income inequality came to the forefront of public discussions. Consequently, the concern that trade with low-wage developing countries (such as China) has eroded the American middle class once again received attention.

This fourth edition of *Free Trade under Fire* has been updated to deal with a host of new developments, ranging from protectionism and the Great Recession to the latest evidence on trade, wages, and jobs. As noted in the first edition, this book draws upon the vast amount of economic research on international trade policy that lends insight into these issues. As before, I wish to acknowledge all of the scholars who have made contributions to this field in recent years. In addition to those mentioned in previous editions, I would particularly like to thank Chad Bown, Nina Pavcnik, and Robert Johnson for providing valuable advice on this edition. I am also indebted to Maha Malik, Andres Isaza, and Konrad von Moltke, my trustworthy Dartmouth research assistants, who helped with the preparation of this new edition. Thanks also go to Peter Dougherty and Seth Ditchik at Princeton University Press for their continued support of this ongoing project.

FREE TRADE
UNDER FIRE

Introduction

Free trade, one of the greatest blessings which a government can confer on a people, is in almost every country unpopular.
  —Thomas Babington Macaulay (1824)

Nearly two centuries after Macaulay made it, this observation by one of Britain's great historians still rings true. Growing world trade has helped lift standards of living around the world, and yet today, as in Macaulay's time, free trade does not win many popularity contests. Indeed, public opinion surveys in the United States and Europe reveal widespread skepticism about the benefits of international trade and trade agreements. Trade policy remains a highly controversial subject, a source of never-ending public debate.

In almost every country, international trade brings out anxieties and insecurities. With each passing decade, some of the old fears about trade recede and new ones take their place. In the 1980s, many Americans were convinced that Japan would achieve economic dominance by wiping out industry after industry in the United States, from automobiles to semiconductors to supercomputers, and thereby diminish America's position in the world. Such concerns vanished by the early 1990s when Japan entered a prolonged economic slump. But in 1993 fears arose that the North American Free Trade Agreement (NAFTA) would result in a "giant sucking sound" of jobs lost to Mexico due to its low wages. (We owe this memorable phrase to Texas billionaire and 1992 presidential candidate Ross Perot, who was a leading anti-NAFTA activist.) Then, in 1999, the streets of Seattle were filled with large protests against the World Trade Organization (WTO) for its promotion of free trade and alleged indifference to the world's workers and environment. Today, few Americans view Mexico as an economic threat or know or care about what the WTO does.

In the first decade of the twenty-first century, concern shifted to China. China has become a goliath in the production of manufactured goods, and—it is often argued—responsible for huge job losses in the United

States. Around the same time, the offshoring of white-collar jobs (from call centers to software programming) to India sparked new worries of a "service-sector sucking sound." While concerns about white-collar job loss due to foreign competition have receded, many still believe that China poses a serious threat to the American economy.[1]

These fears of trade exist in good times and in bad. The 1990s were a period of robust economic growth and the lowest U.S. unemployment in thirty years, yet NAFTA and actions taken by the WTO generated heated debates. And economic downturns invariably continue to bring out cries that foreign countries are stealing our jobs and therefore protectionist trade policies are required to protect American workers and the industries that employ them.

Even today, trade agreements reached decades ago are still very controversial. NAFTA was signed in 1993, more than twenty years ago, but during the 2008 Democratic primaries, Hillary Clinton called NAFTA a mistake and proposed a "time out" on further trade agreements. Meanwhile, to the consternation of Canada and Mexico, candidate Barack Obama promised to renegotiate the agreement. (In office, he wisely did no such thing.) NAFTA has left a bitter residue in American politics. "Outside of corporate boardrooms and D.C. think tanks, Americans view NAFTA as a symbol of job loss and a cancer on the middle class," said Lori Wallach, director of Public Citizen's Global Trade Watch.[2] This perception partly accounts for Congress's reluctance to embrace President Obama's goal of new trade agreements with Europe and the Pacific. In fact, in response to the president's 2015 plea for trade authority, Rep. Keith Ellison (D-MN), the chair of the House's progressive caucus, said, "I was looking for the president to explain to me why this is going to be different than the North American Free Trade Agreement of 1994."

Yet the NAFTA-bashing is somewhat puzzling because U.S. tariffs on imports from Mexico had been at very low levels for many decades prior to NAFTA; what NAFTA really did was abolish Mexico's high tariffs on U.S. exports to that country. Furthermore, NAFTA has contributed to the

---

[1] Perhaps not surprisingly, many people in Japan, Mexico, China, India, and the rest of the world have seen things very differently. They fear economic domination by the United States and wonder how local producers can ever compete against large, wealthy, and technologically sophisticated American companies.

[2] http://www.citizen.org/pressroom/pressroomredirect.cfm?ID=4086.

slow transformation of Mexico, helping it to become a modern economy that is integrated with the rest of the world. Since NAFTA passed, Mexico has become a multiparty democracy with a growing middle class, which has helped reduce pressures for illegal immigration into the United States.

Still, the many vociferous critics of free trade see only a policy that brings pervasive harm. A wide range of groups, from environmentalists to religious organizations to human rights activists, have joined in protesting against free trade. These groups rail against trade agreements and the WTO as benefiting corporations, harming workers, decimating manufacturing industries, sweeping aside environmental regulations, and undermining America's sovereignty.

In his book *Myths of Free Trade* (2006), Sen. Sherrod Brown, an Ohio Democrat writes, "An unregulated global economy is a threat to us all—to the child in Avon Lake, Ohio, who eats raspberries grown in Guatemala by poorly paid farmers who use pesticides banned in the United States; the unskilled, minimum wage worker in Los Angeles who loses her job to an unskilled, five-dollar-a-day worker in Yucatan; the machinist in New York who takes a wage cut because of his company's threat to move to China; the Chinese prison camp laborer; the tomato grower in Florida who has to sell his farm; and the peasant in Chiapas who must flee the native village where his family had made its home for dozens of generations. But our national leaders—particularly Republican congressional leaders and Presidents Clinton and Bush, economists and newspaper editors, business executives and tenured economics professors—continue to ignore the uncomfortable consequences of free trade, hoping the American public will not take notice."[3]

In an October 2014 op-ed in the *New York Times*, Jeff Madrick writes that "free trade creates winners and losers—and American workers have been among the losers." Free trade policies, he argues, have been a "major" factor in the erosion of wages and the loss of job security.[4]

Opponents of free trade are not confined to one segment of the political spectrum. From the Tea Party on the right to Naomi Klein on the left, trade skeptics can be found everywhere. And the litany of complaints placed on the doorstep of free trade goes well beyond the perennial

---

[3] Brown 2006, 4.

[4] Jeff Madrick, "Our Misplaced Faith in Free Trade," *New York Times*, October 3, 2014.

objection—emphasized regularly by most opponents to the current system—that trade forces painful economic adjustments such as plant closings and layoffs of workers. Liberal Ralph Nader charges that "the Fortune 200's GATT and NAFTA agenda would make the air you breathe dirtier, and the water you drink more polluted. It would cost jobs, depress wage levels, and make workplaces less safe. It would destroy family farms and undermine consumer protections." Conservative Patrick Buchanan chimes in with the claim that "broken homes, uprooted families, vanished dreams, delinquency, vandalism, crime—these are the hidden costs of free trade."[5] The group Public Citizen says that "the real-life devastation being caused by the implementation of the WTO's terms—and the growing social and political backlash this pain is generating worldwide—is the reason the WTO is wracked by the severe crisis that burst into view in Seattle and Cancún."[6]

Why is such hostility directed at free trade policies and the World Trade Organization? The rapid increase in international trade in recent decades may have unleashed a "globalization backlash." In this view, increased global integration has accelerated the pace of economic change and has brought with it painful economic adjustments. Meanwhile, the reach of world trade rules has gone beyond trade barriers to encompass internal regulatory policies regarding health, safety, and the environment. As a result, groups disturbed by these changes, whether directly in terms of their jobs or indirectly in terms of the community values they believe are at stake, have questioned the effects of global economic integration and the institutions associated with it. These groups have raised legitimate concerns about commerce and our local communities, and whether sovereignty has shifted from elected representatives at home to faceless and unaccountable bureaucrats abroad.

Clearly, the debate over trade policy remains intense and shows little prospect of abating. The debate has raised many fundamental questions. Why is free trade considered by some to be a desirable policy? Do the most frequently made criticisms of free trade, such as its adverse impact on employment and the environment, have merit? Do the circumstances of developing countries make free trade particularly undesirable for them?

---

[5] Nader 1993, 1. Buchanan 1998, 286.
[6] Wallach and Woodall 2004, 283.

What is the World Trade Organization, and do world trade rules erode a country's sovereignty and undermine its health and environmental regulations?

This book aims to address these basic questions and demystify some of the complex issues that arise in discussions of trade policy. These questions will be examined mainly through the lens of economics. Despite widespread skepticism about free trade among the public at large, economists generally take a positive view of international trade and believe that reducing government-imposed trade barriers is desirable. In the eyes of economists, trade between countries is usually mutually beneficial, just like the exchange of goods within a country, even though the goods happen to cross national boundaries. While some groups lose from trade, at least temporarily, people around the world are generally much better off with trade than they would be without it.

Trade skeptics often accuse economists of having a religious faith in free trade, of blindly clinging to the doctrine in the face of contrary evidence. In fact, the economic case for free trade is based not on faith, but on logic and evidence. As Paul Krugman has written, "The logic that says that tariffs and import quotas almost always reduce real income is deep and has survived a century and a half of often vitriolic criticism nearly intact. And experience teaches that governments that imagine or pretend that their interventionist strategies are a sophisticated improvement on free trade nearly always turn out, on closer examination, to be engaged in largely irrational policies—or worse, in policies that are rational only in the sense that they benefit key interest groups at the expense of everyone else."[7]

Still, the logic and evidence behind the case for free trade deserve to be put under searching scrutiny, as do the logic and evidence behind alternative policies. Even advocates of free trade need to be reminded of the case, lest they simply restate stale arguments that fail to persuade. As John Stuart Mill argued, "Even if the received opinion be not only true, but the whole truth; unless it is suffered to be, and actually is, vigorously and earnestly contested, it will, by most of those who receive it, be held in the manner of a prejudice, with little comprehension or feeling of its rational grounds." Consequently, "however true [a proposition] may be, if

[7] Krugman 1995, 31.

it is not fully, frequently, and fearlessly discussed, it will be held as a dead dogma, not a living truth."[8]

So the views of economists deserve critical scrutiny, but first they deserve a fair hearing. Economists have studied trade for a very long time and have noticed that the same worries and fears about trade tend to get repeated generation after generation. "With America's high standard of living, we cannot successfully compete against foreign producers because of lower foreign wages and a lower cost of production." This claim is heard today, but this particular quote comes from President Herbert Hoover in 1929 as he urged Congress to pass what became known as the Smoot-Hawley Tariff on the eve of the Great Depression. Among the claims heard yesterday and today is that trade will destroy jobs, leading to higher unemployment and lower wages, or that trade deficits will siphon away a country's wealth. To economists, these are economic fallacies that history and experience have refuted time and again. One observer has quipped that "free traders are trapped in a public policy version of [the movie] *Groundhog Day*, forced to refute the same fallacious arguments over and over again, decade after decade."[9] Or perhaps one could say that defending free trade is like playing the arcade game "Whac-a-Mole": when one argument is beaten down, another pops up in its place.

Chapter 1, "The United States in a New Global Economy?" sets out basic facts about international trade and the U.S. economy. World trade has expanded rapidly in recent years, and this development provides the context in which to consider the issue of trade policy. This chapter discusses the reasons for the increase in trade, how trade has changed with the fragmentation of production and the increase in trade of intermediate goods and components, and the state of public opinion on the question of globalization.

Chapter 2, "The Case for Free Trade: Old Theories, New Evidence," examines the economic logic of free trade and recent empirical evidence reinforcing the case for it. Ever since Adam Smith and David Ricardo described the gains from trade in a systematic way, economists have stressed the higher income that results from improved resource allocation as the main advantage of trade. But economists have discovered that

[8] Mill [1859] 1982, 116, 97.
[9] Sanchez 2003.

trade not only helps to allocate existing resources properly but also makes those resources more productive. These productivity gains from trade, overlooked in the standard calculations, appear to be substantial. The welfare benefits of a greater variety of products as a result of trade have also been ignored until recently, and yet a growing body of evidence suggests that they are also quite important.

Chapter 3, "Protectionism: Economic Costs, Political Benefits?" considers the flip side of the case for free trade—that trade interventions are usually misguided and often costly. Tariffs and quotas on imports redistribute income from consumers to producers, but do so inefficiently. That is, trade barriers produce a net economic loss because the costs to consumers far exceed the benefits to producers. In addition, trade barriers reduce exports and harm downstream user industries. The chapter also raises the question of why, despite its costs, trade protectionism is often politically attractive. Finally, the chapter examines situations in which protection may be justified in theory, even if governments are often inept in trying to take advantage of those situations.

Chapter 4, "Trade, Jobs, and Income Distribution," focuses on the most frequent argument in favor of limiting trade—that jobs will be saved in industries that compete against imports. As we shall see, reducing trade saves those jobs only by destroying jobs elsewhere in the economy. Opponents of free trade have also argued that imports have replaced good, high-wage jobs with bad, low-wage jobs. The truth turns out to be quite the opposite: jobs in industries that compete against imports are mainly low-skill and consequently low-wage jobs. This chapter also examines the extent to which trade with low-wage developing countries can be held responsible for the rise in economic inequality within the United States.

Chapter 5, "Relief from Foreign Competition: Antidumping and the Escape Clause," describes the legal framework that allow firms to petition the government for the imposition of tariffs on competing imports. The antidumping law is the most commonly used measure to block so-called unfair imports. The government's definition of "dumping" is a lower price charged in the United States than in a foreign exporter's home market, but it is not clear that this is a problem requiring trade restrictions, or that the government calculates the dumping margin in a fair manner. This chapter also examines the case for providing domestic industries with temporary relief from imports so that they can adjust to foreign competition.

Chapter 6, "Developing Countries and Open Markets," takes a look at the special circumstances of developing countries. Is free trade always beneficial in the case of poor countries? What type of trade policy is most likely to promote economic development? Did countries such as Japan and Korea grow rich by rejecting free trade and instead pursuing closed markets and industrial policies? The chapter also addresses the issue of fair trade and how rich-country agricultural subsidies and import tariffs harm developing countries, as well as how developing countries harm themselves with their own antitrade policies.

Chapter 7, "The World Trading System: The WTO, Trade Disputes, and Regional Agreements," focuses on the current controversies about the multilateral trading system, particularly the World Trade Organization. Since its inception, the WTO has come under intense criticism from nongovernmental organizations (NGOs), which attack it as an antidemocratic institution that has struck down domestic environmental regulations by ruling them inconsistent with world trade laws. This chapter examines the WTO's rules and dispute settlement system, as well as the environmental cases that have come before it. Finally, it considers the Doha Round of trade negotiations and the rise of regional trade arrangements such as NAFTA.

As Macaulay so aptly noted long ago, despite the palpable benefits of free trade, it is frequently the object of condemnation rather than approbation. That condemnation is often the result of misconceptions about the benefits of international trade, the impact of trade policies, and the role and function of the WTO. This book seeks to dispel these misconceptions and is offered in the modest hope that it may improve our understanding of the trade policy issues that confront us.

1

The United States in a New Global Economy?

International trade has become an integral part of the U.S. economy over the past few decades. The United States imports electronics from China, apparel from Mexico, oil from Saudi Arabia, and steel from Korea, and exports aircraft from Washington, wheat from Kansas, software from California, and machinery from Illinois. The United States sells financial and information-technology services to customers around the world and buys data entry, software programming, and call center services from India. There is hardly a sector of the economy or a region of the country that is unaffected by international markets. Over the past quarter century, the United States may even have achieved a historically unprecedented degree of economic integration with the rest of the world. Perhaps it is not surprising, therefore, that the rapid growth of trade has been accompanied by an intense debate over U.S. trade policy. To establish a context in which we can later examine trade policy issues, this chapter briefly looks at the role of trade in the U.S. economy.

The Increasing Importance of Trade

How important is trade in merchandise goods to the U.S. economy? The simplest way to answer this question is to look at its share in gross domestic product (GDP). In 2014, for example, exports of goods amounted to roughly $1.6 trillion, about 9.2 percent of GDP. At the same time, merchandise imports were almost $2.4 trillion, about 13.7 percent of GDP.[1]

---

[1] www.bea.gov (accessed January 30, 2015).

_____Figure 1.1

U.S. Merchandise Exports and Imports as a Percentage of GDP, 1870–2014

Sources: For 1929 to 2014, from Bureau of Economic Analysis. For GDP from 1869 to 1928, see Balke and Gordon 1998; and for merchandise trade information see U.S. Bureau of the Census 1975.

By looking at these numbers in a historical perspective, we can determine whether they are large or small. Figure 1.1 presents U.S. merchandise exports and imports as a share of GDP from 1870 to 2014. As the figure shows, merchandise trade was fairly stable at about 7 percent of GDP in the period just after the Civil War until the outbreak of World War I in 1914. Exports surged during the war, but the trade shares declined sharply during the period from 1919 to 1939 and on through World War II. Between the world wars, many countries pursued inward-looking economic policies, including protectionist trade policies, restrictions on international labor migration, and limitations on international capital flows. These policies substantially reduced world economic integration.[2] For about a quarter century after 1945, exports and imports remained lower than they had been prior to World War I. But as European and Asian countries began to recover from the war, and many of the trade barriers

[2] Estevadeordal, Frantz, and Taylor (2003) examine the reasons for the rise and fall of world trade over this period.

were gradually dismantled, trade began to rise in importance in the early 1970s. Further trade liberalization in the 1980s and 1990s, the opening of the previously closed economies of China and India, and technological improvements in shipping such as containerization, have pushed trade to record levels. By the early 2000s, the United States exceeded the degree of integration that prevailed before World War I.

Will the current trend toward a higher trade share continue? There is certainly no law in economics that dictates an inexorable rise in the ratio of trade to GDP over time. In fact, some economists, from Robert Torrens in the nineteenth century to Dennis Robertson in the twentieth century, expounded a "law of diminishing international trade." They believed that the spread of industrial technology around the world would result in smaller differences in industrial efficiency across countries. Each country would eventually come to produce manufactured goods just as efficiently as any other, and so international trade would diminish. But this theory has been proven false: over time, the division of labor in manufacturing and in other sectors has become more refined, increasing trade even between those countries with comparable technology. For example, the spread of industrial technology has enabled an increasing number of countries to produce automobiles. Rather than reducing international trade in cars, this development has stimulated a large amount of trade in automobile products, especially parts and components.

A more plausible version of the idea of diminishing international trade is that the trade share would fall as countries grew richer, because the composition of demand would shift away from traded goods (such as food, clothing, and manufactures) toward nontraded goods (such as housing, healthcare, education, and other services). And to some extent, this has taken place. In many high-income countries, the share of personal consumption expenditures devoted to services has risen steadily at the expense of expenditures on durable and nondurable goods. This shift in demand has helped move the U.S. economy away from the production of goods and toward the production of services. (The more rapid productivity growth in goods-producing sectors, which has reduced the prices of goods relative to those of services, has also contributed to this result.) For example, the traded-goods sectors of the U.S. economy—agriculture, mining, and manufacturing—have declined from 26 percent of current-dollar

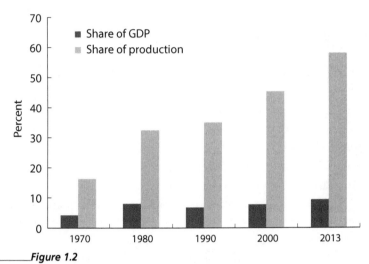

_____*Figure 1.2*

U.S. Merchandise Exports as a Share of GDP and Merchandise Production, Selected Years
    Source: U.S. Bureau of Economic Analysis (www.bea.gov).

GDP in 1980 to 16 percent in 2013.[3] The service sectors of the economy,
comprising transportation and public utilities; wholesale and retail trade;
finance, insurance, and real estate; and government have grown more
rapidly than the traded-goods sectors. Although in the past most of these
service activities could not be traded internationally, an increasing number of them are now tradable, as will be discussed shortly.

Even though the share of merchandise goods in the economy has
fallen significantly, the merchandise trade share has not. The gradual rise
in the share of merchandise trade to GDP therefore masks the vastly increased importance of trade within the traded-goods sector. This is seen
most strikingly by comparing merchandise exports to merchandise production rather than to total GDP. As figure 1.2 indicates, merchandise
exports as a share of merchandise production soared from about 15
percent in 1970 to nearly 60 percent in 2013, while relative to GDP it has
changed only modestly. This implies that the increase in the size of the
nontraded sector can sharpen the degree to which countries specialize in
the traded-goods sector and therefore increase trade.[4] Thus, a close analy-

[3] www.bea.gov.
[4] This is precisely what the analysis by Flam (1985) predicted.

_____Table 1.1.
Composition of U.S. Exports and Imports, 2014

	Exports	Imports
Food, feeds, & beverages	9	5
Crude materials	6	2
Mineral fuels	12	15
Chemicals & manufactured goods	33	36
Machinery & transport equipment	40	42

Source: U.S. Bureau of the Census, Report FT-900. http://www.census.gov/foreign-trade/data/index.html.

sis of the merchandise trade figures indicates that international trade is substantially more important now than in the recent past for those sectors engaged in trade.

The rise in trade relative to production is also evident in the case of specific commodities. Both the share of domestic production shipped to other markets and the ratio of imports to domestic consumption are much higher today than just a few decades ago, especially for perishable products, such as fruits, flowers, and vegetables, which only recently have become widely traded across countries.

What is the commodity composition of U.S. foreign trade? Table 1.1 addresses this question by looking at the shares of exports and imports in various categories. Given the agricultural land and natural resource endowments of North America, it should come as no surprise that food and raw materials make up a larger share of U.S. exports than imports. And given the country's high level of energy consumption, the United States is still a significant net importer of mineral fuels. (The energy situation is rapidly changing now that new technology for extracting natural gas has led to substantial increases in fuel production in North Dakota and elsewhere.) Yet the vast majority—roughly 75 percent—of U.S. exports and imports are manufactured goods. In the cases of machinery (electrical, general industrial, power generating, and scientific), motor vehicles, and office equipment, the value of both exports and imports is high. In other categories, there is less overlap: leading manufactured exports also include airplanes and aircraft parts and various chemicals, while leading manufactured imports include televisions and consumer electronics, clothing and footwear, iron and steel mill products, and toys and sporting goods.

Many of these imports of manufactured goods are not final goods sold to consumers, but intermediate components and parts sold to other businesses. These capital goods are inputs into the production process. As chapter 3 will explain, this fact has important implications for trade policy: protectionist policies will directly harm employment in domestic industries by raising their production costs, in addition to forcing consumers to pay a higher price for the products they buy.

Though trade is more important than ever for the merchandise-producing sector, this is not necessarily the case for the overall economy. Production and employment have shifted toward the service sector, where international trade does not play as large a role. In fact, only about 9 percent of American workers are directly exposed to international competition by being employed in the goods-producing sectors of the economy (mining and manufacturing). In contrast, about 26 percent of workers were employed in those sectors in 1970.[5] This means that a smaller part of the U.S. economy, in terms of output and employment, is directly affected by merchandise trade flows.

Yet this interpretation is not entirely accurate because many previously nontraded services are now becoming more tradable. In 2014, the value of these U.S. service exports—excluded from the merchandise trade figures considered so far—amounted to about $720 billion, more than 40 percent of the value of merchandise exports. The United States is a large net exporter of services, having imported just $488 billion in that year. The major categories of services trade include shipping and tourism, royalties and fees (receipts from intellectual property rights, such as trademarks, patents, and copyrights), and military transfers.

The addition of trade in services has raised the overall economic significance of trade.[6] In 2014, exports of goods and services were 13.4 percent of GDP, of which merchandise exports were 9.2 percent and service exports were 4.2 percent. (In 1970, by contrast, service exports were only about 1 percent of GDP.) Also in that year, imports of goods and services stood at 16.5 percent of GDP, of which merchandise imports were 13.7 percent and service imports were 2.8 percent.[7] Figure 1.3 pro-

---

[5] Council of Economic Advisers 2014, tables B-14.

[6] François and Hoekman 2010.

[7] From the Bureau of Economic Analysis, Department of Commerce (www.bea.gov).

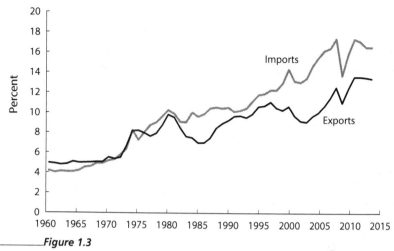

_____Figure 1.3
U.S. Trade in Goods and Services as a Percentage of GDP, 1960–2014
Source: Bureau of Economic Analysis (www.bea.gov).

vides a closer look at exports and imports of goods and services as a percentage of GDP since 1960. (The trade deficit will be discussed in chapter 4.)

The most rapidly growing category of U.S. service exports are those listed as "other private services," which include education, finance, insurance, telecommunications, and business, professional, and technical services. Despite recent fears that "offshoring" will harm the employment prospects of white-collar workers, the United States continues to export more than it imports in these "other private services." In 2013, U.S. exports of "other private services," including legal work, computer programming, engineering, management consulting, and more, were $304 billion. U.S. imports of such services were $201 billion. This is true even in the narrower category of "business, professional, and technical services," which includes computer and information services, management and consulting services, and so forth. In this category, the United States exported about $153 billion and imported about $116 billion in 2013.[8]

Unlike the case of merchandise, trade in services tends to be a small part of total service production, although the share is rising. In 1970, the

[8] http://www.bea.gov/international/index.htm#trade.

ratio of service exports to private services value-added was less than 2 percent, but by 2013 that ratio had risen to more than 6 percent.[9] While small in comparison to the merchandise sector, this ratio has been rising slowly even though everyone expects greater trade in services in the future.

Yet even services that cannot be traded are increasingly subject to international competition. This is because direct investments enable U.S. firms to enter foreign markets and allow foreign service-firms to compete in the U.S. market. U.S. direct investments abroad increased from 6 percent of GDP in 1960 to 27 percent in 2013, and many of these investments were in the service sector. For example, Google has set up its European Union headquarters in Ireland and maintains many offices and labs around the world. Yale University recently set up a campus in Singapore in collaboration with the National University of Singapore, and New York University has a branch campus in Abu Dhabi. Major U.S. law firms such as Sidley Austin have offices in Europe, Asia, and Latin America to extend its global reach.

Similarly, the value of foreign direct investment in the United States increased from 1 percent of GDP in 1960 to 16 percent in 2013. Many foreign banks have established a presence in the U.S. market to provide financial services, and foreign automobile firms (such as Honda, Toyota, BMW, Mercedes, and Volkswagen) have set up plants to produce in—and even export from—the U.S. market. The British sandwich shop Pret A Manger, founded in 1986, entered the U.S. market in New York in 2000 and has gradually expanded to other major cities. In addition, domestic service firms are increasingly the target of mergers and acquisitions as foreign firms seek entry into the U.S. market. As an indication of the increased foreign presence in the U.S. economy, the foreign-owned affiliates' share of value added originating in private industry in the United States increased from 3.8 percent in 1988 to 6.1 percent in 2012. In addition, the foreign-owned affiliates' share of private industry employment rose from 3.5 percent to 5.0 percent over the same period.[10]

Thus, firms have a choice in how they can sell products to foreign residents: either by exporting domestically produced goods, or by producing

[9] From the Bureau of Economic Analysis, Department of Commerce (www.bea.gov).

[10] Anderson 2012. Direct investment figures are from the Bureau of Economic Analysis (www.bea.gov).

and selling directly in the foreign country. This gives us another way to look at international commerce—based on company ownership rather than production location. In 2013, U.S. companies sold $2,280 billion worth of goods and services to foreign consumers through exports and earned $460 billion in net income from sales to foreign consumers through their foreign affiliates. Meanwhile, foreign companies sold $2,757 billion to U.S. consumers through exports to the United States and earned nearly $169 billion in net income through sales by their U.S. affiliates. The resulting U.S. deficit in goods, services, and net receipts from sales by affiliates in 2013 was about $290 billion smaller than the deficit in goods and services in the conventional international accounts based solely on location of production. The ownership-based deficit was smaller because U.S. companies earned more in net income from sales to foreign consumers through their foreign affiliates than foreign companies earned in net income selling through their U.S. affiliates.[11]

_____**Trade and the Fragmentation of Production**

Yet could the recent rise in the trade share be an anomaly of how trade statistics are collected? The increased trade in intermediate components requires that we ask this question. Every time a component is shipped across a border, it gets recorded by customs officials as an export or an import. When components are repeatedly shipped across the border at different stages of production, the official recorded value of trade rises with each crossing, but there may be no more final goods output than before. Thus, the value of trade relative to production may be inflated if intermediate products cross national borders multiple times during the production process. For example, there is substantial two-way trade between the United States and Canada in automobiles and parts. About 60 percent of U.S. auto exports to Canada are engines and parts, whereas 75 percent of U.S. auto imports from Canada are finished cars and trucks.[12]

---

[11] Bureau of Economic Analysis, "An Ownership-Based Framework of the U.S. Current Account, 2002–2013," _Survey of Current Business_, January 2015. http://www.bea.gov/scb /pdf/2015/01%20January/0115_ownership_based_current_account.pdf.

[12] Hummels, Rapoport, and Yi 1998, 84. The coordination involved in this cross-border movement of auto parts is mind-boggling. To keep a Ford factory in Toronto producing 1,500 Windstar minivans a day, a logistics subcontractor "organizes 800 deliveries a day

The increase in automobile trade between the United States, Canada, and other countries does not itself indicate that more and more cars are being built; rather, various parts and components that used to be produced domestically are now produced in other countries and traded multiple times across international borders.

This phenomenon is known as *vertical specialization*. Vertical specialization refers to the fragmentation of the production process as intermediate goods and components become a greater part of world trade. According to some estimates, vertical specialization accounts for about half of the growth in U.S. trade since the 1960s and about a third of the increase in world trade since 1970.[13] As the Canada auto trade example suggests, a non-negligible portion of the value of U.S. imports is simply the value of U.S. exports of domestically produced components that are shipped abroad for further processing or assembly and then returned to the United States for additional work before sale or export.

Such vertical specialization, or production sharing, means that the origin of any particular manufactured product cannot be attributed to a single country. The new Boeing 787 aircraft may be assembled at the company's production facility near Seattle, Washington, but the center fuselage is made in Italy, the engines in the United Kingdom, the wings in Japan, the passenger doors in France, the cargo doors in Sweden, the wing tips in South Korea, and the landing gear doors in Canada. For one particular car produced by an American manufacturer, 30 percent of the car's value is due to assembly in Korea, 17.5 percent due to components from Japan, 7.5 percent due to design from Germany, 4 percent due to parts from Taiwan and Singapore, 2.5 percent due to advertising and marketing services from Britain, and 1.5 percent due to data processing in Ireland. In the end, 37 percent of the production value of this American

---

from 300 different parts makers. . . . Loads have to arrive at 12 different points along the assembly lines without ever being more than 10 minutes late. Parts must be loaded into trucks in a prearranged sequence to speed unloading at the assembly line. To make all this run like clockwork takes a team of ten computerwielding operations planners and 200 unskilled workers, who make up the loads in the right sequence at a warehouse down the road." *The Economist*, December 5, 2002.

[13] See Yi 2003 and Hummels, Ishii, and Yi 2001. For more recent work on this phenomenon, see Johnson and Noguera 2012 and Johnson 2014.

car came from the United States even though the car was imported.[14] Most of the cost is incurred in the United States.

The classic example of this phenomenon is the Apple iPhone. The back of an iPhone says: "Designed in California, Assembled in China." That is because the iPhone is not "made" anywhere: it is composed of hundreds of individual parts made all over the world and all brought together for final assembly in China. For example, the iPhone's flash memory and display module are made by Toshiba (Japan), the application processor by Samsung (Korea), the camera module and GPS by Infineon (Germany), the Bluetooth and WLAN by Boradcam (United States), and so forth. The various parts are assembled by Foxconn, a Taiwanese company, at its plant in Shenzhen, China.

This makes U.S. import statistics quite misleading as to the true origin of a particular product. In 2009, the United States imported iPhones from China at a unit cost of $179, adding $1.9 billion to the recorded U.S. trade deficit that year. Yet the assembly cost incurred in China was only about $6.50 per unit, roughly 3.6 percent of the unit cost. But U.S. import statistics attribute the entire unit cost to China because that is where the product arrived from when it entered the United States. This means that the actual U.S. trade deficit with China is overstated and the actual trade deficit with Japan and Germany, which were exporting components to China, is understated.[15]

---

[14] World Trade Organization 1998, 36. Similarly, one type of Barbie doll is manufactured with $0.35 in labor from China; $0.65 in materials from Taiwan, Japan, the United States, and China; $1.00 in overhead and management from Hong Kong. The export value from Hong Kong is $2.00, and, after shipping, ground transportation, marketing, and wholesale and retail profit, the doll is sold in American stores at $9.99. See Robin Tempest, "Barbie and the World Economy," *Los Angeles Times*, September 22, 1996, A-1.

[15] Xing and Detert 2010. Similar calculations have been done on the iPod and the iPad. For example, a 30-gigabyte Apple video iPod, which sold for $300 in late 2005, is assembled in China. Although counted in U.S. trade statistics as a $150 import from China, only about half of that cost was incurred in China, mainly the $73 hard drive (made in a Toshiba plant) and $4 for assembly and testing. The rest of the iPod's material inputs came from Japan, Korea, Taiwan, and the United States, and most of the margin was captured by retail, distributor, and Apple profits in the United States. Of the $300 that a consumer would spend on this product imported from China, only a quarter of that price was actually incurred in China (Linden, Kraemer, and Dedrick 2007). These calculations are imperfect because it is difficult to know the countries where the Japanese, Germany, and American firms are making their components.

In fact, a sizable fraction of China's exports are processed goods that require many foreign inputs and components. One recent study found that the overall level of foreign content in China's exports was about 50 percent. Of course, there is a great deal of variation in this ratio across products: sophisticated or high-technology goods such as computers and telecommunication equipment have a high fraction of foreign content, while labor-intensive goods such as apparel have a high fraction of domestic content.[16] Mexico is another country that plays a big role in the global supply chain. On average, about two-thirds of the value of Mexico's manufactured exports consists of foreign-produced intermediate goods. In about 80 percent of its manufactured exports, Mexico's foreign content is more than 50 percent. Foreign components are particularly important in computer and peripheral equipment, and audio, video, and communications equipment.[17]

This specialization in the production and trade of components and intermediate goods may account for the fact that world trade has grown much more rapidly than world output. Even if world production of cars (a final good) is only expanding modestly, world trade in car components is increasing rapidly. This rapid growth in trade may also be related to the large role that multinational firms play in world trade. Multinationals are key in coordinating international production networks and putting complex goods together. Therefore, it may not be surprising to learn that a sizable part of U.S. trade is simply the exchange of goods between affiliated units of a multinational company. For example, in 2010, 18 percent of U.S. exports of goods and 14 percent of U.S. imports of goods were "intrafirm" transactions between affiliated companies.[18] International trade between "related parties," in which one firm has an ownership stake in another, is even larger: in 2013, 50 percent of U.S. imports and 30 percent of U.S. exports were between entities with such a relationship.[19]

Thus, by simply looking at the sheer volume of goods leaving and entering the country, one can say that the United States engages in significantly more international trade today than in the recent or distant past.

---

[16] Koopman, Wang, and Wei 2014.

[17] De La Cruz, Koopman, Wang, and Wei 2011.

[18] Barefoot 2012, table 6.

[19] https://www.census.gov/foreign-trade/Press-Release/2013pr/aip/related_party/.

But the statistics on trade can also be misleading for two reasons: a final good may be produced with inputs that cross national borders multiple times, each time getting recorded as an export or an import, and imports may actually have a significant degree of content that does not come from the country of origin.

_____Why Is Commercial Integration Greater Today?

International trade has increased rapidly during the postwar period, particularly in the past two decades. What accounts for this growth? One simple answer is that the factors previously inhibiting trade, and preventing exchanges from taking place, are now less important than before. These impediments to trade include transportation costs, transactions costs, and government policies.

Transportation costs have always been an important factor in world trade.[20] In the late nineteenth century, the expansion of global trade was propelled by a significant decline in shipping costs due to the introduction of steam ships. And it appears that the expansion of trade in the late twentieth century was also propelled by shipping developments, notably the container, which could be easily moved on and off ships. Introduced in the late 1960s and widely adopted in the 1970s and 1980s, containerization produced a huge increase in port labor productivity (tons moved per hour) and a substantial increase in ship size. One recent study finds that containerization helped increase trade, mainly among developed countries, by about 700 percent over a twenty-year period, a much larger effect than free trade agreements.[21]

Containerization may make shipping more efficient, but ocean-borne freight is still relatively slow. It takes roughly fourteen days for a cargo ship to go from Hong Kong to Long Beach, a massive U.S. port south of Los Angeles. The rise of air transport as a means of moving goods between countries has cut delivery times in ways that have brought an ever-increasing variety of perishable goods (cut flowers from Central America, lobsters from Maine) into world commerce. About 20 percent of world trade (by value) is now transported by air, with the share higher in North

---

[20] See Hummels 2007 for an overview of research on trade and transportation costs.
[21] Bernhofen, El-Sahli, and Kneller 2013.

America and East Asia. As the old adage says, time is money. According to one estimate, each day saved of shipping time is worth 0.6 to 2.1 percent of the value of the products.[22] Trade in intermediate goods is very time-sensitive because of its importance in the production process. According to one calculation, faster methods of transport over the past fifty years have been equivalent to reducing tariffs from 20 to 5 percent. This is because each day of delay reduces trade by one percent. This has enormous implications for landlocked developing countries, where transport is difficult, discouraging trade in time-sensitive agricultural and manufactured goods. It takes an average of forty-eight days in sub-Saharan Africa to get a container from the factory and loaded onto a ship. Cutting ten days off of that process could have a bigger impact on trade than any reduction in formal trade barriers.[23]

Other transactions costs—any expense that must be incurred to bring about exchange—are harder to quantify, but are now lower in potentially important ways. The costs of acquiring information, for example, can limit the extent of market integration. A century ago, before the age of mass communication, obtaining information about distant markets was more difficult than today. Producers are now more likely to have better information about local tastes and demands than they did in the past, which makes them able to service demand in those markets more efficiently. In addition, consumers used to have good information only about the attributes of locally produced goods, but now they are likely to be equally well informed about the products of foreign firms.

Finally, trade has expanded because government restrictions on the importation of foreign goods have been reduced. Tariffs, import quotas, and exchange controls that originated during the Great Depression of the 1930s have been gradually relaxed in the decades after World War II. Average tariffs on manufactured goods have dropped to less than 5 percent in most developed countries over the postwar period. Figure 1.4 shows that high U.S. tariffs were the norm prior to the 1940s, but that import duties fell sharply and have remained at very low levels in recent decades.

---

[22] Hummels and Schaur 2013.
[23] Djankov, Freund, and Pham 2010.

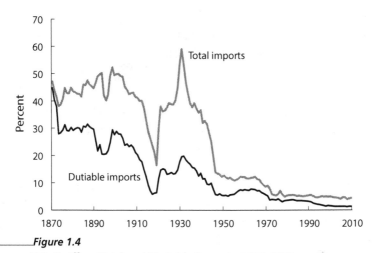

Figure 1.4

Average U.S. Tariff on Total and Dutiable Imports, 1870–2013

Sources: U.S. Bureau of the Census 1975, updated with the U.S. International Trade Commission dataweb (www.usitc.gov).

Furthermore, whole geographic areas, such as Europe and North America, have abolished customs duties and become free trade areas. Many developing countries have also undertaken important unilateral trade policy reforms in recent decades. For example, after having been closed to trade and foreign investment for decades, China and India—two of the world's most populous nations—starting opening up to global commerce in 1978 (China) and in 1991 (India). Some developing countries have also liberalized their import regimes as they joined the World Trade Organization. Although nontariff measures are still used to protect domestic producers from import competition, it is nonetheless true that trade barriers have fallen significantly around the world.

Quantifying the precise contribution of all these factors to the expansion of world trade is difficult. One study finds that about two-thirds of the postwar growth in the trade of countries belonging to the Organization for Economic Cooperation and Development (OECD) is due to income growth, a quarter to tariff reductions, and about 10 percent to transportation cost reductions.[24] This calculation, however, does not take into account production sharing or vertical specialization.

[24] Baier and Bergstrand 2001.

_____Limits to Globalization

What percent of American consumption expenditures is devoted to Chinese goods? Would you be surprised if it was slightly over 1 percent? That is the answer according to the data in table 1.2.

This table presents a breakdown of U.S. personal consumption expenditures for 2010. The first column presents the expenditure shares, and the next two columns show the fraction of the products "made in the USA" or "made in China" (not showing the residual, which are made elsewhere). The final two columns show the actual domestic content in those categories; some "made in the USA" goods have foreign content and some "made in China" goods have non-Chinese content.

The first thing to note is that nearly 90 percent of consumption spending is on domestic goods, not imported goods. That is because two-thirds of consumption spending is on services, such as housing, medical care, and recreation, the import content of which is very small. Nearly a quarter of consumption spending is on nondurable goods, such as food and gasoline, where the import content is not from China. The major categories where the China content is high is clothing and footwear and furniture and household equipment, but these categories amount to only 8 percent of total consumption spending. Even in these categories, it is easy to exaggerate how much comes from China because of the iPhone phenomenon: China assembles products for shipment to the United States, but much of the value of the product is the cost of intermediate goods that China did not produce itself. Take clothing and footwear: 35 percent of spending in this category is on goods from China, but after stripping out the foreign components (cotton, yarn, etc.) made elsewhere, only 14 percent of spending in this small category is really going to China.

This finding is a reminder that most of what we buy in America is made in America. Partly because we spend so much on services, which are difficult to trade internationally, most of our spending remains domestic. There is a natural limit to how far globalization can go.

In fact, even though world economic integration has increased rapidly in recent decades, the world remains far from fully integrated. Trade within a country dominates trade between countries by an order of magnitude. The United States may be more integrated with the rest of the world than in the past, but we are far from the point at which trade between New

_____*Table 1.2.*
Composition of U.S. Personal Consumption Expenditures, 2010

	Expenditure share	Share spent on		Import content	
		Made in USA	Made in China	Total	Chinese goods
Total	100	88.5	2.7	7.3	1.2
Less food & energy	86.1	88.0	3.1	7.7	1.4
Durable	9.9	66.6	12.0	18.7	6.2
Motor vehicles	3.4	74.9	1.2	17.5	0.6
Furniture & household equipment	4.7	59.6	20.0	21.4	10.6
Non-Durables	23.2	76.2	6.4	12.1	2.6
Food	8.0	90.8	0.4	5.2	0.2
Clothing/shoes	3.4	24.9	35.6	29.5	13.8
Gasoline & energy	3.6	88.4	0.1	7.4	0.0
Services	66.9	96.0	0.0	4.0	0.0
Housing	16.6	100.0	0.0	0.0	0.0
Household operations	7.2	99.7	0.0	0.3	0.0
Transportation	1.6	90.4	0.0	9.6	0.0
Medical care	18.4	99.3	0.0	0.7	0.0
Recreation	8.2	99.6	0.0	0.3	0.0
Other services	14.9	84.3	0.0	15.7	0.0

Source: Hale and Hobijn 2011.

York and Rio de Janeiro is carried on as easily as trade between New York and Los Angeles. It remains the case that more than 85 percent of what the United States consumes is produced in the United States.

One economist has used the following analogy to illustrate how far we are from perfect trade integration: if Americans were just as likely to purchase goods and services from foreign producers as from domestic producers, then the U.S. import-to-GDP ratio should equal the non-U.S. share of world GDP. In other words, the United States would spend as much on foreign products as the average foreign resident, or roughly 75 percent, which is about the non-U.S. share of world GDP. Since the current trade share is about 15 percent, while that hypothetical trade share would be 75 percent, one can conclude that we are only about one-sixth of the way to the point at which "it would literally be true that Americans did business as easily across the globe as across the country."[25]

[25] Frankel 2000.

A leading empirical model of trade, the so-called gravity equation, shows that there are numerous factors that shape bilateral trade flows: distance between countries; geographic location; language, currency, and political ties; and so on. Results from this model indicate that the mere presence of a national border acts as a powerful impediment to trade. The implication is that even when countries share a common language and a common border, similar institutions and a similar culture, the mere existence of a national border creates a significant bias in favor of intranational trade as opposed to international trade, even if trade barriers are low.[26]

_____*Public Views on Globalization: The Trade Policy Controversy*

What are the public's views about international trade? A survey of public opinion in forty-four countries in 2014 by the Pew Research Center found widespread support for international trade.[27] As figure 1.5 shows, nearly half of those polled in Nigeria, Lebanon, Israel, and India believe that growing trade is "very good" for their country, while a majority in all countries believe trade is "very good" or "somewhat good."

Interestingly, Americans are among the least supportive of international trade. Yet it is still the case that 68 percent of Americans said that trade was good for the United States, an improvement from previous years. Only 28 percent said that trade was bad or somewhat bad, down from 41 percent in 2008. However, this support has declined from 2002, when 78 percent said trade was good and only 18 percent said trade was bad.

Since 1993, Gallup has asked people in the United States whether they view foreign trade more as an opportunity for growth through exports or as a threat to the economy because of imports. As figure 1.6 shows, the more positive view of trade in the 1990s gave way to a more negative view of trade in the 2000s, but the positive view has reappeared since the 2013 poll. The poll also reveals that the more education a person has the

[26] Anderson and van Wincoop (2003) find that the border effect (the difference between intranational and international trade) implies a 45 percent reduction in trade, after controlling for other factors affecting trade, such as country size, distance between countries, language, and currency. On the issue of trade costs, see Anderson and van Wincoop 2004.

[27] Pew Research Center, "Faith and Skepticism about Trade, Foreign Investment," September 16, 2014, www.pewresearch.org. Question 27: What do you think about growing trade and business ties between (survey country) and other countries—do you think it is a very good thing, somewhat good, somewhat bad, or a very bad thing for our country?

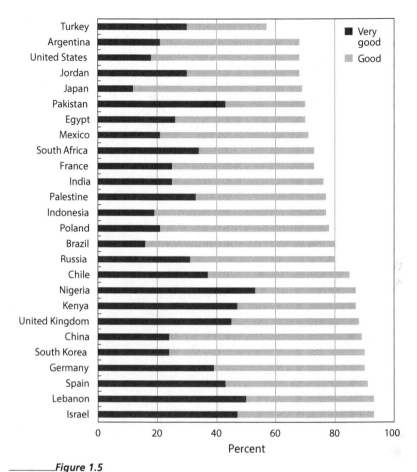

_____*Figure 1.5*
World Opinion on International Trade, 2014
    Source: Pew Global Attitude Project (http://www.pewglobal.org/2009/07/23/chapter-5
-views-on-trade-and-globalization/).

more favorable his or her view of trade: 64 percent of those with a college education thought trade was an opportunity for growth (and only 26 percent a threat) as opposed to 49 percent of those with a high school education (of whom 41 percent thought trade is a threat).

This is not a surprise. Surveys have consistently found that years of formal education are closely linked to an individual's view of trade: those with at least some college education were much more likely to have positive attitudes about globalization and trade than those with only a high school degree. As we will see in chapter 4, this association might arise because individuals with less education are more likely to be employed

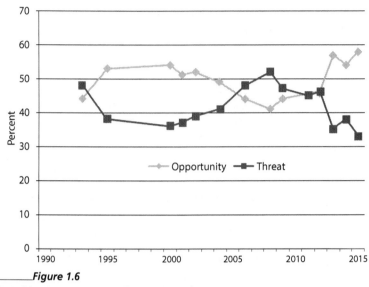

_____Figure 1.6

U.S. Public Opinion on Trade, 1993–2014

Note: Question asked: What do you think foreign trade means for America? Do you see foreign trade more as an opportunity for economic growth through increased U.S. exports or a threat to the economy from foreign imports?

Source: http://www.gallup.com/poll/167516/americans-remain-positive-foreign-trade .aspx.

in sectors that compete against imports and have greater difficulty becoming reemployed once displaced compared to those with a higher level of education.

While Americans are generally favorable toward trade, they are less enthusiastic about trade agreements with other countries. An April 2014 poll found that about 50–55 percent of those surveyed believe that new trade agreements with the European Union and Pacific Rim countries would be good for the United States and about 20–25 percent thought they would be bad.[28] With the passage of time, however, Americans have

[28] See http://www.pewglobal.org/2014/04/09/support-in-principle-for-u-s-eu-trade-pact/. An earlier poll, conducted when the United States was still coming out of the recession, indicated less support for trade agreements. A November 2010 poll found that 44 percent of those surveyed thought trade agreements like NAFTA were bad for the United States while only 35 percent thought they were good. An overwhelming number of those surveyed said that trade agreements would lead to job losses, lower wages, and lower economic growth. Pew Research Center for the People and the Press, "Public Support for Increased Trade, Except with South Korea and China," November 9, 2010, http://www

even taken a more positive view of NAFTA. In 2004, only 42 percent of Americans surveyed thought that NAFTA was beneficial for the U.S. economy, but 50 percent did in 2014.[29] (Interestingly, people in the United States think that Mexico gained the most from the agreement, whereas people in Mexico think that the United States gained more.)

These findings suggest that the public is willing to accept increased international trade driven by the anonymous force of technology, but a little more hesitant to support integration driven by specific policy initiatives. Even though economists have not untangled the precise degree to which recent trade integration has been technology-driven or policy-driven, the public appears to view this distinction as important. This tendency is consistent with the finding that the public appears to care about jobs destroyed because of imports, but does not care as much about jobs destroyed due to the invisible hand of technology or changing market prices.

The public opinion polls also reveal an interesting divergence between the two political parties and their supporters. Recent polls have shown that Democratic voters have been more favorable of trade agreements than Republican voters. Republicans and Republican-leaning independents who agreed with the Tea Party have had a particularly negative view of the impact of trade agreements. Yet Democratic politicians tend to oppose trade agreements due to labor unions, while Republican politicians tend to support freer trade due to business interests. Thus, the views of both Democratic- and Republican-voting constituents seem to be different from those of the politicians who represent their respective parties.

In fact, congressional voting over trade legislation has become quite partisan and highly contentious. Figure 1.7 shows the share of each party's vote in the House of Representatives for trade liberalization (for bills that reduced tariffs or against bills that raised tariffs). Prior to World War II, the Democrats supported freer trade while the Republicans supported high tariffs. By the 1950s, the Republicans had begun to support trade agreements to reduce tariffs for foreign policy reasons and due to the

---

.people-press.org/2010/11/09/public-support-for-increased-trade-except-with-south-korea
-and-china/.

[29] Smeltz and Kafura 2014.

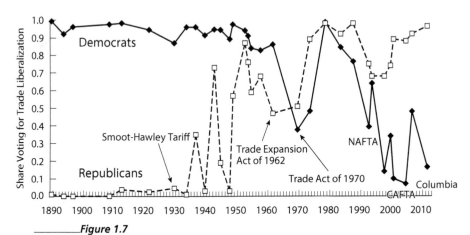

_____Figure 1.7
Partisan Division in Congressional Trade Votes, U.S. House of Representatives,
1890–2013
Source: Compiled by the author.

support of big business. For many years thereafter, a bipartisan consensus
favored reducing tariffs in trade agreements.

However, particularly since the NAFTA vote in 1993, Democrats have
become more opposed to free trade agreements. The switch in the Democrats' position, which first became evident in the early 1970s, is largely
due to the opposition of organized labor to increased foreign trade. The
increased polarization of trade voting in Congress reflects the heightened
political conflict over the issue in recent years. For example, the House
of Representatives voted in October 2012 to pass the free trade agreements with South Korea and Colombia. In both cases, more than 90
percent of House Republicans supported the agreements. However, of
the House Democrats, 85 percent voted against the Colombia agreement
and 70 percent voted against the South Korea agreement.

The public support for trade in the abstract and skepticism about trade
policy in the particular is a key aspect of the political controversy over
free trade. Trade policy has always been contentious, but it has come to
involve complex economic, political, and legal factors, making it increasingly difficult to understand. This book aims to examine how these factors affect U.S. trade policy. The appropriate place to begin is with the
economic case for free trade.

2

The Case for Free Trade: Old Theories, New Evidence

For more than two centuries, economists have pointed out the benefits of free trade and the costs of trade restrictions. As Adam Smith argued more than two centuries ago, "All commerce that is carried on betwixt any two countries must necessarily be advantageous to both," and therefore "all duties, customs, and excise [on imports] should be abolished, and free commerce and liberty of exchange should be allowed with all nations."[1] The economic case for free trade, however, is not based on outdated theories in musty old books. The classic insights into the nature of economic exchange between countries have been refined and updated over the years to retain their relevance to today's circumstances. More important, over the past decade economists have gathered extensive empirical evidence that contributes appreciably to our understanding of the advantages of free trade. This chapter reviews the classic theories and examines the new evidence, noting as well the qualifications to the case for free trade.

Specialization and Trade

The traditional case for free trade is based on the gains from specialization and exchange. These gains are easily understood at the level of the individual. Most people do not produce for themselves even a fraction of the goods they consume. Rather, we earn an income by specializing in certain activities and then use our earnings to purchase various goods and services—food, clothing, housing, healthcare—produced by others.

[1] Smith [1763] 1978, 511, 514.

sence, we "export" the goods and services that we produce with our own labor and "import" the goods and services produced by others that we wish to consume. This division of labor enables us to increase our consumption beyond that which would be the case if we tried to be self-sufficient and produce everything for ourselves. Specialization allows us to enjoy a much higher standard of living than otherwise possible and gives us access to a greater variety of goods and services.

Trade between nations is simply the international extension of this division of labor. For example, the United States has specialized in the production of aircraft, industrial machinery, and agricultural commodities (particularly corn, soybeans, and wheat). In exchange for exports of these products, the United States purchases, among other things, imports of crude oil, clothing, and iron and steel mill products. Like individuals, countries benefit immensely from this division of labor and enjoy higher real incomes than they would by forgoing such trade. Just as there seems no obvious reason to limit the free exchange of goods within a country without a specific justification, there is no obvious reason why trade between countries should be limited in the absence of a compelling reason for doing so. (Popular arguments for limiting trade will be examined in subsequent chapters to see if they are persuasive.)

Adam Smith, whose magnificent work *The Wealth of Nations* was first published in 1776, set out a case for free trade with a persuasive flair that still resonates today. Smith advocated the "obvious and simple system of natural liberty" in which individuals would be free to pursue their own interests, while the government provided the legal framework within which commerce would take place. With the government enforcing a system of justice and providing certain public goods (such as roads, in Smith's view), the private interests of individuals could be turned toward productive activities, namely, meeting the demands of the public as expressed in the marketplace. Smith envisioned a system that would give people the incentive to better themselves through economic activities, where they would create wealth by serving others through market exchange rather than through political activities, where they might seek to redistribute existing wealth through brute force or legal restraints on competition. Under such a system, the powerful motivation of self-interest could be channeled toward socially beneficial activities that would serve the general interest rather than toward socially unproductive activities that might advance the interests of a select few but would come at the expense of society as a whole.

Free trade is an important component of this system of economic liberty. Under a system of natural liberty in which domestic commerce is largely free from restraints on competition, though not necessarily free from government regulation, commerce would also be permitted to operate freely between countries. According to Smith, free trade would increase competition in the home market and curtail the power of domestic firms by checking their ability to exploit consumers through high prices and poor service. Moreover, the country would gain by exchanging exports of goods that are dear on the world market for imports of goods that are cheap on the world market. As Smith put it,

> What is prudence in the conduct of every family can scarce be folly in that of a great kingdom. If a foreign country can supply us with a commodity cheaper than we ourselves can make it, better buy it of them with some part of the produce of our own industry, employed in a way in which we have some advantage. The general industry of the country . . . will not thereby be diminished . . . but only left to find out the way in which it can be employed with the greatest advantage. It is certainly not employed to the greatest advantage, when it is thus directed towards an object which it can buy cheaper than it can make.[2]

Smith believed that the benefits of trade went well beyond this simple arbitrage exchange of what is abundant in the home market for what is abundant in the world market. The wealth of any society depends upon the division of labor. The division of labor, the degree to which individuals specialize in certain tasks, enhances productivity. And productivity, the ability to produce more goods with the same resources, is the basis for rising living standards. But, as he put it, the division of labor is limited by the extent of the market. Smaller, more isolated markets cannot support a high degree of specialization among their workforce and therefore tend to be relatively poor. Free trade enables all countries, but particularly

---

[2] Smith [1776] 1976, 457. Free trade made this possible: "The interest of a nation in its commercial relations to foreign nations is, like that of a merchant with regard to the different people with whom he deals, to buy as cheap and to sell as dear as possible. But it will be most likely to buy cheap, when by the most perfect freedom of trade it encourages all nations to bring to it the goods which it has occasion to purchase" (464).

small countries, to extend the effective size of their market. Trade allows such countries to achieve a more refined division of labor, and therefore reap a higher real income, than if international exchange were artificially limited by government policies.[3]

_____Comparative Advantage

In 1799, a successful London stockbroker named David Ricardo came across a copy of *The Wealth of Nations* while on vacation and quickly became engrossed in the book. Ricardo admired Smith's great achievement, but thought that many of the topics deserved further investigation. For example, Smith seemed to believe that a country would export goods that it produces most efficiently and import goods that other countries produce most efficiently. In this way, trade is a mutually beneficial way of increasing total world output and thus the consumption of every country. But, Ricardo asked, what if one country was the most efficient at producing everything? Would that country still benefit from trade? Would disadvantaged countries find themselves unable to trade at all?

To answer these questions, Ricardo arrived at a brilliant deduction that became known as the theory of comparative advantage.[4] Comparative advantage implies that a country could find it advantageous to *import* some goods even if it could produce them more efficiently than other countries. Conversely, a country is able to *export* some goods even if other countries could produce them more efficiently. In either case, countries stand to benefit from trade. Ricardo's conclusions about the benefits of trade were similar to Smith's, but his approach contains a deeper insight.

At first, the principle of comparative advantage seems counterintuitive.[5] Why would a country ever import a good that it could produce

---

[3] For a more complete discussion of Smith's ideas about trade and trade policy, see Irwin 1996a.

[4] For speculation on how Ricardo discovered the theory, see Ruffin (2002).

[5] When challenged by a distinguished mathematician to name "one proposition in all of the social sciences which is both true and non-trivial," the Nobel laureate economist Paul Samuelson (1972, 683) famously replied by mentioning the theory of comparative advantage. In a marvelous essay, Krugman (1998a) examines why many noneconomists have difficulty grasping the essential logic of comparative advantage.

more efficiently than another country? Yet comparative advantage is the key to understanding the pattern of world trade. For example, imagine that you were hired to examine the factors explaining international trade in textiles. You might start by examining the efficiency of textile producers in various countries. If one country was found to be more efficient than another in producing textiles, you might conclude that this country would export textiles and other countries would import them. Yet this conclusion could well be wrong because simply comparing the efficiency of production in one industry across countries is insufficient for determining the pattern of trade.

According to Ricardo, international trade is not driven by the *absolute* costs of production, but by the *opportunity* costs of production. The country most efficient at producing textiles might be even more efficient than other countries at producing other goods, such as shoes. In that case, the country would be best served by directing its labor to producing shoes, in which its margin of productive advantage is even greater than in textiles. As a result, despite its productivity advantage in textiles, the country would export shoes in exchange for imports of textiles. In the absence of other information, the absolute efficiency of one country's textile producers in comparison to another country's is insufficient to determine whether that country produces all of the textiles it consumes or imports some of them.

To put it differently, a country can obtain textiles either *directly* through domestic production, or *indirectly* by producing something else and exporting it in exchange for imports of textiles. The most efficient way of getting textiles is whichever way yields the country the greatest quantity of such goods at the least cost. So returning to the textile question, the real choice facing a country is whether it should devote its resources to producing textiles, or to producing other goods that can be exported in exchange for textiles. A direct comparison of the efficiency of domestic and foreign textile producers will not by itself help us determine the pattern of trade.[6]

[6] As James Mill, a close friend of Ricardo's, explained, "When a country can either import a commodity or produce it at home, it compares the cost of producing at home with the cost of procuring it from abroad; if the latter cost is less than the first, it imports. The cost at which a country can import from abroad depends, not upon the cost at which the foreign country produces the commodity, but upon what the commodity costs which it

Although the concept of comparative advantage can be counterintuitive when applied to countries, individuals base their actions on it every day. The brilliant Barcelona football (soccer) player Lionel Messi might be the best on the field at any position, whether forward striker or midfield defender (i.e., he could have an absolute advantage over all other players). But his on-field advantage is greatest as a right wing, where he can use his uncanny abilities to be the most effective against defenders. It is this position where his comparative advantage is the greatest. Similarly, the author of this book might be inferior to his spouse in both cooking and cleaning up, but regrettably that is not an excuse to do nothing; instead, I am compelled to work where my margin of inferiority is the least (i.e., where I have a comparative advantage). Without information on alternative activities, a person's absolute efficiency in one activity should not determine where that individual chooses to direct his or her (scarce) labor time. Yet absolute efficiency is still frequently discussed as if it alone determines the pattern of resource allocation and international trade. Domestic steel and textile producers insist that they are the world's most efficient producers of their products, implying that something must be wrong or unfair when they are beset by competition from imports.

Indeed, from the standpoint of a domestic industry competing against imports, the trade patterns dictated by comparative advantage can sometimes seem unfair. The U.S. textile and apparel industry has been hard hit by foreign competition for many decades, going back to imports from Japan in the 1950s when that country was a low-wage developing nation. American clothing-firms are much more productive than their foreign counterparts, in terms of output per hour, yet this does not guarantee them success in the market. It seems wrong that an American industry can be more efficient than any of its foreign competitors in absolute terms and yet fail to export—and even struggle against imports. But comparative advantage tells us that those sectors with the greatest *relative* efficiency advantage (compared to other countries) will be the ones that export with the greatest success.

To take another example, Lee Iacocca, the charismatic chief of Chrysler in the 1980s, once admitted that American automakers had fallen behind

---

sends in exchange, compared with the cost which it must be at to produce the commodity in question, if it did not import it" (quoted in Irwin 1996b, 91).

their Japanese rivals in the past, but proudly proclaimed that the U.S. auto industry had met the competitive challenge and had finally matched the efficiency of Japanese producers. (This claim may stretch the truth, but let us accept it for the sake of argument.) Unfortunately, the theory of comparative advantage tells Iacocca that he has a problem: it may not be enough for an industry that competes with imports merely to match or even to exceed the productive efficiency of foreign producers to overcome that competition and recapture market share. The reason is that Chrysler and other U.S. automakers were not really competing against Japanese automakers as much as they were against other American industries that enjoyed an even greater productive superiority over their counterparts in Japan. U.S. auto producers might be able to match the productive efficiency of Japanese auto producers, but if American farmers and telecommunications equipment producers remain vastly more efficient than their Japanese counterparts, the United States will continue to export agricultural goods and telecom products to Japan in exchange for imports of automobiles.

For developing countries, the theory of comparative advantage is good news in terms of their ability to trade profitably with advanced countries. Even if a developing country lacks an absolute productive advantage in any field, it will always have a comparative advantage in the production of some goods. Most countries, from Argentina to Zambia, are unable to match the productive efficiency of any U.S. industry, and yet still they are able to export some goods to the United States. Such countries will export goods where their relative disadvantage is least and use those export revenues to improve their standard of living by purchasing other foreign-produced goods, from fuel to capital equipment to medicine. There is no country whose economic circumstances prevent it from engaging in mutually beneficial trade with other countries. (Chapter 6 examines developing countries in more detail.)

What determines a country's comparative advantage? There is no single answer to this question. Sometimes specialization is based on climate or natural resources, sometimes on accumulated skills and capital, sometimes on an abundance of cheap labor, sometimes on government promotion of a particular industry. Some sources of comparative advantage are relatively immutable, while others—based on technology, education, and worker skills—can evolve over time. Entrepreneurship and the business environment can also be critical factors. A country could have an ideal climate for producing wine, but unless someone invests in the capital and skills necessary for its production, that climatic advantage will remain latent and unexploited. Whatever the underlying reasons, these differences across countries are the primary driving force behind trade.

Critics of free trade sometimes insist that the theory of comparative advantage is obsolete because Ricardo did not consider capital mobility or technology transfer between countries. But modern economists have altered many of the assumptions underlying Ricardo's analysis, and the main result—that international exchange is mutually advantageous—remains intact.[7]

Figure 2.1 illustrates the concepts of comparative and absolute advantage by comparing labor productivity (output per worker) in the United States and Japan across industries in 1990. Even though the productivity of several Japanese manufacturing industries exceeded that of the United States, such as those making steel, automobiles, and consumer electronics, having this absolute advantage did not make Japan a richer country than the United States. In fact, per capita income in Japan was only about 80 percent of that in the United States in 1990, more or less where it remains today. This can be explained by looking at the width of the bars, which indicate the share of employment in those sectors. A large share of Japan's labor force is employed in sectors where Japan's productivity is low in comparison to that of the United States. Japan's weighted average productivity was only about 80 percent of that in the United States, because it was dragged down by low productivity in the retail services, construction, and food processing.

For example, food processing employed 11 percent of manufacturing workers in Japan, but their total factor productivity was just 40 percent of that in the United States. This low productivity is due to the small scale of Japanese firms in this sector; Japan has six times more food-processing firms per capita than the United States. Insufficient domestic competition

---

[7] In fact, the United States is a large free trade area with labor and capital mobility and transferable technology across regions. Yet despite lower wages in the South for much of the late nineteenth and early twentieth centuries, high-wage regions of the country did not suffer from a "race to the bottom," and the South did not get rich at the expense of the North, but rather a slow process of convergence to higher incomes occurred across regions. See McLean and Mitchener 1999.

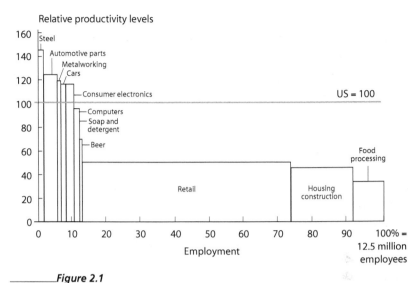

_____*Figure 2.1*

Employment-Weighted Relative Productivity Level, Japan Relative to the United States, 1990

Source: Lewis 2004, 25.

in this sector means that there has not been enough pressure to consolidate production and improve efficiency. Trade protection limits competition and encourages this inefficiency. Japan's vegetable oil sector is protected by just a 5 percent tariff and its level of productivity is 85 percent of what the United States can produce, whereas the dairy industry is protected by a stiff 227 percent tariff and its level of efficiency is less than half of that in the United States.[8]

Thus, Japanese steel and automobile producers may be significantly more efficient than their American counterparts, but that does not make Japan a rich country because those sectors are a small part of the overall economy. Japan will match U.S. per capita income only when the average productivity of its overall workforce matches that of the United States.

Today, more people are worried about competition from China, where wages are much lower than in the United States but where productivity growth has been rapid. Figure 2.2 presents industry-level labor productivity in China compared to the United States in 1995 and 2004. (The United

[8] These data are from a 1990 McKinsey study; see "Rotten," *Economist*, August 17, 2000. See also Lewis 2004.

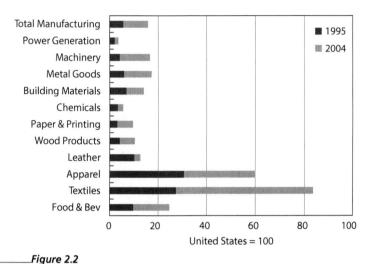

_____**Figure 2.2**
China's Labor Productivity, Relative to the United States', by Industry, 1995 and 2004 (United States = 100)
  Source: Deng and Jefferson 2011, table 5.

States is benchmarked at 100 in both years.) Not surprisingly, China has an absolute productivity disadvantage, and the United States has an absolute productivity advantage, in every industry in both years. That is, in every industry, China's labor productivity is significantly lower than that of the United States, although it had closed the gap in many of them by 2004. Yet, despite lagging in absolute productivity, China has a *comparative* advantage in some industries. In 2004, the four industries in which China came closest to achieving U.S. levels of productivity were apparel (60 percent of U.S. level), textiles (84 percent), metal goods (17 percent), and machinery (17 percent). It should come as no surprise that China's export success has been greatest in these industries, in addition to others that were not calculated, such as footwear and the assembly of consumer electronics.

How can China export clothing and footwear when its industries are significantly less efficient than their U.S. counterparts, even if that is where its comparative advantage lies? The answer is that wages in China are significantly lower than in the United States. In 2009, average hourly compensation in Chinese manufacturing was about $2.85 per hour in city manufacturing and $1.15 in rural town and village enterprises, in contrast to $34.19 in average hourly compensation costs for workers in U.S. manufacturing. Thus, urban workers in China earn about 8 percent of what American workers earn, up from 3 percent in 2002.[9] Therefore, China can easily export apparel because its productivity is 60 percent of the U.S. level while its wages are only about 8 percent of the U.S. level. This means that its unit labor costs—the costs of labor relative to its productivity—are very low in these goods compared to those in the United States.[10]

Given that China's wages are only about 8 percent of U.S. wages, on average, why doesn't China export everything to the United States? That is because its productivity in other industries is less than 8 percent of the U.S. level, meaning that it does not have a unit labor cost advantage over U.S. producers. For example, China cannot easily export chemicals because its productivity level is only 5 percent of the U.S. level, whereas it must pay wages that are 8 percent of the U.S. level. (This link between wages and productivity will be examined further in chapters 4 and 6.) Thus, even though its wages are a small fraction of those in the United States, China's unit labor costs in this industry are high by international standards. Furthermore, labor costs are only one component of the total costs of production.

As China's productivity improves over time, its wages will rise as well. In 1995, China's average productivity in manufacturing was just 6 percent of the U.S. level; by 2004 it was nearly 16 percent of the U.S. level. Over that same period, its average wage rate has also more than tripled.[11] This is not a coincidence. Therefore, it may not be surprising to learn that China is actually losing its export advantage in low-cost, labor-intensive industries such as apparel and footwear as its workforce becomes more productive and it moves into more sophisticated industries. Not only are Chinese wages rising rapidly, but domestic inflation and the appreciation of its currency (the renminbi) against the dollar have made those labor-

[9] http://www.bls.gov/fls/china.htm. Rural workers have lower wages, but the productivity of inland firms is lower than that of coastal firms and the transportation costs required to deliver their goods to the coastal ports are high.

[10] Actually, because wages for production workers in the U.S. apparel industry, at about $12 per hour, are much below the average U.S. wage, China's wage is about a fifth of the U.S. apparel wage. But since China's productivity is nearly three-fourths that of the United States, paying one-fifth the wage still gives the country a large unit labor cost advantage.

[11] Deng and Jefferson 2011 and http://www.bls.gov/fls/china.htm#manufacturing.

intensive goods increasingly expensive in world markets.[12] Wages are rising because productivity has increased and firms need to pay higher wages to retain their workers and prevent them from leaving for other firms.[13] In addition, other countries, such as Vietnam and Cambodia, have wage rates less than half of those in China and can come close to matching its productivity in similar labor-intensive industries.[14] The apparel and footwear industries are beginning to migrate from China to Vietnam and Cambodia, where the unit labor costs are lower. This is a natural cycle of economic development. Just like the United States, Japan, Taiwan, and Korea before it, China will eventually lose its textile, apparel, and footwear industries as it begins to produce more sophisticated goods and its wages and productivity level rise.

Figure 2.3 illustrates this process by showing the share of Nike's footwear production in various Asian countries. In the late 1980s, about two-thirds of its footwear was made in South Korea, with a smaller fraction made in Taiwan. But as wages rose in those countries, Nike shifted its production to places with lower wages, such as China and Indonesia. The share of Nike's production in China peaked around 2000. Because wages in China have been rising rapidly, Nike started moving production to Vietnam. When Vietnam's wages rise and begin to push up Nike's costs, the company will move production to countries with lower wages, such as Cambodia or Bangladesh. That will not be a disaster for Vietnam.

---

[12] Ceglowski and Golub (2012) find that China's unit labor costs fell between 1998 and 2003, but have been rising since then due to wage growth and the appreciation of its currency against the dollar. China's exchange rate policy has been very controversial and will be discussed in the context of trade deficits in chapter 4.

[13] "Cheng Chunmeng, the general manager of a manufacturer of colorful children's chairs in east-central China, gave his workers a 30 percent raise last year to keep them from leaving." Keith Bradsher, "Even as Wages Rise, China's Exports Grow," *New York Times*, January 9, 2014.

[14] "In coastal provinces [of China] with ready access to ports, even unskilled workers now earn $120 a month for a 40-hour workweek, and often considerably more; wages in inland provinces, where transport is costlier, are somewhat lower but also rising fast. While Chinese wages are still less than $1 an hour, factory workers in Vietnam earn as little as $50 per month for a 48-hour workweek, including Saturdays. . . . When those increases are combined with a currency rising against the dollar at an annual pace of up to 10 percent, labor costs in China are now climbing at 25 percent a year or more. . . . A popular saying among Western investors is that Vietnam is the next China. Cambodia, with even lower wages attracting garment manufacturers, is called the next Vietnam." Keith Bradsher, "Investors Seek Asian Options to Costly China," *New York Times*, June 18, 2008.

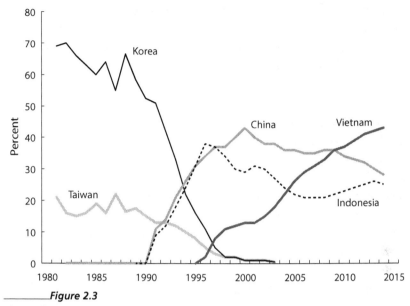

Figure 2.3

Share of Nike's Production of Shoes, by Country, 1982–2014
  Source: Annual Reports, Nike.

When Nike pulled out of Korea and Taiwan, it did not leave those countries destitute; rather, it pulled out because those economies were doing so well in providing higher-wage jobs to workers.

In sum, the United States has an absolute productivity advantage in producing apparel, but still imports almost all of its apparel consumption from abroad. So what good is having high labor productivity? Simply put, a country that has an absolute productivity advantage over other countries will be richer than other countries. An absolute advantage in productivity does not determine the pattern of trade, but it does translate into higher per capita income. In other words, the reason why Americans enjoy one of the highest per capita incomes in the world is that its labor force is highly productive. Conversely, the reason why China's per capita income is low is that its overall labor productivity is low. China has become richer, however, by improving its labor productivity, as Japan and Korea did before it. China's overall labor productivity was just 3 percent of the United States in 1990, 6 percent in 2000, and 14 percent in 2010. By 2011, China's labor productivity was nearly 15 percent of that in the United States. Not surprisingly, China's per capita income has also risen very rapidly and was about 13 percent of the U.S. level in 2013.[15] As Paul Krugman has put it, "Productivity isn't everything, but in the long run it is almost everything. A country's ability to improve its standard of living over time depends almost entirely on its ability to raise its output per worker."[16]

_____The Gains from Trade

While the idea that all countries can benefit from international trade goes back to Smith and Ricardo, subsequent research has described the gains from trade in much greater detail. In his book *Principles of Political Economy* (1848), John Stuart Mill, one of the leading economists of the nineteenth century, pointed to three principal gains from trade. First, there are what Mill called the "direct economical advantages of foreign trade." Second, there are "indirect effects" of trade, "which must be counted as benefits of a high order." Finally, Mill argued that "the economical benefits of commerce are surpassed in importance by those of its effects which are intellectual and moral."[17] What, specifically, are these three advantages of trade?

The "direct economical advantages" of trade are the standard gains that arise from specialization, as described by Smith and Ricardo. By exporting some of its domestically produced goods in exchange for imports, a country engages in mutually beneficial trade that enables it to use its limited productive resources (such as land, labor, and capital) more efficiently and therefore achieve a higher real national income than it could in the absence of trade. A higher real income translates into an ability to afford more of all goods and services than would be possible without trade.

Economists suspect that these static gains from specialization are sizable. But it is difficult to measure the overall gains from trade because most countries have always been open to world trade to some extent. We usually do not observe countries moving abruptly from situations of no trade to trade, or vice versa, so that we can calculate the benefits of trade.

[15] Asian Productivity Organization 2013, 58. The per capita income figure is based on market exchange rates rather than the purchasing power parity exchange rate.

[16] Krugman 1990, 9.

[17] Mill [1848] 1909, 580ff.

Fortunately, history provides a few examples of such changes that allow us to get a glimpse of the total static gains from trade.

The classic illustration of the direct gains from trade comes from Japan's opening to the world economy. In 1859, as a result of American pressure, Japan opened its ports to international trade after two centuries of self-imposed economic isolation (autarky). The gains from trade can be estimated by examining the prices of goods in Japan before and after the opening of trade. For example, the price of silk and tea was much higher on world markets than in Japan prior to the opening of trade, while the price of cotton and woolen goods was much lower on world markets. With the introduction of trade, prices of those goods in Japan converged to the prices on the world market. As a result, Japan began exporting silk and tea in exchange for imports of clothing and other goods. According to one calculation, Japan's national income was 8–9 percent higher as a result of the static reallocation of resources in response to the opportunity to trade.[18] (Of course, the long-run dynamic gains from acquiring better technology and improving its productivity were many multiples of this, and will be discussed shortly.)

The early United States provides another example, this time of a country that was open to trade and then deliberately shut its borders for a short period. In 1807, President Thomas Jefferson ordered an economic embargo to prevent the harassment of American shipping by British and French forces that were engaged in a bitter military conflict. While America's ports were closed to international commerce, the domestic price of imported goods rose 33 percent and the domestic price of exported goods fell 27 percent. The static welfare loss from this embargo was about 5 percent of U.S. GDP. It is little wonder that the embargo was highly unpopular and, as a result, abandoned after just fifteen months.[19]

A more recent example is the Israeli blockade of the Gaza Strip from 2007 to 2010, which pushed the small territory into autarky. A study of the blockade found that average welfare loss for a household in Gaza was equal to between 14 and 27 percent of the value of its pre-blockade expenditure. The welfare loss was disproportionally larger for wealthier households, who were more likely to purchase foreign goods. In addi-

[18] Bernhofen and Brown 2005.
[19] Irwin 2005b.

tion, labor productivity fell 36 percent in manufacturing because Gaza firms were cut off from the ability to source inputs and sell output abroad, but labor productivity hardly fell at all in services because they were not as dependent on foreign trade.[20] The impact of autarky on Gaza was much larger than in the earlier cases of Japan and the United States because it is a small country that is very dependent on trade. (Just imagine what would happen to the New Hampshire economy if it was prevented from trading with the rest of the United States and the world.)

Today, economists use various methods to estimate the gains from increased trade as a result of the reduction in trade barriers. The estimated gains are much smaller than the total gains from trade because existing trade barriers are relatively modest. One study that simulates the effects of removing all barriers to trade in agricultural and manufactured goods finds that the worldwide gains would be about $287 billion, or 0.7 percent of world income.[21] (This does not include liberalization of services trade or improvements in trade facilitation in developing countries.) For the United States, the real income gain would be $16 billion, or 0.1 percent of its GDP. This gain combines the benefits to the United States of reducing its own trade barriers and the benefits of lower foreign trade barriers. However, most of the gains to the United States from lower trade barriers around the world would likely come from opening up trade in services, which is not taken into account in this calculation.

As these examples indicate, the calculated welfare gains that emerge from these simulations are sometimes small as a percentage of GDP. Some have interpreted these calculations to mean that trade liberalization is not especially valuable. But the small numbers arise partly because these agreements usually lead to modest policy changes for the United States. For example, what the United States undertook in signing NAFTA or might undertake as a result of the current multilateral trade negotiations, essentially making already-low import tariffs somewhat lower, can-

[20] Etkes and Zimring 2015.

[21] Anderson, Martin, and van der Mensbrugghe 2006. These calculations arise from computable general equilibrium models, which are complex computational models used to simulate the impact of various trade policies on specific industries and the overall economy. These models calculate the gains that arise from shifting resources between various sectors of the economy; specifically, the shift of labor and capital away from industries that compete against imports toward those in which the country has a comparative advantage as a result of changes in trade policy.

not be compared to Japan's move from autarky to free trade or to Jefferson's embargo on shipping or to the Gaza blockade. In looking at the potential liberalization of trade going forward, these numbers do not reflect the entire gains from trade, just the marginal gains from an additional increase in trade as a consequence of a partial reduction in trade barriers.

More important, the reallocation of resources across industries as calculated in most simulation models does not take into account the other channels by which trade can improve economic performance. What are these other channels?[22] There is overwhelming evidence that free trade improves economic performance by increasing competition in the domestic market. This competition diminishes the market power of domestic firms and leads to a more efficient economic outcome. This benefit does not arise because foreign competition changes a domestic firm's costs through changes in the scale of output, but by changing the pricing behavior of imperfectly competitive domestic firms. Firms with market power tend to restrict output and raise prices, thereby harming consumers while increasing their own profits. With international competition, firms cannot get away with such conduct and are forced to behave more competitively. In fact, a survey of several studies concludes the following: "In *every* country studied, relatively high industry-wide exposure to foreign competition is associated with lower [price-cost] margins, and the effect is concentrated in larger plants."[23] Numerous studies confirm this finding in other countries, providing powerful evidence that trade disciplines domestic firms with market power. Yet the beneficial effects of

---

[22] Feenstra (2006) discusses some of the new sources of gains from trade.

[23] Roberts and Tybout 1996, 196. One view had been that greater openness to trade allows firms to sell in a potentially larger market, and that firms are able to reduce their average costs of production by expanding the size of their output. The lower production costs resulting from these economies of scale are passed on to consumers and thereby generate additional gains from trade. But economists have found that the importance of scale economies is overstated. Evidence from both developed and developing economies suggests that economies of scale at the plant level for most manufacturing firms tend to be small relative to the size of the market. As a result, most plants have attained their minimum efficient scale. Average costs seem to be relatively unaffected by changes in output, so that a big increase in a firm's output does not lead to lower costs, and a big reduction in output does not lead to higher costs. For example, many firms are forced to reduce output as a result of competition from imports, but these firms' production costs rarely increase very much. See Tybout 2003.

increasing competition are not always taken into account in the simulation models discussed above because they often assume that perfect
competition already exists.

Another problem with the standard estimates of the gains from trade
is that they largely overlook the benefits to consumers from exposure to
a greater variety of goods. This neglect comes from the traditional emphasis on the effects of trade on production, which is easily calculated,
whereas the gains to consumers from choice among a wider variety of
goods are more difficult to quantify. (Consumer utility is an amorphous
concept, and detailed product-level data are difficult to come by.) Yet the
few intriguing attempts to explore this benefit have suggested that it is
tremendously important. For example, tariffs may affect not just the
amount but also the range of foreign goods imported. When the selling
of a product in a market has a fixed cost, a tariff reduces the size of the
market and therefore the potential profits of engaging in trade. Because
the smaller size would not allow firms to recoup the fixed costs of selling
in that market, some varieties of goods would be excluded from it. In this
way, barriers to trade can reduce the range of goods available to an
economy and limit the availability of specialized consumer and producer
intermediate goods.

When trade restrictions reduce the number of traded goods, the welfare costs of those restrictions are much larger than in the standard analysis, where the number of traded goods is assumed to be fixed. The reason
is this: if a tariff eliminates imports of a particular variety of good, then
all the consumption benefits are lost with no offsetting gains. Although
the standard computable models do not account for this loss, we know
that variety is highly valued. For example, consider consumers in East
Germany and Poland who, after the collapse of Communism, found ex-
otic and affordable fruits such as bananas and oranges in the marketplace
for the first time in their lives. Or consider their newfound ability to purchase apples and cabbages without worms and rot. The effect of such
changes on aggregate output and income was negligible, but the welfare
gains from the availability of new and improved goods were not insignifi-
cant at all.

If a tariff simply reduces the quantity of an imported good, the loss to
consumers is a much smaller, second-order loss to overall welfare, be-

cause most of what consumers lose is transferred to producers or paid to the government in the form of tariff revenue. If a computable model assumes that a tariff just reduces the quantity of existing goods, when it actually reduces the range of imported goods, the welfare cost is understated—by as much as a factor of ten, according to one calculation.[24]

One study simulated the experience of a small open economy that reduces its import tariff from 20 to 10 percent. With constant returns to scale and no product variety, the welfare gain is 0.5 percent of the present value of consumption. With product variety, the welfare gain is about 10 percent of the present value of consumption over the infinite horizon. This is because the tariff reduction induces entry into the production of intermediate goods, and the resulting increase in variety reduces the cost of intermediates to final goods producers.[25]

These welfare effects need not imply an enormous change in national income: domestic output (measured GDP) may not change much as a result of the tariff. But the welfare cost can be substantial when consumers value the consumption of different varieties of goods. To the extent that economists focus only on trade's effect on production or income, they understate the gains from trade.

Is there systematic evidence that tariffs reduce the range of consumer and intermediate varieties available to an economy? Can we be sure that this reduction in variety of goods is costly to economic welfare? A growing body of evidence suggests that the answer is yes. For example, over the past three decades, the number of varieties imported by the United States has increased by a factor of four. The number of countries supplying each imported good has doubled. As a result, according to one study, consumer welfare is about 2.6 percent of GDP higher over this period simply due to the gains from variety.[26]

Furthermore, trade is responsive to tariff reductions, especially on the variety dimension. After trade barriers are reduced, not only do countries trade more of the same goods, but also trade expands most rapidly in goods that were previously not traded or traded only at low levels. In other words, goods on the margin are those that respond most to reduced

[24] Romer 1994.
[25] Rutherford and Tarr 2002.
[26] Broda and Weinstein 2006.

costs of exchange. The high sensitivity of trade flows to reductions in trade barriers may be due to this factor.[27]

Variety is just as valuable for producers as it is for consumers. Free trade expands the range of intermediate goods available for domestic firms to use as inputs. The availability of different specialized inputs can increase the range of goods produced and the efficiency of the industry that produces the final goods. For example, after India reduced its tariffs on intermediate goods in the 1990s, giving domestic firms access to previously unavailable inputs from the world market, the firms responded by increasing product scope significantly; about one-third of new product introductions have been attributed to lower tariffs, implying large dynamic gains from trade.[28] Furthermore, the use of new imported inputs by Korean business groups (chaebol) helped to promote total factor productivity growth at the industry level, even after controlling for other factors such as research-and-development expenditures.[29]

Finally, there are important gains from trade in terms of the quality of imported goods. One study looked at India's imports of computer printers between 1996 and 2005, when it abolished its 20 percent import tariff. It found that consumers reaped large gains from being able to purchase higher-quality goods, significant gains from lower prices, and small gains from increased variety.[30]

_____Productivity Gains

Trade improves economic performance not only by allocating a country's resources to their most efficient use, but also by making those resources more productive in what they are doing. This is the second of John Stuart Mill's three gains from trade, the one he called "indirect effects." These indirect effects include "the tendency of every extension of the market to improve the processes of production. A country which produces for a larger market than its own can introduce a more extended division of

[27] Hummels and Klenow 2005.

[28] Goldberg, Khandelwal, Pavcnik, and Topalova 2010.

[29] Feenstra, Markusen, and Zeile 1992. See also Kasahara and Rodrigue (2008) for evidence from China.

[30] Sheu 2014. She finds that consumers would require a 65 percent decrease in all 1996 prices to be as well off as they were with the quality available in 2005.

labour, can make greater use of machinery, and is more likely to make inventions and improvements in the processes of production."[31]

In other words, trade promotes productivity growth. The higher an economy's productivity level, the higher its standard of living. International trade contributes to productivity growth in at least two ways: it serves as a conduit for the transfer of foreign technologies that enhance productivity, and it increases competition in a way that stimulates industries to become more efficient and improve their productivity, often by forcing less productive firms out of business and allowing more productive firms to expand. After neglecting them for many decades, economists have finally studied these productivity gains from trade more systematically.

The first contribution, international trade serving as a conduit for the transfer of foreign technologies, operates in several ways.[32] One is through the importation of capital goods. Imported capital goods that embody technological advances can greatly enhance an economy's productivity. For example, the South Carolina textile magnate Roger Milliken (once a financier of anti–free trade political groups) bought textile machinery from Switzerland and Germany because domestically produced equipment was more costly and less sophisticated.[33] This imported machinery enabled his firms to increase productivity significantly. Between a quarter and half of growth in U.S. total factor productivity may be attributed to new technology embodied in capital equipment. To the extent that trade barriers raise the price of imported capital goods, countries are hindering their ability to benefit from technologies that could raise productivity. In fact, one study finds that about a quarter of the differences in productivity across countries can be attributed to differences in the price of capital equipment.[34]

Advances in productivity are sometimes the result of investment in research and development (R&D), and the importation of foreign ideas

---

[31] Mill [1848] 1909, 581.

[32] Keller 2004.

[33] Ryan Lizza, "Silent Partner: The Man Behind the Anti–Free Trade Revolt," *New Republic* 222 (January 10, 2000): 22–25.

[34] Eaton and Kortum 2001. Lee (1995) finds that the ratio of imported to domestically produced capital goods is significantly related to growth in per capita income, particularly in developing countries, and Mazumdar (2001) reaches similar conclusions.

can be a spur to productivity. Sometimes foreign research can be imported directly. For example, China has long struggled against a devastating disease known as rice blast, which in the past destroyed millions of tons of rice a year, costing farmers billions of dollars. Under the direction of an international team of scientists, farmers in China's Yunnan province started planting a mixture of two different types of rice in the same paddy. Through this simple technique of biodiversity, farmers nearly eliminated rice blast and doubled their yield. Foreign R&D enabled the Chinese farmers to increase yields of a staple commodity and to abandon the chemical fungicides they had previously used to fight the disease.[35]

At other times, the benefits of foreign R&D are secured by importing goods that embody it. Countries more open to trade gain more from foreign R&D expenditures because trade in goods serves as a conduit for the spillovers of productive knowledge generated by that R&D. Several studies have found that a country's total factor productivity depends not only on its own R&D but also on how much R&D is conducted in the countries that it trades with. Imports of specialized intermediate goods that embody new technologies, as well as reverseengineering of such goods, are sources of R&D spillovers. Thus, developing countries that do not conduct much R&D themselves can benefit from R&D done elsewhere, because trade makes the acquisition of new technology less costly.[36] These examples illustrate Mill's observation that "whatever causes a greater quantity of anything to be produced in the same place, tends to the general increase of the productive powers of the world."

The second way in which international trade contributes to productivity is by forcing domestic industries to become more efficient. We have already seen that trade increases competition in the domestic market, diminishing the market power of any single firm and forcing it to behave more competitively. Competition also stimulates firms to improve their efficiency; otherwise they risk going out of business. Over the past decade, study after study has documented this phenomenon. After the Côte d'Ivoire reformed its trade policies in 1985, overall productivity growth tripled, growing four times more rapidly in industries that became less sheltered from foreign competition. Industry productivity in Mexico in-

[35] Carol K. Yoon, "Simple Method Found to Increase Crop Yields Vastly," *New York Times*, August 22, 2000.

[36] See Madsen 2007 and Acharya and Keller 2007.

creased significantly after its trade liberalization in 1985, especially in traded-goods sectors. Detailed studies of Korea's trade liberalization in the 1980s, Brazil's during 1988–90, and India's in 1991 reached essentially the same conclusion: trade not only disciplines domestic firms and forces them to behave more like a competitive industry, but it also helps increase their productivity.[37]

Competition can force individual firms to adopt more efficient production techniques. But international competition also affects the entry and exit decisions of firms in a way that helps raise the aggregate productivity of an industry. In any given industry, productivity is quite heterogeneous among firms: not all firms are equally efficient. Trade strengthens high-productivity firms and eliminates those that are low-productivity firms. On the export side, exposure to trade allows firms that are more productive to become exporters and thereby expand their output. In the United States, plants with higher labor productivity within an industry tend to be the plants that export; in other words, more efficient firms are the ones that become exporters.[38] For example, one study of the U.S.-Canada Free Trade Agreement found that Canadian plants that were induced by the U.S. tariff cuts to start exporting (or to export more) increased their labor productivity, engaged in more product innovation, and had higher adoption rates for advanced manufacturing technologies.[39] The opportunity to trade, therefore, allows more-efficient firms to grow.

On the import side, competition forces the least productive firms to reduce their output or shut down. For example, when Chile began opening up its economy to the world market in the 1970s, exiting plants were, on average, 8 percent less productive than plants that continued to produce. The productivity of plants in industries competing against imports grew 3 to 10 percent more than in non–traded goods sectors. Protection had insulated less productive firms from foreign competition and allowed them to drag down overall productivity within an industry, whereas open trade weeded out inefficient firms and allowed more efficient firms to expand.[40] Thus, trade brings about certain firm-level adjustments that

---

[37] Harrison 1994; Tybout and Westbrook 1995; Kim 2000; Ferreira and Rossi 2003; Krishna and Mitra 1998; and Sivadasan 2009.

[38] See Bernard, Jensen, Redding, and Schott 2007 for a survey of this literature.

[39] Lileeva and Trefler 2010.

[40] Pavcnik 2002. Similarly for Colombia, see Fernandes 2007.

increase average industry productivity in both export-oriented and import-competing industries.

The impact of the U.S.-Canada Free Trade Agreement on Canadian manufacturing is suggestive. Tariff reductions helped boost labor productivity by a compounded rate of 0.6 percent per year in manufacturing as a whole and by 2.1 percent per year in the most affected (i.e., high-tariff) industries. These are astoundingly large effects. This amounts to a 17 percent increase in productivity in the post-FTA period in the highly affected sectors, and a 5 percent increase for manufacturing overall. These productivity effects were not achieved through scale effects or capital investment, but rather due to a mix of plant turnover and rising technical efficiency within plants. By raising productivity, the FTA also helped increase the annual earnings of production workers, particularly in the most protected industries.[41]

Recent work has highlighted the important distinction between tariffs on final goods (output) and tariffs on intermediate goods (capital goods and material inputs). Tariffs on final goods may harm consumers, but trade policies that increase the price of imported capital goods may be more damaging because they can affect the productivity of domestic firms. Tariffs and other trade barriers that raise the cost of capital goods mean that each investment dollar buys less capital. This reduces the efficiency of investment spending and can reduce overall investment and growth.[42] For example, a study of Indonesia found that a 10 percent reduction in input tariffs increased industry productivity by 3 percent, whereas a similar reduction in final goods tariffs increased industry productivity by less than 1 percent.[43] The reason for the difference is the channel by which the lower tariffs increase productivity: in the case of final goods, the gain comes from intensifying domestic competition, whereas with intermediate tariffs the gains arise more directly from importing higher-quality or different varieties of inputs. Indeed, the firms that actually imported intermediate inputs saw an 11 percent rise in productivity.

To sum up, traditional calculations of the gains from trade stress the benefits of shifting resources from protected industries to those with an

[41] Trefler 2004.
[42] Lee 1995.
[43] Amiti and Konings 2007.

international comparative advantage. But trade may affect the allocation of resources among firms within an industry as much as, if not more than, it affects the allocation of resources between different industries. New evidence shows that large productivity differences exist between plants within any given industry, and therefore shifting resources between firms within an industry may be even more important for productivity than shifting resources between industries. In addition, allowing domestic firms to import the best and cheapest capital goods and intermediate products in the world allows those companies to improve their performance. In doing so, trade helps improve productivity.

While difficult to quantify, these productivity effects of trade may be on an order of magnitude more important than the standard gains. Countries that have embraced trade liberalization over the past few decades, such as Chile, New Zealand, and Spain, have experienced more rapid growth in productivity than before. Free trade contributes to a process by which a country can adopt better technology and exposes domestic industries to new competition that forces them to improve their productivity. As a consequence, trade helps raise per capita income and economic well-being more generally.

Can We Measure the Gains from Trade?

We have seen that there are gains from trade and that trade raises productivity through a variety of mechanisms. But is there really a payoff in terms of higher income? Is it true that countries that engage in more trade, or reduce their trade barriers, will have a higher per capita income as a result? Can this be empirically verified in studies using cross-country data?

These questions may seem straightforward, but they are deceptively difficult to answer. Until recently, empirical analysis of these issues was unsatisfactory. The usual approach was to examine the statistical relationship between trade (typically measured by the ratio of exports to GDP) and income across many countries. Although studies usually uncovered a positive correlation between trade and income, the meaning of this result is uncertain. Perhaps countries that trade more have higher incomes, or perhaps countries with higher incomes engage in more trade because they have better ports and other infrastructure that support trade or because they have better economic policies in general.

Fortunately, creative research by Jeffrey Frankel and David Romer has overcome this ambiguity. They demonstrated that the reason higher incomes are associated with more trade is not simply because highincome countries trade more.[44] Indeed, they find that the effect of trade on income is strikingly higher once the part of trade that is not driven by income is isolated: the standard estimates suggest that a 1 percent increase in the trade share increases per capita income by about 0.8 percent, but using only geographic determinants of trade raises the estimated effect to about 2 percent (although this is imprecisely estimated). Frankel and Romer find that the effect of trade on income works mainly through higher productivity, but also by increasing the capital stock.

The Frankel-Romer approach has been extended and improved by subsequent researchers. One recent study introduces time-varying distance instruments that allow for the inclusion of country-specific effects.[45] This allows the researcher to control for all time-invariant factors that may be correlated with income, such as distance from the equator, the disease environment, and colonial history. The study finds a smaller impact of trade on income than Frankel and Romer—a 10 percent increase in trade leads to a 5 percent increase in per capita income—but it is much more robust. Furthermore, almost all of the effect of trade on income comes from higher productivity, not more physical or human capital.

Although differences in trade resulting from policy may not affect income the same way as differences resulting from geography, these results are suggestive for trade policy. One study therefore used dozens of statistical specifications to examine the link between various indicators of a country's trade policy and its per capita income. Almost invariably, more open trade policies are associated with higher per capita income, although

---

[44] The fundamental problem is that trade affects income and income affects trade. To isolate the effect of trade on income, a measure of trade that is unrelated to income must be found. Noting that distance from trade partners is a key determinant of trade but is unrelated to income, Frankel and Romer (1999) used a country's geographic attributes to identify the relationship between trade and income. Frankel and Rose (2002) later controlled for other variables and estimated somewhat lower coefficients of trade on income. Using the geographic determinants of trade produced an impact estimate of 0.43, and a long-run estimate of 1.6, lower than the earlier estimate of 2.

[45] Feyrer 2008.

the magnitude and significance of the relationship varied considerably depending upon the indicator used.[46]

According to the theories discussed earlier in this chapter, freer trade can be expected to lead to higher levels of income or consumer welfare, but not necessarily a higher rate of economic growth. Yet in the transition from a lower to a higher level of income, the growth rate should increase. What sort of growth effect from trade liberalization is plausible? Suppose trade barriers are reduced such that the share of imports in GDP rises from 10 to 14 percent. This move to free trade allows the economy to purchase an additional 4 percent of GDP's worth of imports. If we assume that the average surplus gain from these imports is half the export cost, then the real value of consumption rises 2 percent. If the reduction in trade barriers is phased in over a decade, this corresponds to an increase in growth of about 0.2 percent annually.[47]

In this case, the trade policy change would not have a decisive, or even noticeable, impact on the overall rate of economic growth in any given year. But the magnitude of the impact on growth does not need to be large to generate substantial welfare benefits over time. A permanent increase in the steady state growth rate of an economy of just 0.2 percent can yield a welfare gain equivalent to a 5 percent increase in the present value of consumption over a long horizon.[48]

What is the empirical link between trade liberalization and economic growth? While several studies have found a positive relationship between lower trade barriers and more rapid economic growth in the postwar period, others have questioned these results.[49] One obstacle that hampers these empirical studies is the absence of a single variable that accurately measures trade policy.[50] The relationship between trade policy and eco-

[46] Jones 2001. However, Rodríguez and Rodrik (2001) have countered that reverse causality precludes this conclusion because richer countries have chosen to have lower trade barriers.

[47] I owe this example to Brad DeLong.

[48] Rutherford and Tarr 2002, 268.

[49] Rodríguez and Rodrik (2001) dissect many of the studies and question the robustness of their results and whether changes in trade barriers are responsible for the observed growth performance. More recent papers described in the following paragraphs take greater care in addressing their concerns and find a robust relationship running from trade liberalization to economic growth. Chapter 6 addresses this issue as well.

[50] There is no single metric that ideally describes the stance of a country's trade policy. Import tariffs can be measured imperfectly, but they are not necessarily the most important

nomic growth may be hard to pin down in the context of cross-country growth comparisons, partly because trade policy is poorly measured, and partly because the effects of trade policy may be swamped by other factors that are difficult to measure.

Recent studies have addressed many of the flaws that have plagued previous research. Most previous studies estimated the growth effects of trade liberalization by examining a cross-section of countries, that is, by comparing country X's experience with country Y's. But the difference in these countries' growth rates could be due to a host of reasons that economists cannot adequately control for. Instead, a more recent study uses a panel of data from 1950 to 1998 to estimate the *within*-country response of per capita income, investment, and trade share to the date of major trade policy changes.[51] After controlling for time-invariant country characteristics, the study shows the average within-country growth rate to be 1.5 percentage points higher after periods of trade liberalization in comparison to the no-reform period.[52] However, there is considerable heterogeneity in the growth effect—although the average effect is positive and statistically significant, in about half of the countries growth was zero or negative in the post-liberalization period. The within-country effect of trade reform on the investment rate is also positive and around 1.5 to 2.0 percentage points.[53] And the ratio of exports and imports to GDP is found to rise about 5 percentage points as a result of trade liberalization.

Another recent study of liberalizing and nonliberalizing countries during the 1990s finds that countries that reduced import duties on capital goods and intermediate inputs grew about 1 percentage point faster than other countries that did not.[54] Relative to their baseline growth experience from 1975 to 1989, the liberalizing countries saw their GDP per worker rise 15 to 20 percent relative to nonliberalizers, consistent with an extra

---

feature of trade policy today. Nontariff barriers can be an even more important impediment to trade in many countries, but they cannot be measured precisely. See the World Bank (2008a) for an attempt to provide benchmark indicators of trade policy across the world.

[51] Wacziarg and Welch 2008.

[52] They are also able to control for the fact that many reforms are undertaken during periods of economic crisis and therefore growth may rebound after a stabilization that includes trade reform.

[53] See also Wacziarg 2001.

[54] Estevadeordal and Taylor 2013.

1 percentage point of growth per year. Reducing tariffs on final consumption goods did not have such a strong impact on economic growth. This reinforces the point that trade barriers on capital goods and intermediate products are especially harmful to economic performance. And yet another study of economic policy liberalization, focusing largely on trade policy and a country's openness to world trade, found that reforming countries grew more rapidly than similar but non-reforming countries, although there was significant heterogeneity in the outcome, particularly after the 1990s.[55]

What should be concluded from this research? While there is no guarantee that trade liberalization will increase the level of income or the rate of economic growth under all circumstances, the repeated finding of a positive relationship between them is more than just coincidence. Despite shortcomings in method and measurement, cross-country and within-country studies support the conclusion that economies with more open trade policies tend to perform better than those with more restrictive trade policies. Additional, striking evidence comes from individual country experiences. These event studies clearly dramatize the benefits of deregulating imports, and the experience of countries such as China, Chile, South Korea, India, and Vietnam will be considered in chapter 6.

Additional Benefits of Trade

The economic gains from trade are substantial, but they are not the only benefits that come to countries with a policy of open trade. John Stuart Mill's third and final claim was that "the economical advantages of commerce are surpassed in importance by those of its effects which are intellectual and moral."[56] Mill did not elaborate, but he may have been referring to the idea of *deux commerce*, exemplified by Montesquieu's observation in *The Spirit of the Laws* (1748) that "commerce cures de-

---

[55] Billmeir and Nannicini 2013.

[56] "It is hardly possible to overrate the value . . . of placing human beings in contact with persons dissimilar to themselves, and with modes of thought and action unlike those with which they are familiar," Mill continues, because "there is no nation which does not need to borrow from others, not merely particular arts or practices, but essential points of character in which its own type is inferior" ([1848] 1909, 581).

structive prejudices."[57] Trade brings people into contact with one another and, according to this view, breaks down the narrow prejudices that come with insularity. Commerce can also force merchants to be more responsive to customers, as greater competition gives consumers a wider choice. This may be a quality margin on which producers compete for the patronage of consumers.

For example, a study on the effects of fast-food restaurant chain McDonald's on Asian culture noted that restrooms in Hong Kong previously had the reputation for being unspeakably filthy. When McDonald's opened in the mid-1970s, it redefined standards, setting a new, higher benchmark for cleanliness that other restaurants were forced to emulate. In Korea, McDonald's established the practice of lining up on a firstcome, firstserve basis to purchase food, rather than the rugby scrum that had been the norm. When McDonald's first opened in Moscow, a young woman with a bullhorn stood outside its doors to explain to the crowd that the servers smiled not because they were laughing at customers but because they were happy to serve them. Sanitation, queuing, and friendly service have their advantages and surely make for more pleasant living, whatever your opinion of McDonald's food.[58]

There is also a longstanding idea that trade promotes peace among nations. Many Enlightenment philosophers in the eighteenth century and classical liberals in the nineteenth century endorsed this view. Montesquieu argued that "the natural effect of commerce is to lead to peace" because "two nations that trade with each other become reciprocally dependent." John Stuart Mill endorsed this view: "It is commerce which is rapidly rendering war obsolete, by strengthening and multiplying the personal interests which are in natural opposition to it. And it may be said without exaggeration that the great extent and rapid increase of international trade, in being the principal guarantee of the peace of the world,

---

[57] Montesquieu [1748] 1989, 338.

[58] See Watson 1997. Some globalization critics revile McDonald's for destroying local cuisine and foisting homogeneous, unhealthy, processed food on the public. Yet Watson (1997) points out that McDonald's restaurants located in foreign countries are locally owned and highly attuned to local culture and tastes. One recent survey indicated that nearly half of all Chinese children under the age of twelve identified McDonald's as a domestic brand. See Elisabeth Rosenthal, "Buicks, Starbucks and Fried Chicken: Still China?" *New York Times*, February 25. 2002.

is the great permanent security for the uninterrupted progress of the ideas, the institutions, and the character of the human race."[59]

Political scientists, and a few economists, have examined whether economic interdependence mitigates conflict between nations. Most empirical studies have tended to support the idea that there is a positive link between trade and peace.[60] While the link between trade and peace is intriguing, there are many difficulties in establishing a statistical relationship between them. The methodological obstacles include making political concepts operational and representing them numerically, as well as establishing causal relationships. For example, countries that are at peace with one another are also more likely to be trading partners; which is the cause and which is the effect? Countries that are less aggressive are probably more likely to join international institutions, raising the same question. One recent study finds countervailing effects: increased bilateral trade increases the cost of conflict between the partners and thereby promotes peace, but increased multilateral trade may reduce the cost of conflict (because a country would have alternative sources of supply) and hence may increase the risk of conflict.[61]

If the trade-peace link is eminently plausible though not definitively established, a stronger finding is that democracies are more peaceful than autocratic countries. While we do not know whether democratic regimes are inherently more peaceful than other types of government, overwhelming evidence shows that democracies rarely go to war against one another. Does increasing trade contribute to peace indirectly, by promoting political reform and democratization? Untangling the links between trade and democratization is difficult because each is related to the other. Trade may indeed promote democracy, but democracies are also more likely to pursue open trade policies and therefore trade more.[62]

---

[59] Mill [1848] 1909, 582.

[60] See Hegre, Oneal, and Russett 2010. In his essay "Perpetual Peace" (1795), the great philosopher Immanuel Kant suggested that durable peace could be built upon the tripod of representative democracy, international organizations, and economic interdependence.

[61] Martin, Mayer, and Thoenig 2008. It is sometimes thought that World War I demonstrates the failure of trade to ensure peace, but more careful scholarship shows that this was not the case: the conflict started among countries that were less well integrated into world trade (Austria-Hungary and Serbia). See Gartzke and Lupu 2012.

[62] Mansfield, Milner, and Rosendorff (2000) examine this relationship.

Even after accounting for this effect, it appears that trade does indeed promote democracy. Examining the period after 1870, one study detects a positive impact of openness on democracy from about 1895 onward. Late nineteenth-century globalization may have helped to generate the "first wave" of democratization. Between 1920 and 1938, countries more exposed to international trade were less likely to become authoritarian. These results hold for the post–World War II period as well. However, there is some variation in the impact of openness by region, and commodity exporters and petroleum producers do not seem to become more democratic by exporting more of such goods.[63] Recent research also indicates a relationship between free trade agreements and the strengthening of democracy in developing countries.[64] By destroying the rents that come from protectionist policies, such agreements reduce the incentive of authoritarian groups to seize power. Thus, governments in unstable democracies may have an incentive to seek such agreements to consolidate their position.

This view of nineteenth-century classical liberals appears to have gained new support in recent years as well: as Chile, Taiwan, South Korea, and Mexico have been integrated into the world economy, they have also moved toward more democratic political systems. Those opposed to the U.S. trade embargo against Cuba believe that greater trade with that country would increase the prospects of political reform there too.

The big question today is whether economic development and expanding trade will lead China to move away from its authoritarian political regime and toward a more pluralistic political system that includes improvements in human rights. The link between trade liberalization and political liberalization was a contentious issue in the debate over extending Permanent Normalized Trade Relations (PNTR) to China and allowing it to join the WTO in 2000. Proponents of normalized trade argued that expanding commerce would enhance the power and influence of the private sector in China at the expense of the government. Opponents disagreed, arguing that more trade would simply enrich and strengthen the Chinese government. Although greater openness has operated very

---

[63] Lopez-Cordova and Meissner 2004. See also Eichengreen and Leblang 2008.
[64] Liu and Ornelas 2014.

slowly in the case of China, there is some evidence of potentially important political changes at local levels.[65]

Even if trade fails to generate a movement toward democracy, it can still promote better performance in other domestic institutions. For example, countries that are more open also tend to be less corrupt, a finding that holds even after accounting for the fact that less corrupt countries may engage in more trade.[66] Conversely, protectionist policies have been found to breed corruption, particularly when bureaucrats have discretion in allocating import licenses to those who wish to import goods.[67] A study of India finds that freer trade led to a reduction in violent crime, because trade restrictions led to smuggling and gang violence; in particular, murder rates fell significantly after the 1991 trade reforms, especially in industrial states more affected by the lifting of import barriers.[68]

While the statistical relationships among trade, peace, and democracy are difficult to sort out, the existing evidence suggests that they share beneficial links. In sum, Mill's observations about the noneconomic benefits of trade—including peace and political reform—appear to be broadly valid, although they may not hold in every case.

_____*Free Trade and the Environment*

Among the most vocal of free trade's many critics are those who worry about its impact on the environment. Some environmentalists believe that freer international trade will lead to more economic activity, and more economic activity will lead to greater environmental degradation. In other words, with trade comes more logging, more fishing, more soil erosion, more industrial pollution, and so on. But what, in fact, is the relationship between trade and the environment? Must trade lead to environmental damage, or might it in some ways actually benefit the environment? And do restrictions on trade improve the environment?

To answer these questions, we must recognize that the link between trade and the environment is indirect. Some of the greatest environmental disasters in recent decades have taken place in communist countries, par-

---

[65] See Thorton (2008) for an assessment of the prospect for democracy in China.
[66] Ades and Di Tella 1999.
[67] Dutt 2009.
[68] Prasad 2012.

ticularly in Eastern Europe and the former Soviet Union. The horrible air pollution caused by state-run, coal-burning, capital-intensive industries and the destruction of lakes and streams with toxic chemicals owed nothing to free trade but resulted from a system of centralized decision-making that valued resources less wisely than a system of decentralized markets with well-established property rights and prudent government regulation. This is also the underlying problem in China: the political authorities are not accountable to the people and hence they are not responsive to citizen demands for a clean environment. The communist leaders of China reward provincial officials solely on the basis of economic growth, not on the quality of life of the people in the province. As a result, China has been systematically destroying its air and water resources.

In other countries as well, trade is not the underlying cause of environmental damage. The burning of the Amazon rain forests is largely motivated by local inhabitants clearing land for their own use, not international trade. And simple observation demonstrates that more trade and commerce does not always create more pollution: air quality in Delhi and Mexico City prior to economic liberalization was much worse than in most advanced countries, even though those cities had fewer cars and generated less electricity.

Environmental damage results from poor environmental policies, not poor trade policies. Environmental damage arises from the inappropriate use of our natural resources in the land, sea, and air. The overuse of these resources is commonly related to the lack of well-defined property rights. When property rights are not well established, that is, when no one has ownership rights and control over a resource, then open access to the resource frequently leads to its exploitation beyond the socially optimal level. For example, if ownership of a forest is not well defined, then anyone can chop down trees for his or her own use without paying the costs associated with utilizing the resource.[69] If control of the forest were established through property rights, then the owners would regulate and charge for the use of the timber. Obviously, the ownership and overuse problems are particularly acute for the air and ocean, where government

---

[69] Ferreira (2004) finds that openness to trade alone does not promote deforestation, but that it can do so in countries with poor government institutions that fail to define and protect property rights.

regulation of the right to use the resource, reflecting public ownership of it, may be called for.

In many such cases, because environmental problems stem from the failure to clearly establish and enforce private or public property rights, trade policy is not the first-best means by which to achieve environmental objectives. Trade is only indirectly related to environmental problems, and therefore trade policy is an indirect, inefficient, and often inefficacious way of addressing environmental problems.

Fortunately, the objectives of free trade and a cleaner environment often work together. For example, numerous studies have traced the relationship between pollution emissions and a country's per capita income. They have generally found a relationship shaped like an inverted U: as per capita incomes rise from low levels, pollution increases, but beyond a certain point (about $5,000), further increases in income tend to diminish pollution.[70] The initial increase in pollution is due to industrialization, while the decrease is due to cleaner production technologies and more effective environmental regulation that come with higher incomes. Both Delhi and New York City have traffic jams, for example, but the locally made cars and scooters in developing countries tend to belch out worse fumes than those with cleaner exhaust systems in the United States.

Beyond the threshold, higher incomes do not mean more pollution and lower incomes do not mean less pollution. To the extent that trade increases a country's income beyond the turning point in the inverted U relationship, it helps indirectly to improve the environment. More directly, new technology is cleaner technology and trade facilitates the diffusion of new technology. Furthermore, the "dirty industry migration" hypothesis, that polluting industries will move to developing countries where environmental regulations are lax, has received little empirical support. There is no "race to the bottom" in environmental standards because the costs of abating pollution are not a significant determinant of industries' location, and consequently not a significant determinant of trade flows.[71]

[70] This is also known as the environmental Kuznets curve; see Dasgupta, Laplante, Wang, and Wheeler 2002.

[71] See Jaffe et al. 1995 and Karp 2011. A recent study of the pollution haven hypothesis with respect to China found that equity joint ventures in highly-polluting industries funded through Hong Kong, Macao, and Taiwan are attracted by weak environmental standards in

One important study examined three channels by which trade can affect sulfur dioxide (SO_2) emissions: the scale effect (increases in economic activity increase SO_2 emissions), the technique effect (increases in income lead to cleaner production methods and reduce emissions), and the composition effect (trade alters the composition of activity and hence the average pollution intensity of national output). The authors were surprised to conclude that free trade is good for the environment because, as an empirical matter, the technique effect outweighs the scale and composition effects.[72] The effect of income growth on pollution depends largely on the underlying source of growth: growth achieved through capital accumulation tends to raise pollutants, while growth achieved by trade and technological change appears to reduce pollutants. This could also account for the inverted-U-shaped relationship of pollution to income—developing countries initially tend to achieve growth through (dirtier) capital accumulation, whereas growth in developed countries is based on human capital accumulation and technology (cleaner methods).

Another study focused on the issue of causality in estimating the effect of trade on the environment for a given level of income.[73] This study looked at the links between trade and seven measures of environmental quality and found that trade had a strongly beneficial impact in reducing SO_2 emissions, and a less significant but still positive impact in reducing NO_2 emissions and total suspended particulate matter. Trade also reduced energy depletion and increased access to clean water, while having no impact on deforestation. The one exception was CO_2 emissions, where increased openness was related to greater emissions, perhaps because of the free-rider problem afflicting countries that seek to limit greenhouse gas emissions. But the study found no evidence for a "race to the bottom" in environmental standards or the "pollution haven" hypothesis, in which trade encourages some countries to specialize in dirtier industries.

China. In contrast, joint ventures funded from non-ethnically Chinese sources are not significantly attracted by weak standards, regardless of the pollution intensity of the industry (Dean, Lovely, and Wang 2009).

[72] Antweiler, Copeland, and Taylor 2001. Their empirical estimates of the scale effect indicate that a 1 percent increase in the scale of economic activity increases SO_2 emissions by 0.3 percent, but that the technique effect suggests that a 1 percent increase in income decreases emissions by 1.4 percent.

[73] Frankel and Rose 2005.

In terms of the United States, real manufacturing output has increased by more than 70 percent over the past thirty years, while pollution emissions have fallen significantly (ranging from 30 percent for nitrogen oxides to 66 percent for sulfur dioxides). The United States even reduced its carbon dioxide emissions from energy sources by 12 percent between 2005 and 2012, although those emissions rose 2 percent in 2013. Most of this overall decline is due to improved production technology or abatement processes, not importing dirtier products from abroad to avoid domestic regulation. Indeed, the average pollution content of U.S. imports has fallen over time, and the United States does not seem to have been offshoring pollution by importing polluting goods.[74]

Unfortunately, U.S. trade policy sometimes supports special interests at the expense of the environment. For example, to reduce its dependence on imported oil and reduce greenhouse gas emissions, the United States has encouraged the use of ethanol, an agricultural-based product that is blended with gasoline. U.S.-produced ethanol, which is primarily based on corn, is subsidized by Congress with a fifty-one-cent-per-gallon tax credit (which has been one factor in rising corn prices). But sugar-based ethanol is significantly cheaper and generates eight times more energy per unit of input than corn-based ethanol. Yet Congress imposed a tariff of 2.5 percent plus fifty-four cents per gallon on sugar-based ethanol (which comes primarily from Brazil) in order to protect Midwestern corn farmers and agri-businesses from foreign competition. Using sugar ethanol is energy-efficient and environmentally sustainable, would reduce fuel prices and help friendly nations like Brazil, and limit dependence on imported oil from Venezuela and the Middle East. The Bush administration proposed eliminating the tariff in 2006, but Congress rejected this idea, thereby discouraging the use of sugar ethanol.

The case of solar panels is another instance in which protectionist trade policies have conflicted with environmental goals. The federal government has spent billions of dollars in production subsidies and consumer tax credits to encourage the use of alternative energy sources, such as solar. Low-cost solar panels and modules are essential to making it cost competitive with fossil fuels. Yet in 2012, the United States imposed stiff tariffs—ranging from 34 to more than 260 percent—on solar panels im-

---

[74] Levinson 2009; Levinson 2010; Kahn 2003.

ported from China. (The rationale for the tariffs is that the imports were being dumped and subsidized in the U.S. market; see chapter 5 for a discussion of antidumping and countervailing duties.) By making solar panels more expensive, these tariffs have reduced planned installation of solar power systems since steadily falling prices have been driving the adoption of solar power by households and businesses alike.

The environmental degradation associated with China's trade and economic growth has been a particular concern. The 2008 Olympic Games highlighted the problem of intense smog around Beijing, and there are many stories of lakes and rivers being poisoned by industrial pollution, fertilizer runoff, and algal bloom. Unfortunately, in its push for growth the Chinese government has not valued the environment (which underscores the importance of accountable governance), although this is beginning to change. But has trade per se exacerbated the problem? One recent study shows that industrial emissions have stabilized while rapid growth in trade has continued—a result that can be explained by the declining pollution intensity of output.[75] The study examined the direct emissions of four pollutants for about thirty Chinese industries and found that the pollution intensity of almost all sectors has fallen in terms of water pollution (chemical oxygen demand) and air pollution (measured by SO_2, smoke, or dust). The study also revealed that China's export bundle is shifting toward relatively cleaner sectors over time, such as office and computing machinery and communications equipment as opposed to textiles and apparel. The most polluting sectors, such as paper and nonmetallic minerals, have very low and declining shares in China's manufacturing exports. Furthermore, China's exports are less water pollution intensive and generally less air pollution intensive than Chinese import-competing industries, and both Chinese exports and imports are becoming cleaner over time.[76]

[75] Dean and Lovely 2010.

[76] Furthermore, some calculations of the pollution content of China's exports ignore the distinction between China's domestic exports and its processed exports (related to production fragmentation). Processed exports account for half of China's exports and generate relatively little domestic value added but also relatively few environmentally harmful emissions. Dietzenbacher, Pei, and Yang (2012) find that China's emissions as embodied in its exports are overestimated by more than 60 percent if the distinction between processing exports and normal exports is not made.

Across the world, governments tend to protect and support heavy industries, such as steel and petrochemicals, which are among the dirtiest and most polluting industries. State-owned enterprises in China, for instance, are much dirtier than their private counterparts because they are much less efficient and technologically up-to-date. Therefore, reducing subsidies and trade barriers can help shut these polluters down and shift production to more efficient producers that use cleaner technologies. A recent study that examined trade in high-efficiency and clean coal technologies, efficient lighting, solar photovoltaics, and wind power found that tariff and nontariff barriers are significant impediments to the diffusion of clean energy technologies to developing countries.[77]

International negotiators are attempting to limit many government trade policies that are harmful to the environment. Three specific cases provide an illustration of the environmentally damaging effects of trade barriers and subsidies: fisheries, agriculture, and forestry trade. Ocean fishing is a classic example of a common resource that is overutilized, and yet fishing is a heavily subsidized activity. A study prepared for the European Parliament estimates that world fishing subsidies amounted to $35 billion in 2009, much of it in the form of fuel and capacity subsidies, and particularly in Asian countries, such as Japan and China.[78] Many of these subsidies have led to excess capacity in fishing fleets, which in turn promotes overfishing. In this way, such subsidies directly harm efforts to conserve fishing stocks and promote sustainable development. Clearly there is no tradeoff in eliminating fishing subsidies and preserving the environment. In fact, the United States, Iceland, Australia, and New Zealand have pressed the membership of the World Trade Organization to discuss an international agreement to limit or abolish fishing subsidies, not just because such subsidies distort trade but also because they contribute to the depletion of ocean resources.

In the agricultural sector, the governments of advanced countries commonly intervene through import restrictions, domestic price supports, and export subsidies. These trade barriers and price subsidies tend to be implemented in countries that do not have a comparative advantage in agricultural goods and cause producers there to intensify their efforts in

---

[77] World Bank 2008b.
[78] Sumaila, Lam, Le Manach, Swartz, and Pauly 2013.

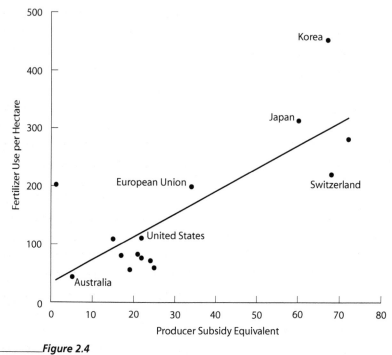

_____Figure 2.4

Figure 2.4

Producer Protection and Fertilizer Use in Agriculture, 2000
  Sources: OECD 2008, table 3.3; and FAO 2002, table 14.

environmentally harmful ways. As figure 2.4 indicates, the more a country protects its domestic agricultural producers, the more those producers rely on pesticides and fertilizers. Korea, Japan, Switzerland, and, to a lesser extent, the European Union heavily protect agriculture and must rely on chemicals to boost yields because these regions are not particularly well suited for all types of agricultural production.[79] As a result, trade barriers and production subsidies have "intensified land use, increased applications of agrochemicals, [and caused] adoption of intensive animal

[79] As Anderson (1998, 74) notes, "Land-scarce Western Europe and Japan crop twice as much of their total land area as does the rest of the world on average, so the extent of contamination of their soil, water, and air from the use of farm chemicals is even greater. . . ." Thus, "the relocation of crop production from densely populated protectionist countries to the rest of the world would cause a much larger reduction in degradation in the former compared with any increased degradation in the latter, where chemical use would expand from a low base and to still-modest levels."

production practices and overgrazing, degradation of natural resources, loss of natural wildlife habitats and bio diversity, reduced agricultural diversity, and expansion of agricultural production into marginal and ecologically sensitive areas."[80] Countries that have a comparative advantage in agriculture, whether they are developed, such as Canada and Australia, or developing, such as Argentina and Brazil, do not depend as heavily on fertilizers and pesticides to maintain output.

Liberalizing trade in agricultural products would therefore benefit the environment by allowing countries with a comparative advantage in agriculture to expand production and forcing countries with a comparative disadvantage to contract output. One economist has noted that "an international relocation of cropping production from high-priced to low-priced countries would reduce substantially, and quickly, the use of chemicals in world food production."[81] In addition, the relocation of meat and milk production from intensive grain-feeding enterprises in densely populated rich countries to pasture-based enterprises in relatively lightly populated poorer countries would reduce the use of growth hormones and medicines for animals.

A related issue is the effort to minimize "food miles" (the distance food travels) and to encourage consumers to buy local produce. The goal of reducing greenhouse gas emissions has led many people to conclude, erroneously it turns out, that buying locally produced food is better for the environment than importing food over long distances. As Adrian Williams, an agricultural researcher at Cranfield University in the United Kingdom, explains, "The idea that a product travels a certain distance and is therefore worse than one you raised nearby—well, it's just idiotic. It doesn't take into consideration the land use, the type of transportation, the weather, or even the season," or other factors such as cultivation and harvesting methods, water use, fertilizer use, and packaging.[82]

In fact, greenhouse gas emissions are dominated by the production phase, not the transport. For example, the environmental cost of air-freighting roses from Kenya to Britain is much less than importing them across the English Channel from the Netherlands because heated greenhouses in Europe have a very high carbon footprint, whereas Kenya's

[80] Sampson 2000, 55.
[81] Anderson 1992, 163.
[82] Specter 2008.

natural climate is much less energy- and fertilizer-dependent. Lamb produced in New Zealand and shipped eleven thousand miles by boat has one-fourth the CO_2 emissions of British-produced lamb because of New Zealand's greater production efficiency and cleaner production methods (less energy intensive, less fertilizer, etc.). The same applies to the production of New Zealand apples, which requires less fertilizer than elsewhere and uses electricity generated from renewable resources.[83] Finally, in terms of environmental impact, New Yorkers might consider consuming more wines from France as opposed to California because the carbon intensity of transporting wine by sea is substantially less (per unit) than transport via truck across the country.

With regard to forest products, the United States sought without success to eliminate all tariffs on such goods in recent multilateral trade negotiations. Environmental critics have charged that liberalizing trade in forest products will merely accelerate an unsustainable rate of deforestation around the world. Yet trade in timber and timber products is a minor cause of deforestation in tropical countries. Almost all the annual logging in developing countries is for the domestic production of fuel and charcoal—for the simple reason that fuel and charcoal are the cheapest source of energy for poor people. About 77 percent of forest timber production in Asia, 70 percent in South America, and 89 percent in Africa is for domestic fuel and charcoal.[84] As with all open-access resources, better forestry management is the key to reducing the rate of deforestation.

In fact, not only are policies that reduce trade in forest products ineffective in reducing deforestation, but also limiting trade in forest products may exacerbate the problem. Without the timber trade, which raises the value of forests by providing external demand for its products, the investment value of these forests would fall. This smaller value would give local users less of an incentive to conserve the resource. In addition, eliminating trade restrictions would directly improve the efficiency of wood use. For example, Indonesia maintains high export taxes on logs to promote domestic forest-based industrialization. These export taxes have generated a large but inefficient domestic lumber industry. Every cubic meter of Indonesian plywood produced requires the cutting of 15 percent more

[83] Saunders, Barber, and Taylor 2006. Webb, Williams, Hope, Evans, and Moorhouse 2013.
[84] World Resources Institute 1999, table 11.3.

trees than if plywood mills elsewhere in Asia were to process the logs. Not only has Indonesia's policy of protecting plywood mills failed to reduce total log demand, but gross operational inefficiencies have also led to a much higher rate of logging than if log exports were allowed.[85] Thus, a ban on imports of raw tropical forest lumber by developed countries would not only fail to counter the underlying cause of deforestation, but also might accelerate it due to the inefficiency of local processors.

Despite all of this evidence, critics of free trade are often quick to oppose trade agreements ostensibly on the basis of their environmental impact. Controversy about the environmental impact of free trade was particularly intense during the debate over NAFTA in 1993. Yet there were reasons to expect that NAFTA would lead to environmental improvements in Mexico. Aside from increasing income and promoting the adoption of newer, cleaner production technologies, Mexico has a comparative advantage in unskilled labor-intensive goods rather than in capital-intensive goods. Hence, freer trade may force dirtier capital-intensive industries in Mexico to contract as a result of competition. With protective tariffs eliminated, these industries are forced to shut down or adopt better technology to stay in business.

Furthermore, an environmental side agreement to NAFTA was negotiated. As a result, environmental groups that represented approximately 80 percent of the membership of the entire environmental community agreed to support the agreement.[86] But more militant organizations, such as the Sierra Club, Friends of the Earth, Greenpeace, and Public Citizen, continued to oppose NAFTA. These groups generally oppose any growth-oriented trade policy, regardless of its environmental provisions. Steward Hudson of the National Wildlife Foundation testified before Congress that "a fair and objective reading of the NAFTA leaves you with one uncompromising conclusion: the environment is far better off with this NAFTA than without . . . those who want to kill NAFTA are hiding behind the environment. The environmental critics of NAFTA, those who would forever be holding out for more, even at the expense of making progress on the environment in dealing with problems that concern all of us, are out

---

[85] Barbier, Bockstael, Burgess, and Strand 1995, 419.

[86] These groups included the World Wildlife Fund, the National Wildlife Federation, the Environmental Defense Fund, the National Audubon Society, and others (Audley 1997, 90).

to kill trade. . . . No amount of fine tuning or renegotiation will satisfy these opponents of NAFTA. The bar will continue to be raised because the goal is to kill NAFTA."[87]

In fact, recent assessments have concluded that NAFTA did not lead to a deterioration in Mexico's environment, but unfortunately it has not spurred many improvements either. A trade agreement itself cannot reverse decades of abuse. Environmental conditions along the U.S.-Mexican border remain poor despite the institutions and programs created to improve the situation.[88] One study illustrates the mixed picture by looking at trade in used automobiles, which opened up between the two countries in 2005. Since then, Mexico has imported over 2.5 million used vehicles from the United States. Average vehicle emissions per mile fell in both countries because traded vehicles are dirtier than the average car in the United States and cleaner than the average car in Mexico. However, trade may have increased total lifetime emissions because older cars have a longer life in Mexico.[89]

None of this evidence should be interpreted as minimizing the importance of taking effective measures to improve the environment. But free trade and a cleaner environment are not incompatible. Because trade in itself is not a driving force behind pollution, a policy of free trade rarely detracts from such goals, and in many instances may help. (The link between world trade rules and environmental regulation is also considered in chapter 7.)

_____*Free Trade in Perspective*

The benefits of free trade appear to be substantial, although precise quantification of those benefits is sometimes difficult. In extreme cases, governments that force their citizens to forgo the advantages of international trade, particularly in developing countries (as will be discussed in

[87] U.S. House of Representatives 1994, 368–70. In the end, the major congressional critics of NAFTA, such as Richard Gephardt, David Bonior, and Marcy Kaptur, made no reference to the environment in their floor speeches against the agreement, but rather focused on job loss in the United States (Audley 1997, 106). The more extreme opponents of NAFTA were prone to exaggeration and hyperbole. The Sierra Club, for instance, said that NAFTA would be "a major step toward ending democracy" in America.

[88] Hufbauer and Schott 2005.

[89] Davis and Kahn 2011.

chapter 6), do not sacrifice just a couple of percentage points of national income, but risk impoverishing their people. The higher real income that comes with trade is valuable not just to allow the consumption of more goods for crass material reasons, but to help people afford food and medicine. Free trade and higher incomes give people access to better healthcare, better education, and better technologies that will help improve the environment. Regrettably, the United States, the European Union, and other developed countries impose stiff import barriers on agricultural products and labor-intensive manufactured goods, such as clothing and leather, in which developing countries have a comparative advantage. This not only harms consumers in their own country, but reduces income in developing countries as well.

But several caveats should be offered. Free trade is beneficial because it allows a country to take advantage of the opportunity to trade, but it is not the only—or even the most important—determinant of whether a country achieves economic prosperity. Free trade is not a "magic bullet" that can solve all economic problems. The real and substantial gains from trade should not be exaggerated when other fundamental economic problems are pressing. Stable macroeconomic policies, the rule of law, and the protection of property rights that enable the market mechanism to function properly are preconditions for reaping the full benefits of international trade.[90] As Thomas Macaulay stated back in 1845, "It is not one single cause that makes nations either prosperous or miserable. No friend of free trade is such an idiot as to say that free trade is the only valuable thing in the world; that religion, government, police, education, the administration of justice, public expenditure, foreign relations, have nothing whatever to do with the well-being of nations."[91]

At the same time, restricting trade entails real economic costs. These losses may appear to be abstractions, but they are in fact harmful for real

[90] According to Adam Smith, "Commerce and manufactures can seldom flourish long in any state which does not enjoy a regular administration of justice, in which the people do not feel themselves secure in the possession of their property, in which the faith of contracts is not supported by law, and in which the authority of the state is not supposed to be regularly employed in enforcing the payments of debts from all those who are able to pay. Commerce and manufactures, in short, can seldom flourish in any state in which there is not a certain degree of confidence in the justice of the government" ([1776] 1976, 910).

[91] From a speech on "The Corn Laws," delivered December 2, 1845, at a public meeting in Edinburgh. Reprinted in Macaulay 1900, 89.

3

Protectionism: Economic Costs, Political Benefits?

Economic analysis has long established free trade as a desirable economic policy. This conclusion has been reinforced by mounting empirical evidence on the benefits of trade, and yet protectionism is far from vanquished in the policy arena. Of course, this is nothing new: as Adam Smith observed more than two hundred years ago, "not only the prejudices of the public, but what is much more unconquerable, the private interests of many individuals, irresistibly oppose" free trade.[1] Indeed, interest groups opposed to free trade often have a political influence that is disproportionate to their economic size. This chapter describes the economic costs of trade restrictions and examines why, despite these costs, protectionism is often a seductive and politically attractive policy. The chapter concludes by considering instances in which trade protection might actually be beneficial.

The Costs of Tariffs and Quotas

In *The Wealth of Nations*, Adam Smith not only developed a powerful case for free trade, but he also issued a scathing attack on contemporary mercantilist policies that restricted trade. The ostensible purpose of these government policies was to promote national wealth, but Smith argued that such policies were ill conceived and detracted from that objective. Smith observed that policymakers too frequently equated the interests of producers with the interests of the nation as a whole. Under mercantilism, almost any policy that helped existing producers expand output,

They don't care abt people

[1] Smith [1776] 1976, 471.

↑Ṗ

such as limits on imports or restrictions on competition, was deemed beneficial. But Smith pointed out that this approach confused the means with the end:

> Consumption is the sole end and purpose of all production; and the interest of the producer ought to be attended to only so far as it may be necessary for promoting that of the consumer. The maxim is so perfectly selfevident that it would be absurd to attempt to prove it. But in the mercantile system the interest of the consumer is almost constantly sacrificed to that of the producer; and it seems to consider production, and not consumption, as the ultimate end and object of all industry and commerce.[2]

Tariffs = less effect.

Furthermore, Smith argued that policies such as trade barriers would not expand total output but merely divert resources to less productive uses. As he put it, "No regulation of commerce can increase the quantity of industry in any society beyond what its capital can maintain. It can only divert part of it into a direction into which it might not otherwise have gone; and it is by no means certain that this artificial direction is likely to be more advantageous to the society than that into which it would have gone of its own accord."[3]

While governments often justified trade restrictions as serving the public interest, Smith noted that such restrictions did not benefit the public as much as they served the private interests of influential merchants who had captured government policy for their own advantage. In fact, he believed that trade restrictions "may . . . be demonstrated to be in every case a complete piece of dupery, by which the interests of the State and the nation is constantly sacrificed to that of some particular class of traders."[4]

> In every country it always is and must be the interest of the great body of the people to buy whatever they want of those who sell it cheapest. The proposition is so very manifest that it seems ridiculous to take any pains to prove it; nor could it ever have been called in question had

---

[2] Smith [1776] 1976, 660.
[3] Smith [1776] 1976, 453.
[4] Adam Smith, letter to William Eden, written in 1783 at the end of the American Revolution; reprinted in Smith 1977, 272.

not the interested sophistry of merchants and manufacturers con-
founded the common sense of mankind. Their interest is, in this respect, directly opposite to that of the great body of the people. As it is
the interest of the freemen of a corporation to hinder the rest of the
inhabitants from employing any workmen but themselves, so it is the
interest of the merchants and manufacturers of every country to secure to themselves the monopoly of the home market.[5]

Policies that give preferential treatment to domestic producers in the
home market still exist today. For example, in the American Recovery and
Reinvestment Act of 2009, Congress included "Buy American" rules that
all public projects funded by the stimulus spending must use iron and
steel produced only in the United States. While this may have been good
for domestic steel producers, it is hard to see the benefit for American
taxpayers. The provision potentially raised the cost of investment projects
to state and local governments, making their infrastructure investment
spending buy less than it might otherwise, or take funds away from other
valuable uses, such as health and education. Furthermore, one analyst
argued that the provision would not create many jobs, because steel production is very capital intensive, and could harm exports if other countries retaliated against the United States.[6] In fact, Canada was outraged by
the provision and threatened to do exactly that, until it received an exemption from the law a year later.

Despite the gradual decline in trade barriers over the past half century,
the array of protectionist policies around the world is still quite large. The
principal means of blocking trade include tariffs (taxes on imports), quotas (quantitative restrictions on imports), and nontariff barriers of various
sorts (such as product standards and technical regulations). The easiest
policy to measure is tariffs. Table 3.1 shows the average applied tariff on
all manufactured and agricultural imports for selected countries in 2011.
Developed countries have relatively low average tariffs, usually less than

[5] Smith [1776] 1976, 493–94. "That this monopoly of the homemarket frequently gives
great encouragement to that particular species of industry which enjoys it, and frequently
turns towards that employment a greater share of both the labour and stock of the society
than would otherwise have gone to it, cannot be doubted. But whether it tends either to
increase the general industry of the society, or to give it the most advantageous direction,
is not, perhaps, altogether so evident" (453).

[6] Hufbauer and Schott 2009.

_____Table 3.1.

Average Applied Tariffs for Selected Countries, 2011 (percent, unweighted average)

	All products	Manufactured products	Primary products
Developed countries			
United States	2.8	2.6	2.9
European Union	1.5	0.7	4.3
Japan	2.5	2.0	4.9
Canada	2.9	3.2	1.7
Australia	2.8	3.1	1.3
Middle-income countries			
Argentina	9.8	10.0	7.3
Korea	10.3	7.3	26.3
Brazil	13.6	14.1	8.2
Thailand	11.2	10.5	15.9
Egypt	12.6	9.4	37.6
Iran	25.3	25.7	22.2
Russia	7.5	7.5	7.4
Developing countries			
India	11.5	10.2	20.0
China	7.9	7.9	8.0
South Africa	7.1	7.5	4.7
Tanzania	12.8	12.3	16.6
Bangladesh	13.9	13.6	16.3

Source: World Bank, *World Development Indicators 2013*, http://wdi.worldbank.org/table/6.6#.

5 percent. (Only certain places, such as Hong Kong and Singapore, have zero tariffs.) Developing countries are much more diverse in their average tariff rates, but they are invariably higher than in most rich countries. And nearly every country imposes higher tariffs on agricultural goods than on manufactured goods.

In the case of the United States, the 2014 Harmonized Tariff Schedule consists of 10,514 tariff lines for itemized imports, each with an associated tariff rate. (About 37 percent of the tariff lines have a duty of zero.) A simple average of the applied rates is 4.8 percent, with 4.0 for nonagricultural goods and 6.7 for agricultural goods. There are many tariff peaks, including tobacco at 350 percent, sour cream at 177 percent, and peanuts at 164 percent.[7] Yet it is also the case that almost 70 percent of imports

[7] About 5 percent of the lines in the U.S. tariff code exceed 15 percent. World Trade Organization 2014, 50.

(by value) enter the country without paying any duties, partly because of free trade agreements such as NAFTA, which applies to America's two largest trading partners, Canada and Mexico.

The tariff figures in table 3.1 are simple unweighted averages of each country's tariff code and significantly understate the magnitude of protection. Tariff peaks may apply to only a few lines of imports, but may severely restrict trade. In addition, the indicators ignore other nontariff forms of protection, such as quotas and quantitative restrictions. A study that looks at the overall trade restrictiveness of a country's import policy, including tariffs, quotas, and nontariff barriers, has calculated the overall tariff average that replicates the anti-import effect of all these policies. This overall tariff is much higher than simple tariff averages. For example, India's average tariff on all goods is about 14 percent, but the restrictiveness of its trade regime is equivalent to a 22 percent across-the-board tariff. Similarly, Japan's average tariff is less than 3 percent but its trade restrictiveness is equivalent to an 11 percent tariff. For the United States and European Union, average tariffs of less than 3 percent yield restrictiveness equivalents just shy of 7 percent.[8]

*less trade &
efficiency*

These anti-import policies reduce trade and tend to distort economic activity, leading to inefficient outcomes. Their effects can be separated into two components. First, import barriers redistribute income from domestic consumers to domestic producers. When imports of a product are restricted, the product becomes scarcer in the domestic market. Scarcity drives up the price, benefiting domestic producers of the product but harming consumers who are forced to pay more for it.

For example, in September 2009, President Barack Obama imposed new duties on car and truck tires imported from China. The tariffs were set to last three years, and the existing tariffs of 3–4 percent were augmented by an additional 35 percent in the first year, 30 percent in the second year, and 25 percent in the third year. U.S. importers shifted their source of supply away from China to other countries, such as Indonesia, which could not produce tires as cheaply as China could. Domestic tire producers were able to increase their prices as consumers shifted their purchases from imported tires to domestic tires. One study estimates that the total net cost to consumers was $1,112 million per year, $817 million as a result of the higher cost of imported tires and $295 million

[8] Kee, Nicita, and Olarreaga 2009.

due to the higher cost of domestically produced tires.[9] The study also estimates that a maximum of 1,200 jobs were "saved" as a result of the tire tariff, amounting to $900,000 in consumer cost per job saved. (Average worker compensation in the tire industry is $40,000 per year.) Thus, $1,112 million was extracted from consumers to give $48 million to tire workers, only some of whom might have been laid off had the tariffs not been imposed. However, the study continued, consumer spending on other goods might have been $1,064 million lower as a result of the higher cost of tires, resulting in the loss of an estimated 3,731 jobs in other sectors of the economy. Thus, the policy may have destroyed jobs overall.

This redistribution and employment reshuffling is usually hard to justify. For example, the United States helps the domestic sugar industry through price supports and import restrictions in the form of a tariff-rate quota. Under a tariff-rate quota, sugar-exporting countries are given a certain (small) quantity that they can bring into the United States at the regular tariff rate, and any exports beyond that specified quantity are subject to a tariff rate of nearly 150 percent. Because of the import restrictions, the price of sugar in the United States has been roughly two to three times that on the world market. Domestic sugar-producers reap about $1 billion annually as a result of this policy. However, 42 percent of the total benefits to sugar growers goes to the top 1 percent of all farms.[10] The rationale for rewarding a few large sugar-producers with hundreds of millions of dollars every year at the expense of consumers has never been made clear.

Second, and even worse, protectionist policies distort prices and therefore economic incentives. This distortion leads to wasted resources, known as a deadweight loss. As import restrictions push the domestic price of a good above the world price, domestic firms produce more, while consumers reduce their overall purchases and suffer a real income loss as a result of the higher prices. The inefficiency associated with these distortions of incentives imposes a deadweight loss on the overall economy. Trade barriers are like an income transfer in which ten dollars is taken from consumers while giving only eight dollars to producers, result-

[9] Hufbauer and Lowry 2012.
[10] U.S. General Accounting Office 2000a; 1993, 32–33. See also Beghin et al. 2003.

ing in a two-dollar loss to the economy as a whole. The sugar policy benefited producers of sugar to the tune of $1 billion, but it imposed far greater costs—about $1.9 billion, according to the General Accounting Office—on consumers. The result is a deadweight loss to the economy of $900 million.[11]

Economists have made rough estimates of the income transfers and the deadweight losses associated with trade barriers. Although the average tariff on imports is low, the United States has significant restrictions on agricultural imports, particularly beef, canned tuna, dairy products, and sugar and sugar-containing goods. In addition, the average tariff on apparel is 14 percent and on footwear is 11 percent.[12] The U.S. International Trade Commission (ITC) has calculated that the net cost—that is, the deadweight loss—of these trade barriers was about $1.1 billion in 2013.[13] (This net cost comes from calculating the overall costs to consumers, who pay more for both the imported good and domestic substitute products as a result of the import restriction, and deducting the income transferred to domestic producers and the government in the form of tariff revenue. It is a measure of the efficiency lost as a result of restricting trade.) Because the average tariff is quite low, the elimination of these barriers would increase overall U.S. imports by only 0.2 percent (or roughly $54 billion), although imports of some products, such as cheese and sugar, might increase by as much as 40 percent.

The net cost of $1.1 billion in 2013 is significantly lower than the $16.4 billion that the ITC calculated a decade earlier in 2002. The reason for the reduction is the expiration of the Multi-Fiber Arrangement (MFA). Until its demise in January 2005, the MFA was the biggest piece of pro-

---

[11] A more recent estimate by Beghin and Elobeid (2013) puts the consumer cost at $3 billion.

[12] When it comes to manufactured goods, the United States essentially has a two-tiered tariff system: average tariffs of 10 to 15 percent on light consumer goods (clothes, shoes, suitcases) and 0 to 1 percent on everything else. For example, clothes and shoes account for less than 7 percent of all imports yet bring in nearly half of all tariff revenue (Gresser 2007).

[13] U.S. International Trade Commission 2013. This figure excludes the cost of antidumping duties, which will be considered in chapter 5. In addition, this figure is based on a highly aggregated view of trade. Because the variance of tariff rates across imports matters for its welfare cost, a more refined study yields a higher welfare loss of $7 billion (Kee, Nicita, and Olarreaga 2009).

tectionist cholesterol blocking the arteries of world trade.[14] The MFA restricted imports of foreign textiles and apparel through a complex maze of country and productspecific quotas. Under the MFA, the United States maintained more than three thousand separate quotas on imports from more than forty nations. The narrowly defined quotas include cotton diapers from China, men's and boys' cotton coats from Sri Lanka, women's and girls' wool coats from the Czech Republic, women's bras from Mexico, men's trousers from Guatemala, women's and girls' manmadefiber woven blouses from the United Arab Emirates, and so on. In 1989, the Treasury Department's Customs Service prohibited the import of thirty thousand tennis shoes from Indonesia because the boxes contained an extra pair of shoelaces, which, it was decided, fell in a separate import quota category.[15]

The result was severely distorted trade and significantly higher prices of clothing for U.S. consumers.[16] The combined effect of tariffs and quotas raised domestic prices of apparel by 18 to 24 percent and prices of finished textile products by about 14 percent in 2002.[17] Indeed, according to virtually every study on the matter, the economic benefits to the United States from eliminating the MFA were enormous. The direct consumer cost of this protection amounted to $24.4 billion in 1990, a burden of over $260 per household.[18] The tax is generally believed to have been quite regressive because lower-income households devote a greater share of their expenditures to clothing than those with higher incomes.

The high costs of the MFA illustrate an important difference between an import tariff and an import quota. When the United States imposes a tax on imports, the government collects as tariff revenue the difference between the world price and the higher, tariff-inclusive domestic price charged to consumers. But when a country limits the quantity of imports

[14] Under the Uruguay Round trade agreement of 1994, the United States and other countries vowed to abolish the MFA by January 2005.

[15] Customs later decided that an extra pair of shoelaces would be permitted so long as they were laced into the shoes and color-coordinated with them (Bovard 1991, 45).

[16] The restrictiveness of the MFA varied considerably across commodity products, ranging from 7 to 12 percent for apparel overall, 12 to 28 percent for women's and girl's cotton knit shirts, 44 to 47 percent for cotton bed sheets, etc. (U.S. International Trade Commission 2006, 70).

[17] U.S. International Trade Commission 2006, 71.

[18] Hufbauer and Elliott 1994.

with a quota, the difference between the world price and the higher domestic price becomes a scarcity rent rather than tariff revenue. This scarcity (or quota) rent is captured by foreign exporters as a markup if they have obtained the right to export a certain amount under the quota in the import-restricting market, where they get to charge a higher price than on the world market.

The transfer of quota rents is a national loss because money is taken from consumers and handed to foreign exporters (in the form of a higher markup) instead of the government (in the form of tax revenue), as would have happened if a tariff had been imposed. Almost all of the roughly $12 billion net cost to the United States of the MFA was due to the transfer of quota rents to foreign exporters and very little due to domestic deadweight efficiency losses.

The transfer of quota rents also distorts the incentives of the exporters, particularly in developing countries. When the United States imposes an import quota, foreign governments are usually responsible for determining which exporters will be allowed to sell in the U.S. market (and thus receive the quota rent) and which exporters will be prohibited from exporting. The allocation of quota rights, except when those rights are auctioned off, is inherently arbitrary and increases the power of government bureaucrats, thereby fostering corruption. The politically well-connected firms, who perhaps are not averse to sharing the quota rents with the bureaucrats, are most likely to obtain export licenses, whereas other firms are shut out. This gives entrepreneurs in developing countries the wrong signal: the way to get rich is to invest in political influence, not to invest in productive efficiency.

As the MFA example indicates, the quota rents can be extremely valuable. In some cases, the quota rent received by foreign producers helps them compete against American firms. For example, when the United States persuaded Japan to limit its automobile exports in 1981, Japan's auto exporters were able to raise the average price of their cars by about $1,000, part of which they invested in product improvements that enabled them to compete even more effectively against their American rivals.[19] When the United States forced Japan to maintain high minimum prices on its semiconductor exports in the late 1980s, some of Japan's

[19] Feenstra 1984.

electronics producers were pleased that the American government, in order to help domestic semiconductor producers, was also helping them raise their prices in the U.S. market. Japanese companies that produced one-megabyte dynamic random access memories (DRAMs) made an additional $1.2 billion in profits in 1988 because of the U.S. trade intervention.[20]

Yet simply documenting the economic costs of protection often has a limited impact on policy. One reason could be that the calculated welfare gains from additional trade liberalization are quite small as a share of GDP. In the case of the United States, the ITC's estimate of $1.1 billion in gains from unilaterally removing U.S. import restraints in 2013, for example, amounts to only 0.007 percent of that year's GDP. This is the cost of existing trade barriers and should not be confused with the gains from trade. Still, it is almost a trivial sum—it is equivalent to an extra $3 pay for a worker who earns $50,000 a year—even though it is an annual gain that accrues in perpetuity. But the small number reflects the fact that average tariff barriers are low, due in part to free trade agreements with Canada and Mexico, America's largest trade partners, and that the United States has avoided the use of costly import quotas.

However, these "static" calculations of the cost of production understate the true cost of trade barriers for many reasons, such as the failure to consider the productivity and variety benefits of trade. In addition, it does not reflect the gains to the United States from a multilateral trade agreement in which this nation benefits from greater market access in other countries. And, of course, just because the cost of protection is relatively low for the United States does not mean that it is low for other countries, particularly many developing countries. For those whose trade barriers are much more pervasive and restrictive, the potential gains from liberalization are much more substantial.[21] For example, the static deadweight loss due to trade restrictions amounts to 3.1 percent of GDP in Egypt, 2.8 percent of GDP in Ghana, and 2.2 percent of GDP in Tunisia, according to a recent study. Once again, these costs are understated be-

[20] Flamm 1996, 277.

[21] Messerlin (2001) reports that the costs of protection in the European Union are equivalent to about 6–7 percent of the EU's GDP, or about the same as the annual value of output in Spain. The net cost of trade protection in Japan (circa 1989) has been estimated to be anywhere from $8 billion to $17 billion, according to Sazanami, Urata, and Kawai (1995).

cause they ignore the productivity gains from trade and the benefits of international agreements that would give these countries greater access to other markets.[22]

The estimates of the cost of protection are also understated because they do not take into account the resources devoted to political pressure. Expenditures on campaign contributions and legal fees may generate private benefits for those making the expenditures, if they can persuade policymakers to restrict trade on their behalf. Those expenditures are socially unproductive because the goal is to redistribute wealth rather than create it.

Indeed, the impact of trade barriers can be significantly larger when the political determinants of those barriers are taken into account. A standard statistical method of gauging the effect of trade restraints on imports is to examine the determinants of import demand, such as the relative price of imports, domestic income, and other explanatory variables. But this approach ignores the simultaneity of imports and protection: higher tariffs may reduce imports, but more imports also lead to greater political pressure for higher tariffs. This confounds any attempt to isolate the effect of tariffs on imports and, unless corrected for, leads one to understate the effect of tariffs on imports. When one study confronted this problem by examining the politicaleconomic determinants of trade barriers in the United States and using the results to help explain imports, the statistical coefficient representing the negative impact of nontariff barriers (such as quantitative restrictions) on imports was increased by a factor of ten. The conventional estimate suggests that removing nontariff barriers would increase manufactured imports by $5.5 billion (in 1985), whereas after controlling for the political determinants of those barriers, the impact was estimated to be closer to $50 billion.[23]

The numbers assigned to the welfare costs of trade barriers often have an abstract feel to them that makes them difficult to grasp. What may be more distressing is the rarely exposed seamier details of the protectionist racket, which allow one to go behind the numbers and see how firms and sectors actually get the government to intervene on their behalf. The sugar program is a classic example. Sugar imports are restricted to maintain domestic price supports for sugar beet and cane producers. The

[22] Kee, Nicita, and Olarreaga 2008.

[23] Trefler 1993.

[handwritten: important/also going to a profit-connect firms]

benefits of these restrictions are highly concentrated because Congress has not limited the amount of support that large firms can receive. For example, one farm received over $30 million in benefits from the sugar program in 1991, and just 0.2 percent of all sugarcane farms—thirty-three in total—received 34 percent of the entire program benefits.[24] The family of Alfonso Fanjul singlehandedly supplies the United States with about 15 percent of its sugarcane through its land holdings in south Florida and the Dominican Republic, collecting somewhere between $52 to $90 million in benefits from the price supports on U.S. production and the quota rents on Dominican sugar exports.[25] Not surprisingly, the Fanjul family could afford to make nearly $300,000 in campaign contributions in 1988.[26] *[handwritten: they control to favor politics]* At the same time, the Fanjul farms were being investigated for chronic violation of U.S. labor laws. Government support for the sugar industry has also harmed the environment because chemical runoff from the intensive farming of sugarcane in south Florida has seeped into the Everglades.

The sugar program is not just an economic, political, and environmental inequity, but it prevents desperately poor sugar-producing countries from exporting to the United States. Countries such as Colombia and Guatemala are deprived of valuable foreign exchange earnings that could be spent on food, fuel, and medicine. Congressional opponents of the sugar policy have suggested that Andean farmers, who have been prevented from selling their sugar in major markets, have turned their cropland toward the production of coca used in cocaine production and other illegal drugs. The Caribbean and Latin American farmers who find themselves cut out of the American sugar market may be forced to turn to illegal crops as a way to make a living. *[handwritten left margin: Share global $ to those who need it.]*

When politics and trade meet, the result not only harms consumers, but may even jeopardize national security. Shortly after the terrorist attack on the United States on September 11, 2001, President Pervez Musharraf of Pakistan requested the suspension of tariffs and quota on Pakistan's exports of textiles and apparel to the United States in an effort to lift its economy. After debate within the Bush administration, Commerce De-

[24] U.S. General Accounting Office 1993.

[25] Jane Mayer and Jose de Cordoba, "Sweet Life: First Family of Sugar Is Tough on Workers, Generous to Politicians," *Wall Street Journal*, July 29, 1991.

[26] Alfonso Fanjul is so politically powerful that President Bill Clinton interrupted a "meeting" with Monica Lewinsky to take a phone call from him. This is according to Lewinsky's testimony as presented in the Kenneth Starr report.

we stopped trading w/ Pakistan

partment officials informed Pakistan that the United States would be unable to grant trade concessions; pressure from the domestic textile and apparel industry successfully blocked any expansion of imports. In fact, Pakistan's textile exports to the United States actually fell sharply in the months after 9/11 because of a sharp rise in insurance premiums, costing Pakistan over $1 billion in exports and throwing untold numbers of workers out of their jobs at a delicate time in the region.[27]

steel example

When examined up close, trade policy is not pretty. Steel industry lobbyists, for example, have induced members of Congress to change U.S. trade laws for the specific benefit of their industry, which has received pension bailouts, loan guarantees, environmental exemptions, decades of trade restrictions—and continues to press for more.[28] When powerful industries push politicians to intervene on their behalf, the picture is often an ugly one. And the problem is even worse in developing countries, where outright corruption is more of a problem. As the last chapter pointed out, protectionist trade policies tend to generate more corruption as private firms seek to bribe government officials to impose (or exempt them from) import restrictions.[29]

So far we have examined the direct costs of import barriers. But the indirect effects of import barriers are also important, though not always readily apparent. The indirect consequences of import restrictions include a reduction in exports and lower employment in downstream industries, and we consider each in turn.

_____Import Barriers Harm Exports

Imagine taking a poll of Americans and asking, "Should the United States impose tariffs on foreign goods to prevent imports from low-wage coun-

---

[27] According to one report, the reason for the rejection of Pakistan's request was that Congressional Republicans decided that they wanted to give the president trade negotiating authority without Democratic support to show the business lobbies that pro-trade Democrats were not trustworthy on the issue. To get a majority, Ways and Means Chairman Bill Thomas needed to woo protectionist Republicans to support the bill with promises that key industries in their districts would be protected. House Republican leaders secured the deciding vote of Robin Hayes (R-NC) only by promising not to increase quotas on Pakistani textile imports. See Franklin Foer, "Fabric Softener," *New Republic*, March 4 and 11, 2002, 19–21.

[28] See Barringer and Pierce 2000.

[29] Dutt 2009.

tries from harming American workers?" A sizable fraction of the respondents would probably answer "yes." If asked to explain their position, they would probably reply that import tariffs would create jobs for Americans and thereby reduce unemployment. (The validity of this opinion will be examined in chapter 4.)

Then suppose you asked the same people, "Should the United States levy an export tax on domestically produced goods such as aircraft, grains, machinery, software, and the like?" The answer would probably be a resounding and unanimous "no!" After all, they would argue, export taxes would destroy jobs and harm important industries.[30]

Yet according to an important proposition known as the Lerner symmetry theorem, these two policies are equivalent in their economic effects.[31] The Lerner symmetry theorem holds that a tax on imports is functionally equivalent to a tax on exports. In other words, any restriction on imports also operates as a restriction on exports. This theorem helps us understand another aspect of import tariffs—how they destroy jobs in export industries.

Some participants in the debate on trade tend to believe that a country's exports and imports are independent of one another, and therefore one can reduce imports without having an adverse effect on exports. In fact, exports and imports are the flip side of the same coin. Exports are the goods a country must give up in order to acquire imports. Exports are necessary to generate the earnings to pay for imports. The past century illustrates the close relationship between exports and imports in the United States. Looking back at figure 1.1, which plots U.S. merchandise exports and imports as a percentage of GDP from 1870 to 2013, we see that exports and imports have been highly correlated, except in recent years. (The trade deficit will be discussed in chapter 4.)

Additional evidence of the Lerner symmetry theorem comes from the recent experience of developing countries. Figure 3.1 depicts China's exports and imports as a share of its GDP from 1952 to 2012. Most people

---

[30] In addition to being unconstitutional under Article 1, section 9 of the U.S. Constitution.

[31] The theorem is named after Abba Lerner, who published a short but brilliant paper on the subject as a graduate student at the London School of Economics in 1936. Lerner's paper established the formal truth of the proposition, but it had been a feature of trade policy debates long before then.

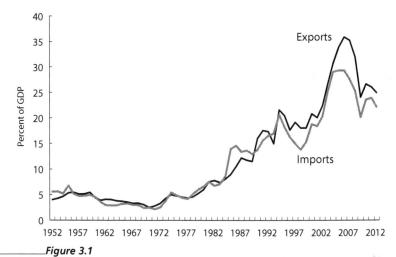

_____*Figure 3.1*

China's Exports and Imports, as a Percentage of GDP, 1952–2012
Source: International Monetary Fund, International Financial Statistics.

are well aware that China has become a major exporter. Few realize that China's astounding growth in exports has been matched by astounding growth in imports. This simply demonstrates that trade is indeed a two-way street, not a one-way flow.

As another example, consider two South American countries, Chile and Brazil. These countries have pursued quite different types of commercial policies in recent decades. Chile undertook an extensive liberalization of its trade policy in the 1970s, dramatically cutting its import tariffs. As figure 3.2 indicates, this change in policy helped Chile's imports surge from about 15 percent of GDP in 1970 to 30 percent of GDP in 2000. And yet this period also witnessed a surge in exports on the same order of magnitude: the import expansion was matched by an export expansion. As in the case of other countries, Chile's experience also suggests that export diversification is an additional benefit that comes with lifting the implicit export tax that is inherent in import tariffs.[32]

[32] By reducing import taxes, a country is lifting an implicit tax on the export sector. This tax relief allows marginal exports, previously suppressed by the tax, to become profitable. As a result, countries do not simply export more of the same things, but other goods that were previously unprofitable to export. This implies that trade liberalization allows exports to become more rather than less diversified, thereby reducing the risk of adverse export

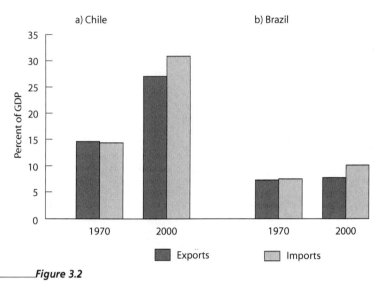

_____Figure 3.2

Exports and Imports as a Share of GDP, Chile and Brazil, 1970 and 2000
Source: International Monetary Fund, International Financial Statistics.

By contrast, Brazil has pursued "import substitution" policies since the 1960s. These policies aimed to promote industrialization by severely restricting imports. In 1970, Brazil's exports and imports amounted to about 7 percent of its GDP. Brazil's trade policy did not change dramatically in the subsequent twentyeight years, and thus, Brazil's exports and imports remained at 7 percent of GDP in 2000 despite the tremendous growth in world trade over this period. The Brazilian government has made great efforts to expand exports, but substantial import barriers have indirectly constrained exports and undermined those efforts.

At one level, the idea that import restraints will reduce exports is straightforward. If foreign countries are blocked in their ability to sell their goods in the United States, they will be unable to earn the dollars they need to purchase U.S. goods. The mechanisms that link a country's exports and imports to one another are complex and not always readily apparent, but can be illustrated by focusing on the foreign exchange market. Suppose the United States were to reduce its tariff on Chilean goods unilaterally. One would expect U.S. demand for Chile's goods to

price shocks. Chile, for example, reduced its export dependence on metals (mainly copper) from 64 percent of exports in 1980 to 46 percent in 1996.

—explanation (handwritten)

increase. To make these purchases, consumers in the United States will (indirectly) have to sell dollars on the foreign exchange market to purchase Chile's currency, the peso. In response to the increased demand for pesos from those holding dollars, the value of the dollar will fall in terms of the peso, or conversely the peso's value will rise in terms of dollars. This change tends to raise the price of Chilean goods in the United States, dampening demand for those goods.

But here is the flip side: although it was the United States that lowered its tariffs while Chile left its tariffs unchanged, Chile will now purchase more goods from the United States. This is because the cheaper dollar tends to lower the price of U.S. goods in pesos, stimulating Chilean demand for them. Therefore, the foreign exchange market is one of several mechanisms that link exports and imports, ensuring that a country's exports increase when it unilaterally reduces its own import tariffs.[33]

The pattern of U.S. exports and imports shown in figure 1.3 also illustrates this relationship. The ratio of exports and imports to GDP was fairly stable in the 1950s and 1960s, but in the early 1970s and again in the late 1970s there was a pronounced jump in both of these ratios. These jumps coincide with large increases in world oil prices. (As late as 1980, almost 30 percent of U.S. imports by value were mineral fuels.) The big increase in the import bill is seen in the higher ratio of imports to GDP, but—since those imports must be paid for with something—the export ratio also rose in each case. In both instances the increase in exports was brought about by a depreciation in the value of the dollar.

This link between exports and imports also explains why the employment effects of trade intervention tend to cancel each other out. Throughout U.S. history, large tariff increases have failed to stimulate greater employment because any increase in employment in import-competing industries was offset by a decrease in employment in industries that are export oriented. The Smoot-Hawley tariff of 1930, for example, significantly reduced imports but failed to create jobs overall because exports fell almost one-for-one with imports, resulting in employment losses in those industries.[34]

adverse employment effect (handwritten)

---

[33] A change in the exchange rate is only one of several ways in which symmetry will hold; for example, it still holds for countries with fixed exchange rates or in single currency areas such as Europe, but through a different mechanism.

[34] Irwin 2011.

Thus, the connection between imports and exports cannot be overlooked when evaluating trade policy. Governments that undertake policies to reduce imports will find themselves also reducing exports. This reduction in imports may expand employment in industries that compete with them, but the reduction in exports tends to contract employment in those industries dependent upon foreign sales. An appreciation of the Lerner symmetry theorem is particularly important when assessing the claim that import tariffs have a beneficial effect on overall employment.

_____Import Barriers Harm Downstream Industries

Not only do import restrictions reduce the number of jobs required to produce exports, but they also destroy jobs in downstream industries that use the imports. Recall from table 1.2 that the majority of U.S. imports are not final consumer goods, but intermediate goods used by domestic firms in their production. Any trade restriction that raises the price of an intermediate good directly harms downstream user industries and thus adversely affects employment in those industries. In other words, when domestic firms have to pay a premium on their productive inputs, particularly when they are competing with foreign rivals who do not pay those taxes, employment in those industries suffers.

more expense in intermediary too

Restrictions on imported sugar, for example, have produced sour results for those employed in the sugar-refining and candy-making industries. When food manufacturers who produce sugar-intensive products are forced to pay a higher price for sugar than their foreign rivals, their competitive position suffers. In 2002, a LifeSavers candy plant that employed 650 workers in Michigan was closed and relocated to Canada. Before the shutdown, the plant produced about 3 million rolls of LifeSavers per day using 250,000 pounds of sugar. Due to the high price of sugar in the United States, the company would save over $10 million a year in sugar costs just by relocating across the border. Canada is the location of choice for large sugar-using food manufacturers because the country does not have any sugar farmers and hence does not artificially inflate the price of sugar on their behalf.

Limits on sugar imports have had repercussions throughout the American food manufacturing industry. In 1990, Brachs Candy Company announced that because of the high domestic price of sugar, it would close a factory in Chicago that employed three thousand workers, and expand production in Canada. According to Chicago's former mayor Richard Daley, as of 2001 the city's confectionary industry had lost 11 percent of its jobs over the previous ten years. "The continuation of domestic sugar price supports," Daley said, "[was] a key reason these companies [(confectioners) were] considering leaving Chicago and relocating their facilities outside of U.S. borders."[35]

After noting that the U.S. price of sugar had been at two to three times the world price for twenty-five years, a Commerce Department report in 2006 concluded that "this price difference results in a significant competitive cost disadvantage for domestic sugar-containing products manufacturers."[36] It reported that employment in the sugar-refining and sugar-containing products industry had fallen by more than eleven thousand between 1997 and 2002, even as employment in the non–sugar-containing food products industry had risen by more than thirty thousand. Of the ten thousand jobs lost, the Commerce Department attributed at least 6,400 to plant closings and relocation related to the high domestic price of sugar. In fact, sugar policy has jeopardized many more workers in sugar-using industries than it protects in the sugar-growing industry: in 2002, employment in sugar-using industries was 987,810, whereas there were only 61,000 workers employed growing and harvesting sugarcane and beets. Trade barriers were thought to protect only 2,260 of those sugar-growing jobs, which meant that the consumer cost per job saved was $826,000. As a result, the report noted, "nearly three confectionery manufacturing jobs are lost for every job protected in the sugar-growing sector due to the price gap between U.S. and world refined sugar prices."

More recent estimates of the sugar program conclude that between 17,000 and 20,000 jobs would be created in the food industry with the removal of the sugar quotas, while 2,700 jobs would be lost in sugarcane farming and sugar processing.[37]

There are numerous examples of the adverse effect that trade restrictions have on employment in related industries. In 1991, the United States imposed antidumping duties on imported flat-panel displays, used by domestic manufacturers of laptop computers: specifically, 62.67 percent

[35] Groombridge 2001, 5.

[36] U.S. Department of Commerce 2006.

[37] Beghin and Elobeid 2013 and U.S. International Trade Commission 2013, 2–9.

duties on active matrix LCD displays and 7.02 percent duties on electrolu-minescent displays. Producers of laptops could no longer afford to pur-chase the expensive displays in the United States and still compete ef-fectively against overseas rivals, who could buy the same displays at much lower prices on the world market and then export their laptops freely to the United States. To avoid the higher domestic prices, several manufacturers decided to shift production abroad. Immediately after the imposition of the antidumping duties, Toshiba announced that it would cease production of laptops in California and shift production to Japan, Sharp announced that it would cease production of laptops in Texas and move production to Canada, and Apple announced that it would relocate its assembly of laptops from California to Ireland or Singapore.[38] Simi-larly, after the United States imposed price floors on Japanese DRAM semiconductors, computer manufacturers shifted their assembly opera-tions outside of the United States to take advantage of the lower prices for memory chips in other markets. In these and numerous other cases, import restrictions benefiting one industry have only harmed another industry.

When the purchasers of imported intermediate goods organize politi-cally, they can alter the debate over the desirability of protection on employment grounds. In the case just mentioned, firms that used semi-conductors (particularly computer manufacturers IBM, HewlettPackard, Sun Microsystems, and others) formed a coalition to oppose the renewal of the price floors on Japanese memory chips. As a result of this con-sumer coalition, U.S. trade officials no longer heard a single voice—that of semiconductor producers—regarding America's trade policy. The gov-ernment did not know how to deal with the sharply conflicting domestic interests, so it simply let the price floor agreement expire.[39]

The same political process played out in the steel industry. In 1984, the United States negotiated voluntary restraint agreements (VRAs) that lim-ited steel imports from all major foreign suppliers. The VRAs raised the domestic price of steel and helped steel producers, but harmed the pro-duction, employment, and exports of the far more numerous domestic users of steel, including the automobile, machine tool, and construction

[38] Hart 1993.
[39] Irwin 1996b.

industries. To fight the VRAs, these downstream industries formed the Coalition of American Steel-Using Manufacturers (CASUM), led by Caterpillar, the manufacturer of heavy earthmoving equipment, and by the Precision Metalforming Association, a small business group whose members process raw steel for industrial users such as the automobile industry. The VRAs were allowed to expire in 1991 in part because CASUM posed an extremely difficult question to government officials: How are Caterpillar, John Deere, and other domestic steel-using firms supposed to compete at home and abroad against such foreign competitors as Komatsu when they are forced to pay a hefty premium for the steel they must purchase? If Caterpillar laid off workers because higher domestic steel costs led to sales being lost to foreign producers, those workers could justifiably ask whether the government believed that jobs in the steel industry were more important to the economy than jobs in the equipment-manufacturing industry.[40]

The U.S. steel industry used to get its own way when lobbying government officials for import relief. Now it has to battle steel-consuming industries for political influence. When the steel industry filed massive antidumping suits in 1998–99, steel-using groups formed the "40-to-1" coalition, referring to the fact that the fewer than two hundred thousand steelworkers are outnumbered by eight million employees in steel-using industries, particularly in construction, metal fabrication, heavy machinery, and transportation equipment. The jobs of workers in steel-using industries would be at risk if steel prices were artificially increased. General Motors, which purchases over seven million tons of steel annually, warned that imposing tariffs on imported steel would make GM's domestic operations "less competitive in the international marketplace to the extent that those operations are subjected to costs not incurred by offshore competition, and to the extent that U.S. import barriers impede access to new products and materials being developed offshore, or remove the competitive incentives to develop new products in the United States."[41]

In 2002, when the Bush administration was considering whether to impose special safeguard tariffs on imported steel, the steel-users coalition—the Consuming Industries Trade Action Coalition, or CITAC—re-

---

[40] Moore 1996.
[41] Lindsey, Griswold, and Lukas 1999, 7.

sponded once again. According to a study commissioned by CITAC, the proposed import relief would save between four thousand and eight thousand jobs in the steel industry. But, by increasing steel prices and imports of steel-containing products, the import restrictions would reduce employment by thirty-six thousand to seventy-four thousand in other sectors of the economy. The higher prices would force steel consumers to pay between $2 billion and $4 billion in extra costs, would cost the economy eight jobs for every one steel job created, and cost consumers about $425,000 per job saved in the steel industry.[42]

A year after the Bush administration imposed tariffs of up to 30 percent on certain steel imports in March 2002, the International Trade Commission surveyed steel consumers about the impact of this action. About half of steel purchasers reported an increase in contract or spot prices after the tariffs were imposed. Based on the survey responses, roughly 8 percent of the decline in employment in steel-consuming firms between 2002 and 2003 was attributed to the safeguard measure.[43] Once again, in deciding whether to limit steel imports, the government faced the choice of protecting jobs in the steel industry or protecting jobs in automobiles, commercial building, wire products, electronic equipment, heavy machinery, oil and gas drilling, and other steel-using industries.

These examples demonstrate the first lesson of economics: there is no such thing as a free lunch. Every government intervention involves a tradeoff of some sort. Higher sugar prices increase employment in sugar production, but reduce employment in food-manufacturing industries. Higher semiconductor prices increase employment in the semiconductor industry, but decrease employment in the computer industry. Higher steel prices increase employment in the steel industry, but decrease employment in the steel-using industries. When a domestic industry asks the government to impose trade barriers that would raise the domestic price above the world price, the choice means trading off jobs in one sector of the economy for jobs in another sector, not creating or losing jobs overall.

Why do policymakers usually fail to see themselves as facing such a tradeoff? For one thing, if downstream consumers do not organize politi-

---

[42] François and Baughman 2001.
[43] U.S. International Trade Commission 2003, 2–50.

— people might not say anything

cally, the indirect consequences of trade barriers may never be brought to legislators' attention. And the nature of the political process gives members of Congress and officials in the executive agencies responsible for trade policy a strongly biased view of the effects of trade. Constituents who lose their jobs in import-sensitive industries, such as steel, invariably complain to their representatives and government agencies about foreign competition. Legislators and bureaucrats cannot ignore these voters, and it is hard for them to resist the temptation to help by "doing something" about the situation, even if that imposes hardship on others who are often silent. Meanwhile, those who owe their jobs and high wages to exports or to industries that depend upon inexpensive intermediate goods almost invariably fail to express their appreciation to policymakers for not interfering in the process of trade. As a result, those seeking to limit trade tend to be more vocal than those who benefit from open markets.   *protectionists*
— have
louder voices

_____**The Politics of Protection**

If free trade is so beneficial and protectionism so costly, then what explains the attractiveness and persistence of trade barriers? One reason why free trade is so controversial is that, in the short run, not everyone stands to benefit from the policy. Changes in trade flows and in trade policy have a ripple effect through the economy and alter the distribution of income. Because some groups are harmed by trade and benefit from trade barriers, it is not clear that free trade policies will always be adopted. The actual policy will depend upon the relative political strength of those supporting and opposing trade restrictions, based on underlying economic interests or any other motivation.

Indeed, specific groups that benefit from protectionist barriers usually exert political influence beyond their numbers. Political influence tends to be skewed in favor of those seeking government assistance because those who stand to gain have more at stake than those who stand to lose. As Vilfredo Pareto pointed out long ago, "a protectionist measure provides large benefits to a small number of people, and causes a very great number of consumers a slight loss."[44] This circumstance makes it easier to enact such measures. Pareto's idea that the benefits of trade protection

owe
is stake to em

[44] Pareto 1971, 379.

are highly concentrated, while the costs are widely diffused, has been a central point of departure for explaining the existence and persistence of import restrictions.

The U.S. sugar program, once again, illustrates this imbalance in costs and benefits. Import restrictions have kept domestic sugar prices at roughly twice the world price. The General Accounting Office estimated that domestic sugar producers reaped about $1 billion in 1998 as a result of this policy. However, 42 percent of the total benefits to sugarcane and sugar beet growers went to just 1 percent of all producers; indeed, just seventeen sugarcane farms collected over half of all the cane growers' benefits. Clearly, the owners of these few farms have a powerful incentive to maintain the import restrictions. Although the sugar policy imposes far larger costs on consumers of sweeteners ($1.9 billion according to the GAO) than are distributed to growers, consumers are far more numerous, and these costs are spread widely among them.

This combination of concentrated benefits and dispersed costs leads to an enormous imbalance in the relative size of the political forces opposing and favoring any change in the sugar policy. The incentive for household consumers to oppose the policy is virtually nonexistent: even though the total cost across all consumers is large, the cost to each individual consumer is small: only about $10 per person per year. On the other hand, the policy creates large, tangible benefits for a few producers, who are willing to devote substantial resources to defend the policy. In 2012, the sugar industry spent $7.9 million in lobbying to keep import restrictions in place. On top of that, sugarcane and sugar beet political action committees spent $5.3 million in campaign contributions, split evenly between Democrats and Republicans, in the 2012 election cycle. Since 1990, the sugar industry has made campaign contributions totaling nearly $42 million.[45] As a result, such special interests have an influence on policy that is disproportionate to their size.

Another example of concentrated benefits and dispersed costs is the program to protect American manufacturers of wire clothes hangers used by dry cleaners. In 2008, M&B Metal Products Co. of Leeds, Alabama, succeeded in getting the government to impose antidumping tariffs of

---

[45] See data available at http://www.opensecrets.org; http://www.opensecrets.org/industries/background.php?cycle=2014&ind=A1200.

15.44 percent and 94.06 percent on two major exporters from China.
(Chapter 5 covers antidumping policy.) The manufacturer argued that the
cost to consumers of the additional tariffs would be trivial, only a penny
or two per hanger, so that if someone paid $12.95 to have his or her suit
cleaned, the price would rise to just $12.96 or $12.97. As a result, it was
argued, consumers would not notice the difference. Yet the costs add up.
With 30,000 dry cleaners in the United States, each paying an additional
$4,000 per year due to the hanger tariff, the annual cost to consumers
would be about $120 million. Even though individual consumers might
not notice, the tariffs would allow the domestic producer to capture a
share of this amount, giving it a powerful financial incentive to press for
the duties. Furthermore, according to the International Trade Commission, U.S. employment in wire hanger manufacturing was just 564 workers in 2004; if each of those 564 jobs were "saved" by the tariff, the cost
per job saved would be $212,765 per year in an industry where the typical
full-time worker earns about $28,000 per year.[46]

Yet such imbalances in the concentration of costs and benefits are not
the whole story. Many small groups could benefit from special government policies, but few actually succeed in organizing and obtaining it.
Why are some special interests able to form a political organization or
interest group while others are not? And why do only some of those that
organize succeed in influencing policy? The formation of interest groups
is a critical element of the politics of trade policy. Unfortunately, economists and political scientists have not been very successful in revealing
much about the organization of economic interests.[47] However, several
hypotheses are worth exploring.

One difficulty in forming a successful political interest group is the
"free-rider" problem. If a tariff benefits all firms in an industry regardless
of whether they contributed to the political effort to get the tariff imposed, then some firms may choose not to contribute. They would prefer
that others undertake the burden because, if protection is secured, the
shirking firms cannot be excluded from the benefits of higher prices as
imports are squeezed out of the market. But at the same time, the fewer

[46] U.S. International Trade Commission 2007b.

[47] Rodrik (1995) and Gawande and Krishna (2003) survey the economic literature on
the political economy of trade policy.

Free-rider problem

firms participating in seeking protection, the lower the probability of obtaining protection.

Industries that are relatively concentrated, either economically (a small number of firms) or geographically (the same regional location), are best positioned to overcome the costs of collective action. They can monitor the political contributions of others and attempt to punish or exclude free riders. The freerider problem also explains the difficulty of mobilizing the dispersed opponents of programs. The numerous but widely dispersed consumers who pay higher prices for sugar have a collective interest in changing the current policy, but there is a strong incentive to shirk from any organized effort to do so.

For other economic interests, however, political organization is not even necessary. For example, wheat farmers in Kansas and Nebraska, tobacco farmers in North Carolina, and citrus producers in Florida do not require much political organization to ensure that their elected representatives take their interests to heart. Legislators represent the preferences of important unorganized constituents in order to raise the probability that they will be reelected. In addition, with the spread of antidumping and other bureaucratic mechanisms for obtaining protection, described in chapter 5, it is not even clear that political contributions by interest groups are the predominant means by which trade policy is affected. The freerider problem is less of an obstacle in antidumping cases because the definition of an industry is often so narrow that even a single firm has the standing to file a petition.

Thus, because of the conflicting interests of specific groups, there is no reason to believe that free trade will necessarily be adopted as a country's trade policy. But what if citizens could actually vote on trade policy matters? An interesting benchmark to consider is the trade policy that would emerge in a democratic vote under majority rule. While trade policy is rarely determined in this way, this is a useful starting point for thinking about the policy that would arise in a competitive, representative political system.

In a direct democracy, trade policy would be determined by the preferences of the median voter.[48] If free trade raises aggregate income but

---

[48] See the classic analysis by Mayer (1984). The median voter is the decisive marginal voter whose views determine which side will win under majority rule.

reduces the income of the median voter, then free trade would probably not get a majority vote to pass in a referendum. This points to the distribution of workers' skills across the electorate as a potentially important determinant of the median voter's interests. Suppose workers with a high school education lose one dollar as a result of free trade, while those with a college education gain two dollars. If workers with a college degree constitute at least one-third of all voters, free trade would raise overall income. But if the less-educated workers make up more than half of the electorate, the median voter would oppose the policy, unless guaranteed a compensatory income transfer.

As noted in chapter 1, educational attainment appears to be an important factor in shaping the American public's views of trade policy. Several studies have shown that the more education a person receives, the more likely that person is to support open trade policies.[49] This is consistent with the view that economic interests are at stake: the United States exports goods and services that require a highly educated workforce, whereas it imports more labor-intensive goods that, in the competing domestic industry, require few years of formal education. Because the fraction of the population receiving advanced education has risen in recent decades, support for freer trade might be expected to grow over time.[50]

Other factors affecting the median voter's views on trade include the manner in which voters perceive their economic interests to be related to trade policy. One such factor is the degree to which workers are potentially mobile between different sectors of the economy or different regions of the country. For example, a worker who over time has built up industry-specific skills (such as a blast-furnace worker in the steel industry) will probably view trade policy differently than someone whose skills are useful in several different industries (such as a financial accountant who happens to work in the steel industry). A coal miner in West Virginia

[49] See Blonigen 2011 and the references therein.

[50] In 2013, for example, 53 percent of persons aged sixty-five to seventy-four had received some college education or had earned a higher degree, while 63 percent of persons aged twenty-five to thirty-four had reached this level of educational attainment (http://www.census.gov/hhes/socdemo/education/data/cps/2013/tables.html). There is also evidence that home ownership is a factor that shapes an individual's preferences on trade policy. Even highly educated individuals tend to express support for protectionist policies if they own a home in a region that is adversely affected by imports.

who refuses to consider relocating to another part of the country is going to think about economic change differently from someone who is willing to move thousands of miles in search of a new opportunity.

In most countries, however, trade policy is not determined by voters in a referendum, but by elected representatives voting in the legislature. In this case, the distribution of economic interests across electoral districts can interact with the rules of the political system (a winner-take-all versus a proportionate representative system) and shape the outcome. If a sizable minority of the electorate is opposed to free trade but is uniformly distributed across districts, then a winner-take-all system might result in the election of few opponents to free trade, whereas their political strength might be greater in a proportional system.

Politicians can be crafty in exploiting the geographic variation in trade interests by using selective promises of protection to win votes. To help get NAFTA passed by the House of Representatives in 1993, President Bill Clinton negotiated a special safeguard agreement for citrus producers just to win the support of Florida's congressional delegation. During the 2000 election campaign, candidate George Bush promised to aid steelworkers in West Virginia, which helped swing the state to the Republicans for the first time in decades and helped him win the election. (The Bush administration followed through on its promise by imposing tariffs on imported steel in 2002.) In the 2008 Democratic primaries, candidates Barack Obama and Hillary Clinton questioned the wisdom of NAFTA in Ohio, where many manufacturing jobs had been lost, but not in Texas, where the agreement is viewed favorably. In general, the states of North Carolina, Alabama, and Idaho have a high concentration of economic activity in commodities that are protected by import restrictions. The states of Washington and California have a large stake, and many other states have a smaller stake, in open trade due to the export orientation of local producers.

Finally, trade policy outcomes also depend upon how the conflict between these competing groups is mediated by policymaking institutions in the government. These institutions may be biased in favor of one group over another, either because certain groups have better access to decision makers or because those decision makers are more sensitive to the interests of some groups. This can obviously affect the direction that trade policy takes. For example, antidumping policy is essentially nonpolitical and administered in a routine, bureaucratic way by government agencies. Small, narrowly defined industries tend to choose the anti-dumping route to trade protection, whereas larger industries may have the political clout to secure protection directly from the president and Congress. Because of all these variables, generalizations about the politics of trade policy are difficult to make. So it should not be surprising that political economists have failed to answer basic questions about how firms achieve political influence.

But one generalization seems fairly robust: once policies are in place, they are difficult to change, particularly if change involves taking benefits away from any industry. In a classic essay, Gordon Tullock called this the "transitional gains" trap.[51] Any new tariff or subsidy creates a short-term, transitional benefit for a particular group, but no long-term benefit because costs rise, benefits get capitalized (in higher land prices, in the case of agriculture, for example), and conditions become normalized. But the termination of these schemes would generate large losses for the entrenched interests. Hence, the beneficiaries of the policy will fight against any effort to eliminate a tariff or subsidy, even if the apparent benefit from the policy is no longer very large.

For example, during the Korean War, Congress introduced support measures for owners of mohair goats, whose wool was useful for making warm army uniforms. These subsidies persisted for forty years after the end of the war because farmers adamantly opposed their withdrawal and politicians did not want to fight them. Although the government program was abolished in 1994, saving $200 million, it was revived just a few years later. Wool growers did not flourish with the subsidies, but they were definitely harmed by their removal. Experience with other industries in the past—such as steel, textiles and apparel, and semiconductors—have also shown that once the government gives a certain group a special program, that program can become institutionalized at various levels of government and very difficult to take away.

For this reason, it has been said that voting for freer trade is an "unnatural act" for a politician because he or she would be taking away tangible benefits for some in exchange for uncertain benefits for others. That the beneficiaries of a policy change are uncertain who they are cre-

---

[51] Tullock 1975.

ates problems in itself. When imports increase, some groups know with a high degree of certainty that their jobs and incomes are at stake. Yet it is often not clear which individuals and industries stand to gain jobs and income when exports increase. Uncertainty about whether an individual will benefit from or be harmed by trade can lead to a status quo bias in favor of maintaining trade restrictions. Even if the entire electorate recognized that a clear majority would benefit from free trade, a reform in which most voters would benefit might not pass in a popular vote if a large number of these voters considered themselves unlikely to be part of the majority that would gain from the reform. This uncertainty means that the expected value of reform could be negative for a majority of voters, in which case they would block it. In addition to the transitional gains trap, this phenomenon gives the political system a status quo bias.[52]

The status quo bias is simply reinforced if voters are risk averse (wherein they prefer a lower but certain return over a higher but less certain return) or loss averse (wherein they are more sensitive to losses than to equivalentsized gains, and thus prefer to avoid any loss). These factors might help explain why countries with trade restrictions find it politically difficult to eliminate them. In such cases, tariffs may be viewed as a social welfare mechanism to prevent substantial reduction of real incomes in certain sections of the community. This function might explain why so many tariffs in the past seem to have had income maintenance as their goal and why they have continued, even when designed to be only temporary. For example, if the goal is to keep real incomes of certain farmers, steelworkers, or textile manufacturers higher than they would be otherwise, there is less of a motivation to reduce trade barriers, even though other income transfer policies would be more efficient than restricting trade.

Despite the forces that favor the imposition and maintenance of trade barriers, political leaders in many countries have recognized the economywide benefits of free trade and have been able to overcome political

---

[52] Fernandez and Rodrik 1991. Rodrik (1995, 1479) gives this example: suppose there are 100 voters and a policy reform will increase the incomes of 51 individuals by $5 and decrease the incomes of 49 individuals by $1. The policy produces a net gain of (5 X 51)— (1 X 49) = $209. But suppose the 49 know that they will lose, while the 51 do not know whether they will win or lose. Not only will the 49 losers vote against the policy, but so will some of the potential winners, and thus a majority will reject the reform.

inertia, throw off existing measures, and adopt more open trade policies. The United Kingdom eliminated virtually all of its protectionist policies in the mid-nineteenth century when export-oriented cotton textile interests grew powerful enough to defeat import-competing agricultural producers. The United States significantly reduced its tariffs in the mid-twentieth century as it came to dominate world trade in manufactured goods. As chapter 6 discusses, many developing countries—from Korea in the 1960s to Chile in the 1970s to China in the 1980s to India in the 1990s—have undertaken radical changes in economic policies in the direction of open markets.[53] Often these changes require creative political leaders who respond to a crisis or form new political coalitions in a way that breaks through the inertia of the status quo.

_____Is Protection Ever Beneficial?

The theory and evidence reviewed thus far have failed to address the idea that, in certain instances, import restrictions might be economically beneficial.[54] In fact, economists have identified certain conditions under which trade protection can actually improve welfare. Broadly speaking, trade interventions can be beneficial when they are used to improve the terms of trade, to promote industries with positive externalities, or to capture rents in international markets.[55] Although these theoretical cases exist, daunting political problems remain in actually having government implement policies that can capture these benefits. Let us consider each case in turn.

When a country has the ability to influence the prices of its exports and imports on the world market, then trade restrictions can potentially raise national income by improving the ratio at which a country exchanges exports for imports, something known as a country's terms of trade. An improvement in the terms of trade, either through higher export prices or lower import prices, increases the purchasing power of exports

---

[53] For a set of case studies on unilateral moves to free trade, see Bhagwati 2002.

[54] Adam Smith fully conceded that there are sound noneconomic rationales for restricting trade, such as protecting industries essential for national defense.

[55] Corden (1974) provides a good overview of the various cases in which protection might be economically justifiable. Irwin (1996a) explores the debate among economists about these cases.

in terms of the imports they procure. This translates into higher income because the country can acquire more imports for the same amount of exports. For example, oil exporting countries benefit from a higher price for oil (i.e., their terms of trade improve), whereas oil importing countries suffer from a higher price for oil (i.e., their terms of trade deteriorate).

Power to affect Price-huge

The power to influence the world market price is usually held by a country or group of countries that dominate production of a certain good, often a natural resource commodity. For example, the United States produced 80 percent of the world's cotton prior to the Civil War. Southern cotton producers collectively had a significant impact on the world price, but each producer alone had no particular influence. The United States might have been better off if producers had formed a cartel to restrict exports or, barring that, if the government had imposed an export tax to force up the world price of cotton. The Organization of Petroleum Exporting Countries (OPEC) has used limits on production to help increase the world price of oil, and its members have reaped billions of dollars in additional revenue as a result. (Of course, it is always difficult for such *Cheating can happen* cartels to prevent smaller members from cheating and to prevent nonmembers from increasing production.) Similarly, the number of large exporters of gold, diamonds, and some metals is limited by natural resource endowments, giving some countries the power to influence prices on world markets.

Except in such special cases, the terms-of-trade motive for trade restrictions has little relevance for most countries' policies.[56] Few countries have the clear-cut ability to manipulate their terms of trade to much advantage, except for those commodity examples, and most policymakers probably have little idea what conditions would have to be met for tariffs to be set optimally.[57] Most governments are highly sensitive to domestic political concerns about trade and seek to minimize adjustment

---

[56] Most government officials are probably not aware of the impact their policies have on the country's terms of trade. Panagariya, Shah, and Mishra (2001) provide evidence that developing countries are price-takers on world markets and therefore cannot improve their terms of trade by restricting exports or imports. After estimating a slew of export supply elasticities facing various importing countries, Nicita, Olarreaga, and Silva (2014) find that the median "optimal tariff" on imports (to improve the terms of trade by forcing exporters to reduce their prices) is just 4 percent.

[57] If domestic producers are aware of their market power, they can appropriately determine the price of their exports with less need for government interference (Rodrik 1989).

costs to producers rather than search out goods in which optimal tariffs might be employed.

To the extent that countries can influence the price of their exports, the appropriate response is an export tax, something that is unlikely to be popular. In addition, any gains from such a policy could disappear if competing suppliers emerged or if other countries imposed retaliatory duties. Finally, such a trade restriction is not desirable from the standpoint of world welfare and global efficiency. An improvement in the exporting country's terms of trade implies a deterioration in the importing country's terms of trade and actually leaves the world as a whole worse off.

[margin note: Just Bad]

Another situation in which trade interventions can, in principle, yield economic benefits is when they serve as a second-best measure to promote industries that generate positive externalities. In the case of positive externalities, the private costs of production are higher than the social costs of production because producers do not take into account the benefits of their actions for other sectors of the economy. As a result, the domestic industry produces less of a good than is socially desirable. These benefits can be captured if the private and social costs of production are properly aligned, which can sometimes be achieved through domestic subsidies. If subsidies cannot be used, there may be a second-best case for promoting the industry through protection. Recent theoretical cases have considered optimal trade policy for industries in which there are static or dynamic external economies, such as learning-by-doing or R&D spillovers, in which the production experience or research of one firm benefits others in the industry, as is alleged to be the case in certain high-technology industries. In theory, circumstances can arise in which some government promotion may be appropriate.

But as a practical matter, using trade policy to correct for such market failures is problematic. Correctly identifying these externalities is, by their very nature, extremely difficult.[58] Even if the externality can be identified,

---

[58] Industrial policy advocates propose various criteria for determining which industries are better than others and therefore deserve promotion. One proposed criterion was industries with high value-added per worker, but as Krugman (1994) notes, these are really just capital-intensive industries. This would lead one to support the cigarette industry and the oil pipeline industry. Sometimes it is argued that the presence of external economies of scale is demonstrated by geographically concentrated industries. Just because most U.S.-made carpets come from one county in Georgia, to use a commonly cited example of this

Not a very go [handwritten annotation]

the first-best policy of a subsidy has to be ruled out. Using tariffs to promote a targeted industry has been likened to acupuncture with a fork: the relevant market failure may be corrected, but at the cost of introducing a by-product distortion, such as a higher price for domestic consumers. Finally, the relevant externality must be external to the firm and internal to the country. The R&D or learning benefits could spill over between countries, particularly if foreign firms maintain a presence in the domestic market or have an ownership stake in the domestic firms, or when the knowledge cannot be limited geographically. In this case, any promotion scheme benefits all firms around the world, not just domestic ones, significantly narrowing the cases in which intervention would produce purely a national advantage instead of simply providing an international public good. It is particularly difficult for the United States, where policy is determined largely by lawyers who are responding to self-interested producers, to discern impartially which industries exhibit such dynamic externalities and which do not, let alone the degree to which the knowledge spills over to foreign firms.

Many industries that are touted as creating positive externalities fail to do so. For example, in the late 1980s and early 1990s, high-definition television (HDTV) was widely believed to be a "technology driver" for the high-technology industry: if the United States failed to dominate the underlying technology, it would lose its competitive position in commercial applications and in related industries, such as semiconductors and workstations. Whichever country invested in the "right" technology first was expected to have a strategic advantage over latecomers in what was projected to be a lucrative new market. To this end, Europe and Japan moved quickly to subsidize their producers. Japan invested nearly $1.2 billion in HDTV research (much of it from the Ministry of International Trade and Industry and the state broadcaster, NHK), while taxpayers in the European Community spent about $1 billion on HDTV research through 1991.[59]

Fearing the United States would be left behind, in 1989 the American Electronics Association proposed that Congress appropriate $1.35 billion

---

phenomenon, does not mean that the carpet industry deserved to be subsidized at its inception or deserves to be subsidized now.

[59] See Hart 1994 and Dai, Cawson, and Holmes 1996.

in direct subsidies and loan guarantees to support HDTV research. Congress authorized $30 million in research grants through the Defense Department and promised more, but the first Bush administration opposed the funding. The ensuing stalemate prevented any further spending. Yet gridlock not only saved American taxpayers millions of dollars, it proved to be the best policy. The European and Japanese technologies were developed first, but they settled on an analog standard that was soon viewed as obsolete. Meanwhile, frustrated by the impasse in Washington, American firms set to work themselves on HDTV research and, by entering the field somewhat later, were able to improve upon foreign research. Ultimately, American firms created a digital system that was later selected as the industry standard by the Federal Communications Commission. Moreover, only now has HDTV become commercially available, and it has failed to become the driving or profitable technology that many influential commentators thought it would be twenty years ago.

More recently, the federal government has guaranteed loans to "innovative technologies," but it is not clear that bureaucrats are good venture capitalists. Taxpayers are on the hook for $529 million after the solar firm Solyndra failed. It had been given a government-sponsored loan in an effort to produce cleaner energy technologies, but declared bankruptcy in 2011 amid claims that it might have misrepresented its finances to the government.

The final rationale for trade intervention is to capture rents or profits in the international market. To understand this process, consider a firm that is competing against a single foreign rival in an imperfectly competitive market (i.e., one in which there are abovenormal profits) in a third country. In this case, a government export subsidy for the firm could induce the foreign rival to cut its output, thereby shifting profits from the foreign to the domestic firm. This practice is known as strategic trade policy, in which the government undertakes a precise, strategic intervention on behalf of domestic firms in a way that increases national welfare.[60] For example, European support for Airbus is commonly believed to be an attempt to shift profits away from Boeing in the lucrative market for wide-body aircraft.[61]

[60] Brander (1995) provides a comprehensive survey of this literature.

[61] Irwin and Pavcnik (2004) examine the impact of Airbus's A-380 super jumbo on Boeing sales of the 747.

Although there was much enthusiasm for strategic trade policy in the 1980s, numerous theoretical and practical objections have diminished its appeal. First, successful intervention depends crucially upon key parameters in the market's structure that make it difficult for governments to determine the best policy. For example, one study showed that if the firms competed by setting prices rather than quantities, then the optimal policy would switch from an export subsidy to an export tax. The introduction of asymmetric information between the firms and the government further increases the range of possible outcomes and makes clear-cut predictions even more difficult. Setting aside theoretical issues, calibrated simulation models of strategic trade policy reveal that the potential gains from implementing the optimal policy are exceedingly small. When the right policy is excruciatingly difficult to determine in the first place and depends upon getting parameters of industry structure and competitive interaction exactly right, the small potential payoff suggests that such interventions are not worthwhile, especially when the potential outlays are high.

really ain't even worth it

Theoretical work on optimal trade interventions is usually developed in the context of an omniscient government that has full information and the capability of setting policy in an optimal manner. In the real world, governments are neither omniscient nor immune to external pressure. Do the theoretical results stand up when the government is confronted with political pressure to use policy on behalf of certain industries? Not surprisingly, the answer is no. Research has shown that the case for such interventions is substantially weakened when government policy is subject to strategic manipulation by politically active firms.[62] Thus, there are many reasons to be skeptical about whether a government can determine where strategic intervention will be worthwhile among the many industries competing for government assistance, especially in a representative

too much politics

[62] Grossman and Maggi (1998) examine whether a welfare-maximizing government should pursue a program of strategic trade intervention or instead commit itself to free trade when domestic firms have the opportunity to manipulate the government's choice of the level of intervention. Domestic firms, for example, may overinvest in physical and knowledge capital in a regime of strategic intervention in order to influence the government's choice of subsidy. They find that this manipulation can make a commitment to free trade desirable even in settings where profit-shifting opportunities are available.

democracy, where trade policy is often driven by the interests of politically active domestic producers.[63]

It is sometimes said that free trade is right in theory but wrong in
practice. Actually, the opposite is true. Any clever graduate student in
economics can quickly come up with half a dozen reasons why free trade
fails as a theoretical proposition. In theory, a lot of things can happen. In
practice, the economic benefits of trade and the costs of protection are
tangible.

The three theoretical possibilities for trade intervention discussed here
depend upon particular circumstances in special cases and require constant adjustment to changing market conditions. Free trade is a much
simpler policy because it does not need changing when the underlying
economic conditions change. Furthermore, any government that undertakes large, systematic sectoral interventions creates a great deal of concentrated political and economic power, not just to do good but also to
make costly mistakes.

---

[63] Krueger (1990, 21) argues that "in the real world of scarce information, uncertainty,
and pervasive rent-seeking, policy makers will inevitably miss the crucial and subtle distinctions between profits that are high because of rents and those that are high because of risk;
between wages that are high because of rents, and those that are high because of skills; and
between sectors that provide inputs, and those that result in spillover externalities."

4

Trade, Jobs, and Income Distribution

The argument against free trade that resonates most strongly with the public and with politicians is that imports destroy jobs. Indeed, the greatest fear about international trade in general, and imports in particular, is that it can harm workers, reduce wages, and lead to unemployment. But is this an accurate view of trade as a whole? And if so, are import restrictions the remedy? This chapter addresses the relationship between trade, jobs, and wages, and examines government policies to assist displaced workers. The chapter also considers the underlying causes of trade deficits to see if a country suffers when it imports more than it exports.

_____How Does Trade Affect Employment?

The claim that trade should be limited because imports destroy jobs has been around at least since the sixteenth century.[1] Why should we import something produced abroad, it is commonly asked, when we can produce it here at home with our own workers?

Of course, not all imports destroy jobs. The United States imports coffee, bananas, and tin, but these imports do not directly harm domestic industries or cause job losses, because these products are not produced at home.[2] Furthermore, few people complain about U.S. fuel imports, aside from a few small oil drillers in Texas and Oklahoma, because for-

[1] See Irwin 1996b, 36ff.

[2] However, the U.S. apple industry once complained that cheap banana imports were hurting them because apples and bananas are substitutes. In the late 1920s, the apple industry proposed that banana imports be taxed to shift consumer demand toward the purchase of apples.

eign suppliers give us access to low-cost energy imports that enable us to have cheaper electricity, heat our homes, and fuel our cars.[3]

But imports do indeed destroy jobs in certain industries: for example, employment in the shoe industry in Maine, the steel industry in Pennsylvania, the textile and apparel industry in South Carolina, and the furniture industry in North Carolina is much lower because these industries have faced stiff competition from imports. So we can understand why the plant owners and workers and the politicians who represent them would like to change this situation by imposing trade barriers.

But just because imports destroy some jobs does not mean that trade reduces overall employment or harms the economy. (Technology also destroys jobs, such as the replacement of bank tellers with ATM machines, office assistants with computers and voice mail, and manual workers with machines, yet these innovations are not viewed as a bad thing.) As we saw in chapter 3, blocking imports may protect jobs in industries that compete against imports, but it also diminishes employment in other industries by reducing exports and raising costs for import-using industries. Therefore, the statement that imports destroy jobs is incomplete because trade also creates jobs in export industries and import-using industries. In 2013, exports of goods and services "supported" 11.3 million American jobs, directly and indirectly, according to the Department of Commerce.[4]

Since trade both creates and destroys jobs, one question is whether trade has any effect on overall employment. Unfortunately, attempts to quantify the overall employment effect of trade are largely an exercise in futility.[5] This is because the impact of trade on the total number of jobs in an economy is best approximated as zero. Total employment is not a function of international trade, but the number of people in the labor force. As figure 4.1 shows, employment in the United States since 1950 has closely tracked the number of people in the labor force.

---

[3] Of course, the rapid expansion of domestic production of oil and natural gas in recent years due to fracking and other new technologies has changed the U.S. position in energy trade. It has also put pressure on Congress and the administration to lift the ban on American oil exports, which was imposed in the 1970s during the era of shortages.

[4] Johnson and Rasmussen 2014.

[5] For one recent attempt, see Groshen, Hobijn, and McConnell 2005.

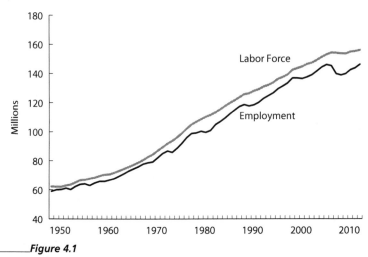

_____*Figure 4.1*

Civilian Labor Force and Civilian Employment in the United States, 1950–2014
   Source: FRED, Federal Reserve Economic Data, Federal Reserve Bank of St. Louis
(http://research.stlouisfed.org/fred2/).

Of course, there is always some unemployment, represented by the
gap between the two series. For example, the large recent gap starting in
2008 is due to the financial crisis and the subsequent Great Recession,
from which the United States has slowly emerged. But the level of unemployment is determined more by the business cycle than by changes in
trade flows or trade policy. And the business cycle has a rhythm of its
own, driven by factors largely independent of trade.

To see this more directly, figure 4.2 compares the unemployment rate
with the ratio of imports of goods and services to GDP since 1970. Except
for the period from 1970 to 1975, higher unemployment rates are not associated with increases in imports as a share of GDP. Since the early
1980s, the unemployment rate has moved lower even as the imports-to-
GDP ratio has increased. When unemployment rose in the early 1980s,
the early 1990s, the early 2000s, and the late 2000s because of recessions
in each of those periods, imports were not surging but actually falling off
because of declining demand. For example, the financial crisis of 2008
and the subsequent Great Recession led not only to a sharp rise in unemployment, but also to a collapse in U.S. imports.

As figure 4.1 demonstrates, overall job creation has exceeded job destruction over time. Although the net change in employment is relatively

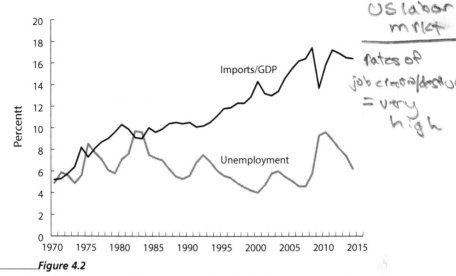

US labor mrkt

rates of job creation/destruct = very high

_____**Figure 4.2**

Unemployment and Import Penetration in the United States, 1970–2014
   Source: FRED, Federal Reserve Economic Data, Federal Reserve Bank of St. Louis
(http://research.stlouisfed.org/fred2/).

small in any given year, a striking feature of the U.S. labor market is that
gross rates of job creation and destruction are very high. In a dynamic
and rapidly changing economy, jobs are continuously created and eliminated, at a rate of about four to five million per month. In 2014, for example, there were 55.1 million job separations (36 percent of which were
layoffs and discharges, the remainder being quits) and 57.9 million hires.
National employment rose by about 2.8 million over the year, but the net
change in jobs was a small fraction of the gross flows of workers in and
out of the labor force and moving between jobs.[6]

extne. fluid

   How much are imports to blame for the job losses experienced in any
given year? Not much. Changes in consumer tastes, domestic competition,
productivity growth, and technological innovation, in addition to international trade, all contribute to the churning of the labor market. It is virtually impossible to disentangle all of the reasons for job displacement
because they are interdependent; for example, technological change may
be stimulated by domestic or foreign competition. Yet to the extent that
such attributions are made by the Bureau of Labor Statistics, trade is a tiny
factor in the displacement of labor. As table 4.1 shows, import competi-

WHAT REALLY EFFECTS LABOR MARKET

[6] Bureau of Labor Statistics, Job Openings and Labor Turnover Survey, January 2014.

- Δ in cons. tastes
- productivity growth
- tech. innovation
- int'l trade
— interdep. factors

_____Table 4.1.
Number of Workers Affected by Extended Mass Layoffs, 1996–2012

Year	Total number of workers, all reasons	Due to import competition	Percentage of total due to imports	Due to overseas relocation	Percentage of total due to imports & relocation
1996	948,122	13,476	1.4	4,326	1.9
1997	947,843	12,019	1.3	10,439	2.4
1998	991,245	18,473	1.9	8,797	2.8
1999	901,451	26,234	2.9	5,683	3.5
2000	915,962	13,416	1.5	9,054	2.5
2001	1,524,832	27,946	1.8	15,693	2.9
2002	1,272,331	15,350	1.2	17,075	2.5
2003	1,216,886	23,734	2.0	13,205	3.0
2004	993,909	8,064	0.8	16,197	2.4
2005	884,661	11,112	1.3	12,030	2.6
2006	935,805	10,458	1.1	13,367	2.5
2007	965,935	11,589	1.2	n.a.	n.a.
2008	1,516,978	9,679	0.6	n.a.	n.a.
2009	2,108,803	3,192	0.2	n.a.	n.a.
2010	1,257,134	1,199	0.1	n.a.	n.a.
2011	1,112,710	1,214	0.1	n.a.	n.a.
2012	1,257,212	n.a.	n.a.	n.a.	n.a.

Source: Bureau of Labor Statistics, Mass Layoff Statistics (www.bls.gov/mls).
Note: Displaced workers are those who face involuntary separations due to plant clos-ings, mass layoffs, etc., and do not include those who lose their jobs due to temporary layoffs or voluntary separations. Due to budget cuts, the BLS has stopped collecting these data.

tion and overseas plant relocations accounted for about 3 percent of total employment separations due to mass layoffs in recent years. During the recent Great Recession, layoffs topped two million in 2009, but less than 1 percent of those job losses were due to import competition.

In fact, study after study has confirmed that the trade-induced turn-over in U.S. labor markets is small in comparison with the overall turn-over.[7] Trade is only slightly related to cross-industry variation in worker displacement rates. Although industries with high displacement rates are often import sensitive, not all import-sensitive industries have high dis-placement rates. One respected study concludes that there is "no system-

[7] See Addison, Fox, and Ruhm 1995. Kletzer (1998b, 455) also concludes that "increas-ing foreign competition across industries accounts for a small share of job displacement" across industries because there are "high rates of job loss for industries with little trade."

Trade's effect isn't
as high as others

atic relationship between the magnitude of gross job flows and exposure
to international trade. . . . On balance, the evidence is highly unfavorable
to the view that international trade exposure systematically reduces job
security."[8]

But how can we be sure that the number of jobs destroyed by imports
will be matched by the number of jobs created elsewhere in the economy? One reason is that macroeconomic policy can be adjusted to offset
any imbalance in the forces that drive job creation and destruction. If
imports begin rolling in and trigger widespread layoffs, for example, the
unemployment rate may begin to rise. If the unemployment rate rises,
and with it the risks of a recession, the Federal Reserve Board is likely to
ease monetary policy and reduce interest rates, other things being equal.
This action not only stimulates the economy in the short run, but also
leads to a depreciation of the dollar on foreign exchange markets, which
in turn makes U.S. exports less expensive to foreign consumers and imports more expensive to U.S. consumers. As a result, employment goes
back up and returns to its long-run relationship with the labor force. (The
trade deficit will be discussed at the end of this chapter.)

Yet the effect of trade on jobs is a politically sensitive issue and one
that is prone to exaggeration in political discourse. For example, the debate over the North American Free Trade Agreement in 1993 largely
consisted of claims and counterclaims about whether the agreement
would add to or subtract from total employment. NAFTA opponents
claimed that free trade with Mexico would destroy jobs: the Economic
Policy Institute put the number at 480,000 workers. NAFTA proponents
countered with the claim that it would create jobs: the Institute for International Economics suggested that 170,000 jobs would be created.[9]
Those stressing the job losses gave the impression that there would be a
permanent reduction in the number of people employed in the economy.

---

[8] Davis, Haltiwanger, and Schuh 1995, 48–49. They find that there is a higher rate of
gross job destruction in very high import-penetration sectors, but that this disappears after
controlling for industry wages. "This is evidence that import-intensive industries exhibit
greater gross job flows because their workers have relatively low levels of specific human
capital—not because foreign competition subjects these industries to unusually large and
volatile disturbances" (49). Simply put, workers who lack industry-specific skills are more
apt to switch jobs and are less apt to remain in any given industry than workers who have
industry-specific skills.

[9] Orme 1996, 107.

Those stressing the positive employment effects gave the impression that more trade would lead to a higher level of employment and that this should be the motivation for pursuing more open trade policies.

Both of these impressions were false because at the end of the day it is virtually impossible to know the precise effect of the trade agreement on employment changes. (Furthermore, as we saw in chapter 2, the reason for pursuing more open trade policies is not to increase employment, but to generate more productive employment that will raise aggregate income.) Every estimate of the medium-term impact of NAFTA on employment was a fraction of the monthly turnover in U.S. labor markets. And as demonstrated by the experience after 1994, when NAFTA went into effect, the fears of massive job losses in the United States as a result of free trade with Mexico proved to be unwarranted. The "giant sucking sound" of jobs being lost to Mexico, as famously predicted by Ross Perot, was never heard. In 1998, four years after NAFTA went into effect, several analysts noted the following:

> By any reasonable measure, even the gross job turnover induced by the agreement has been slight. According to the Department of Labor, over the nearly four years from January 1994 through midAugust 1997, 220,000 workers had petitioned for adjustment assistance (cash and training allowances) under the legislation enacted when the trade deal was signed. Of this total, 136,000—an average of about 40,000 workers per year—were certified as eligible for assistance (under both the more general trade adjustment assistance program and that created as part of NAFTA). Even this figure overstates NAFTA's true impact, because to be eligible under both programs workers only need to show that "imports" have contributed to their losses, but not specifically as a result of NAFTA. By way of comparison, the gross monthly turnover of jobs in the United States exceeds 2 million. Since NAFTA, overall employment in the United States has risen by more than 10 million.[10]

Even when judged by the liberal standards of the NAFTA assistance program, only 2.4 percent of displaced workers on permanent layoff required assistance as a result of being harmed by the agreement.[11]

[10] Burtless, Lawrence, Litan, and Shapiro 1998, 57.
[11] Schoepfle 2000, 115.

The claims of large employment gains were equally flawed. Analysts at several Washington think tanks (both favorable and unfavorable to NAFTA) settled upon the rule of thumb that every $1 billion in exports generates or supports thirteen thousand jobs (implying conversely that every $1 billion in imports eliminates the same number of jobs) as a way of evaluating the employment effects of trade agreements. Some NAFTA proponents argued that, because Mexico was to eliminate relatively high tariffs against U.S. goods while U.S. tariffs against Mexican goods were already very low, the agreement would generate more exports to, than imports from, Mexico. Using the rule of thumb, it was therefore reasoned that NAFTA would result in net job creation. For example, President Clinton's trade representative claimed that the agreement would create two hundred thousand new jobs within two years.

Such formulaic calculations and predictions were made to fight the dire forecasts that thousands of jobs would be lost as a result of NAFTA, but there was never any reason to believe any of these figures. Even if tariff reductions are asymmetric, exports may not grow more rapidly than imports.[12] And it is a further mistake to think that changes in the trade balance translate into predictable changes in employment; a booming economy with low unemployment may be accompanied by a growing trade deficit because people have more money to spend on imports. In any case, these claims for the job-creation benefits of NAFTA soon boomeranged. When the peso collapsed in late 1994, for reasons that had nothing to do with NAFTA, imports from Mexico surged and the U.S. trade surplus evaporated.[13]

More recently, the performance of the U.S. labor market was relatively weak in recovering from the 2001 recession, particularly in comparison to the late 1990s. When juxtaposed with the growth in trade, many have suspected that foreign competition and imports might be responsible for

[12] Trade agreements themselves have little effect on bilateral trade balance or the overall trade balance, as we will see later.

[13] NAFTA opponents then argued, using the ruleofthumb formula endorsed by NAFTA proponents, that thousands of jobs had been lost as a result of trade with Mexico because the trade surplus had become a trade deficit. An analyst at the Economic Policy Institute, for example, claimed that the trade deficit with Mexico and Canada destroyed 440,172 American jobs between 1994 and 1998.

the disappointing outcomes. Yet a study of trade and offshoring in the 2000 to 2003 period concluded that

> weakness in U.S. payroll employment since 2000 has not been caused by a flood of imports of either goods or services. It should certainly not be attributed to any trade agreements the United States has signed. Rather, the weakness of employment is primarily the result of inadequate growth of domestic demand in the presence of strong productivity growth . . . to the extent that trade did cause a loss of manufacturing jobs, it was the weakness of U.S. exports after 2000 and not the strength of imports that was responsible—the share of imports in the U.S. market actually declined.[14]

The weakness of exports was in part due to the strength of the dollar on foreign exchange markets over this period.

Finally, the sharp rise in the unemployment rate during the Great Recession (which officially lasted from December 2007 to June 2009, although the recovery has been slow) can be attributed to the financial problems associated with the collapse of housing prices, not a sudden intensification of import competition. The U.S. unemployment rate rose from 5.4 percent in January 2008 to a peak of 10.6 percent in January 2010. At the same time, the volume of U.S. imports fell 3 percent in 2008 and 14 percent in 2009 due to the sharp fall in demand.

Despite trade and trade policy having little relationship to a country's overall level of employment, trade policy debates in Washington and elsewhere are often framed through the lens of jobs alone. That is why one still sees efforts made to quantify the relationship between trade and jobs—usually with a political point to be made. As noted earlier, the Department of Commerce reckons that exports supported 11.3 million jobs in 2013.[15] They came up with this figure based on the calculation that every billion dollars in exports is associated with 5,590 jobs, but they do not perform an analysis of jobs lost as a result of imports. On the other hand, the Economic Policy Institute routinely issues reports about how the trade deficit with China costs American jobs. For the year 2013, they reported that exports to China supported 767,500 workers

[14] Baily and Lawrence 2004, 213.
[15] Johnson and Rasmussen 2014.

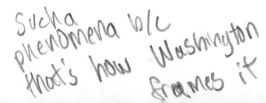

US weak recovery vs session ≠ Trade rising indic Domestic weakness

Such a phenomena w/c that's how Washington frames it

and imports from China had displaced 4.890 million workers, meaning that America had lost 4.1 million more jobs than it had gained because of the trade deficit.[16] However, this calculation assumed that a dollar of imports from China displaces a dollar of domestic production, when in fact (as chapter 1 documented, using the iPhone example and others) a sizable proportion of China's exports are simply assembled foreign-made components, including parts from the United States. Then again, there is the study sponsored by the U.S. Chamber of Commerce, the National Retail Federation, and others showing that imports support sixteen million U.S. jobs, not only in terms of shipping, handling, and selling the goods, but in providing essential components and intermediate goods for U.S. exports.[17]

a lot of studies are leaving out factors

Each of these studies looks at just one part of the overall complicated relationship between trade and jobs. Each is seriously incomplete and has shortcomings in its method of analysis. For example, the Economic Policy Institute study just mentioned assumes that a dollar's worth of imports from China displaces a dollar's worth of U.S. production and the jobs that go with it. The implication is that stopping those imports from China with trade barriers might create jobs for Americans. But if it restricted imports of certain goods from China, the United States would likely start importing those goods from other Asian countries rather than produce them at home. (As pointed out earlier, this is what happened in 2009 when the Obama administration imposed tariffs on automobile tires from China; rather than produce more tires domestically, the United States started importing more from Indonesia.)

The battle over trade and jobs will be repeated when the United States completes the Trans-Pacific Partnership (TPP), currently being negotiated with Pacific Rim countries. If trade barriers decline and trade expands between the United States and Pacific Rim countries, government officials will emphasize the job gains from increased exports while opponents will emphasize the job losses from increased imports. John F. Kerry, Secretary of State in the Obama administration, wrote that the TPP would increase exports by $123 billion and "help support an additional 650,000 jobs."[18]

---

[16] Scott and Kimball 2014.

[17] Baughman and François 2013.

[18] http://www.project-syndicate.org/commentary/american-alliances-international-cooperation-by-john-f--kerry-2015-01#4bxmfbYemSPg1fzI.99 (accessed February 4, 2015).

(Note that the slight change in language since the NAFTA debate; then government officials spoke of jobs being "created" by exports, but now it is jobs being "supported" by exports.) Yet the lead economist who wrote the study on which this claim is based noted that no employment projects were made because "like most trade economists, we don't believe that trade agreements change the labor force in the long run. The consequential factors are demography, immigration, retirement benefits, etc. Rather, trade agreements affect how people are employed, and ideally substitute more productive jobs for less productive ones and thus raise real incomes."[19]

Yet even if the quest to identify trade's impact on the overall number of jobs is largely futile, trade does have important implications for employment in different sectors of the economy and even the wages paid to workers.

Trade and the Manufacturing Sector

Even those who may agree that trade has no effect on total employment may oppose free trade in the belief that it shifts jobs into less desirable sectors. One of the greatest concerns in recent decades has been that trade has sacrificed good jobs in manufacturing for bad jobs in services and has thereby contributed to the "deindustrialization" of the U.S. economy. Indeed, through American history, policymakers and the public have always taken a special interest in the health of the manufacturing sector.[20]

From the 1970s through the 1990s, the number of jobs in manufacturing held steady. In 2000, there were 17.2 million workers in manufacturing, about the same as the 17.8 million workers in 1970. (Of course, the share of the labor force employed in manufacturing fell significantly over this period because the labor force grew in size.) Yet there was a vast increase in manufacturing output over this period. Large advances in labor productivity made this possible. Just as U.S. agricultural output has increased steadily even as the number of farmers has declined, the manu-

---

[19] http://www.washingtonpost.com/blogs/fact-checker/wp/2015/01/30/the-obama-administrations-illusionary-job-gains-from-the-trans-pacific-partnership/ (accessed February 4, 2015). The study is Petri, Plummer, and Zhai 2012.

[20] See Baily and Bosworth 2014.

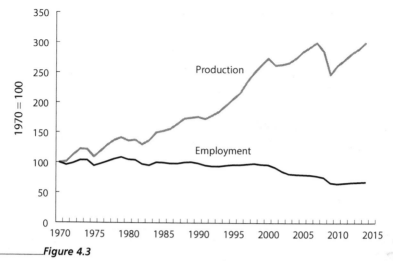

_____Figure 4.3

U.S. Manufacturing Production and Employment, 1970–2014

Source: FRED, Federal Reserve Economic Data, Federal Reserve Bank of St. Louis (http://research.stlouisfed.org/fred2/).

[handwritten: US agri/manufact: ↑ product. w/ same workers]

facturing sector was able to increase output significantly without any need to hire additional workers. *[handwritten: until 2000]*

Since 2000, however, the manufacturing sector has run into difficulties. Between 2000 and 2003, around the time of the mild recession of 2001, the manufacturing sector shed nearly three million jobs, while output stagnated. Then the economy shed another two to three million manufacturing jobs when production dropped in the Great Recession of 2008–9. Since then, manufacturing output recovered to its pre-crisis peak only in 2014, while the number of manufacturing jobs has increased only slightly, leaving the U.S. economy with a little more than twelve million manufacturing workers in that year. *[handwritten: from '01-'14 manu = struggling]*

Figures 4.3 and 4.4 show these trends. Figure 4.3 shows U.S. manufacturing production and employment from 1970 to 2014, where all of these developments are depicted. Figure 4.4 shows the steady decline in manufacturing's share of total employment, from 25 percent of the nonfarm workforce in 1970 to 9 percent in 2014. At the same time, real manufacturing output share of real GDP has remained steady throughout this period. Manufacturing has maintained its share of U.S. production, but its share of employment has fallen because the sector's productivity has exceeded

[handwritten: → employ = lower now ✶ product = maintained ✶]

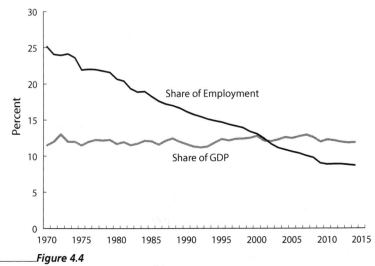

_____Figure 4.4

U.S. Manufacturing as a Share of GDP and Employment, 1970–2014

    Source: FRED, Federal Reserve Economic Data, Federal Reserve Bank of St. Louis (http://research.stlouisfed.org/fred2/).

that of other parts of the economy. (Manufacturing's share in nominal GDP has declined over time because the price of manufactured goods has fallen more than other prices in the economy.)

    The flip side to these developments is that a growing share of the labor force is employed in the service sector. As consumers have shifted their spending to such services as healthcare, education, recreation, and personal finance, the economy has responded by devoting more resources to those sectors. Because of the relatively poor productivity performance in these service sectors, a greater share of the labor force has to be devoted to these occupations in order to increase output and meet consumer demands. This is not a unique American phenomenon, but one that has taken place (sometimes to an even greater extent) in most developed countries.

    Thus, the decline in the share of employment in manufacturing—an experience shared with other high-income countries—is largely due to strong productivity growth in manufacturing and the shift of consumer demand away from goods and toward services. But has trade also contributed to the shift of employment away from manufacturing in the United States? As table 1.1 showed, the United States is both a big exporter and a big importer of manufactured goods. In 2014, the United States exported $1.193 trillion and imported $1.957 trillion in manufactured goods. The trade deficit in manufactured goods, at $763 billion, is slightly smaller than the overall merchandise trade deficit because the United States is a net importer of mineral fuels. Yet it is still quite sizeable at about 4.0 percent of GDP.

If that deficit were to be magically erased and the United States exported as much manufactured goods as it imported, how many more manufacturing jobs would there be? One calculation indicates that balanced trade in manufactured goods would increase U.S. manufacturing employment by 2.7 million in 2010.[21] This amounts to about a quarter of all jobs in manufacturing, a pretty significant figure, but only 2 percent of total nonagricultural employment in that year.

How much of the decline in the share of employment in manufacturing—shown in figure 4.4—would have been prevented if the United States had had balanced trade in manufactured goods over this period? The answer is very little. Between 1970 and 2014, the share of nonfarm employment in manufacturing fell sixteen percentage points, from 25 to 9 percent. If manufacturing productivity remained fixed at its 1970 level, manufacturing's share of employment would have to have risen eight percentage points in order for output to have matched its 2014 level. Alternatively, if the United States had balanced trade after 1970 but labor productivity grew as rapidly as it did, manufacturing's employment share would have been only one percentage point higher than it actually had been—10 percent, instead of 9 percent. Thus, the impact of long-term productivity improvements is far more important than increased manufactured imports in explaining the employment shift to services.

These calculations are rather mechanical and seem to imply that reducing imports might be a good thing for manufacturing employment. In fact, if imports of manufactured goods were to fall, that doesn't necessarily mean that domestic production of manufactured goods would be higher. To some extent, imports and domestic production may be complements rather than substitutes. As figure 4.5 indicates, annual changes in domestic manufacturing output and in real manufactured imports are positively correlated: an increase in imports is positively related to an

---

[21] Lawrence and Edwards 2013.

productivity shifts not import shifts explain Δ's in employ to srv.

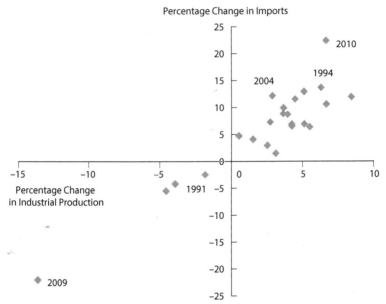

Percentage Change in Imports

_____*Figure 4.5*

Percentage Change in Production and Imports of Manufactured Goods, 1991–2013

Source: FRED, Federal Reserve Economic Data, Federal Reserve Bank of St. Louis (http://research.stlouisfed.org/fred2/).

increase in domestic production. This is because a strong and growing economy brings about more domestic production and more imports, whereas a weak economy tends to see a falloff in both. If imports only displaced domestic production, one would expect to see a negative relationship in the figure.

Furthermore, even in labor-intensive industries highly affected by trade, job losses occur much more because of technological change—the substitution of capital for labor and the introduction of new technology—than from imports. Trade protection cannot stop this process of mechanization and change. For example, the apparel industry has experienced a secular decline in the number of workers that even relatively high trade barriers have been powerless to stop.

Still, some people justify import restrictions as a way of slowing the movement of workers out of manufacturing industries. Here, two points should be recognized: jobs are "saved" in the industry only by destroying jobs elsewhere, as we have already seen, and protection is a costly and inefficient jobs program. The consumer cost per job saved as a result of trade restrictions can be calculated by dividing the total cost of protection to the consumer (due to the higher prices that they pay) by the number of jobs that protection maintains in the industry. During the 1980s, for example, restrictions on the importation of textiles and apparel cost consumers about $24 billion annually and prevented the loss of roughly 170,000 jobs in the domestic industry. Therefore, consumers paid $140,000 a year for every job saved in the textile and apparel industry. This was a stiff price for society to pay merely to keep workers employed in relatively low-wage occupations. The cost per job saved is even higher in the industries typically associated with high-paying manufacturing jobs, such as the machine tool industry ($350,000 per job) or the sugar industry ($600,000 per job).[22] And, as pointed out in chapter 3, the 2009 tire tariff had a consumer cost of $900,000 per job saved.

The China Shock

The issue of manufacturing jobs is particularly controversial when it comes to China because of the rapid growth in imports from that country. In fact, the United States has faced three "waves" of imports over the past thirty years, but has never quite faced an import shock of the magnitude of that associated with China in the 2000s.

Figure 4.6 shows the value of U.S. imports from Japan, Mexico, and China as a percent of GDP. A wave of imports came from Japan in the early 1980s. Everyone during that decade was worried that Japan was stealing our jobs and, indeed, trade created a big adjustment problem for firms and workers in the automobile, steel, and semiconductor industries. The appreciation of the U.S. dollar against the yen and other major currencies contributed to the rise in imports and the slower growth of exports. These events also generated a great deal of political pressure for protectionism and many imports were in fact restricted. By the late 1980s, the U.S. economy had recovered from a severe recession in the early 1980s, the dollar depreciated on foreign exchange markets, imports from Japan receded, and protectionist pressures abated.

A second wave of imports from Mexico can be seen in the 1990s after NAFTA took effect. Once again there was a big scare about Mexico taking

[22] Hufbauer and Elliott 1994.

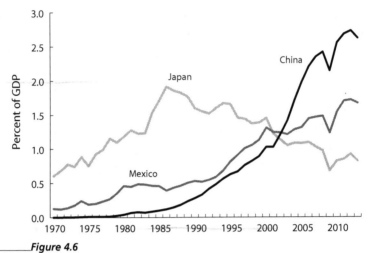

_____Figure 4.6
Imports from Japan, Mexico, and China as a Percentage of GDP, 1970–2013
Source: International Monetary Fund, Direction of Trade Statistics (www.imf.org).

all of our jobs. Yet imports from Mexico were not as disruptive to the U.S. economy as imports from Japan had been. Mexico tended to export labor-intensive goods, such as textiles and apparel, and engage in labor-intensive activities, such as the assembly of electronics, where the counterpart U.S. industries were already relatively small and declining. Furthermore, these imports from Mexico came at a time (late 1990s) when the U.S. economy was doing well and creating many job opportunities for displaced workers.

The wave of imports from China in the 2000s has far exceeded the earlier waves from Japan and Mexico, as figure 4.6 shows. While imports from China began to increase in the 1990s, as imports from Japan were declining in importance, they grew particularly rapidly in the 2000s, to some extent displacing imports from Mexico. Of course, as noted in chapter 1, the gross value of imports from China exaggerates the country's importance, because many of its exports are assembled final products made from components produced in other countries. Even allowing for this fact, the expansion of imports from China has been remarkable.

Have these imports created much difficulty for manufacturing workers in the United States? Recent research suggests that the answer is yes. One study finds that imports from China explain 21 percent of the decline in

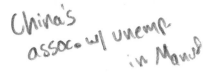
U.S. manufacturing employment over the period 1990 to 2007—a loss of 1.5 million jobs.[23] According to these results, manufacturing employment fell by 548,000 between 1990 and 2000 and by another 982,000 between 2000 and 2007 due to imports from China. Many of these workers were forced to take lower-paying jobs in the service sector, or dropped out of the labor force and went on government disability programs. At the same time, if imports from China resulted in the involuntary displacement of ninety-seven thousand manufacturing workers per year (adjusted to account for voluntary separations), they accounted for less than one-fifth of involuntary job loss in manufacturing and less than 5 percent of involuntary job loss in the overall economy over the same period.[24]

Another study suggests that China's entry into the World Trade Organization in December 2001 may have played a role in the sharp drop in U.S. manufacturing employment between 2000 and 2002.[25] By joining the WTO, China was now guaranteed low-tariff access to the U.S. market; it had that access prior to 2001, but the privilege was never guaranteed and had to be renewed by Congress on regular basis. The resolution of uncertainty about whether China's goods would continue to receive favorable tariff treatment in the U.S. market may be related to the surge of imports from China in the early 2000s. In fact, imports from China grew more rapidly in categories where the threat of higher tariffs (if China had not been granted continued market access) was higher, and employment losses were also larger in those categories of goods.

Which sectors were most affected by imports from China? Of course, textiles and apparel constitute one of the largest categories of China's exports, as well as other sectors such as furniture. Both of these industries are located in the south central United States. Hence, much of the adverse impact of imports from China has been geographically concentrated, in Tennessee, Missouri, Arkansas, Mississippi, Alabama, Georgia, North Carolina, and Indiana.[26]

Other studies blame the trade deficit with China for even larger job losses, but rely on suspect methodologies. According to the Economic

---

[23] Autor, Dorn, and Hanson 2013a.

[24] Lawrence 2014, 86.

[25] Piece and Schott 2012. See also Acemoğlu, Autor, Dorn, Hanson, and Price 2015 on import competition and the employment sag of the early 2000s.

[26] Autor, Dorn, and Hanson 2013b.

Policy Institute, the trade deficit with China was responsible for the loss of 3.2 million U.S. jobs from 2001 to 2014.[27] This number is inflated, for several reasons pointed out earlier in this chapter. First, China's leading exports to the United States include consumer electronics, sporting goods and toys, apparel and footwear, and furniture. As chapter 1 pointed out, the Chinese content in the consumer electronics exports tends to be relatively small (it imports the components and exports the assembled goods), and so using the dollar value of imports from China to calculate the effect on employment grossly overstates its impact on the U.S. labor market. The EPI study assumes that if the United States did not import these goods from China, they would be produced in the United States, thereby creating jobs. But if not imported from China, the United States would probably have imported the goods from another Asian country, as was done well before China's economic rise.

In fact, the Congressional Budget Office found that "roughly one-third of the increase in the share of imports from China in U.S. markets from 1998 through 2005 was offset by reduced growth and, in some cases, declines in the shares of imports from other countries," an offset that was even higher prior to 1998.[28] To some extent, China has simply displaced other East Asian countries—Hong Kong, Taiwan, and Korea—as a source of U.S. imports. U.S. employment in industries such as sporting goods, toys, apparel, and footwear had already been declining rapidly since the 1960s as a result of foreign competition in general. It is unlikely that reducing imports from China would have boosted domestic employment very much because China took over those markets from other foreign suppliers. Furthermore, in product categories that overlap with existing U.S. industries, U.S. and Chinese producers tend to sell in different markets: China has tended to specialize in selling cheaper, lower-quality goods whereas U.S. manufacturers have specialized in selling more expensive, higher-quality goods.[29]

Most of these studies focus on the period prior to 2007, when China was widely accused of "currency manipulation" in keeping the value of its currency, the renminbi, artificially low against the dollar. By keeping its currency undervalued on foreign exchange markets, the Chinese gov-

---

[27] Scott and Kimball 2014.
[28] Congressional Budget Office 2008, 9.
[29] Schott 2008.

ernment reduced the price of its exports and hence facilitated their rapid growth. This controversial policy will be discussed later in the chapter. However, the practice may be less important now that China has allowed the renminbi to appreciate on foreign exchange markets, which is part of the reason why its trade surplus has fallen significantly. Possibly as a result of these changes, figure 4.6 suggests that imports from China have begun to level off, perhaps indicating that the import surge from China has peaked.

The lesson from recent experience is that large surges in imports can cause problems for domestic workers. In addition, in all three cases, the wave of imports was related to a relatively weak foreign currency. A strong dollar may make imports cheaper for consumers, but it can also create problems for U.S. firms and workers competing against imports or trying to export their goods. A standing mantra of every Secretary of the Treasury has been that "a strong dollar is good for America," but at least one leading economist has argued that it is in the country's interest to have a "competitive" dollar instead.[30]

Strong vs. competitive Dollar?

_____Offshoring and Trade in Services

Many of the fears about trade and manufacturing employment are now being echoed with respect to the service sector. In the past, most service workers were completely insulated from foreign competition. But, as discussed in chapter 1, many services are now tradable. A recent concern has been that white-collar service workers will see their jobs "outsourced" or "offshored" to low-wage countries such as India because of the Internet and other communication technologies. Although many of the offshored jobs involve relatively low-skill work, such as manning phone banks at call centers, even highly paid professionals, such as architects and software programmers, have found that their work can be shifted to much lower paid but technically qualified English-speaking workers in India. Such offshoring has been shown to increase the productivity of domestic firms, but the question of the impact of domestic jobs is the key concern.[31]

offshoring:
Domestic productivity=↑ ☺
jobs = ??? ☹

[30] Feldstein 2006.
[31] Amiti and Wei 2009.

Estimates vary widely as to the number of service workers whose jobs are potentially offshorable. One leading economist, Alan Blinder, has estimated that the jobs performed by thirty to forty million American workers could be done abroad.[32] Although Blinder fears for the consequences, he notes that "despite all the political sound and fury, little servicesector offshoring has happened to date." Indeed, the actual number of service-sector jobs lost so far appears to be small. The Bureau of Labor Statistics began asking about the overseas transfer of jobs in collecting data on mass layoffs in the first quarter of 2004. In that quarter, 8.7 percent of all layoffs were due to the movement of work and 2.5 percent (a total of 4,633 jobs) related to the movement of work to another country.[33] Unfortunately, the BLS discontinued collecting these statistics right at that time.

Recent research has also suggested that offshoring has not had large impacts on the U.S. labor market. One study focused on the impact of trade in services on white-collar workers in the United States between 1996 and 2007, the period in which outsourcing concerns were very high.[34] Focusing on the decade-long impact of services trade with India and China and whether increased trade forced more workers to "switch" their jobs or occupations, the study found that service exports to India and China reduced switching while service imports increase switching. However, the export effect was slightly stronger leading to the implication that rising services trade led to less worker dislocation, on average. Furthermore, there was no increase in worker switching in tradable sectors relative to nontradable sectors. Those who were forced to switch jobs because of service imports, however, were more likely to be unemployed and remain so for an extended period. What happened to the wages of workers who were forced to switch jobs and found work elsewhere? That depended on the on the assumption made: if workers were assumed to get sorted based on their characteristics not in the data (i.e., the least-able workers are those forced into other sectors), there was no statistically significant wage impact; if there was no such sorting, wages fell by 14

---

[32] Blinder 2006. For a debate among economists about whether we should worry about offshoring or not, see Bhagwati and Blinder 2009.

[33] Bureau of Labor Statistics 2004.

[34] Liu and Trefler 2011.

percent. The wages of those who managed to stay employed in the sectors affected by service outsource did not change.

Another recent study examined the interrelationship between offshore workers, immigrants in the United States, and native-born U.S. workers. The study found that offshore workers were a close substitute for immigrants working in the United States and not a good substitute for native workers due to the different tasks that they perform. A decline in offshoring costs led to task-upgrading of natives and task-downgrading of immigrants; that is, offshore workers are assigned the most complex among the low-complexity tasks previously performed by immigrants, as well as the least complex among the high-complexity tasks previously performed by natives. The result was not so much harm to native workers but an increase in task polarization between immigrants and natives in the domestic labor market.[35]

Furthermore, it should be remembered that international trade—in services, as in goods—is not a one-way flow but a two-way street. The estimate of jobs lost due to offshoring mentioned above does not take into account the projected increase in demand for skilled information-technology workers in the United States due to work for export. The BLS does not collect statistics on the number of jobs created by work that is offshored from other countries to the United States, otherwise known as "inshoring." As chapter 1 noted, the United States is a major net exporter of services to other countries. The United States has roughly balanced trade in the subcategory of "telecommunications, computer and information services," where the concern about outsourcing has been the greatest. The United States is likely to begin exporting many more services to other countries as a result of technological developments that also allow for more imports of services.

In addition, there are natural equilibrating forces that limit how much work will be offshored. While Indian wages remain much lower than American wages, higher demand for skilled Indian workers has put upward pressure on costs that will diminish the advantage of offshoring.[36] Wages in India's software industry, a major center of offshored work from

---

[35] Ottaviano, Peri, and Wright 2013.

[36] Noam Scheiber, "As a Center for Outsourcing, India Could Be Losing Its Edge," *New York Times*, May 2, 2004.

[handwritten: Wages for India workers = Rising]

the United States, had been rising at double-digit rates over the past two decades, significantly increasing the cost of hiring Indian workers. Hourly compensation costs in manufacturing, for example, doubled in India between 2002 and 2010.[37] Furthermore, the quality of the Indian workforce has been an issue; one report indicates that 75 percent of technical school graduates and 85 percent of regular graduates are unemployable by their information technology (IT) sector.[38] In addition, the quality concerns and the cultural divide have been more problematic than many anticipated.

[handwritten margin: Quality ain't that nice w/ it]

As a result, a number of leading firms, such as Bank of America, Honda, Aviva, and Delta Airlines, have brought back a significant amount of their IT spending to North America. In fact, the United States has even received "inshoring" contracts from India. For example, in March 2004, IBM won a ten-year, $750 million contract from Bharti Tele-Ventures, India's largest private telecommunications company, which will transfer some jobs from Asia to the United States and France. IBM will service Bharti's hardware and software requirements and take over its customer billing and relations operations. Wipro and other Indian firms are offshoring some work to "underdeveloped" parts of the United States, such as Idaho and Georgia, because they have found it cheaper to do it there.[39]

[handwritten margin: people spread offshoring]

Thus, the fears about a "service-sector sucking sound" have been exaggerated. One analysis concludes that, "similar to manufacturing, it is highly unlikely that a significant share of high-wage, skill-intensive service activities will move to emerging markets in the short term and even in the long term."[40] It is likely that many of the easily offshorable jobs have already been lost, and some have even returned as companies discover that cheaper English speakers abroad ultimately may not be cost-effective or good enough to maintain quality. And some scare stories, such as the offshoring of the work of highly paid radiologists, have turned out to be false.[41]

[handwritten margin: high-wage, high-skill jobs won't shift too much; still needed]

[37] U.S. Bureau of Labor Statistics, International Labor Comparisons, August 2013. http://www.bls.gov/fls/ichcc.pdf.

[38] Geeta Anand, "India Graduates Millions, but Too Few are Fit to Hire," *Wall Street Journal*, April 5, 2011.

[39] Anand Giridharadas, "Outsourcing Works, So India Is Exporting Jobs," *New York Times*, September 25, 2007.

[40] Jensen and Kletzer 2008.

[41] Levy and Goelman 2005.

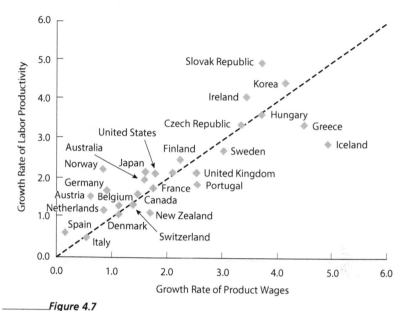

_____**Figure 4.7**

Changes in Labor Productivity and Product Wages, Selected OECD Countries,
Annual Growth Rates, 1995–2006
  Source: Sharpe, Arsenault, and Harrison 2008, 52.

_____**Trade and Wages**

Another concern is that trade puts downward pressure on U.S. wages as
firms strive to match lower wages in developing countries, unleashing a
"race to the bottom" in cutting labor costs. As a general matter, such fears
overlook the fact that high American wages are based on the high productivity of U.S. workers. And the growth in a country's average wages is
determined by the growth of a country's productivity, as figure 4.7 shows.
Foreign competition does not suppress this growth. Rather, as chapter 2
described, trade can foster growth in productivity through several channels. Foreign competition cannot take away the advantages that give rise
to this high productivity, namely, the availability of sophisticated technology, the substantial stock of human capital, and the many other advantages of operating in the U.S. market.
   The relationship between rising productivity and increasing worker
compensation also holds within countries over time. In the case of the

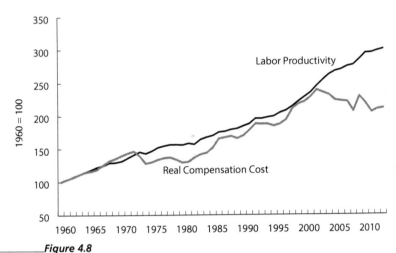

_____Figure 4.8

Labor Productivity and Labor Compensation Costs, 1960–2013

Note: Productivity is output per hour worked in the non-farm business sector. Real compensation cost is compensation per hour in the non-farm business sector divided by the produce price index.

Source: FRED, Federal Reserve Economic Data, Federal Reserve Bank of St. Louis (http://research.stlouisfed.org/fred2/).

United States, as figure 4.8 shows, the growth of worker compensation (deflated by the producer price index) tracks growth in productivity remarkably well, at least until the early 2000s.[42] Economists have been investigating why the two series have diverged over the past decade.[43] Part of the explanation has to do with an increase in the share of profits in national income and a disproportionate share of real income gains accruing to the top 1 percent of the income distribution.[44] The rise in the share of income going to capital, and the decline in the share of income going to labor, is a global phenomenon, not one confined to the United States.[45] There are also important measurement problems regarding productivity

[42] Thus, workers have been compensated for the growth in output per worker in terms of the revenue received by firms. See Feldstein 2008

[43] Pessoa and Van Reenen 2013.

[44] See Lawrence 2008 and Dew-Becker and Gordon 2005. The top 1 percent of income earners captured 21 percent of the real income gains between 1997 and 2001, according to the latter study.

[45] Karabarbounis and Nieman 2014 attribute it to the decline in the price of capital goods, which induced firms to substitute capital for labor. However, looking at the U.S. labor share, Elsby, Hobijn, and Sahin (2014) suggest that industries facing greater foreign

(normally based on gross output, not output net of depreciation, which has become increasingly important) and how compensation treats housing and government income; after making adjustments, the gap can largely be accounted for.[46] Still, it remains to be seen whether the gap in figure 4.8 continues to run counter to historical experience; the two series have sometimes deviated in the past only to return to the same level.

Although average wages are determined by the underlying factors that make American workers productive, trade can affect the *distribution of* wages in an economy. And here, a very basic point must be stressed: the perception that imports destroy good, high-wage jobs in manufacturing is almost completely erroneous. It is closer to the truth to say that imports destroy bad, low-wage jobs in manufacturing. This is because wages in industries that compete against imports are well below average, whereas wages in exporting industries are well above average.

For example, the United States tends to import labor-intensive products, such as apparel, footwear, leather, and goods assembled from components. These labor-intensive sectors tend to employ workers who have a lower-than-average educational attainment, and who therefore earn a relatively low wage. For example, in 2006 average hourly earnings of Americans working in the apparel industry were 37 percent lower than in manufacturing as a whole. Average hourly earnings were 32 percent lower in the leather industry and 25 percent lower in textile mills than in the average manufacturing industry.[47] Figure 4.9 shows the relationship between the share of imports from low-wage developing countries in a given industry and the average U.S. wage. The United States tends to import more from developing countries in industries that pay relatively low wages.[48] (The category of computers and electronic products is an

competition may have reduced the share of income going to labor more than other industries.

[46] See Scott Winship, "Has Inequality Driven a Wedge between Productivity and Compensation Growth?" October 20, 2014, http://www.forbes.com/sites/scottwinship/2014/10/20/has-inequality-driven-a-wedge-between-productivity-and-compensation-growth/.

[47] U.S. Bureau of the Census 2008, table 613.

[48] Bernard, Jensen, and Schott (2006) examined how U.S. manufacturing plants responded to import competition from low-wage developing countries. They found a variety of adjustments: some labor-intensive operations reduced output or closed, while more capital-intensive plants adjusted their product mix to more sophisticated goods and actually grew.

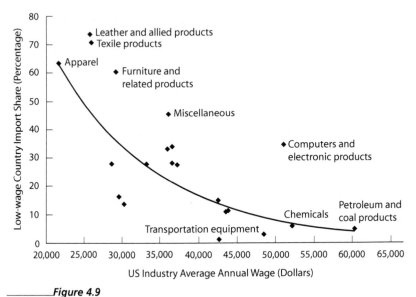

_____Figure 4.9
U.S. Wages and Import Competition from Low-Wage Countries
Source: Jensen and Kletzer 2008.

outlier because these items are assembled in low-wage developing coun-tries from components produced elsewhere, as noted in chapter 1.)

By contrast, the United States tends to export more skill-intensive man-ufactured products, such as aircraft, construction machinery, engines and turbines, and industrial chemicals. Workers in these industries earn rela-tively high wages. For example, in 2006 average hourly earnings in the aircraft and aerospace industry were 56 percent above the average in manufacturing, 11 percent higher in metalworking machinery, and 27 percent higher in pharmaceuticals. Figure 4.10 shows the positive rela-tionship between exports per worker and the average wage by industry.

Because exports increase the number of workers in relatively more-productive, high-wage industries, and imports reduce the number of workers in relatively less-productive, low-wage industries, the overall im-pact of trade in the United States is to raise average wages.[49] Conversely, any policy that limits overall trade and reduces both exports and imports

[49] One often reads that median household income has stagnated in recent decades, but the composition of the median household has changed quite a bit over this time. Fitzgerald (2008) discusses the difficulties in measuring income inequality and shows that real median

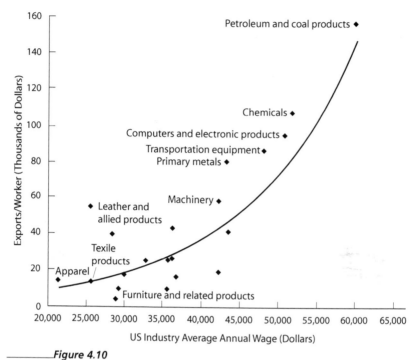

_____**Figure 4.10**

Exports per Worker and U.S. Industry Wages, Manufacturing
  Source: Jensen and Kletzer 2008.

What Protect Policies do

tends to increase employment in low-wage industries and reduce employment in high-wage industries. Restricting trade would shift American workers away from things that they produce relatively well (and hence export and earn relatively high wages in producing) and toward things that they do not produce so well (and hence import and earn relatively low wages in producing) in comparison with other countries. Employment gains for the low-wage textile machine operators in the factory mills would be offset by employment losses for the high-wage engineers in aircraft and pharmaceutical plants.

This raises the concern that trade has contributed to increased income inequality in the United States. In theory, trade can have sharply different effects on the wages of different types of workers. In a classic article, Wolfgang Stolper and Paul Samuelson connected the distribution of

household income for most household types increased somewhere between 44 and 62 percent from 1976 to 2006.

wages in an economy to the prices of traded goods that are determined by the world market. They reached the unambiguous conclusion that the real income of some factors of production will rise absolutely as a result of free trade, while the real income of other factors will fall absolutely.[50] This is implicit in what we have discussed: trade creates jobs in high-wage industries in which the United States exports (aircraft, machinery), and reduces jobs in low-wage industries in which the United States imports (apparel, footwear).

There is no doubt that wage and income inequality have increased in recent decades. In the 1980s and the early 1990s, the wage premium for college-educated workers relative to workers with less education (high school degree or dropout) rose substantially, but then leveled off after 2000.[51] In addition, there is evidence of wage stagnation in the middle of the income distribution and an absolute decline in the real wages of workers with very few years of formal education. Has international trade contributed to the increase in wage inequality in the United States, as theory suggests it might?

The impact of international trade and wages and the wage structure has proven to be one of the most difficult things to untangle of all of economics.[52] The consensus among economists seems to be that increased demand for educated workers due to technological changes is mostly responsible for the rising wage premium. By contrast, the role of trade in generating wage inequality appears to be modest. How has this conclusion been reached? If trade had been driving the changes in relative wages in the United States during the 1980s, then theory suggests that the price of unskilled labor-intensive goods should have fallen relative to

[50] Stolper and Samuelson 1941. For example, if we consider only skilled and unskilled labor, a rise in the relative price of skill-intensive goods increases the real wage of skilled workers and decreases the real wage of unskilled workers. While the precise relationship between product prices and factor rewards depends upon many other factors, such as the degree to which labor can move between sectors, the key conclusion is that trade can have sharp consequences for income distribution.

[51] See Haskel, Lawrence, Leamer, and Slaughter 2012 for a recent review.

[52] There are various measures of economic inequality, but wage inequality will be the focus here. Income and wealth inequality have also increased substantially in recent years, but are less directly related to international trade. Instead, factors such as asset holdings and capital gains, as well as the "superstar" phenomena in certain industries (hedge funds, CEOs, sports, and entertainment), have been driving the income distribution at the very top 1 percent.

the price of skilled labor-intensive goods. But after examining the data, researchers failed to detect such a decline. In addition, they found that manufacturing firms were consistently choosing to employ more skilled labor relative to unskilled labor, despite the rising cost of hiring those skilled workers. This evidence is consistent with an increase in the demand for educated workers.[53]

Another way of looking at the question examines the quantities of imports of labor-intensive goods as a factor that may cause the displacement of less-educated workers and reduce their wages. In this case, the volume of traded goods, rather than their prices, is the focus. This approach yields essentially the same conclusion. Examining the period from 1980 to 1995, one study finds that the wages of college graduates rose 21 percent relative to those of high school graduates. At the same time, trade and immigration accounted for only about two percentage points (or 10 percent) of this change.[54] The relatively small contribution of trade is related to the fact that imports of manufactured goods from developing countries, presumably the primary source of unskilled labor-intensive goods, rose from just 1.0 percent of GDP in 1970 to 3.2 percent in 1990, hardly a dramatic increase in light of the spectacular increase in the labor market returns to education during this period.

Studies are just emerging of the more recent period from the late 1990s in which there was a large increase in imports from low-wage developing countries, such as China and Mexico after NAFTA. Yet the preliminary evidence also suggests that the contribution of trade to wage inequality is relatively small. One estimate puts the contribution of trade with low-wage countries from 1980 to 2006 at something shy of 10 percent of the overall rise in the college wage premium.[55] Another study concludes that "without the impact on wage inequality between 1981 and 2006, the wages of blue-collar workers would have been 1.4 percent higher than they were in 2006 and that almost all of this took place before 2000."[56]

---

[53] See the papers in Collins 1998, Feenstra 2000, and Feenstra and Hanson 2003 for an overview of this literature.

[54] Borjas, Freeman, and Katz 1997. However, they found that these factors are somewhat more important in explaining the wage gap between high school graduates and high school drop outs.

[55] See Lawrence Katz's comments in Krugman 2008.

[56] Lawrence 2008, 37.

Furthermore, "the timing of wage inequality is not what might have been expected if increased trade penetration in the U.S. economy always gives rise to increased wage inequality" because inequality grew rapidly in the 1980s when trade with developing countries was growing slowly, whereas inequality leveled off when imports from low-wage countries were accelerating.[57]

Because the college premium that increased so much in the 1980s has leveled off since then, those theories are less useful. More recent work has suggested a polarization of the labor force, based less on education level than on the skills used at work. Recent studies have identified a hollowing out of the middle of the wage distribution, in which highly educated workers have done very well, low-skilled workers have done all right, but workers in the middle have done very poorly.[58] The leading hypothesis is that information and communication technologies polarize labor markets by increasing demand for the highly educated at the expense of the middle educated, with little effect on low-educated workers who do routine work. While this hollowing out has apparently occurred in a number of advanced economies, research has failed to link it to international trade.[59]

Trade, then, does not appear to be primarily responsible for increased wage inequality in recent decades. Evidence instead points to technological change as having raised the demand for more highly educated workers and having significantly altered the skill set and the type of work that is valued (e.g., routine versus nonroutine). For example, the advent of ATM machines and personal computers reduced the demand for bank tellers and office assistants and increased the demand for skilled technicians and highly trained or educated personnel. Whereas international

[57] "After 2000, the share of imports from non-OPEC developing countries continued to grow rapidly, while the share of imports from developing countries actually declined. . . . Yet this was a period of slow wage growth for almost all workers, with very little additional inequality." Lawrence 2008, 31, 34. One hypothesis for trade's lack of impact on wage inequality more recently is that the factor content of imports appears to be roughly similar to that of the U.S. economy overall, so it does not have a disproportionate impact on unskilled workers in particular. See Lawrence and Edwards 2013.

[58] Autor, Katz, and Kearney 2008. See also Lemieux 2010 and Goos, Manning, and Salomons 2014, who find that this is a pervasive phenomenon across Western European countries as well.

[59] Michaels, Natraj, and Van Reenen 2014.

trade would shift the demand for skills between sectors of the economy, skill-biased technical change would increase the demand for skilled workers in all sectors.[60] In fact, the relative wage of educated workers in many developing countries has been increasing as well, a pattern that can be explained by skill-biased technical change but is more difficult to explain as a result of international trade.[61]

But if trade has contributed even modestly to increased wage inequality, we can understand why adversely affected workers would oppose free trade. Workers who are laid off from their job tend to experience a large and persistent loss of income. This is especially the case for workers who have to shift to another sector of the economy. In particular, manufacturing workers who lose their jobs and get reemployed in the service sector suffer a significant wage cut. One recent study, using data from 1984 to 2002, found that workers forced to switch occupations as a result of trade suffered a real wage loss of about 15 percent.[62] Furthermore, when job losses are highly concentrated in a certain region, the laid-off manufacturing workers seeking employment in services depress the wage of other service workers. In other words, the whole local community suffers. And, as previously noted, those workers are likely to leave the labor force and get government disability payments.

Interestingly, however, a domestic industry faced with intense foreign competition typically does not reduce the wages of its workers. The evidence suggests that such firms reduce employment but not wages.[63] This makes sense: if a firm tried to cut wages, the best workers would leave because they have skills that give them opportunities elsewhere in the economy. The least desirable workers would stay because they have no attractive alternatives. In addition, firms respond to competition by improving their technology and upgrading the quality of their products, all of which requires more skilled labor. Rather than cut wages, firms usually adjust to competition by reducing employment. Then they can choose

---

[60] Berman, Bound, and Griliches (1994) found that nearly three-quarters of the overall shift in labor demand (for nonproduction workers) was a change in demand within industries rather than between industries.

[61] Goldberg and Pavcnik 2007.

[62] Ebenstein, Harrison, McMillan, and Phillips 2014.

[63] Revenga 1992 and Ebenstein et al. 2014. If the industry is unionized and the firm pays an above-market wage, however, there is scope for the firm to reduce wages to the competitive level.

which workers to keep and which to lay off in an attempt to raise productivity and position the company to survive.

Survey evidence indicates that workers with less educational attainment, those whose wages have lagged the most in recent decades, are also the most skeptical of the benefits of free trade.[64] Although these workers may have a legitimate economic interest in preventing trade, it does not make sense to deal with their concerns by harming the overall economy. It is no more reasonable to help them by imposing barriers to trade than it would be to ban ATM machines or word processing so as to increase the demand for bank tellers and office assistants. This might help them in the short run, but it would also reduce economic opportunities for others now and for their children in the future. A more constructive response would be to encourage workers to make investments in education and, where possible, cushion the blow for those who are adversely affected by trade. One reason the debate over trade policy is never-ending, however, is that policies to cushion the blow are often viewed as inadequate.

Displaced Workers and Trade Adjustment Assistance

Although free trade may be good for the economy as a whole, some workers in import-competing industries will be displaced from their jobs as a result of foreign competition. Without some policy to help these workers, opposition to free trade will always be politically potent. What government programs exist to help workers who lose their jobs as a result of imports? Do these programs work well, and should trade-displaced workers get better treatment than workers who are unemployed for other reasons?

As discussed earlier in this chapter, import competition accounts for only a small fraction of workers who lose their job every year. Even so, who are the displaced workers in import-competing industries and what is being done to help them? Workers in import-sensitive industries "are similar to other displaced manufacturing workers—slightly older, with virtually no difference in educational attainment or job tenure"—but are

---

[64] Scheve and Slaughter 2001.

more likely to be women.[65] And even among import-sensitive industries, workers in very high import-share industries tend to have less education, have shorter job tenure, and are more likely to be female than workers in medium and low import-share industries.[66] The two most salient of these characteristics are gender and relatively low levels of education. These underlying characteristics tend to determine the labor market experiences of these workers, not the fact that they are employed in industries that compete against imports.

For example, workers displaced from high import-share industries are less likely to find new employment within a certain time period. This fact could be interpreted as indicating that the reemployment prospects of workers who have been laid off from industries that compete against imports are worse than average. But this correlation disappears once one controls for the higher proportion of female workers in those industries. In other words, women in general tend to have lower reemployment rates after being laid off any job. They may opt to leave the labor force, for example, or take more time off between jobs than men do. It is this characteristic, rather than anything special about import-competing industries per se, that accounts for the lower reemployment rate of workers displaced from high import-share industries. As one researcher concludes, "Trade-displaced workers may have more difficult labor-market adjustments, but the source of the difficulty is their otherwise disadvantaged characteristics, not the characteristics of their displacement industry."[67]

What about the wage losses suffered by workers thrown out of work as a result of imports? The plight of displaced workers cannot be trivialized because numerous studies have shown that their earnings losses are sizable and persistent.[68] The losses are largely based on how long the workers had been employed in the jobs from which they were displaced

---

[65] "The most striking difference between import-competing displaced workers and other displaced manufacturing workers is the degree to which import-competing industries employ and displace women. Women account for 45 percent of import-sensitive displaced workers, relative to 37 percent of the overall manufacturing displaced. Some industries stand out: Women account for 80 percent of those displaced from apparel, 66 percent from footwear, and 76 percent from knitting mills (part of the textile industry)" (Kletzer 2001, 3).

[66] Kletzer 1998b, 450.

[67] Kletzer 2000, 375.

[68] Kletzer 1998a.

Worse for older & longer-tenured [handwritten annotation]

(the longer they were employed, the greater the earnings loss) and whether the workers found reemployment in the same industry or in a different industry (if reemployed in a different industry, then the earnings losses are greater). For example, displaced workers with one to three years of tenure experienced an average drop of 10 percent in earnings after four years relative to their prior earnings trajectory; workers with three to six years of tenure experienced an average drop of 23 percent in earnings; and workers with more than six years of tenure experienced a loss of more than 30 percent in earnings.[69]

As it turns out, several studies have found that workers displaced from industries in which import penetration was increasing rapidly had lower earnings losses than other displaced workers.[70] Because workers in import-sensitive sectors tend to be low-wage workers with shorter job tenures, workers displaced from industries that compete with imports generally have lower earnings losses than the average displaced worker. This is particularly true in one of the most trade-sensitive industries, the textile and apparel industry, which lost more than nine hundred thousand jobs between 1990 and 2014, due to technological change as well as imports.[71]

While most workers displaced from industries that compete against imports eventually find employment in the same industry, in related manufacturing industries, or in the nontraded service sector, they almost never find employment in export-oriented industries.[72] A worker laid off from the apparel industry, for example, is extremely unlikely to find em-

[handwritten margin note: *Shift from import to export*]

---

[69] Jacobson, Lalonde, and Sullivan 2011.

[70] Addison, Fox, and Ruhm 1995. However, Autor, Dorn, Hanson, and Song (2014) find that earnings losses among trade-displaced workers are higher for individuals with low initial wages, low initial tenure in their jobs, and low attachment to the labor force.

[71] According to Field and Graham (1997), in contrast to displaced workers in other manufacturing industries, who experienced an average 10 percent drop in wages after finding new employment, displaced apparel workers who found new jobs actually received higher wages, while textile workers experienced little change in their wages. The explanation is that apparel workers receive very low wages in the first place and that over 60 percent of laidoff apparel workers found reemployment in another manufacturing industry. However, this occurred in the 1980s and 1990s when the economy was doing well, creating many new employment opportunities for those who lost their jobs.

[72] Autor, Dorn, and Hanson (2013) and Autor, Dorn, Hanson, and Song (2014) find many low-wage displaced workers leave the labor force and retire, receive unemployment compensation, or go on disability.

ployment in the aircraft industry, because a different skill mix is required. Furthermore, trade-displaced workers generally do not move geographically in search of new employment. These patterns create a problem for workers and policymakers: those harmed by imports will not reap the benefits of new employment opportunities in export-oriented industries, particularly if they are in different regions of the country. Telling these workers that rising employment in export industries located elsewhere will offset the decline in their current industry of employment is not likely to persuade them that free trade is a good thing.

There is little debate about whether unemployed workers should receive some form of government assistance. The question is whether workers displaced for reasons of trade should receive more benefit than the far more numerous workers who lose their jobs for other reasons. Special adjustment assistance for workers laid off as a result of imports has been justified on efficiency, equity, and political grounds, but all three rationales are open to question.

The efficiency rationale is that government assistance can speed up the process of adjusting to trade and thereby make it more efficient. This is doubtful on both theoretical and empirical grounds. In theory, the government should intervene to accelerate adjustment only if some market failure is associated with that process. The simple fact that the adjustment process sometimes operates slowly and with friction is insufficient grounds for intervention. In addition, the empirical studies of displaced workers alluded to earlier generally suggest that the labor-market experiences of workers displaced from trade-sensitive industries are not much different from those of workers with similar characteristics who have been displaced from industries not sensitive to trade. Therefore, efficiency considerations do not seem to justify singling out trade-affected workers for more generous treatment than that given to other displaced workers. Then there is the more general point related to the potential inefficiency of any government program that attempts to redistribute income to a targeted group. The costs of administering a compensation program might well be much higher than the losses incurred by displaced workers.[73]

[73] Jacobson (1998, 476) suggests that the "transactions costs associated with [compensation] are likely to be many times larger than the costs imposed on those adversely affected by change."

The equity rationale—that fairness requires giving workers displaced by imports special treatment—is also questionable. Workers may lose their jobs for any number of reasons: increasing domestic competition, fluctuations in the weather, substitution of capital for labor, changes in technology, shifts in consumer tastes, and so on. Even if it were possible to single out workers who have been dislocated for trade-related reasons, there is no compelling reason for treating them differently than those who have lost their job for other reasons. In fact, it seems unfair to provide a more comfortable cushion for the workers displaced because of imports and not for those laid off because of, say, a painful recession brought on by the collapse of a bubble in housing prices. What is the reason for providing more generous compensation to the apparel worker in Georgia who loses a job to imports than to the typewriter assembler at SmithCorona displaced because of computers or the Kellogg's worker laid off because General Mills begins producing tastier cereals?

The political argument for trade adjustment assistance is that the public views these various causes of employment loss as different. Job loss due to trade is much more politically controversial than job loss due to domestic competition or technological change or a recession. Therefore, trade adjustment assistance might be able to reduce the opposition to trade legislation by compensating for concentrated losses from liberalization. Congress made trade adjustment assistance (TAA) a matter of U.S. policy ever since the Trade Expansion Act of 1962 for that very reason. Since the 1970s, however, there is almost no evidence that TAA has been able to "buy off" labor groups who are opposed to the passage of trade agreements.

The TAA program, which must be renewed regularly, currently works the following way:[74] Unemployed workers can typically receive up to twentysix weeks of unemployment insurance, although this period was lengthened during the Great Recession of 2008–9. If a group of unemployed workers believe they have lost their job due to trade, however, they can apply for TAA with the Department of Labor. The Labor Department must certify that the workers lost their jobs because of an increase in imports or a shift in the location of production to another country. If they are certified, the workers are eligible for training assistance, job

[74] See Collins 2012 for a full description.

search and relocation allowances, and a health coverage tax credit. Most importantly, they can receive financial support under the trade readjustment allowance (TRA), which is income support for those who have exhausted the standard unemployment insurance and are enrolled in a job training program. Workers can receive unemployment insurance and the TRA for a combined total of 117 weeks, more than two years, and even 130 weeks under certain circumstances.[75]

In recent years, the Labor Department has certified about 80 percent of the petitions it has received. For example, in fiscal year 2013, about 1,480 petitions were filed and 79 percent were certified, covering 104,158 workers. About 60 percent of the petitions are from workers in the manufacturing sector. The top states receiving TAA benefits are Michigan, North Carolina, Pennsylvania, Ohio, and Wisconsin. In fiscal year 2013, the Labor Department spent about $186 million in TRA assistance, although total spending on trade adjustment programs was $756 billion.[76] These expenditures are a fraction of total spending on unemployment insurance. The program is inexpensive because few workers are actually involved in it; workers declared eligible for TRA do not necessarily collect benefits. In fact, usually less than half of all workers who are declared eligible for some form of trade adjustment assistance actually take advantage of it. For example, in fiscal year 2011, about 103,000 workers were certified as eligible to receive TAA benefits, but only about 18,000 new participants were recorded.[77] This is because workers were either rehired or reemployed in the interim, received union compensation, or do not wish to enroll in a training program.

eligibility ≠ benefits

[75] A special NAFTA assistance program was set up in 1994, relating only to those affected by trade with Canada and Mexico. Under this program, workers could receive benefits even as a result of trade diversion. In other words, if NAFTA diverts trade to Mexico in such a way that higher imports from Mexico substitute for lower imports from another country, workers may be eligible for assistance. As long as Mexican imports have increased, no causal link from NAFTA to the job loss is required. For example, when a sawmill in the state of Washington shut down because federal forest lands were declared off limits to save the spotted owl, the 135 workers affected were declared eligible for NAFTA-TAA because timber imports from Canada subsequently increased. See Bill Richards, "Shaky Numbers: Layoffs Not Related to NAFTA Can Trigger Special Help Anyway," *Wall Street Journal*, June 30, 1997, A1.

[76] http://www.doleta.gov/tradeact/.

[77] See Collins 2012.

takes away incentive

While the budgetary outlays are relatively small, the TAA program is not perfect. Workers provided with benefits over a longer period of time do not have an incentive to find a new job quickly. And prolonging the period of unemployment—as the TAA does—does not usually result in better labor market matches for those workers. In fact, to say that TAA is imperfect is an understatement: it actually does harm, according to an external review of the program commissioned by the Labor Department

financially
not
long we
but maybe
politically
doing well

and conducted by the respected consulting firm Mathematica Policy Research. The 2012 report concluded that "the net benefit to society of the TAA program as it operated under the 2002 amendments was negative $53,802 per participant."[78] The net cost to participants was a whopping $26,837 per participant because they earned lower wages than those in a match comparison group. The net cost to the rest of society was $26,965 per participant, which included program costs and the training and reemployment costs. However, this calculation did not take into account the

Imp.
Note

possibility that TAA made freer trade policies more politically feasible and therefore those gains from trade should be included in the calculation. The study noted that "if TAA made even a relatively modest contribution to the ease of enacting free trade policies, the program's total benefits would outweigh its costs."[79]

Other studies offer little grounds for thinking that the TAA has a positive impact.[80] This bleak assessment is not unique to TAA: there is little evidence that any government training program works well. After studying many such training programs, the OECD reached the sober conclusion that "broad training programs aimed at large groups of the unem-

---

[78] Dolfin and Schochet 2012, i. The estimated program impacts by comparing TAA participants who filed for unemployment insurance benefits to a matched comparison group of unemployment insurance claimants in the manufacturing sector living in the same or similar local areas who were not eligible for the program. The net cost was lower if the comparison group was other non-TAA workers who had exhausted their unemployment insurance.

[79] Dolfin and Schochet 2012, 69. As noted earlier, however, there is not much evidence that TAA has made it easier for Congress to vote for free trade agreements.

[80] Reynolds and Palatucci (2012) find that there was no evidence that TAA recipients had better employment outcomes than comparable non-TAA individuals. However, the TAA recipients who went through a training program did do better than TAA recipients who received a waiver and did not go through such a program. The first finding is similar to the earlier study of Decker and Corson 1995, although they also found the training program had little value.

ployed have seldom proved a good investment, whether for society or for the program participants."[81]

Thus, as currently designed, TAA is far from ideal. To the extent that the program merely provides an incentive for trade-displaced workers to remain unemployed for a longer period of time than other displaced workers, it fails to help workers or improve economic efficiency. This leaves policymakers in a frustrating dilemma: some workers are definitely being harmed by imports, and yet government programs have failed to help them. So how should the system be changed? Some argue that the training requirement should be dumped: workers do not like it anyway, and it seems to provide no economic value. The benefits should not be tied to time out of work because doing so only prolongs the period of unemployment. Since it is not the case that a longer search leads to a better job match for workers, assistance programs should encourage quick reemployment. *What about wage insurance?*

The 2002 trade adjustment assistance legislation contained an interesting pilot program—wage insurance—that deserves careful study. Because the current TAA discourages work and fails to compensate for income losses, since payments cease when a worker takes a lower-paying job, time-limited earnings insurance was introduced to provide compensation while preserving the incentive to find work. This Alternative Trade Adjustment Assistance (ATAA) gives selected workers over fifty years old cash benefits equal to 50 percent of the difference between their old pay and their new pay (capped at $10,000) if they are reemployed at a lower wage within twenty-six weeks of being laid off and earn less than $50,000 in their new job. Under this scheme, workers would receive these special payments only when they became reemployed.

Any proposal that seeks to provide compensation while preserving the incentive of workers to find employment is worth exploring. It is too soon to say how well the wage insurance and other new provisions of the 2002 TAA have worked.[82] Such a scheme, however, would force a reexamination of the entire concept of unemployment insurance. A potential prob-

---

[81] Organization for Economic Cooperation and Development 1994, 37. Card, Kluve, and Weber (2010) examine 97 studies between 1995 and 2007 on training programs and offer cautious support for the idea that they can improve labor market outcomes.

[82] Kletzer (2004) reports that a wage insurance trial in Canada had modest effects in accelerating reemployment.

lem with earnings insurance is that it could be costly, although it could replace existing programs rather than be added to them. Aside from the high costs of such a program, basing a compensation program on past earnings runs the danger of trying to create a riskless society. Should the government insure against all losses that individuals incur in the labor market, particularly when the individuals themselves do not seem interested in purchasing such insurance?[83]

The Trade Adjustment Assistance Act of 2011 was due to expire at the end of 2014, but has been extended until new TAA legislation can be formulated. Among the proposals being considered are expanding eligibility to include service workers (who may find their job has been offshored), relaxing eligibility criteria, raising benefit levels, and extending and expanding the wage insurance program. The Congressional Budget Office priced out these changes as costing about $600 to $700 million per year. Although this would nearly double expenditures on TAA, it is still relatively inexpensive in comparison to the gains from keeping markets open to trade. Other public policies geared toward helping workers best manage their lives in this period of rapid economic change include such things as ensuring the portability of health and pension benefits in order to reduce the adverse impact of changing jobs, which must inevitably happen in an ever-changing economy.

The lamentable conclusion is that there is no easy solution and no obvious government policy that can address all of the concerns of workers adversely affected by economic change, whether it be due to imports or new technology. Trade adjustment assistance has not worked as promised, and may even be an impediment to economic efficiency. A broader government program to help displaced workers should be examined and might be a small price to pay to reduce anxieties about international trade and maintain political support for open markets. But even if such a program is affordable and gets the incentives right, there is absolutely no guarantee that demands for import barriers by labor groups in import-competing sectors (such as the steelworkers union) will diminish. Even if

[83] As Jacobson (1998, 475) notes, "Neither society at large nor members of the risk pool potentially affected by costly job loss appear willing to pay for such (earnings) insurance . . . individuals adversely threatened by trade and other factors appear to lack the willingness to pay actuarially fair insurance," although this may be due in part to the existence of government compensation programs. However, see Kaivanto (2007) for an economic rationale for wage insurance.

fully compensated for losing their jobs, these workers simply may not want to move to a different job in a different location when there is a chance they can stay employed where they are by pressuring government to stop imports.

_____*What about the Trade Deficit?*

In every year since 1976, the value of goods and services imported into the United States has exceeded the value of goods and services exported. Does the trade deficit injure domestic industries and have adverse effects on employment? Should the trade deficit be a matter of concern and reversing it an objective for trade policy?

The connection between the trade deficit and employment is much more complex than the simple view that jobs are lost because imports exceed exports. As figure 4.11 shows, the correlation between the merchandise trade deficit and the unemployment rate is actually negative. Most of the time, the trade deficit has risen during periods of falling unemployment and has fallen during periods of rising unemployment. A booming economy, in which many people are finding employment, is also an economy that draws in many imports, whereas a sluggish economy with higher unemployment is one in which spending on imports slackens. There is no better example of this than the Great Recession of 2008–9: the trade deficit fell sharply when falling housing prices led to a financial crisis, deep recession, and significantly higher unemployment.

Of course, the imports that a country receives are not free. In order to acquire them, a country must sell something in return. Imports are usually paid for in one of two ways: the sale of goods and services or the sale of assets to foreign countries. In other words, all of the dollars that U.S. households and businesses hand over to other countries in purchasing imports do not accumulate there, but eventually return to purchase either U.S. goods (exports) or U.S. assets (foreign investment). Both exports and foreign investment create new jobs: employment in export-oriented sectors such as farming and aircraft production is higher because of those foreign sales, and foreign investment either contributes directly to the national capital stock with new plants and equipment or indirectly promotes domestic capital accumulation by reducing the cost of capital.

A deeper understanding of the trade deficit, however, requires some familiarity with balance-of-payments accounting. Balance-of-payments

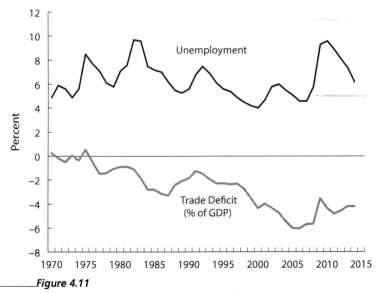

_____*Figure 4.11*

Unemployment and the Trade Deficit, 1970–2014

Source: FRED, Federal Reserve Economic Data, Federal Reserve Bank of St. Louis (http://research.stlouisfed.org/fred2/).

accounting may be a dry subject, but it helps lift the fog that surrounds the trade deficit. This accounting also suggests which remedies are likely to be effective in reducing the deficit, should that be a policy objective.

The balance of payments is simply an accounting of a country's international transactions. All sales of U.S. goods or assets to nonresidents constitute a receipt to the United States and are recorded in the balance of payments as a positive entry (credit); all purchases of foreign goods or assets by U.S. residents constitute a payment by the United States and are recorded as a negative entry (debit). The balance of payments is divided into two broad categories of transactions: the current account, which includes all trade in goods and services, plus a few smaller categories; and the financial account, which includes all trade in assets, mainly portfolio and direct investments.

The first accounting lesson is that the balance of payments always balances. By accounting identity, which is to say by definition, the balance of payments sums to zero. This implies that

$$\text{current account} + \text{financial account} = 0.$$

Because the overall balance of payments always balances, a country with a current account deficit must have an offsetting financial account surplus. In other words, if a country is buying more goods and services from the rest of the world than it is selling, then the country must also be selling more assets to the rest of the world than it is purchasing.[84]

To make the link clearer, consider the case of an individual. Each of us as individuals exports our labor services to others in the economy. For this work, we receive an income that can be used to import goods and services produced by others. If an individual's expenditures exactly match his or her income in a given year, that person has "balanced trade" with the rest of the economy: the value of exports (income) equals the value of imports (expenditures). Can individuals spend more in a given year than they earn in income; in other words, can a person import more than he or she exports? Of course, by one of two ways: either by receiving a loan (borrowing) or by selling existing financial assets to make up the difference. Either method generates a financial inflow—a financial account surplus—that can be used to finance the trade deficit while also reducing the individual's net assets. Can an individual spend less in a given year than that person earns in income? Of course, and that individual exports more than he or she imports, thereby running a trade surplus with the rest of the economy. The surplus earnings are saved, generating a financial outflow—a financial account deficit—due to the purchase of assets for investments.

What does this mean in the context of the United States? In 2013, the United States had a merchandise trade deficit of about $704 billion and a services trade surplus of $229 billion. The balance on goods and services was therefore a deficit of about $475 billion, but owing to other factors (net income payments and net unilateral transfers) the current account deficit was nearly $379 billion, or 2.2 percent of that year's GDP. This implies that there must have been a financial account surplus of roughly the same magnitude. Sure enough, in that year U.S. residents (corporations and households) increased their ownership of foreign assets by $552 billion, while foreigners increased their ownership of U.S. assets by

---

[84] A country therefore cannot experience a "balance of payments deficit" unless one is using the old nomenclature that considers official reserve transactions (an important component of the balance of payments under fixed exchange rate regimes) as a separate part of the international accounts.

finance going towards US

$906 billion. Therefore, the financial account surplus was approximately $354 billion. In other words, foreigners increased their ownership stake in U.S. assets more than U.S. residents increased their holdings of foreign assets, thus forming the mirror image of the current account deficit.[85]

The balance of payments "balances" in the sense that every dollar we spend on imported goods must end up somewhere. Here's another way of thinking about it: in 2013, the United States imported almost $2,746 billion in goods and services from the rest of the world, but the rest of the world only purchased $2,271 billion of U.S. goods and services, leaving a gap of $475 billion. What did the other countries do with this money? First, American assets abroad earned more interest and dividends than foreign assets in the United States, so other countries paid us $229 billion. However, the United States also made $133 billion in net unilateral transfers to the rest of the world in the form of worker remittances, foreign aid, and the like. These two factors reduced the gap to $379 billion, the size of the current account deficit, which foreign countries returned to the United States by purchasing assets here. In essence, for every dollar Americans handed over to foreigners in buying their goods (our imports), foreigners used eighty three cents to purchase U.S. goods (our exports), three cents (net) to pay us interest, and the remaining fourteen cents to purchase U.S. assets. What assets are foreign residents purchasing? Some are short-term financial assets (such as stocks and bonds) for portfolio reasons; some are direct investments (such as mergers and acquisitions) to acquire ownership rights; and some are real assets (such as buildings and land) for the same reasons.

GREAT WAY TO LOOK @ SIMPLY

Is the current account deficit sustainable? As long as foreign investors want to continue purchasing U.S. assets, the deficit can be sustained. Once foreign investors decide to stop buying U.S. assets or to sell them, then the dollar will tend to depreciate on foreign exchange markets, increasing exports and decreasing imports and thus tending to reduce the trade deficit. This process can be slow and orderly and does not require a "hard landing" or involve a sudden collapse in the dollar.[86]

Why it will conta be sustainable

[85] Data from the Bureau of Economic Analysis website; www.bea.gov. The difference between the current account deficit and the financial account surplus is a statistical discrepancy. These figures are based on the initial release of data for 2014 and are subject to revision.

[86] In the mid-1980s, many commentators feared that the current account deficit was

Thus, in running a current account deficit, the United States is selling assets to the rest of the world.[87] These foreign purchases of domestic assets allow the United States to finance more investment than it could through domestic savings alone. In essence, the United States is supplementing its domestic savings with foreign investment and thus is able to undertake more investment than if it had relied solely on domestic savings. The equation that expresses this relationship is

$$\text{current account} = \text{savings} - \text{investment}.$$

Once again, this equation is an identity, meaning that it holds by definition. A current account deficit (the financial account surplus) implies that domestic investment exceed domestic savings. Conversely, countries with current account surpluses have domestic savings in excess of domestic investment, the excess being used to purchase foreign assets via foreign investment (financial account deficit). However, the ability of a country to run a current account surplus or deficit depends upon the degree to which capital is allowed to move between countries, which in turn is a function of the international monetary system and the exchange rate regime. In the absence of international capital movements, domestic savings must equal domestic investment, and therefore the current account will be balanced.

Figure 4.12 illustrates this point by presenting the U.S. current account as a percentage of GDP from 1970 to 2013, along with the evolution of

---

unsustainable and that the economy would face a "hard landing" once foreign capital stopped flowing into the United States. These fears proved to be misplaced: the economy did not suffer a hard landing when capital inflows slowed in the late 1980s, the dollar depreciated in an orderly way, and the current account deficits fell as a share of GDP.

[87] This United States has done this for so long that the value of U.S. assets owned by foreigners is greater than the value of foreign assets owned by U.S. residents. Technically, this makes the United States a "debtor" country, but the U.S. situation is not really comparable to developing country debtors. In developing countries, foreign investment sometimes includes large amounts of short-term government debt, denominated in a foreign currency. It is misleading to compare these debts to the foreign purchase of U.S. assets by saying that the United States is borrowing from other countries. Borrowing implies a specific payback schedule, hence the repayment problems that developing countries sometimes encounter. In the U.S. case, foreign investors are simply choosing to purchase dollar-denominated assets from the owners of those assets. The investors often wish to take a direct, long-term ownership stake in the United States that they do not intend to reverse. For a good discussion of the role of the dollar and dollar-denominated assets in the world economy, see Prasad 2014.

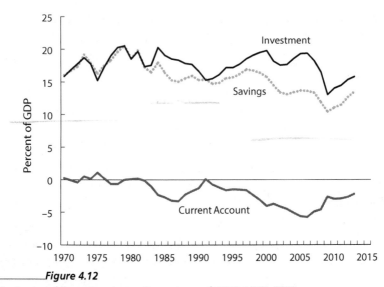

_____*Figure 4.12*

Savings and Investment as a Percentage of GDP, 1970–2013

   Source: FRED, Federal Reserve Economic Data, Federal Reserve Bank of St. Louis
(http://research.stlouisfed.org/fred2/).

savings and investment. The current account was roughly balanced in the
1970s because of restrictions on international capital mobility. Under the
Bretton Woods system of fixed exchange rates, which lasted from just
after World War II until 1971, governments maintained fixed exchange
rates by imposing controls on capital movements. As a result, capital
flows were minimal by present-day standards. When the international
monetary system suppresses financial account transactions, the financial
account balance will be close to zero, and therefore the current account
balance must also be close to zero.

   The Bretton Woods system collapsed in 1971, but restrictions on international capital mobility lingered until the early 1980s. When international capital movements were permitted, relatively large current account
imbalances also began to emerge. The United States became a magnet for
capital from the rest of the world, particularly after the early 1980s. For
example, after Japan eased restrictions on the holding of foreign assets in
1980, Japanese investors took part of their large pool of capital (invested
in its domestic market as a result of its high savings rate) and sought
higher rates of return in foreign capital markets, particularly in the United

US attracts capital

States. Now that they were free to buy U.S. assets as well as U.S. goods, Japanese residents chose to spend some of the dollars they earned in exporting goods to the United States by buying U.S. assets rather than U.S. goods.

As a result, the United States has been a net recipient of foreign investment since the early 1980s, meaning that domestic investment has been greater than domestic savings. The U.S. current account deficit grew even larger in the late 1990s and early 2000s, peaking at about 6 percent of GDP in 2006. Former Federal Reserve Chairman Ben Bernanke proposed the idea that a "global savings glut"—factors outside the United States—was responsible for the growing deficits of this period, reflected in the shift of rapidly growing East Asian economies and oil-producing countries from being net borrowers to being net lenders on international capital markets. The windfall to oil exporters from higher petroleum prices and the buildup of foreign exchange reserves and foreign investment by East Asian countries increased the savings of those countries, which they chose to invest in the United States, resulting in the large U.S. current account deficit. The financial crisis of 2008–9, however, reduced foreign demand for dollar-denominated assets and hence the U.S. current account deficit has fallen to about 2–3 percent of GDP.

The U.S. bilateral trade deficit with China is the most controversial part of the U.S. current account deficit. In 2013, the U.S. trade deficit with China was just about $300 billion, or 1.8 percent of GDP. An important factor behind China's trade surplus is that most of the dollars that it receives from exporting goods to the United States are used to buy U.S. assets rather than U.S. goods. In 2013, China purchased approximately $215 billion in U.S. Treasury bills and other securities. Such purchases have enabled China's foreign exchange reserves to swell from $166 billion in 2000 to an astounding $3.8 trillion by the end of 2014.

For many years, China accomplished this by intervening in foreign exchange markets to peg the value of its currency, the renminbi, against the dollar at a relatively low rate. In essence, China's central bank was selling renminbi and buying dollars, pushing up the value of the dollar and pushing down the value of the renminbi. This policy continues today, but it proved to be particularly controversial in the mid-2000s. As China's accumulation of dollar assets accelerated, particularly U.S. Treasury bonds, China's current account surplus ballooned from 1 percent of GDP

US trade def. wl china = inter dep.

in 2001 to 11 percent of GDP in 2007. Many observers thought that the renminbi was undervalued by a substantial margin, perhaps as much as 40 percent.[88] This has led to charges that China was manipulating its currency to achieve unbalanced, export-led growth, and was suppressing domestic consumption. An undervaluation of the renminbi is an implicit subsidy to Chinese exports. While that makes U.S. imports from China cheaper than they otherwise would be, it also reduces U.S. exports. However, it is also an implicit subsidy to the U.S. Treasury since it enables the government to borrow at a lower interest rate than it otherwise could.

In 2005, partly as a result of U.S. pressure, China began to allow the renminbi to appreciate slowly against the dollar, about 25 percent (or 40 percent in inflation-adjusted terms) in subsequent years. The appreciation of the renminbi helped increase the cost of Chinese goods to the rest of the world, and its current account surplus shrank from 11 percent of GDP in 2007 to about 2 percent of GDP in 2013. However, a July 2014 International Monetary Fund staff report determined that the renminbi was still moderately undervalued, by perhaps 5 to 10 percent.

As we have seen, the U.S. trade deficit is often blamed for job losses. Yet it is difficult to say much about the impact of the trade deficit on the number of jobs in the economy because looking at the trade flows alone ignores the role of financial flows in keeping interest rates low. If the United States took action to reduce the trade deficit in an effort to reduce the number of jobs lost to imports, then net capital inflows from abroad would necessarily have to fall (i.e., China would no longer buy Treasury bills and the renminbi would appreciate and the dollar would depreciate). Then domestic investment would have to be financed by domestic savings, implying higher interest rates, which would reduce the number of jobs created by business investment. In the end, the positive impact of a lower trade deficit on employment might be offset by the negative impact of lower domestic investment and higher interest rates.

So what are the implications for trade policy? The current account is fundamentally determined by international capital mobility and the gap between domestic savings and investment. The main determinants of savings and investment are macroeconomic in nature. Current account imbalances have nothing to do with whether a country is open or closed to

[88] Goldstein and Lardy 2008.

foreign goods, engages in unfair trade practices or not, or is more "competitive" than other countries. If net capital flows are zero, the current account will be balanced. Japan's $11 billion current account deficit in 1980 became an $87 billion current account surplus in 1987 not because it closed its market, or because the United States opened its market, or because Japanese manufacturers suddenly became more competitive. The surplus emerged because of financial and macroeconomic policy changes in Japan and the United States. The current trade imbalance with China is more controversial because it involves efforts by the Chinese government to control the flow of capital between the two countries and influence the value of its currency rather than allow those things to be determined by private financial market participants.

Trade policy does not directly affect the current account deficit because tariffs and quotas have little influence on domestic savings and investment, the ultimate determinants of the current account. If a country wishes to reduce its trade deficit, then it must undertake macroeconomic measures to reduce the gap between domestic savings and investment. Reducing the federal government's fiscal deficit, which acts to absorb domestic savings, could contribute to this result. Long ago it was believed that restrictions on imports would automatically reduce the trade deficit. But that result would follow only if exports remained unaffected, an assumption that the Lerner symmetry theorem suggests, and experience demonstrates, is false. Adam Smith saw through such policies of restriction: "Nothing, however, can be more absurd than this whole doctrine of the balance of trade, upon which, not only these restraints, but almost all the other regulations of commerce are founded."[89]

To conclude, we have seen in the past two chapters that trade is a small part of the everyday shift of workers between various sectors of the economy, creating jobs in some industries but destroying jobs in others. While some workers are adversely affected by imports, government programs are in place to help them. Blocking imports may protect some jobs in industries that compete against imports, but harms employment in export-oriented and import-using industries, as chapter 3 explained. To fully understand trade policy, we must appreciate these oft-ignored indirect effects.

[89] Smith [1776] 1976, 488.

5

Relief from Foreign Competition:
Antidumping and the Escape Clause

We have seen how trade policies aimed at reducing imports also reduce exports and employment elsewhere in the economy. Yet import restrictions are often justified as a way of providing relief to industries suffering from "unfair" foreign competition, particularly dumping and subsidies. The antidumping law allows tariffs to be imposed on low-priced imports and has become the primary instrument for addressing such concerns. This chapter examines antidumping actions and asks whether they provide a remedy for unfair trade, or are merely a convenient mechanism for an industry to protect itself from imports. We will also look at countervailing duties, which address foreign subsidies, and the escape clause, which can provide industries with temporary relief from imports without the claim of unfairness. Finally, we will examine whether trade protection really helps industries such as textiles and steel adjust and become more competitive, or whether it simply delays adjustment to new competition.

Unfair Trade: Subsidies and Dumping

We are all familiar with the claim that imports cost jobs. But many people are also afraid that American industries are being harmed by unfair foreign trade practices. These include export subsidies and the dumping of goods at low prices that divert sales away from U.S. firms. To counter such practices, the United States enforces several "fair trade" laws that allow import tariffs to be imposed. For example, when a foreign government subsidizes its exports to the United States, the subsidy is considered to be an actionable unfair trade practice if it injures domestic producers.

Of course, from a strictly economic point of view, an importing country might well benefit from receiving subsidized goods. Even if the subsidy harms domestic producers, the subsidy allows the importing country to purchase imports at a lower price, thanks to the generosity of foreign taxpayers. By improving the terms of trade, the foreign subsidy adds to the domestic gains from trade. For example, domestic oil producers would be understandably upset if the Organization of Petroleum Exporting Countries (OPEC) decided to subsidize its oil exports to the United States, but the country as a whole would probably welcome the lower gas prices that would follow.

But such subsidies are not desirable from the standpoint of the world economy. For one thing, such subsidies cut into the exports of countries that have a natural comparative advantage in those products, and so distort the world's allocation of resources. Subsidies also generate political friction among trading partners, each viewing the other's government as putting its finger on the scales of international competition to tip the outcome toward its own favored producers.[1]

For these reasons, the United States led the effort to draw up an Agreement on Subsidies and Countervailing Measures among the WTO membership. The subsidies agreement establishes rules on permissible types of subsidies and tries to ensure that such subsidies will not distort trade. Under the agreement, export subsidies and subsidies to industries that compete against imports are prohibited in principle, but subsidies related to research and development, regional development, and environmental compliance purposes are permissible.

In the United States, domestic firms have legal recourse against subsidized imports. The remedy takes the form of tariffs known as countervailing duties (CVDs). Domestic firms initiate the legal process by filing a

---

[1] The United States, it should be noted, provides indirect export subsidies through the Export-Import Bank. In fiscal year 2013, the Export-Import Bank authorized $27 billion in support to U.S. exporters through loans, guarantees, and export credit insurance. Just a small fraction of U.S. exports gets support, but large corporations (the major exporters) receive the bulk of the assistance. Boeing received 65 percent of all loan guarantees, and General Electric, Caterpillar, Bechtel, and John Deere are other major recipients. The bank has been under attack in Congress for providing "corporate welfare." In addition, Delta Airlines has complained that Export-Import Bank financing of sales of Boeing aircraft to foreign airlines amounts to subsidizing foreign competition. Because of these attacks, Congress's renewal of the bank's charter has been contested.

petition with the Department of Commerce and the U.S. International Trade Commission (ITC) alleging that imports have been subsidized by a foreign government. If Commerce determines that the imports have in fact been subsidized and if the ITC decides that the domestic industry has been injured as a result of the imports, tariffs of the magnitude of the subsidy margin (as determined by Commerce) will be imposed.

In recent years the CVD process has been rarely invoked by domestic firms. Are foreign countries subsidizing fewer of their exports to the United States? As a result of the multilateral subsidy agreement, perhaps so. But the more likely explanation is that domestic firms have found other ways to prevent such exports from entering the U.S. market. And in fact domestic firms find it much easier to obtain protection by accusing foreign firms of "dumping" in the U.S. market than by proving the existence of foreign subsidies.

From the standpoint of domestic firms seeking protection from imports, antidumping is where the action is. The number of dumping cases swamps those of other trade remedies: in recent years, roughly five antidumping cases have been initiated for every CVD case. As of mid-2014, the United States had countervailing duties in place on fifty-two products but maintained antidumping duties on 245 products.[2] This emphasis on antidumping instead of countervailing duties exists around the world as well. In 2012, WTO members initiated twenty-three new countervailing duty investigations and 208 new antidumping investigations. By June 2013, the twenty-eight leading members of the WTO had 1,374 antidumping measures in force.[3] What exactly is going on here?

Dumping has been deemed an unfair trade practice by country authorities and world trade agreements, and the antidumping law is intended to combat it. Yet the gap between the rhetoric and the reality of antidumping trade policy is simply enormous. Dumping sounds awful, as though foreign goods were being unloaded on America's docks and priced below cost to force domestic firms out of business. But under the law, dumping simply means that a foreign exporter charges a lower price in the U.S. market than it does in its home market. This is nothing more than price discrimination. If the foreign exporter is found guilty, the United States can impose import duties to offset the difference.

[2] http://www.usitc.gov/trade_remedy/documents/orders.xls (accessed January 21, 2015).
[3] World Trade Organization 2014, 53–54.

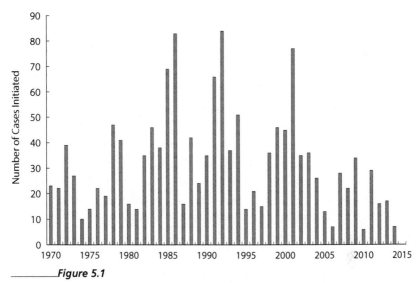

_____*Figure 5.1*

Annual Number of U.S. Antidumping Investigations, 1970–2013

Source: International Trade Administration, U.S. Department of Commerce (http://enforcement.trade.gov/stats/iastats1.html).

Figure 5.1 shows the annual number of U.S. antidumping investigations since 1970. As is evident, the number of investigations is quite cyclical. Fluctuations in antidumping activity are related to such factors as the exchange rate and the unemployment rate; in particular, an appreciation of the dollar and a higher unemployment rate increase the number of cases.[4] The number of petitions filed has dropped off in recent years because some major sectors, such as the steel and chemical industries, have not been using it to block imports as much as they had in the past.

While the details of antidumping (AD) are quite complex, it is important to have a basic understanding of how the law works and why it causes problems for world trade.[5] In the United States, the AD process is activated when a domestic industry, represented by an industry association or in some cases just a single firm, files a petition with the Commerce Department and the ITC. The petitioners must have legal standing to file

[4] Irwin 2005a and Bown and Crowley 2013.

[5] There is now a voluminous literature that finds fault with the antidumping laws. For policy analyses, see Ikenson 2010 and Ikenson 2011. For surveys of academic research on the effects of antidumping duties, see Blonigen and Prusa 2003, Nelson 2006, and Blonigen and Prusa 2015.

a petition. (In 1999, for example, Commerce rejected an antidumping petition filed by a group of Texas oil producers against Saudi Arabia, Mexico, Venezuela, and Iraq on the grounds that the petitioners did not represent the entire domestic industry.) The legal fees associated with filing an AD case typically amount to about $1 million, although more complex cases can cost several million dollars.[6]

The Commerce Department determines whether dumping has occurred and, if so, calculates the dumping margin. Specifically, Commerce ascertains whether a foreign exporter made sales in the United States at prices that are at "less than fair value." Sales are "less than fair value" if the export price—that is, the price charged in the U.S. market—is less than the so-called "normal value." The normal value is determined one of three ways: by the price charged by the foreign exporter in its home market sales, by the price it charged in third-country sales, or by constructed value, which is an estimate of what the price should have been, based on the costs of production plus administrative expenses and a profit margin. The dumping margin is simply the difference between the export price (the price charged in the United States) and the determined normal value divided by the export price. For example, if a foreign firm exports a good to the United States for $80 but charges $100 in its own market, then the dumping margin is 25 percent, or (100–80)/80.

After receiving a petition, Commerce almost always rules that dumping has occurred. In only seven cases out of the roughly four hundred that it considered from 2000 to 2014 did the Commerce Department dismiss a petition on the grounds that there was no dumping. This means that it found dumping in more than 98 percent of all cases. And the dumping margins are usually large: the average AD duty is in the range of 50 percent.[7] However, the average dumping margin varies widely depending upon the method used to calculate the normal value. As table 5.1 shows, during the 1995 to 1998 period, the average margin on (affirmative) cases

[6] In the early 1990s, the U.S. International Trade Commission (1995, 4–3) surveyed petitioners and found a simple petition would cost about $250,000. The price is much higher today, particularly if the petitioner wants the law firm to provide additional support for the petition.

[7] See Blonigen 2006 and Lindsey and Ikenson 2003, 26. The average antidumping duty imposed has risen over time. The average duty was 22 percent in the period from 1981 to 1983 and 56.8 percent in the period from 1991 to 1995. Congressional Budget Office 1998, 25.

_____***Table 5.1.***

Antidumping Margins and Calculation Method, 1995–98

Calculation method	Determinations (affirmative only)	Average dumping margin (affirmative only)
U.S. prices to home	4	4.00%
market prices	(2)	(7.36%)
Constructed value	20	25.07%
	(14)	(35.70%)
Nonmarket economy	47	40.03%
	(28)	(67.05%)
"Facts available"	36	95.58%
	(36)	(95.58%)
Total	141	44.68%
	(107)	(58.79%)

Source: Lindsey and Ikenson 2003, 26.
Note: Not all methods shown.

that compared the U.S. price to the exporter's home market price was just 7.36 percent. When Commerce compared the U.S. price to its constructed value, the average margin was 35.70 percent. In cases involving nonmarket economies, such as China and the former Soviet Union, the average margin was about 67 percent. In cases using "facts available," in which Commerce essentially accepted the data presented by the petitioner, the average margin was nearly 96 percent. Because of a greater reliance on the constructed value method over the price comparison method, the average dumping margin has steadily increased over time.

When U.S. prices are compared to actual foreign market prices, rather than to some constructed value, the dumping margins appear to be quite low. Yet even when a foreign firm charges exactly the same price in the U.S. market as in its home market, Commerce has still been able to find dumping due to a method called "zeroing." To illustrate zeroing, consider this simple example. Suppose a foreign firm always charges $100 for a product in its home market, but its export price to the U.S. market fluctuates and is $90, $100, and $110 in different transactions or at different times. On average, the prices in the two markets are the same at $100 and so you might think that there is no dumping margin. In only one transaction, or in one time period, when the export price is $90, is there "dumping." But the Commerce Department can still find a dumping margin of 11 percent (10/90) because it looks only at that one observation. It ignores—or zeroes out, hence the term "zeroing"—observations in which there is no dumping margin or the export price is higher than the exporter's domestic price.

Of course, this method of comparing the *average* of the exporter's home market prices to the prices charged on *individual* sales in the United States guarantees a finding of dumping, if prices change over time. The zeroing method inflates the dumping margin and does not give the foreign exporter any credit for a negative dumping margin on some sales. America's trading partners have strongly objected to this practice. In several cases brought to the WTO dispute settlement system, panels have ruled that zeroing violates the WTO's rules on antidumping. But Commerce seems reluctant to change its policy. Although the agency states that it has complied with the WTO verdict and no longer uses zeroing, its policy now is to look for "targeted" dumping, which is another way of saying that it will look only for those periods or those transactions where the export price is lower than the home market price.[8]

Yet something is also amiss when a method other than the price comparison approach is employed. When Commerce is unable to collect enough data on the exporter's home market prices, it may resort to the constructed value method. When Commerce undertakes a constructed value calculation, it attempts to estimate the foreign exporter's costs of production plus an allowance for administrative, selling, and general expenses and profits. Prior to 1995, U.S. antidumping practice was to augment the estimated costs of production by at least 10 percent for administrative expenses and at least 8 percent for profits.[9] Under the WTO's Agreement on Antidumping, Commerce cannot tack on these arbitrary amounts to the estimated costs, but must use the actual administrative expenses and the actual profit, when available. However, there is still room for Commerce to use questionable numbers and thereby raise the dumping margin.

When dealing with nonmarket economies, such as China and the states of the former Soviet Union, where prices may not be market-determined, Commerce estimates production costs using wage rates and other factor costs from a surrogate country of similar level of economic development.

---

[8] See Ikenson 2004, Bown and Prusa 2011, and Ahn and Messerlin 2014.
[9] Congressional Budget Office 1994, 31.

For example, in estimating China's costs of producing stainless steel sinks in 2011, Commerce used the cost of production in Thailand and came up with a dumping margin of 33.5 percent. A year later, in estimating China's costs of producing silica bricks, the surrogate country was chosen to be Ukraine and the dumping margin was 63.81 percent. In a 2012 case involving steel wheels from China, the surrogate country was Indonesia and the dumping margins ranged from 44.96 percent to 193.54 percent, with most firms at 63.94 percent. A dumping margin of 63 percent implies that the Chinese firms were generously selling their product for just two-thirds of their "normal" value. Such high dumping margins are typical in cases involving China.[10]

The International Trade Commission's role in an antidumping case is to determine if the domestic industry has suffered or is threatened with "material injury" as a result of the less-than-fair-value imports. The definition of material injury, according to the law, is "harm which is not inconsequential, immaterial, or unimportant."[11] Only the harm to the competing industry is considered, not any harm or injury to consumers or other domestic industries that can result from the imposition of antidumping duties.

While Commerce almost always finds dumping, the injury determination is a more difficult hurdle for the domestic petitioner to clear. This is because of the injury standard itself and because the ITC is a quasi-independent agency (as opposed to Commerce, which is typically an advocate of the domestic industry in the process). Still, the ITC ruled affirmatively in about 83 percent of final determinations during the period 1999 to 2002.[12] Economic factors, such as changes in the industry's out-

---

[10] In another case using the constructed value method, Commerce once determined (with apparent precision) that natural bristle paintbrushes from China were sold at less than their fair value with a dumping margin of 351.9 percent, and imposed tariffs of the same amount. In July 2008, Commerce ruled that the dumping margin on sodium nitrite from China was 190.74 percent. The finding of such high dumping margins is not limited to nonmarket economies. In June 2003, in a case involving polyethylene retail carrier bags (PRCBs, otherwise known as the thin plastic shopping bags one finds at grocery stores), the Commerce Department found margins as high as 123 percent for Thailand, 102 percent for Malaysia, and 77 percent for China.

[11] U.S. House of Representatives 2013, 208.

[12] Lindsey and Ikenson 2003, 3. The ITC ruled affirmatively in 66 percent of final determinations during the period 1980 to 1992. Congressional Budget Office 1994, 50.

put, employment, and capacity utilization, are the main determinants of a favorable injury finding. But political factors, such as whether the industry is a constituent of the chairman of the ITC's congressional oversight committee, also appear to matter.[13]

If dumping is found to exist and the domestic industry is deemed to have suffered material injury, then antidumping duties are imposed. As of August 2014, the United States had 245 AD duty orders in effect on goods coming from thirty-nine countries. The main targets of AD duties are China (94), Taiwan (18), India (15), Japan (13), and South Korea (12). More than 40 percent of the duties are on iron and steel products, with chemicals a distant second. AD orders existed on such goods as ball bearings from Japan and the United Kingdom; raw in-shell pistachios from Iran, steel nails from China and the United Arab Emirates; stainless steel butt-weld pipe fittings from Italy, Malaysia, and the Philippines; preserved mushrooms from Italy, Chile, China, India, and Indonesia; frozen warm-water shrimp and prawns from Thailand, India, Brazil, and China; and large residential washers from Korea and Mexico. China is singled out for duties on its exports of electric blankets, fresh garlic, paper clips, cased pencils, tissue paper, ironing boards, crepe paper, and hand trucks, to name just a few.[14]

Of course, the United States is hardly alone in imposing antidumping duties. Between 1995 and 2013, India imposed the most antidumping measures (519), followed by the United States (319), the European Union (297), Argentina (218), Brazil (165), China (164), and Turkey (154).[15]

What happens when AD duties are imposed? Not surprisingly, imports fall sharply. Looking at table 5.2, we can see that imports subjected to AD duties of over 50 percent fell 73 percent in volume and rose 33 percent in price, on average, from the year before the petition to the year after the petition. Imports subject to AD duties in the 20 to 50 percent range fell 22 percent in volume and rose 2 percent in price. The ITC study on

---

[13] See the survey by Blonigen and Prusa 2003.

[14] For updated statistics and information on the administration of U.S. antidumping laws, see http://enforcement.trade.gov/stats/iastats1.html and http://www.usitc.gov/trade _remedy/731_ad_701_cvd/investigations/active/index.htm.

[15] http://www.wto.org/english/tratop_e/adp_e/AD_MeasuresByExpCty.pdf (accessed January 21, 2015).

_____Table 5.2.
Trade Effects of Antidumping Duties Comparing Year Prior and Following Initiation of AD Investigation, 1989–93

Antidumping duties	Import volume	Import price (unit value)
Over 50 percent	−73%	33%
Between 20 percent and 50 percent	−22%	2%
Under 20 percent	−16%	−10%
Nonaffirmative decision	−3%	3%

Source: U.S. International Trade Commission 1995, 3–9.
Note: Import price effect does not include the antidumping duties.

_____Table 5.3.
Evidence of Trade Diversion in Antidumping Actions, 1989–93

	Import volume	Import price (unit value)
Affirmative, subject country	−32%	5%
Affirmative, nonsubject country	24%	−5%
Nonaffirmative, subject country	−24%	4%
Nonaffirmative, nonsubject country	19%	−3%

Source: U.S. International Trade Commission 1995, 3–15.
Note: Affirmative denotes cases in which antidumping duties were imposed; "subject" refers to imports subject to the duties and "nonsubject" indicates imports from other countries or firms not subject to the duties.

which the table is based also found that developing countries were disproportionately harmed by AD duties: the quantity of their imports tended to fall over twice as much as imports from developed countries.[16]

To a large extent, however, imports from countries not subject to the AD duties fill the void left by those smacked with the AD duties, something known as trade diversion. Because AD duties are imposed only on imports from countries named in the petition, the market is left open to others who can produce similar products. Table 5.3 indicates that while imports from countries affected by the AD duties fell by 32 percent, imports of the same product from countries not subject to the duties rose 24 percent.

[16] Since China is the target of many antidumping actions, recent studies have focused on how such duties affect China's exporters; see Lu, Tao, and Zhang 2013 and Shen and Fu 2014.

Because of this, antidumping petitions are often filed sequentially to squash the imports that arise from other sources as a result of the initial antidumping action. For example, Micron Technology, a producer of dynamic random access memory (DRAM) computer chips in Boise, Idaho, filed an AD petition against DRAM imports from Japan in 1985. After the imposition of restrictions on Japanese exports, foreign DRAM production shifted to South Korea, and so Micron filed an AD petition against Korean producers in 1991. After Korean exports were similarly restricted, Taiwanese producers entered the market, and so Micron filed an AD petition against DRAM exports from that country in 1998. The story is similar in the case of salmon. Antidumping duties were imposed against imports of fresh salmon from Norway in 1991. After Chile began to develop its fishing industry and filled the void left by the Norwegians, they too were hit with AD duties in 1998.

The simplest way for domestic petitioners to avoid this problem is to file multiple petitions against several sources. When the Coalition for Fair Preserved Mushroom Trade filed an AD petition concerning imports of preserved mushrooms in 1998, for example, it targeted imports from Chile, China, India, and Indonesia all at the same time. In 2004, the Shrimp Trade Action Committee filed a case on fresh and canned warmwater shrimp against Brazil, Ecuador, India, Thailand, China, and Vietnam. In 2014, U.S. Steel Corp. and several other companies filed a case on "certain oil country tubular goods" coming from India, South Korea, the Philippines, Saudi Arabia, Taiwan, Thailand, Turkey, Ukraine, and Vietnam.

Congress facilitated the move toward multiple filings by changing the law in 1984. Prior to that time, the injury determination was conducted on a country-by-country basis, even if multiple petitions were filed. After the 1984 change, the ITC had to consider the combined impact of imports from all named countries on the domestic industry. The cumulation provision is estimated to have raised the probability of an affirmative decision by 20 to 30 percent, thereby changing the ITC's determination from negative to positive in one-third of such cases.[17] This, in turn, has given petitioners an additional incentive to file petitions against multiple countries.

---

[17] Hansen and Prusa 1996.

Sometimes petitioners exclude certain countries from petitions as a matter of corporate strategy. For example, in 1994, the Maui Pineapple Company in Hawaii filed an AD petition against imports of canned pineapples from Thailand, resulting in the imposition of AD duties up to 51 percent, depending on the company. Thailand's canned pineapple exports to the United States fell from $101 million in 1993 to $51 million in 1997. Over the same period, imports of canned pineapple from Indonesia jumped from $9 million to $51 million because that country's exports were not subject to AD duties. But Maui did not file an AD petition against Indonesian imports because at that time it was forming a joint venture with one of the country's largest pineapple producers. Similarly, in 1994 Bic filed a petition alleging that disposable lighters from China and Thailand were being dumped in the U.S. market, but did not include Mexico in the petition because Bic had a factory there.[18]

It is important to note that trade diversion occurs even in cases where the final ITC injury decision is negative and no duties are imposed. Even when the domestic industry was found not to have suffered injury, imports from countries that had been the target of the case fell 24 percent on average, while imports from countries not targeted rose 19 percent. Thus, simply filing an antidumping petition can reduce imports from targeted sources even if duties are not imposed. According to one study, when a petition is ultimately rejected, imports from the countries named in the petition fall by about 15 to 20 percent, whereas if the petition is accepted, imports fall about 50 to 70 percent.[19]

A reason for this "chilling effect" on imports is the uncertainty surrounding the AD process: if dumping is found, domestic importers will be liable for the payment of dumping duties after Commerce issues its preliminary determination. To minimize their potential financial exposure, importers quickly stop purchasing from the foreign suppliers named in the petition. There is also an "investigation effect" on imports when an antidumping petition is filed: before Commerce has even made a preliminary determination about dumping, import volumes fall and prices rise by about onehalf of the full effect of imposing duties.[20]

---

[18] *Rushford Report*, September 1999, 3.
[19] Prusa 2001.
[20] See Blonigen and Prusa 2003.

As if there was not already sufficient incentive for firms to file anti-dumping petitions, Sen. Robert Byrd (DW.Va.) opened the door to more mischief in the fall of 2000. Senator Byrd slipped into an agricultural appropriations bill a provision that hands over all the revenue from antidumping duties to the petitioning industry. During the period that the Byrd amendment was in effect, petitioning firms were not only able to charge domestic consumers higher prices for their products, but also received a check from the government for a share of the tariff revenues.

The Byrd amendment led to a scramble for government cash, particularly because the legislation was retroactive. The federal government distributed $560 million to 1,200 firms in 2001–2. The chief beneficiaries have been two ball bearing companies whose lawyers helped write the Byrd legislation. Torrington Company received $63 million in Byrd money in 2001 but has sought reimbursements of $23.4 billion (its sales in 2001 amounted to $1.1 billion).[21] The Byrd provision encourages domestic firms to become bounty hunters and start filing AD petitions to receive tariff revenue payments from the government. Studies have shown that this increased the incentive to file petitions by a significant margin.[22]

However, in a dispute initiated by the EU and seven other countries, a WTO panel ruled in 2002 that the subsidy was inconsistent with the multilateral rules, a finding affirmed by the WTO's Appellate Body in 2003. In 2005, Congress repealed the Byrd amendment, but still allowed the distribution of antidumping tariff revenue to members of the affected U.S. industry who supported the petition for investigation on goods that entered before October 2007. In total, the government disbursed some $1.9 billion in revenue to petitioners. However, the issue is still alive: the original complainants have charged that the United States has not fully complied with the WTO ruling and some members of Congress want to reenact the Byrd amendment.

_____The Costs of Antidumping

Despite the apparent ease with which domestic firms can obtain some form of protection under the antidumping laws, only a tiny fraction of

---

[21] Neil King, "Trade Imbalance: Why Uncle Same Wrote a Big Check to a Sparkler Maker," *Wall Street Journal*, December 5, 2002.

[22] Reynolds 2006.

the value of U.S. imports are covered by AD duties. AD orders covered just 0.07 percent of all imports in 2012.[23] In any given year, the value of imports targeted by antidumping petitions is usually much less than this amount. Given these small figures, is antidumping worth worrying about?

Antidumping continues to merit close scrutiny for several reasons. First, these tariffs quickly add up. The net welfare cost of AD and CVD actions in the United States was a whopping $4 billion in 1993.[24] With the demise of the Multi-Fiber Arrangement in 2005, it is likely that they are collectively the most costly of all U.S. import restrictions.

These costs are only going to mount over time as more cases are filed. This is because AD duties are hard to remove once they are imposed. Starting in 1995, the United States and other WTO members were required to conduct a "sunset" review of their antidumping orders. All AD duties had to be terminated after five years unless a review found that this would lead to a recurrence of dumping and injury. Yet if the domestic petitioning industry objects to the expiration of the duties, Commerce is likely to renew them. In 738 reviews conducted from 1995 to 2011, the U.S. duties were kept in place almost 60 percent of the time.[25] In 2013–14, about 90 percent of the reviews resulted in a continuation of duties.[26]

Yet even the AD review process can become corrupted. For example, between 2006 and 2009, Chinese furniture firms paid $13 million to about twenty U.S. furniture makers at a time when the ITC was reviewing antidumping duties on wooden bedroom furniture. The Chinese firms apparently did this so that their U.S. competitors would not ask for even higher duties when the duties were up for administrative review.[27] One wonders whether domestic firms have ever threatened their foreign rivals with a dumping claim unless they paid some money to avoid such a fate.

A second reason for closely reviewing antidumping measures is that the coverage figures understate the harm in antidumping actions. The

---

[23] World Trade Organization 2012, 47. In 1991, the figure was 1.8 percent; U.S. International Trade Commission 1995, 4–1.

[24] Gallaway, Blonigen, and Flynn 1999.

[25] World Trade Organization 2012, 48.

[26] World Trade Organization 2014, 65.

[27] James Hagerty, "The Price of Trade Peace: Cash Paid to U.S. Rivals Lets Chinese Furniture Makers Skirt Import-Duty Review," *Wall Street Journal*, February 15, 2011.

very existence of the antidumping law allows it to be used as a tool to enforce collusive agreements. For example, in 1989 U.S. producers of ferrosilicon formed a cartel and reduced output. The lower output was used to prove injury and justify the imposition of antidumping duties against five foreign competitors. When Brazil started exporting ferrosilicon in place of the others, their producers were invited to join the U.S. cartel. When they refused, they too were hit with an antidumping case.[28]

When an exporter is confronted with the prospect of potentially severe duties that exporters from other countries will not have to endure, the target has a powerful incentive to negotiate some sort of export restraint agreement that will allow the exporter to avoid the imposition of duties. In some cases, the foreign exporter tries to reach a suspension agreement with Commerce (and approved by the petitioner) that terminates the petition. The quantity of imports falls by the same margin in cases that are settled as those in which duties are imposed, although the import price does not rise as much in settled cases.[29] The Uruguay Round also allows "price undertakings," in which exporters can agree to minimum export prices in order to avoid the imposition of duties. Thus, even when no duties are imposed, antidumping can result in trade restrictions and even collusive outcomes.[30]

Third, the antidumping process is so heavily biased against foreign firms that it is prone to abuse and manipulation by domestic firms. The problem is not that the process is overtly subject to political influence, although that problem has arisen in some high-profile cases. Rather, AD rules are intentionally stacked in favor of the domestic petitioner, both in reaching a conclusion that dumping has occurred and in the size of the dumping margin. Even the Congressional Budget Office notes that the Commerce Department "effectively serves as investigator, prosecutor, judge, and jury in dumping and subsidy determinations." And although it

[28] Eventually, criminal and civil legal actions were taken against the cartel members (Pierce 2001).

[29] Only about 10 percent of all petitions in the United States were withdrawn in the 1990s. Withdrawn petitions used to be considered a signal of a collusive settlement, but Taylor (2004) shows this not to be the case. However, Rutkowski (2006) questions this and shows that withdrawals may be related to collusion in the EU. Reynolds (2013) finds little evidence that AD promotes collusion in two protected U.S. industries.

[30] See Moore 2005.

should be neutral in these roles, Commerce is "actually an advocate of one of the parties to the case."[31]

The antidumping process is riddled with subtle tricks and arbitrary biases that invariably favor the domestic petitioner, making it ironic that AD rules are a part of the "fair trade" laws. The Commerce Department's method of zeroing has already been mentioned. The application of AD measures often hinges on a narrow technicality, such as the definition of the relevant industry. In the case of cut flowers from Colombia, the ITC initially ruled that the domestic industry was not materially injured. After Commerce later accepted petitions maintaining that each individual flower species was a different "industry" (the rose "industry," the chrysan-themum "industry," etc.), the ITC then made an affirmative injury ruling. In the case of frozen concentrated orange juice, Commerce ruled that fresh oranges and industrial concentrate orange juice are "like products" even though the markets and pricing for the two products are quite different.

Even the Commerce Department's Office of Inspector General was critical of the way that the Department's Office of Import Administration handled the eightyfour antidumping and countervailing duty petitions filed by the steel industry in June 1992. The office said that the agency "adopted several controversial and confusing policies that undermined the principles of transparency and consistency . . . [and were] not only inconsistent with past practice, but were also applied inconsistently from one case to the next." The report added that Import Administration "ap-plied policies that made reporting more onerous for respondents, caused confusion among analysts, and made IA's decisions appear arbitrary, even to its own staff."[32]

Finally, perhaps the biggest concern about antidumping is that the antidumping genie is out of the bottle and has spread around the world. Whereas antidumping actions were once instituted mainly by developed countries, now developing countries—such as Mexico, India, China, Ar-gentina, South Africa, and others—have copied them and have become aggressive users of these measures.[33] The more this "legal" form of pro-

---

[31] Congressional Budget Office 1994, 41.

[32] U.S. Department of Commerce 1993, 20.

[33] See Prusa 2001 and Zanardi 2006.

tectionism has been adopted around the world, the harder it will be to contain its adverse effects on trade. Indeed, one study estimates that imports into these aggressive new users of antidumping duties are 6 percent lower than they otherwise would be due to those measures.[34]

Furthermore, the motivation for this spread appears to be retaliation for developed countries' use of antidumping, rather than an increase in unfair trade.[35] This means that U.S. exporters may face more accusations that they are dumping in foreign markets.[36] For example, Micron Technology, previously mentioned as the DRAM producer who filed a series of petitions, was itself accused of dumping memory chips in Taiwan shortly after it succeeded in getting AD duties imposed on Taiwanese exports. And even though the ITC rejected a petition accusing Mexico of dumping emulsion styrenebutadiene rubber, the U.S. petitioner soon faced charges by its Mexican competitor of dumping the same product in that country. And, curiously enough, whenever the United States initiates an antidumping case against China, it is sometimes followed by the announcement of a Chinese antidumping case against an American firm. If antidumping actions remain unchecked, such retaliatory cases can only be expected to multiply in coming years. Yet the United States declined to put antidumping reform on the agenda for future trade negotiations. It is difficult to be optimistic that antidumping policies will change anytime soon.[37]

_____Is Antidumping Defensible?

The antidumping process involves many arbitrary judgments and is subject to abuse. Can any economic rationale be mustered in favor of the AD laws? The problem is that price discrimination, charging different prices in different markets, is a normal business practice and an accepted feature of domestic competition. Exporters often find that competition is

[34] Vandenbussche and Zanardi 2010.

[35] Vandenbussche and Zanardi 2008. While the Congressional Budget Office did not find systematic evidence prior to 1995 that other countries were singling out American firms for antidumping enforcement in retaliation for AD actions, evidence did "lend some credence to fears that U.S. policy may be starting to come back to haunt U.S. exporters as other countries follow its lead." Congressional Budget Office 1998, xiv.

[36] Feinberg and Reynolds 2008.

[37] Moore 2007.

more intense in the international market than in their home market, where they have a more secure position with domestic consumers. Therefore, exporters have to offer price discounts in foreign markets.

On economic grounds, the fact that a firm charges different prices in different markets is neither unfair nor a problem unless it harms competition (such as through anticompetitive actions or predatory practices) or reflects a market-distorting policy. If geared toward preventing these actions, antidumping policy could have some merit as a means of preserving competition or correcting alleged market distortions. Unfortunately, the antidumping laws are not written to identify and respond to such situations. This leaves the impression that the laws exist only to protect domestic firms if they can jump through a few bureaucratic hoops.

For example, the antidumping laws might be worthwhile if they prevented predatory pricing by foreign exporters. Predatory pricing would occur when an exporter prices its goods below cost in an effort to eliminate American producers and achieve a monopoly position. Firms engaging in predatory pricing must be prepared to incur substantial losses initially and then recoup those losses through the future exercise of a monopoly position. But this makes sense only if the firm can effectively knock out most of its competitors in the United States and in other countries. Were the Bangladesh shop towel producers trying to eliminate their foreign rivals and achieve a monopoly position? Were the flower growers from Colombia trying to do the same? Were China's garlic producers aiming for world domination? Most foreign exporters simply want to receive as high a price as possible on their sales. Few companies entertain the delusion of driving all of their competitors out of business in the world market.

In fact, in the overwhelming majority of AD cases, such predatory motives can be ruled out as utterly implausible. One researcher examined the structural characteristics of every one of the 282 industries involved in every dumping case in the 1980s in which duties were imposed or in which the case was suspended or terminated.[38] To isolate the cases in which predatory pricing might be considered plausible, she first eliminated all cases in which the industry in the United States and in the challenged country was relatively unconcentrated. These were excluded on

---

[38] Shin 1998.

the grounds that barriers to entry in such industries are probably not substantial. And without barriers to entry, anticompetitive practices are unlikely to exist because even if the firm drives rivals out of business, it cannot raise prices to finance the losses sustained in the price war if other firms can simply reenter the market once prices go up.

The researcher also eliminated cases in which there were multiple exporters from a single country or from several countries, reasoning that successful collusion by such firms would be unlikely and that there are enough firms to preserve competition. Finally, she eliminated all cases in which the import penetration level was not significant, or in which import growth was not rapid, since the imports would be unlikely to create market power if they did not constitute a large share of the U.S. market. In the end, only thirtynine cases were left, just 14 percent of all those considered, in which the industries were characterized by substantial domestic or foreign concentration. Of these remaining cases in which the preconditions for predation did exist, we cannot say for sure that predation was in fact a motive, only that it could not be ruled out.

The antidumping statute is not employed to prevent predatory conduct or preserve competition, but simply to protect the domestic industry from foreign competition—at the expense of domestic consumers, of course. One legal scholar concludes that while the antidumping laws were "originally marketed as antipredation measures, they are now written in a way that compels the administering authorities to impose antidumping measures in a vastly broader class of cases—all instances in which dumping causes material harm to competing domestic firms."[39] An ITC commissioner once tried to shift the interpretation toward an antipredation remedy. But petitioners appealed to the U.S. Court of International Trade, which ruled that focusing on competition effects "seems to assume that the purpose of the antidumping statute is merely to prevent a particular type of 'injury to competition' rather than merely 'material injury' to industry."[40]

Some antidumping advocates claim that foreign firms have a protected home market in which they can earn high profits, and from which they can subsidize export sales. In this view, any price discrimination due to

[39] Sykes 1998, 29–30.
[40] Sykes 1998, 29–30.

a sanctuary home market counts as a market-distorting practice that antidumping should attempt to remedy. But as one antidumping critic aptly notes, "The [antidumping] law lacks any mechanism for determining whether the price practices it condemns as unfair have any connection to market-distorting policies abroad."[41] The law does not distinguish cases in which there may be a sanctuary market effect, or ask if dumping is at all related to market distortions. If antidumping advocates are sincere in their desire for an antipredation remedy that is not simply protectionism, they should be willing to amend the current law and include an explicit test for the protected sanctuary home market that is often alleged to exist.

The problem with antidumping is not just the way the law is administered. The fundamental problem is that antidumping laws are written with the presumption that price discrimination is a problem. But there is nothing inherently harmful or anticompetitive about price discrimination. Price discrimination is an accepted feature of domestic competition. It would be surprising if domestic prices were *exactly* the same as an exporter's home price.[42] As already noted, the government rarely undertakes direct price comparisons when making a dumping determination, but more frequently makes arbitrary calculations about production costs. The result is that "dumping is whatever you can get the government to act against under the dumping law."[43] It is hard to avoid the conclusion that the antidumping laws are simply a popular means by which domestic firms can stifle foreign competition under the pretense of "fair trade."

Except in cases of gross abuse, antidumping is most frequently used by firms to insulate themselves from falling import prices. Some industries will always be faced with import surges, such as the domestic steel industry in the aftermath of the Asian financial crisis of 1997–98, when a collapse in foreign demand sent world steel prices tumbling. After the domestic computer production outstripped demand in 1985, world prices of

---

[41] Lindsey 2001, 1.

[42] "In the typical antidumping investigation, the DOC compares home-market and U.S. prices of physically different goods, in different kinds of packaging, sold at different times, in different and fluctuating currencies, to different customers at different levels of trade, in different quantities, with different freight and other movement costs, different credit terms, and other differences directly associated selling expenses (e.g., commissions, warranties, royalties, and advertising). Is it any wonder that the prices aren't identical?" Lindsey and Ikenson 2003, 21.

[43] Finger 1993, viii.

semiconductors fell through the floor, triggering a round of dumping complaints. Similarly, temporarily low oil prices led the Texas producers to file the antidumping petition against oil exporters that Commerce rejected. Of course, low prices are bad for producers but good for consumers. It would have been interesting to see Commerce grapple with that petition and explain how OPEC, a production cartel, could possibly be dumping its output in the U.S. market.

In such cases when import prices are falling, the problem facing the petitioning industry is not any price differential between markets, that is, foreign firms charging a higher price in their domestic market than in the United States. The afflicted industry would find no consolation if the U.S. price were higher than the foreign price even as both were falling sharply. Rather, the basic problem for the industry is that prices everywhere are falling due to unforeseen circumstances. It may be reasonable to provide an industry facing such difficulties with temporary protection without any claim that trade is "unfair." And that is precisely what the escape clause is designed to do.

_____The Escape Clause

If a domestic industry is suffering as a result of foreign competition and yet does not allege that the imports are unfairly dumped or subsidized, the industry can still receive temporary protection. Ever since the passage of the Reciprocal Trade Agreements Act in 1934, when the United States embarked on its policy of negotiating tariff reductions with other countries, Congress recognized that trade liberalization might force some sectors of the economy to endure some difficult adjustments. Because of this problem, Congress insisted that if lower tariffs brought about serious injury to particular domestic industries, they should be provided with temporary relief to help them adjust to the new conditions of trade. To this end, the "escape clause" provides a mechanism for domestic industries to get a temporary exception to any negotiated tariff reduction.

Section 201 of the Trade Act of 1974 provides the current statutory basis for the escape clause.[44] It allows representatives of an industry (a

[44] The escape clause is also contained in Article 19 of the GATT and in the Agreement on Safeguards as part of the Uruguay Round negotiations. In 2000, a special "China safeguard" provision was added to U.S. law as a transitional measure when China joined the

trade association, firm, union, or group of workers) to file a petition with the International Trade Commission for temporary relief from import competition. The petition must include a specific plan that details how protection will be used to help the industry adjust. The ITC must then determine if the imports are, or threaten to be, "a substantial cause of serious injury," where "substantial cause" is defined as "a cause which is important and not less than any other cause."[45] Cutting through the legal verbiage, this simply means that imports must be the most important cause of injury. This legalistic language is nontrivial: The ITC rejected a Section 201 petition from the automobile industry in 1980 on the grounds that the most important source of the industry's difficulty was not imports, but the recession of that year.

If the ITC reaches an affirmative finding of injury, it must then recommend an appropriate remedy to the president. This remedy can include action on trade, usually higher tariffs, or other policies that would help facilitate the adjustment efforts of the domestic industry. The president then has wide discretion as to what action is taken, but there are two important requirements. First, the import relief is temporary and can remain in place only for a period of four to eight years. Second, the tariffs must apply equally to imports from all source countries, unlike antidumping duties, which, as we have seen, are applied selectively. (For this reason, Section 201 is sometimes called the Global Safeguard provision.)

Section 201 has been criticized as being merely a protectionist loophole that allows firms to obtain protection, with no allegation of unfair trade, and therefore permits a country to backslide away from open markets.[46] But such provisions function as essential safeguards that make trade liberalizing agreements possible. As other economists have noted,

---

WTO. This provision allowed safeguard duties to be imposed on China alone, in contrast to the usual safeguard requirement that the duties must be nondiscriminatory and apply to imports from all source countries. This provision expired in December 2013, but it was used in about seven cases, including the 2009 case in which President Barack Obama imposed tariffs on automobile tires imported from China.

[45] U.S. House of Representatives 2013, 322.

[46] Expressing skepticism about the "safety valve" explanation for the escape clause, Sykes (2003) argues that the likelihood of direct protectionist legislation decreases if such legislation violates international obligations and results in international sanction. Therefore, "the ability of Congress to resist special interest pressures for protection . . . would likely be greater in the absence of Article XIX." Finger (1996) is equally skeptical about safeguards, dubbing them "legalized backsliding."

"Safeguard provisions are often critical to the existence and operation of trade-liberalizing agreements, as they function as both insurance mechanisms and safety-valves. They provide governments with the means to renege on specific liberalization commitments—subject to certain conditions—should the need for this arise (safety valve). Without them, governments may refrain from signing an agreement that reduces protection substantially (insurance motive)."[47] The presence of the escape clause, it can be argued, has encouraged cautious governments to liberalize trade more than might otherwise be the case.

Section 201 was invoked frequently in the 1970s, but has been used only sporadically in recent decades. Just nineteen cases were filed in the 1980s, ten cases in the 1990s, and three cases in the 2000s. As of early-2015, no safeguard actions were in place. This is partly because it has proven too difficult a way of getting protection: of the nineteen cases considered in the 1980s, for example, the ITC ruled affirmatively in only seven. Even then, there is no guarantee that the president will provide relief to the industry, and in practice presidents are often reluctant to grant it. (Presidents are often reluctant because the tariffs would apply to imports from all countries, adversely affecting many innocent exporters if just a few countries are responsible for the increased imports that cause serious injury.) This record is why Sen. Ernest Hollings (D-S.C.) once made the dismissive quip that "Section 201 is for suckers."[48] The escape clause has been completely overshadowed by antidumping, where the injury standard is not as strict and presidential action is not required. In view of the ease with which antidumping actions can be initiated and affect trade, it comes as no surprise that firms have avoided Section 201.

The steel industry recently discovered two more reasons why escape clause actions are of limited value—administrative exemptions and WTO review. In 2001, as a result of a campaign promise, President George W. Bush initiated a large steel Section 201 case and later imposed duties of up to 30 percent for three years on several types of steel products. But imports from countries having free trade agreements with the United States—Canada, Mexico, Israel, and Jordan—were exempt from the duties, and the Bush administration granted many additional product exclu-

---

[47] Hoekman and Kostecki 2009, 413.
[48] Quoted in Low 1993, 57.

sions that allowed the import of specialized steel products. The European Union and seven additional countries also challenged the steel tariffs at the WTO, claiming they violated the WTO's Agreement on Safeguards. A panel ruled that the safeguard decision was inconsistent with the WTO rules, which allows tariffs to be imposed only when foreign products are being imported in a quantity sufficiently increased so as to cause serious injury. But the safeguard action was taken well after the Asian financial crisis of 1997–98 caused U.S. steel imports to swell, and imports generally declined from 1999 to 2001. In addition, the panel indicated that the U.S. recession rather than imports may have been the major cause of injury.

The Bush administration faced the decision of whether to maintain the safeguard duties and face possible foreign retaliation for violating the WTO agreement, or to rescind the duties and comply with the WTO finding. When the EU threatened to impose tariffs on $2.2 billion of U.S. exports, the government decided to lift the duties in December 2003, after just twenty-one months. The tariffs proved to be much less valuable to the steel industry than it had hoped.[49]

With the increasing abuse of antidumping measures, escape clause actions have come to be viewed in a more benign light. Section 201 is now seen as a potential solution to the problem of the proliferation of antidumping actions. Escape clause actions have several advantages over antidumping measures: there are no bogus claims of unfair trade, they provide greater flexibility in the scope and duration of nondiscriminatory protection, and the president is allowed to take into account the overall economic, security, and political interests of the United States in tailoring a relief package. Relaxing the high standards of the escape clause would make it a more attractive method of obtaining import relief and provide an opportunity to rein in the use of antidumping. The danger, of course, is that Congress might simply expand the use of the escape clause without constraining the use of antidumping. Furthermore, many exporters that are not responsible for any injury-causing surge would strongly object to limits being placed on their exports by a safeguard action.

Clearly, the challenge for policymakers operating in an era of greater economic integration is one of balance—making the escape clause available without compromising open markets: "If the standards for obtaining

---

[49] For an overview of the case, see Read 2005.

import-related remedies are too restrictive, the escape clause mechanism cannot serve as an effective shock absorber for protectionist pressures. On the other hand, if the eligibility criteria are too weak, any domestic industry that faces import competition may become eligible for temporary protection."[50] This tradeoff is one of the most difficult challenges in trade policy.

_____Does Temporary Relief from Imports Work?

Some form of safeguards seems to be a political necessity. And we have seen that the escape clause can be a desirable alternative to antidumping actions. But does temporary relief from imports actually provide a remedy for the ills afflicting the domestic industry? Although protection has been justified as a way of revitalizing certain industries, it may not be able to accomplish this objective. The experience with antidumping duties is that they reduce productivity in an industry by prolonging the life of small, inefficient producers.[51]

Ideally, such relief would offer temporary protection to industries that compete against imports, in exchange for assurances that the industry will undertake measures to adjust to the new competition. But in providing temporary relief, the government encounters a problem with time consistency. The industry would like to reap the benefits of protection without undertaking the costs of adjustment. When the government cannot credibly commit to eliminating protection in the future, an industry may find itself able to perpetuate the protection by not investing sufficiently in cost reductions. If the government bases its decision to renew protection on whether the industry has adjusted to the foreign competition, then the industry may have an incentive not to adjust in order to trigger a renewal of protection. Even making trade relief contingent on such investment does not eliminate the time consistency problem. Temporary, contingent protection may still become permanent protection.[52]

---

[50] Lawrence and Litan 1986, 79.

[51] Pierce 2011. In addition to the discussion of certain industries in the paragraphs that follow, Krueger (1996) presents a series of case studies on protection that examine whether import limits actually helped the domestic industry. Baldwin (1988) also discusses the inefficacy of protectionist measures in helping domestic industries.

[52] Tornell 1991.

This pattern of repeated renewals of protection is sometimes seen in practice. Some industries have used temporary protection to adjust to competition from imports. The automobile, consumer electronics, and semiconductor industries have received temporary protection at one time or another, but adjusted to the new conditions of competition. This does not mean that protection helped promote the adjustment, just that protection was temporary. Indeed, blocking imports failed to solve the fundamental problem these industries faced, either because foreign competition was located in the United States through direct investments or because the industry depended heavily upon foreign export sales and the importation of components. Given the inability of trade policy to solve the underlying problems confronting these industries, domestic firms adjusted by adopting new technology, moving to new market niches, and forming global alliances.[53]

Other industries have essentially received permanent protection over the past few decades by seeking and repeatedly receiving "temporary" protection. Two that stand out are the steel industry and the textile and apparel industry. Both face long-term structural adjustments to domestic and foreign competition and have stubbornly resisted pressures to adapt. The steel industry suffers from excess capacity worldwide, a strong union that has helped price domestic producers out of the world market, and growing domestic competition from smaller mills. The textiles and apparel industry, on the other hand, is struggling against the loss of comparative advantage in labor-intensive manufactures by becoming more capital-intensive, upgrading technology, and outsourcing.

The steel industry has received nearly continuous protection for over thirty years and is still seeking limits on imports. From 1969 to 1974, the large, integrated producers were protected from imports by a series of voluntary restraint agreements (VRAs). From 1978 to 1982, a Trigger Price Mechanism, consisting of minimum import prices, was in effect. From 1982 to 1992, a new round of VRAs was in place. When the industry failed to persuade the government to renew the VRAs, the industry filed a mas-

---

[53] Another way to adjust to import competition is simply to fade away, as has been the fate of the domestic footwear industry. Import penetration in the domestic footwear market rose from 13 percent in 1966 to 90 percent in 1996, while employment fell from 233,400 in 1966 to 46,100 in 1996. See Freeman and Kleiner (2005) on how the remaining firms in the domestic industry have adjusted their labor practices in order to survive.

sive number of AD and CVD complaints in 1992–93. When the Asian financial crisis struck in 1997–98, sharply depressing world steel prices, the industry again filed many AD cases. As a result of the Section 201 escape clause case initiated by President Bush in 2001, the industry benefited from 30 percent tariffs on imports during 2002 and 2003.

Yet all this trade protection has never been enough for the steel industry. In fact, there are two steel industries in the United States—large integrated firms and smaller minimills. The big integrated firms—U.S. Steel, the former Bethlehem Steel, and others—use blast furnaces to create steel from raw inputs and then shape it into various products. Production is concentrated in Pennsylvania, Ohio, and West Virginia, and labor is represented by the United Steelworkers of America. The management and unions of Big Steel perpetually blame their problems on imports and are continually calling for import restraints to allow the industry to revitalize itself.

The smaller minimills take scrap steel and use electric-arc furnaces to produce various final products. Because they do not require iron ore and coal supplies, these firms are not geographically concentrated but spread around the country close to the markets they serve. Minimills have much lower costs than the big integrated steel firms, partly because their workers are not unionized. As a result, the minimills have grabbed U.S. market share away from the big integrated producers. The minimills accounted for about 10 percent of U.S. production in the late 1960s, but nearly 50 percent today. As the market share held by imports has remained steady at about 20 percent, almost all of the erosion in the market share held by the integrated producers is due to the minimills.

Thus, changes in market demand and competition from the minimills are mainly responsible for pushing the large, integrated steel producers into restructuring, which has increased industry productivity.[54] Unlike imports, this domestic competition cannot be stopped at the border and is slowly forcing the integrated producers to adjust. But the process has been prolonged in part due to import restraints and the recalcitrant steelworkers union. The strength of the "steel triangle"—the Big Steel firms, the United Steelworkers union, and their powerful representatives in the Congressional Steel Caucus—have ensured that the large producers continue to receive corporate welfare at the expense of taxpayers and con-

[54] Collard-Wexler and De Loecker 2015.

sumers. In 2002, for example, the Pension Benefit Guaranty Corporation, a U.S. government agency, took over the pension plans of several steel firms whose unfunded pension liabilities exceed $8 billion.[55]

The textiles and apparel industry has also used its political influence to maintain an array of barriers designed to stop foreign competition. The United States negotiated export restrictions on cotton textile products with Japan in the 1950s. Although these trade restrictions were designed as a temporary measure to give the industry some breathing space to become more efficient, the industry always complained that the protection was inadequate. Rather than being eliminated, the temporary restraints slowly spread to include other countries and products, gradually filling in the gaps from which imports were seeping in. The Short Term Arrangement on Cotton Textiles trade was signed in 1961, followed by the Long Term Arrangement on Cotton Textiles in 1962. Set to last for five years, the long-term arrangement was renewed for three years in 1967 and again in 1970. These trade restrictions were extended to wool and manmade textiles products in the first Multi-Fiber Arrangement in 1974. This was followed by the second MFA in 1978, the third MFA in 1982, and the fourth MFA in 1986, each of which continued to tighten the restrictions by expanding the country and product coverage. The MFA was finally abolished in 2005 (after a ten-year phase-out) over the strenuous objections of its proponents, but the industry has not given up the fight for more import restraints.

Unlike the large integrated steel producers, the textile and apparel industry has made some adjustments to compete against foreign imports. The textile industry has become less dependent upon unskilled labor-intensive production techniques by adopting advanced technology and more capital-intensive production methods (often using imported machinery). The consequent increase in productivity has sharply reduced industry employment. The apparel sector, which is less able to substitute capital for labor, has been harder hit and has turned to foreign outsourcing to remain competitive. Despite the plant closings and employment losses at the aggregate level, new firms have entered the industry, and within-plant productivity has increased in both textiles and apparel.[56]

---

[55] For an expose of steel's lobbying tactics and demands for corporate welfare, see Barringer and Pierce 2000.

[56] Levinsohn and Petropoulos 2001.

Despite the inefficacy of import protection in solving an industry's problems, many industries still identify imports as the problem and protection as the cure. Some have even claimed that temporary protection "played a major role in revitalizing key American industries" in the 1980s. For example, the steel and auto industries faced many difficulties in the early 1980s, but received import relief and by the late 1980s had significantly improved their output, employment, and productivity.[57]

This view of protection completely misrepresents the experience of the 1980s. Revitalization was in fact the result of the economic recovery after the recession of 1981–82, which at the time had been the worst economic downturn since the Great Depression. In addition, the appreciation of the dollar in the early 1980s squeezed import-competing and export industries, with relief coming when the dollar began to depreciate after 1985. To conclude from the 1980s that temporary protection is a proven method of boosting industrial competitiveness not only overlooks the more important macroeconomic context of that period, but also ignores the fact that foreign competition is precisely what motivated American manufacturers to cut costs and improve their productivity. Diminishing competition through import restraints takes the pressure off domestic industries and dulls their incentive to improve efficiency.

For example, let us consider the celebrated Harley-Davidson motorcycle case. Even today, this is frequently heralded as a great success of "breathing space" protection. The story, as conventionally told, is that in the early 1980s Harley-Davidson was pushed to the wall by Japanese competition. After receiving temporary import relief in 1983 under the Section 201 escape clause, the company got its act together and came back stronger than ever.[58] In fact, Harley recovered so swiftly that it even requested that the final year of tariff protection be canceled.

The real story is different: import relief had nothing to do with Harley-Davidson's turnaround. At the time, Harley-Davidson produced only "heavyweight" motorcycles with piston displacements of over 1000cc,

---

[57] Tonelson 1994. His article is entitled "Beating Back Predatory Trade," but it is absurd to think that the woes of the steel, automobile, and textile industries were due to foreign predatory practices.

[58] The company's management fully conceded that Harley's production process was far behind the cutting-edge Japanese manufacturing practices at the time the Section 201 petition was filed; see Reid 1990.

while Japanese producers mainly exported medium-weight bikes (700cc to 850cc of piston displacement) to the United States. But in 1975, Kawasaki opened a production plant in Nebraska, and in 1979, Honda opened a plant in Ohio, both of which produced heavyweight motorcycles to compete directly with Harley-Davidson. They did not produce them in Japan because there was virtually no market for such large motorcycles in Asia.

The deep recession of 1981–82 particularly affected blue-collar workers, the main consumer base for Harley's products, and put the company under severe financial pressure. So they filed for import relief under Section 201 in September 1982, making no allegation of unfair dumping or subsidies. The ITC had problems determining that imports were the substantial cause of Harley's injury because imports were plummeting from the recession too. They finally decided that Harley had been injured because unsold inventories of imported medium-weight bikes (700–850cc) were accumulating.[59] The ITC also ruled that Honda's Ohio plant and Kawasaki's Nebraska plant were part of the domestic industry that deserved protection.

The Reagan administration accepted the ITC's recommendation and adopted a tariff-rate quota on imports of motorcycles over 700cc. A tariff-rate quota allows a certain quantity of imports to enter paying the usual tariff, but imports above that quantity have to pay the higher protective tariffs. These were initially set at 45 percent and then declined over five years. The protection had almost no impact on Harley-Davidson because Honda and Kawasaki were already producing heavyweight motorcycles in the United States, production that was not constrained. In fact, Honda and Kawasaki favored the Section 201 case because it could protect them from their Japan-based rivals Suzuki and Yamaha. But even Suzuki and Yamaha were able to evade the tariff-rate quota on imports of motorcycles over 700cc: they simply produced a 699cc version that was not subject to the quota.[60] Then Suzuki and Yamaha had room under the quota

---

[59] The inventory of medium bikes accounted for 80 percent of all unsold motorcycles, and the inventory buildup was much less for models larger than 1000cc because of production cutbacks.

[60] Harley engineers purchased two imported motorcycles because they suspected that only the label on the engine had changed, but to their astonishment the engines were exactly 699cc! Reid 1990, 89.

to export a greater quantity of larger (1000cc) bikes before they had to pay the extra 45 percent duty.

Harley was deeply disappointed with the import relief. Because the final year of tariffs would have been very low and had virtually no effect on the motorcycle market, the company gave up the Section 201 relief a year before it was set to expire. Doing so gained Harley favorable publicity and helped convince President Reagan to visit a Harley plant in Pennsylvania, where he declared, amid a sea of red, white, and blue banners, that his administration was glad to lend Harley a helping hand.

Harley saved itself from bankruptcy and turned itself around because a new management team, appalled at the lax inventory control system and antiquated production methods, dramatically improved the efficiency of the production process. Close attention to production detail, as well as the rebounding economy, helped rejuvenate Harley's economic prospects. Blocking imports contributed virtually nothing to Harley's recovery. A recent counterfactual study of the episode found that the safeguard measures increased Harley's sales by just 6 percent.[61]

Thus, one should not be overly optimistic about the ability of trade protection to help sectors with adjustment problems more severe than coping with a temporary surge of imports. Whether import restraints actually assist the domestic industry in its adjustment efforts is a debatable proposition. But even if protection contributes little to adjustment, the escape clause has been a political necessity and has helped maintain domestic support for the open world trading system.

---

[61] Kitano and Ohashi 2009. Kitano 2013 also finds that the duties were not responsible for the adoption of new technology by Harley. As the chief economist of the ITC during this period later recalled, "If the case of heavyweight motorcycles is to be considered the only successful escape-clause case, it is because it caused little harm and it helped Harley-Davidson get a bank loan so it could diversify." Suomela 1993, 135. In 1986, the company bought a mobile home producer, Holiday Rambler Corp.

6

Developing Countries and Open Markets

Previous chapters have described the benefits of free trade and the costs of import protection, but many observers are skeptical that open trade policies can improve conditions in poor countries, where a majority of the world's population live. This chapter examines whether the case for free trade is qualified by the special circumstances of developing countries. Recent experience suggests that developing countries can reap substantial benefits from adopting more open trade policies, but that such policies alone do not guarantee development, particularly when corruption, civil conflict, excessive regulation, and other institutional failings prevent local entrepreneurs from taking advantage of world markets. This chapter also discusses whether protectionist trade policies contributed to the East Asian growth miracle, whether labor standards should be used to address worker exploitation in sweatshops, and whether "fair trade" offers a satisfactory route to development.

_____Trade Policy and Developing Countries

Until fairly recently, developing countries were reluctant to participate in world trade. Many people in poorer countries feared that rich countries would dominate and exploit them.[1] Powerful foreign multinationals, it was believed, would gain control of small economies unless governments restricted their activities. Furthermore, the prevailing view among economic experts in the 1950s and 1960s was that developing countries

---

[1] "It is sometimes difficult for sophisticated economists and politicians to understand the deep historic and cultural problems some [developing] countries have with the idea of free trade. Some still equate it with oppression from colonial days." This comment comes from Mike Moore, the former director-general of the WTO. Moore 2003, 133.

had limited opportunities to achieve growth through exports. International trade was expected to reinforce their comparative advantage in the production of simple primary commodities, thereby locking them into a pattern of specialization that would forever prevent their economic development.

Over the past three decades, these conclusions have been proven false. Countries that restricted foreign trade and investment may have avoided foreign exploitation, but remained desperately poor nonetheless. Meanwhile, international trade has created opportunities that have promoted economic development and reduced poverty around the world.[2]

It has taken a long time for many people to recognize the transformative power of commerce in improving the lives of the world's poor. Take Bono, the lead singer for U2, who has long been a passionate advocate of foreign aid for developing countries. Recent experience has forced him to change his tune, so to speak. In a speech at Georgetown University in November 2012, Bono talked about the tremendous progress that has been made in reducing poverty in recent years due to strong economic growth in the developing world. Then Bono paused. "Rock star preaches capitalism," he said disbelievingly. Putting his hand on his head, he smiled sheepishly: "Wow, sometimes I hear myself and I just can't believe it!" "But commerce is real," he continued, "aid is just a stopgap. Commerce, entrepreneurial capitalism takes more people out of poverty than aid, of course we know that."[3] But, in fact, he and many others did *not* always know that. Bono admitted that it had been "a humbling thing for me" to realize the importance of capitalism and entrepreneurship in reducing poverty, particularly as someone who "got into this as a righteous anger activist with all the clichés."[4]

However, as a legacy of the past, developing countries have struggled to overcome severe trade-related policy distortions, including high tariffs, quantitative restrictions on imports and exports, overvalued exchange rates, and administrative controls on foreign exchange allocation. Politi-

---

[2] Krueger (1997) provides an excellent analysis of how the old view of trade and development, based on erroneous assumptions and expectations, eventually gave way in the face of contrary evidence.

[3] http://www.youtube.com/watch?v=PUZFgBqcYt8, at 38:13 mark.

[4] http://www.forbes.com/sites/parmyolson/2012/10/22/bonos-humbling-realizations -about-aid-capitalism-and-nerds/ (accessed June 18, 2014).

cally powerful interest groups, including state-owned enterprises that fear competition and government bureaucrats whose power is derived from their decision-making authority, have fiercely resisted trade liberalization and often have been able to block trade reforms. As a result, even after many developing countries have reduced tariffs and liberalized trade policies, they still have much higher tariffs than developed countries. As table 3.1 showed, import tariffs in developed countries are less than 5 percent, on average, while those in developing countries are substantially higher, in the range of 10 to 30 percent, on average. Although developing country tariffs are significantly lower than a decade ago, these tariffs are often just the tip of the iceberg, as many of these countries have in place significant nontariff barriers to trade. Thus, there is ample room for further reforms of trade policy in the developing world.

Of course, free trade is not the single most important factor behind economic development. For many countries, reforms in other areas may be of greater importance and hence a more urgent priority. These include ensuring the security of property rights, providing legal institutions that support market transactions (e.g., enforcing contracts), and encouraging the development of financial markets. In many instances, these goals can be achieved not by proactive government policies, but by eliminating poor policies and counterproductive practices: the government should not arbitrarily confiscate or expropriate goods or property, should not protect monopolies and create obstacles to new business formation, should not scare off foreign investors with uncertainty about taxes, should not suppress financial markets with heavy-handed regulations, and so forth. Other nontrade reforms may require proactive government policies, such as investing in infrastructure and transportation networks and improving public health and access to schools.

Still, trade policy reforms can play an important contributing role in promoting development. Recent experience has demonstrated that reducing trade barriers can bring about striking improvements in economic performance. This in turn leads to improved socioeconomic outcomes, including the reduction of poverty, malnutrition, and infant mortality.

Consider the following statement:

History makes a mockery of the claim that trade cannot work for the poor. Participation in world trade has figured prominently in many of the most successful cases of poverty reduction—and, compared with aid, it has far more potential to benefit the poor. . . . Apart from financial benefits, export growth can be a more efficient engine of poverty reduction than aid. Export production can concentrate income directly in the hands of the poor, creating new opportunities for employment and investment in the process. . . . Experience from East Asia illustrates what is possible when export growth is broad-based. Since the mid-1970s, rapid growth in exports has contributed to a wider process of economic growth which has lifted more than 400 million people out of poverty. In countries such as Vietnam and Uganda, production for export markets has helped to generate unprecedented declines in the levels of rural poverty. Where export growth is based on labour-intensive manufactured goods, as in Bangladesh, it can generate large income gains for women. . . . The benefits of trade are not automatic—and rapid export growth is no guarantee of accelerated poverty reduction. Yet when the potential of trade is harnessed to effective strategies for achieving equitable growth, it can provide a powerful impetus to the achievement of human development targets.

This statement did not come from a globalization cheerleader, but from Oxfam, the British charitable organization that is also very critical of the current system of world trade.[5] Oxfam is among the growing number of nongovernmental development organizations recognizing that open-trade policies enable countries to benefit from the growth of world trade.

The conclusions expressed in Oxfam's statement are supported by empirical analyses of the relationship between trade and growth focusing specifically on developing countries. One study examined the top one-third of all developing countries in terms of the increase in their trade-to-GDP ratio since 1980. These countries—the "globalizers"—cut import tariffs by twice the margin of nonglobalizers and experienced a 5 percent annual increase in real per capita income, whereas the other developing countries—the "nonglobalizers"—saw only a 1.4 percent annual increase in real per capita income.[6] As the authors note, "There are many interesting pair-wise comparisons between the globalising group and the nonglobalising group: Vietnam versus Burma, Bangladesh versus Pakistan,

---

[5] Oxfam 2002, 8–9.
[6] Dollar and Kraay 2004.

Costa Rica versus Honduras. In each of these cases, the economy that has opened up more has had better economic performance."

Indeed, greater trade openness—marked by rising trade and low or declining trade barriers—has been a feature of virtually all rapid-growth developing country experiences in the past fifty years.[7] A more recent study of developing countries found "a significant correlation between tariff reductions and growth acceleration, one that is strong for tariffs on capital and intermediate goods and much weaker for consumption tariffs." In fact, the "liberalizers" grew 1 percentage point more than the "non-liberalizers," a difference that rapidly cumulates to much higher incomes over time.[8]

It is sometimes believed that globalization has been imposed on countries. Yet globalization is also a choice. Through their trade and foreign investment policies, countries can choose the degree to which they want to be a part of the world economy. Cambodia, Vietnam, and Uganda have embraced the world market and have seen their trade-to-GDP ratios soar. Meanwhile, trade has shrunk as a part of the economies of Egypt, Nigeria, and the Dominican Republic. Some of these declines may be due to political instability, macroeconomic mismanagement, or reduction in demand for country-specific goods (such as Zambia's copper), but some also represent government policies that deliberately hinder the ability of citizens to participate in the world economy. For example, Pakistan has an export- (or import-) to-GDP ratio of only about 15 percent, a fraction of what it is for many export-oriented developing countries. The country's own policies have stifled trade and kept this ratio artificially low. Many parts of the world that chose not to participate in the world economy have succeeded in being marginalized.

The greatest example of a country turning its back on the world economy is China in the fourteenth century. The imperial court prohibited any foreign trade (without official permission) for about two centuries after 1371, even going so far as to forbid the construction of new seagoing ships in 1436. While these efforts did not completely eliminate trade, they severely curtailed it at a time when Chinese merchants were very active in the Indian Ocean and Africa. China's action did not stop globalization.

[7] Panagariya 2004.
[8] Estevadeordal and Taylor 2013.

But China lost its technological leadership and fell very far behind the rest of the world in military and commercial strength. Eventually it fell prey to political domination by the West in the nineteenth century.

That lesson still holds true today: countries that deliberately seek to isolate themselves from the world will only find their living standards falling behind those of other countries. The failed, autarkic state of North Korea is a sad reminder of this fact. In the Middle East, too, many countries have resisted joining the world economy. At the time of the September 11, 2001, attack on the World Trade Center and Pentagon, Saudi Arabia, Iran, Iraq, Syria, Afghanistan, Algeria, and other countries in the region had one thing in common: they were not members of the World Trade Organization. With over 150 members, the WTO is not an exclusive club that has shunned them. Instead, these countries did not (until recently) feel compelled to become part of the club, a symptom of their disengagement with the rest of the world.[9] According to the UN's Arab Human Development Report, many societies in the Middle East are closed, their economies stifled, their peoples repressed. They do not encourage business formation or welcome foreign investment, the exchange of goods across borders, or even international trade in ideas. According to the report, the Arab world translates about 330 foreign books annually, one-fifth of the number that Greece alone translates. Perhaps not surprisingly, the report found that one in two Arab youths is dissatisfied with the prospect of living in a closed society and has expressed a desire to emigrate.[10]

In other countries, macroeconomic mismanagement has led to increasingly restrictive trade policies that cut their markets off from the rest of the world. For example, both Argentina and Venezuela have suffered from overvalued currencies in recent years. They have sought to maintain a fixed exchange rate even though high domestic inflation warrants a depreciation of the exchange rate; as a result, the black market exchange rate is very different from the official exchange rate. An overvalued currency makes domestic goods more expensive relative to foreign goods. That kills exports by pricing the country's goods out of the world market. It also leads to excessive spending on imports. To bridge the gap between

[9] Lindsey 2001.
[10] United Nations Development Program 2002, 30.

falling exports and rising imports, while seeking to maintain the artificially high value of their currency, governments often clamp down on spending on imports by using quotas and bureaucratic allocation of foreign exchange. These heavy-handed interventions not only suppress trade, but they also severely distort markets, leading to widespread shortages, growing corruption, and other unfavorable consequences.[11]

Indeed, in South America, there is an interesting experiment taking place between countries that face the Pacific Ocean and those that face the Atlantic Ocean. The Pacific countries—Mexico, Peru, Chile, and Colombia—have embraced economic liberalization and freer trade. The Atlantic countries—Brazil, Argentina, and Venezuela—are suspicious of globalization and continue to have the government play a large role in resource allocation. So far, the Pacific countries have experienced much better economic performance—stronger growth and growing trade—than the Atlantic countries.[12]

_____Two Billion People—China and India

Perhaps the most compelling examples of how more open trade policies can facilitate economic growth and development come from the two most populous countries in the world—China and India. Over the past quarter century, both countries have shifted from economic isolation to economic integration with the rest of the world. Both countries have been growing rapidly and have made remarkable strides in reducing poverty and raising the standards of living of their citizens.

Before 1979, China was virtually closed to world trade. China's trade operated under a strict system of state trading in which about a dozen foreign trade corporations monopolized all international trade. China followed a Soviet-style system of central planning that made import-substitution industrialization (replacing all imports with domestic production) an overriding objective. Imports were minimized and exports were authorized only to the extent required to pay for imports.[13] The policy

---

[11] On overvalued exchange rates and protectionism, see Schatz and Tarr 2002.

[12] David Luhnow, "The Two Latin Americas: A Continental Divide between One Bloc that Favors State Controls and Another that Embraces Free Markets," *Wall Street Journal*, January 3, 2014.

[13] "To achieve the goal of a self-reliant industrial economy, domestic industry was pro-

succeeded in building up domestic manufacturing, but investments in capital-intensive heavy industries failed to improve the welfare of China's citizens.

In December 1978, China began to end its policy of economic isolation. Under the leadership of Deng Xiaoping, the government decollectivized agriculture, freed foreign exchange transactions, allowed private entities to trade, and permitted foreign investment. Although reforms were gradually introduced over the 1980s and 1990s and went well beyond trade policy alone, the opening of China's economy to the world was a critical component of these changes. In 1992, the weighted average tariff on manufactured goods was over 45 percent. Since China joined the WTO in 2001, the country's average tariff will fall to less than 7 percent.[14]

The results have been stunning. China's exports and imports have soared, as figure 3.1 illustrated. China's share of world trade rose from about 1 percent in 1980 to more than 11 percent in 2013. Foreign investment in China has grown from virtually nothing in 1980 to more than $1.3 trillion in 2012. More importantly, as figure 6.1 shows, China's real per capita income has grown at near double-digit rates since the 1980s, making it one of the fastest-growing countries in the world. The dashed line shows China's growth path based on the trend prior to 1979, suggesting that the reforms made an enormous difference to the country's income. As a result of the rapid growth, the poverty rate fell from 84 percent in 1981 to 13 percent in 2008.[15]

Of course, China did not just open up to trade, it fundamentally changed the way its economy was organized. Yet the decision to open to the world was not inevitable; it had a large internal market and could have pursued import substitution or industrial policies in a different way. But its trade policy reforms were a vital component of its broader reforms and have played a critical role in its economic success.

India is another example of a country that dramatically improved its economic performance after moving to freer trade policies. For about

---

tected from foreign competition by direct controls on imports and investment and administrative allocation of foreign exchange combined with an overvalued currency. These policies, enforced by central planners and a central foreign trade monopoly, built an airtight wall between the domestic economy and the world economy" (Shirk 1994, 8).

[14] Ianchovichina and Martin 2004, 9.

[15] www.worldbank.org/enn/china/overview#3 (accessed January 21, 2015). See also Ravallion and Chen 2007 and Bhagwati and Srinivasan 2002.

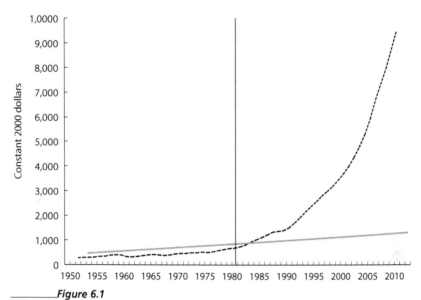

_____*Figure 6.1*

Real per Capita GDP in China, 1952–2012

Source: International Monetary Fund, International Financial Statistics.

four decades after becoming independent in 1947, India pursued a policy of self-sufficiency and industrial planning that required elaborate and complex import restrictions. Importing anything that was not explicitly on a government list of approved items was forbidden. Imports of "nonessential" consumer goods were banned, and those deemed "essential" (food, pharmaceuticals, etc.) were imported and sold only by state agencies. A labyrinth of government requirements—permissions, licenses, and certifications—had to be met before intermediate and capital goods could be imported. This became known as the "license raj" because a license, or government permit, often involving multiple stages, was required to do just about everything, from importing spare parts to expanding the size of one's business.

Bureaucrats and politicians justified these draconian policies on several grounds. Government control over industry and trade was deemed necessary to conserve resources and eliminate wasteful competition. The scarcity of capital was held to justify government approval for investment projects. The shortage of foreign exchange, it was believed, meant that hard currency should be allocated by government officials rather than by the market to ensure its use for projects in the "national interest." The fear of foreign domination lurked behind many of these policies and created resistance to market-based solutions in favor of government-directed ones.

Unfortunately, the outcome was a disgrace—sluggish growth, persistent poverty, inefficient industry, and lagging modernization. The system was deeply corrupt because government officials had to be bribed to get anything done. One estimate puts the value of rents created as a result of the trade restrictions at 5 percent of India's GDP—something very much worth fighting over.[16] According to one quip, India suffered under four hundred years of British imperialism and fifty years of the Fabian socialism of the London School of Economics—and it is not clear which did more damage.[17]

However, an economic crisis in 1991 forced reluctant policymakers to undertake a radical shift in policy.[18] India abandoned parts of its central planning system and abolished the requirement of government permission for all industrial investment expenditures, with some exceptions. Indian firms were permitted to borrow on international capital markets, the rupee was devalued and made convertible, quantitative restrictions on imports were abolished, export subsidies were eliminated, and import duties were slashed from an average of 87 percent in 1990 to 33 percent in 1994. After further cuts, those tariffs are currently about 13 percent. Nontariff barriers covered 95 percent of all imports in 1988 but just 24 percent in 1999.[19] The "license raj"—the rigid and complex system of import controls and foreign investment restrictions administered by government bureaucrats—was dismantled, unleashing the private sector from red tape but also exposing it to international competition.

The outcome has been astonishing. As figure 6.2 shows, growth in real per capita income in India began to pick up in the mid-1980s, when some

[16] Krueger 1974. This figure is just the value of the import licenses. When industrial licensing and other controls are included, Mohammad and Whalley (1984) put the value of rents at 30–45 percent of GDP in the early 1980s.

[17] In the early and middle twentieth century, the London School of Economics was home to Fabian socialist ideas that influenced generations of Indian policymakers (Moore 2003, 132).

[18] The collapse of communism and China's success in opening up its economy also helped convince Indian policymakers that state planning was a failure.

[19] Srinivasan and Tendulkar 2003, 33–39.

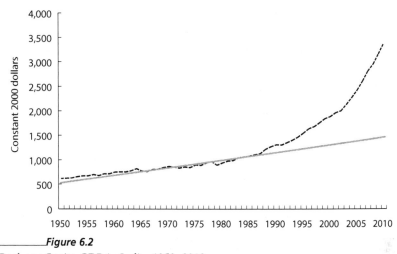

_____**Figure 6.2**

Real per Capita GDP in India, 1950–2012

Source: International Monetary Fund, International Financial Statistics.

tentative steps toward reducing import barriers and investment controls were taken, and accelerated after 1991.[20] (The dashed line indicates India's pre-reform-growth path.) The reduction in trade barriers has also been linked to higher productivity; by one estimate, India experienced a 20 percent increase in aggregate productivity growth and a 30–35 percent increase in intraplant productivity following tariff liberalization.[21] Most important, the poverty rate has fallen from 46 percent in 1983 to 36 percent in 1993–94 to 27 percent in 2004–05, improving the lives of tens of millions of Indians.[22]

The power of economic reform is illustrated by considering seven entrepreneurs who in 1981 started a small business in India with $250 of seed capital. The Indian government created huge obstacles to the setting up of the business. As one of the founders later recalled, "It took us a year to obtain a telephone connection, two years to get a license to import a computer, and 15 days to get foreign currency for travel abroad. . . . The first ten years of our marathon seemed interminable and

[20] Bhagwati and Panagariya 2013.

[21] Sivadasan 2009. There are numerous studies on the productivity effects of India's dismantling of the license raj; on the trade liberalization component, see Topalova and Khandelwal 2011 and Goldberg, Khandelwal, Pavcnik, and Topalova 2010.

[22] World Bank 2011, 5.

frustrating. Although we managed to keep our heads above water, we were floundering."

The lifeboat that rescued the firm and allowed it to flourish was India's deregulation and economic liberalization in 1991. That firm is Infosys Technologies Ltd., now one of the largest and most successful software companies in the world, and that entrepreneur is N. R. Narayana Murthy, the chairman and CEO of Infosys. According to Murthy, the economic reforms of 1991 "changed the Indian business context from one of state-centered, control orientation to a free, open market orientation, at least for high-tech companies." That allowed the company to grow so that it could eventually employ thousands of Indians at relatively high wages. "We at Infosys . . . have never looked back," Murthy says. "The lesson from the Indian experience is a clear clarion call for all who are willing to listen: free trade can bring great benefits to society."[23]

China and India provide dramatic illustrations of the improvement in economic circumstances that can result when poor economic policies are replaced with better ones, particularly with respect to international trade. Higher incomes translate into tangible improvements in the well-being of millions of people. This improvement in well-being cannot be measured in terms of dollars and cents alone, but in the lives that are saved as a result of moving people away from the knife edge of poverty, where a bad harvest or the loss of a job can spell malnourishment or even death. Hunger and malnutrition, illiteracy, and infant mortality persisted for decades after China adopted central planning in 1949 and India received political independence in 1947. Because of the economic opportunities that opened up after the 1978 and 1991 reforms in China and India, respectively, hundreds of millions of people have had a chance to join the middle class.

Thus, the higher income that comes with freer trade is important not just for crass material reasons, but because it can lead to a better life. With higher incomes, families can pay for more and better food, gain access to medicines and better healthcare, and afford schooling for their children. One study examined the direct connections between trade openness and a society's health outcomes, specifically infant mortality and life expectancy. Even after controlling for a country's per capita income, average

---

[23] Murthy 2001.

years of schooling, number of doctors per capita, and other factors, people in countries with lower tariffs had longer life expectancy and experienced lower infant mortality. For example, an eleven-percentage-point reduction in the tariff rate—a change of about one standard deviation in the sample—is associated with between three and six fewer infants dying per thousand live births.[24] Such findings are a powerful reminder of the life-and-death stakes of good and bad economic policies.

The tragedy of India is that, by delaying economic reforms for so many decades, it contributed to the impoverishment of its people for so long. One Indian businessman writes with dismay the following:

> Most people remember the Emergency [suspension of democracy between 1975 and 1977] because it represented a generalized loss of liberty. They do not understand that by suppressing economic liberty for forty years, we destroyed growth and the future of two generations. For the average citizen it was a great betrayal. Lest we forget, we lived under a system where a third of the people went hungry and malnourished, half were illiterate while the elite enjoyed a vast system of higher education, and one of ten infants died at childbirth. Our controls and red tape stifled the entrepreneur and the farmer, and the command mentality of the bureaucrat, which fed the evil system, continues till today to frustrate every effort at reform."[25]

India has paid a very heavy price in human lives for delaying its reforms. But what China and India have accomplished is stunning. Though both countries still have a long way to go, the improvement in human well-being achieved over the past generation is mind-boggling.

Of course, not all of the improved economic performance of China and India can be attributed to more liberal trade policies. China moved away from a system of central planning and collective agriculture, while India freed up bureaucratic obstacles to domestic investment. Nonetheless, trade reforms were a key component of the overall economic reforms. Both countries deliberately shifted from closed economies to ones more open to world trade.

[24] Wei and Wu 2003.
[25] Das 2001, 175.

Trade Policy Reform: Successes and Failures

China and India are dramatic examples of the tangible benefits of economic reform and international trade. On a smaller but no less dramatic scale, other developing countries have changed their economic orientation to the world and have seen improvements in economic performance.

In the mid-1960s, Korea completely changed its trade strategy. The proportion of items automatically approved for import went from zero in June 1964 to 63 percent by December 1965. Korea's currency (the won) was devalued by nearly 50 percent, and a unified exchange rate was adopted. In 1967, many import quotas were abolished and tariffs were sharply reduced. The effective tax on imports fell from nearly 40 percent in 1960 to 8 percent by 1967. Figure 6.3 shows the marked acceleration in Korea's growth of per capita income from around the time of these changes.[26] Indeed, one study suggests that Korea's tariff reductions can explain one-third of the country's catchup to developed countries in terms of output per worker in manufacturing.[27]

In the mid-1970s, Chile also sharply changed its trade policy. Between 1975 and 1979, Chile eliminated all quantitative restrictions and exchange controls and reduced import tariffs from over 100 percent to a uniform 10 percent. After suffering a severe recession due to a banking crisis in the early 1980s, Chile continued trade liberalization. The payoff materialized in a 7 percent average annual growth rate for more than a decade after 1986 and fairly consistent 4–5 percent growth since then.[28]

In the middle and late 1980s, Vietnam adopted economic reforms that helped increase economic growth to an average of more than 7 percent in the late 1990s and early 2000s. As in China, agricultural land reform helped jump-start the growth process, but trade and foreign investment have been important components of Vietnam's success. The poverty rate has been slashed in a remarkably short time. The share of the population living in absolute poverty fell from 75 percent in 1988 to 58 percent in 1993 to 29 percent in 2002 to 15 percent in 2008.[29] The opening of trade contributed directly to this process since exports of

---

[26] Frank, Kim, and Westphal 1975, 75.
[27] Connolly and Yi 2015.
[28] Edwards and Lederman 2002.
[29] World Bank 2012, 17.

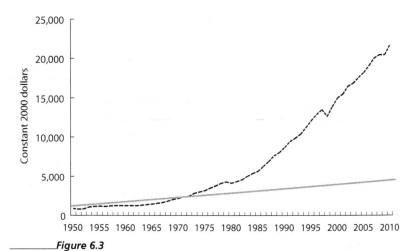

_____***Figure 6.3***

Real per Capita GDP in South Korea, 1953–2011

Source: International Monetary Fund, International Financial Statistics.

rice and labor-intensive manufactured goods are produced by poor households. After the implementation of a U.S.-Vietnamese trade agreement in 2001, Vietnam's exports to the United States doubled in 2002 and again in 2003. Those regions of Vietnam that gained the most from the new market access to the United States also experienced the most poverty reduction.[30]

Is it misleading to draw attention to a handful of success stories and conclude that trade liberalization is broadly beneficial? Are figures 6.1–6.3 simply illustrating a few extreme cases? Not entirely, because a more systematic empirical study looked at the major liberalization episodes around the world between 1963 and 2005 and came to a similar conclusion.[31] The study compared the path of income in a liberalizing country to a counterfactual path of income based on a "synthetic control" group of countries in the same region that did not liberalize. The authors found that "economic liberalization in some countries is associated with a remarkable positive effect on real income." In fact, the study produced many different figures, similar to those just presented, that show large income gains (relative to a plausible counterfactual) for such countries as Barbados, Colombia, Costa Rica, Mauritius, Botswana, and Kenya, among

[30] McCaig 2011. On Vietnam's transition, see Dollar and Ljunggren 1997.

[31] Billmeier and Nannicini 2013.

others. Unfortunately, the study also finds "a lot of heterogeneity in the results across regions and time" with late liberalizers (such as those in Africa and the Middle East that attempted reforms in the early 2000s) not faring as well as early liberalizers.

Indeed, not all countries that have liberalized their trade policies have enjoyed such dramatic successes as those mentioned above.[32] For example, Mexico significantly reduced tariffs and other trade barriers when it joined the GATT in 1985 and signed free trade agreements with the United States and Canada (NAFTA) in 1994 and the European Union in 2000. As a result, Mexico's trade and foreign investment increased significantly. The share of trade (average of exports and imports) in GDP rose from 13 percent in 1985 to 32 percent in 2013. These reforms improved productivity in industries exposed to international competition, as described in chapter 2.

However, Mexico's overall macroeconomic performance has been disappointing since NAFTA.[33] Economic growth, employment growth, and wage growth have all been undistinguished since the early 1990s. NAFTA opponents blame open trade for Mexico's problems. These critics say that NAFTA has harmed farmers and is responsible for the lack of improvement in the standard of living of workers.

The real source of Mexico's malaise is macroeconomic. In December 1994, about a year after NAFTA went into effect, and for reasons not related to the trade agreement, Mexico faced a speculative attack on the peso and was forced to devalue its currency. The peso crisis stemmed from an inconsistency between Mexico's monetary policy and its commitment to maintain a fixed exchange rate. The peso devaluation was a severe setback that slashed real wages overnight and sent the economy into a deep recession.

By keeping trade flows moving, NAFTA helped the Mexican economy through a difficult period. The continued expansion of trade promoted the country's recovery from this traumatic shock. Yet after the initial rebound, the Mexican economy remained weak. The reason for this disappointing performance was a persistent and severe credit crunch, in-

[32] Milner 2013 questions whether falling average tariffs might overstate the extent to which protectionism has actually declined in some developing countries.

[33] Kehoe and Ruhl 2010.

cluding a deterioration in contract enforceability and an increase in non-performing bank loans. Indeed, Mexico's credit-to-GDP ratio fell from 49 percent in 1994 to 17 percent in 2002, preventing any broad-based economic recovery.[34]

A decade after NAFTA went into effect, a Carnegie Endowment for International Peace study concluded, "Put simply, NAFTA has been neither the disaster its opponents predicted nor the savior hailed by its supporters." The report also noted that "NAFTA has accelerated Mexico's transition to a liberalized economy without creating the necessary conditions for the public and private sectors to respond to the economic, social, and environmental shocks of trading with two of the biggest economies in the world."[35] This suggests that other complementary policies are required if trade liberalization is to succeed in improving welfare, a point that will be discussed later.

The twentieth anniversary of NAFTA in 2014 has prompted many reassessments of the agreement.[36] What is sometimes missed in rehashing the old debate is that, despite financial crises, drug violence, and the Zapatista rebellion on the southern Mexican state of Chiapas, Mexico is doing reasonably well. The World Bank reports that 17 percent of Mexico's population joined the middle class between 2000 and 2010 and that measures of inequality have fallen.[37] Furthermore, illegal immigration into the United States from Mexico has dropped to almost zero over the past decade.

While there are good reasons to be optimistic about Mexico's future, its experience, unfortunately, is not unique. Other developing countries significantly reduced tariffs in the 1990s but also have not performed well. In Latin America, Colombia cut its tariffs by more than half in 1991, while Argentina and Nicaragua reduced them from over 100 percent to just 15 percent in one stroke in 1992. In Africa, Kenya reduced its import duties from over 40 percent in the early 1980s to under 15 percent by the late

---

[34] Tornell, Westermann, and Martinez 2004; Kose, Meredith, and Towe 2004; Maurer 2006.

[35] Audley, Papademetriou, Polaski, and Vaughan 2004, 6.

[36] Those critical of the agreement twenty years ago, including groups such as the AFL-CIO, Public Citizen, and the Economic Policy Institute, have called it a "disaster," while supporters continue to defend it. See Hufbauer, Cimino, and Moran 2014.

[37] Ferreira, Messina, Rigolini, López-Calva, Lugo, and Vakis 2013.

1990s.[38] Yet the people of these countries have not seen a dramatic improvement in their standard of living.

This disappointing performance is sometimes interpreted as indicating that trade liberalization and increased integration with the world have failed to help developing countries and that therefore the strategy should be abandoned. This is the wrong conclusion to draw. In the case of Argentina, for example, monetary and macroeconomic instability—arising from excessive borrowing abroad and the resulting buildup of foreign debt—have had devastating effects far beyond any good that open trade could bring. Colombia and other countries have had to endure "shock therapy" to end hyperinflation and hemorrhaging budget deficits, forcing the economy through wrenching adjustments that overwhelmed the impact of trade liberalization. Until the mid-1990s, the overvaluation of West African currencies tied to the French franc severely constrained the ability of West African countries to stimulate growth through exports.[39] Domestic conflict in many of these countries has also deterred investment and has prevented the full benefits of trade from being realized.

In its review of the economic reform and growth experience of the 1990s, the World Bank conceded that "the results of trade reforms have varied and sometimes fallen short of expectations."[40] It went on to say,

> Trade reforms are most likely to stimulate growth when they are part of a comprehensive strategy. Important elements of an effective growth strategy can include sound macroeconomic management, building of trade-related infrastructure and institutions, economy-wide investments in physical and human capital, greater access to developed and developing country markets, and maintenance of a sound rule of law. Because these elements are often difficult to implement, there has

---

[38] World Bank 2001, 51.

[39] "Liberalization of trade in Argentina in the 1980s and 1990s, and in Chile in the early 1980s, for example, was accompanied by an appreciation of the real exchange rate, which reduced the competitiveness of domestic industries and incentive to export—with adverse consequences for the balance of payments and real economy. In many countries of the former Soviet Union and some in Eastern Europe in the 1990s, trade was liberalized while property rights were not well defined and the institutional base for a market economy was not well developed. These, and other institutional issues preventing the free movement of resources, often meant that trade reforms did not expand economic opportunities but restricted them instead" (World Bank 2005a, 137).

[40] World Bank 2005a, 131, 137–38.

been excessive emphasis on trade policy alone, rather than as a component of an overall growth strategy.

One important lesson is that excessive regulation and a poor domestic business environment may prevent trade liberalization from stimulating growth. One study reports that increased openness to trade leads to higher incomes in flexible economies, but not in heavily regulated ones. Specifically, a 1 percent increase in trade is associated with a 0.5 percent rise in per capita income in countries that allow the free entry of firms into sectors that they choose, but has no positive impact on income in countries that restrict business entry.[41] If excessive regulations prevent resources from moving to the economy's most productive sectors and firms, then trade liberalization will fail to improve incomes. A sound domestic environment for business is required for countries to take full advantage of policy reforms that encourage global trade. Highly regulated economies are likely to perform better if they sweep away domestic impediments to economic activity before embarking upon trade reforms.[42]

Indeed, in some developing countries, administrative controls and poor infrastructure may be more important obstacles to trade than tariffs alone. Inefficient customs and tax administration have hampered exporters who require imported components and materials for production. For example, a business in the Central African Republic has to take fifty-seven days to complete all the export formalities, submitting eight documents to different government agencies, and spend $4,581 before a container can leave the port in Yaoundé, in neighboring Cameroon. In Angola, a ship arriving in the port of Luanda must wait an average of eight days before landing, a delay that can stretch to fourteen days during the rainy season. It is estimated that each additional day that an export product is

---

[41] Freund and Bolaky 2008.

[42] The World Bank has started to examine the high costs of business regulation in developing countries. "It takes two days to start a business in Australia, but 203 days in Haiti and 215 days in the Democratic Republic of Congo. . . . A simple commercial contract is enforced in 7 days in Tunisia and 39 days in the Netherlands, but takes almost 1,500 days in Guatemala. The cost of enforcement is less than 1 percent of the disputed amount in Austria, Canada, and the United Kingdom, but more than 100 percent in Burkina Faso, the Dominican Republic, Indonesia, the Kyrgyz Republic, Madagascar, Malawi, and the Philippines" (World Bank 2004, xiii).

delayed reduces exports by more than 1 percent, and the effect on time-sensitive agricultural exports is even more dramatic.[43]

High transport costs and poor infrastructure can prevent trade liberalization from boosting trade in low-income developing countries. Landlocked countries are at a particular disadvantage in world trade since land transport charges have been estimated to be seven times greater than sea transport costs. Studies have found that higher transport costs and weak infrastructure explain much of Africa's poor trade performance.[44] For example, in sub-Saharan Africa, transport costs are five times greater than tariff charges.

Simply chopping import tariffs does not in itself solve these problems. If goods are stranded for weeks at port, or roads are impassable due to the rainy season, cutting tariffs from 20 to 10 percent will not make much difference. As formal barriers fall, the quality and reliability of transport infrastructure (including roads, railways, airports, and seaports) and related services (including telecommunications and business services such as finance and insurance) are increasingly critical to trade. Indeed, one study suggests that developing countries can expand exports more effectively by focusing on trade costs "behind the border" (domestic transport and customs administration) than on trade costs "at the border" (tariffs and quotas).[45]

For this reason, trade facilitation has become a priority in international forums such as the World Trade Organization. Trade facilitation is simply the logistics of moving goods through customs and includes such mundane things as port efficiency, inspections and documentation, transparency of government regulations, and so on. Some policy changes can make a difference. For example, in the early 1990s Argentina began allowing private firms to operate public ports and invest in their infrastructure. As a result, cargo handling increased 50 percent between 1990 and 1995 and labor productivity surged, making Argentine ports among the cheapest in Latin America.[46]

In sum, trade liberalization is not a magic bullet guaranteed to bring about rapid growth in trade and higher incomes. The right conclusion to

---

[43] World Bank 2007, 44–45.
[44] Limão and Venables 2001.
[45] Hoekman and Nicita 2011.
[46] World Trade Organization 2004, Box IIB.5.

draw is that the case for free trade requires a caution: other policies in developing countries can prevent the full benefits of trade liberalization from being realized. Many other factors—political conflicts, macroeconomic instability, a poor domestic business environment—can stand in the way of the beneficial effects of trade and can prevent freer trade from yielding the ultimate payoff of higher living standards.

[handwritten margin note: Other factors against trade (liberal.)]

_____Industrial Policy and the East Asian Miracle

Despite the success that many countries have had with trade liberalization, developing countries still fear the consequences of opening their markets to the world. The old concerns about foreign domination and imports destroying important domestic industries continue to exist. Many people still cling to the view that import substitution and protecting infant industries is the right approach to promoting development.

Import substitution refers to a deliberate policy of encouraging domestic production of manufactured goods in place of imports. Such policies were common in the 1950s and 1960s when industrialization was viewed as the key to economic development. Such policies often succeeded in building up capital-intensive industries and sometimes led to high rates of output growth. But they often failed to improve standards of living because the high investment rates required to maintain growth in the capital stock detracted from growth in consumption. In the case of China prior to 1979, about a third of national income had to be reinvested to maintain growth in the capital stock, leaving little left over for consumers.[47]

[handwritten margin note: more production NOT always better]

These policies often turned out to be self-inflicted wounds. In many instances, capital-intensive industries were unsuited for developing economies that had a comparative advantage in labor-intensive industries. The former required ongoing government support to function profitably. By

[47] "One consequence of this rising capital intensity of production was that gains in per capita consumption were very modest for a country in which per capita output grew relatively rapidly. Between 1957 and 1977, per capita national income rose at an average annual compound rate of 3.4 percent in real terms. Yet, because the share of output that had to be reinvested to sustain that rate of growth rose by fully one-third (from 25 percent in 1957 to an average of 33 percent in the 1970s), improvements in real living standards were quite modest" (Lardy 1992, 34).

sheltering firms from import competition, protectionist policies inhibited export growth and firms became inward-looking, focusing on the domestic rather than the world market. This resulted in small and inefficient firms, since the domestic market was not large enough or competitive enough to promote firms that would be successful on the world market. India is the classic example of a country that built up many manufacturing industries by sheltering them from foreign competition, but failed to deliver a high standard of living to its people.

Although import substitution is widely acknowledged to have failed in comparison to export-promoting policies, export promotion may mean something more than free trade. Many observers point to the stunning growth of several East Asian countries and point to government industrial policies as the key to their success. The economic achievements of Japan in the 1960s and the "four tigers"—South Korea, Taiwan, Singapore, and Hong Kong—in the 1970s have raised new questions about free trade. Many contend that, with the exception of Hong Kong, these countries grew rich not because of free trade, but through wise government use of selective protection and targeted industrial policies.[48]

These countries did many things right—they enjoyed peace and political stability, encouraged high savings and investment rates, emphasized the importance of education and human capital accumulation, provided stable macroeconomic and exchange rate policies, and so on. Korea and Taiwan also pursued important land reforms early in their transition that led to rapid productivity growth in agriculture. In other words, these East Asian countries enjoyed many favorable conditions noticeably absent elsewhere, particularly in Latin America and Africa.

With the exception of Hong Kong, however, these countries did not pursue policies of nonintervention with respect to industry. To varying degrees, governments were involved in the allocation of capital and other resources to promote industrialization, and even employed the tools of trade protectionism. Some observers have concluded that because the Japanese and Korean governments intervened in their economies to promote certain industries, their economic performance can be attributed to these interventions. In this view, the East Asian experience illustrates how

---

[48] Wade 2004. For a recent critique of industrial policy, see Pack and Saggi 2006.

wow! success 'another way'

careful industrial policy and protectionism, not free trade, promote economic development.

Yet there are reasons to be skeptical about this conclusion. It is always tempting to reach a conclusion about causality on the basis of correlation, reasoning that because Japan or Korea intervened in its economy or used protectionist trade measures, the success of the economy is due to that policy. But assessing the contribution of industrial policy to economic growth is a difficult challenge. In a 1993 report on the East Asian miracle, the World Bank noted that

HARD TO PROVE THIS CONNECTION

> their interventions did not significantly inhibit growth. But it is very difficult to establish statistical links between growth and a specific intervention and even more difficult to establish causality. Because we cannot know what would have happened in the absence of a specific policy, it is difficult to test whether interventions increased growth rates.[49]

That is a wishy-washy conclusion, but it makes a fair point. When several factors promoting a good outcome exist simultaneously—a stable political environment, a good educational system, high savings and literacy rates, and so on—it becomes difficult to determine the precise contribution of any one specific factor, such as industrial policy, to the outcome. One cannot rule out the possibility that government intervention actually detracted from the economic success of the country but was more than offset by the other good forces.[50]   *but can't confirm it as reason*

In the case of Japan, the country's success after World War II is sometimes attributed to the selective interventions by the Ministry of International Trade and Industry (MITI). MITI used "administrative guidance" to promote investment in and acquire technology for selected industries. Some argue that MITI was involved not just in "picking" winners by di-

[49] World Bank 1993, 6.

[50] As Adam Smith once opined, "The uniform, constant, and uninterrupted effort of every man to better his condition, the principle from which public and national, as well as private opulence is originally derived, is frequently powerful enough to maintain the natural progress of things towards improvement, in spite both of the extravagance of government and of the greatest errors of administration. . . . But though the profusion of government must, undoubtedly, have retarded the natural progress of England toward wealth and improvement, it has not been able to stop it" (Smith [1776]1976, 343, 345).

verting resources to selected high-growth industries, but in "making" winners by ensuring their success on international markets.

But the actual evidence on MITI's contributions to Japan's success is weak. The two industries that achieved the most notable success on world markets—automobiles and consumer electronics—did not benefit from extensive government support, unlike some other heavy industries such as chemicals and steel. MITI also had notable failures in promoting its biotechnology and computer industries. In fact, one statistical study of Japanese industrial targeting found that a disproportionate amount of support went to low-growth sectors and sectors with decreasing returns to scale. This study failed to find evidence that productivity was enhanced as a result of industrial policy measures.[51]

Qualitative studies of Japan's policies lend support to this skeptical view. The consulting firm McKinsey concluded that robust domestic competition was a source of Japan's success. In many instances, MITI did not foster but actually tried to reduce competition by forming domestic cartels. (In the case of automobiles, for example, it discouraged Honda from entering the market in the 1950s, thinking that there were already too many firms in the industry.) However, in the case of machine tools, MITI helped standardize tolerances used in machines, thereby allowing large-scale assembly of machine tools and applied electronics technology. As one McKinsey analyst reported, "In all our studies of Japan, this is the only action by MITI that we found to have had a significant beneficial impact on the Japanese economy."[52] If this is MITI's one success, the importance of MITI has been vastly overrated.

South Korea may provide a better example of government industrial policy. Under the military dictatorship of Chung Hee Park, the Korean government employed competent technocrats who were directly involved in economic planning and investment allocation. These bureaucrats were insulated from political decisions and thus did not fall prey to corruption. The principal tool at their disposal was directed credit, which they used to promote capital-intensive industries such as chemicals, steel, and shipbuilding. While the government was involved in strategic decisions about

---

[51] Beason and Weinstein 1996. Ohashi (2005) finds that there were few intra-industry knowledge spillovers in the case of Japan's steel industry and that export subsidies did not help the industry's growth.

[52] Lewis 2004, 40.

the economy, it did not implement those decisions through state-owned firms or nationalized industries. Rather, once the government and private sector negotiated economic goals and the means to carry them out, the private firms were responsible for executing them. Furthermore, these firms were not insulated from competition; instead, they were encouraged to export and face the full brunt of international competition.

[handwritten: not any protectionism]

Still, as described earlier in this chapter, what jump-started the Korean economy in the mid-1960s was not industrial policy, but other reforms, including trade and exchange rate policy. One can also question the contribution of the technocrats to Korea's rapid growth since that time. Despite the government's emphasis on building up heavy capital-intensive industries, light labor-intensive industries increased productivity at a more rapid rate during the 1960s and 1970s. Indeed, during the 1970s, the most rapid growth in sectoral shares of value added occurred in lower-wage or low value-added per worker sectors.[53] Furthermore, as in the previously mentioned study of Japan, measures of Korean industrial policy (such as tax incentives and subsidized credit) are not correlated with productivity growth at the industry level.[54] Korea's use of directed credit to promote industrial growth has also led to problems. Korean industry suffered from gross overinvestment and was far too reliant on capital-intensive production methods. Nonperforming loans and weakness in the banking and financial system are related to major economic crises in 1979–81 and 1997–98.

[handwritten: Hang]

Several points stand out from the Korean experience. First, private firms were not shielded from competition but rather exposed to it and forced to meet the test of international markets. The reforms that put Korea on the path of export-led industrialization "did not achieve this result by the conventionally prescribed approach, which is to reduce greatly (if not eliminate) the domestic market's insulation from import competition."[55] Second, bureaucrats were insulated from political pres-

[handwritten: It wasn't that]

---

[53] Dollar and Sokoloff 1990; World Bank 1993, 314.

[54] Lee 1996. Another study concludes that Korea implemented an industrial policy property, promoting infant industries rather than mature ones, but that it failed to pay off because it distorted prices too seriously for too long (Lee 2011).

[55] Rather, it established a "virtual free trade regime for export activity" that also "entailed tremendous openness to imports of raw materials, intermediate inputs, and capital goods" (Westphal 1990, 44).

sures to allocate resources to politically favored projects. The implementation of plans took place by relying on free market institutions and was negotiated with, not imposed on, private firms.

Because of the special historical, political, and cultural circumstances of Korea, even a leading proponent of the view that Korea's economy benefited from government industrial policy has concluded that "one has to be extremely skeptical about the prospects for replicating the Korean government's use of selective intervention."[56] Indeed, the political prerequisites for such judicious intervention are lacking in other Southeast Asian countries, such as Malaysia, Thailand, and Indonesia. The economies of these countries have performed well in recent decades, but corruption and rent seeking have given industrial policy there a bad name. In these countries, industrial policy is virtually synonymous with arbitrary interventions to help out political cronies. However, these countries have also welcomed foreign investment in labor-intensive export industries and have not sought to promote investment in heavy industry to the same degree as Japan or Korea.

The big difference between industrial policy in Japan and Korea as opposed to Malaysia and Indonesia is "export discipline," according to one observer. Export discipline is a policy of "tough love"—giving firms protection and credit subsidies only if they export their goods and meet the test of the global market. If the firm fails, it forfeits its access to government assistance. In this sense, Japan and Korea "did not so much pick winners as weed out losers." But Southeast Asian countries did not enforce such a policy and firms slacked off. "Where export discipline has not been present, development policy has become a game of charades, with local firms able to pretend that they have been achieving world-class standards without having to prove it in the global market place. In Southeast Asia, the energies of entrepreneurs were directed towards fooling politicians [to maintain government support] rather than exporting."[57]

Thus, there is no single East Asian model of economic development. Singapore and Hong Kong are small island states, the latter pursuing an

---

[56] Westphal 1990, 42.

[57] Studwell 2013, 76–77. Simply put, "In Korea, infant industry protection combined with export discipline, plus competition among multiple entrants, made manufacturing policy highly effective in securing technological upgrading. In Malaysia, industrial policy without export-discipline and with insufficient attention to the need to foster competition came unstuck" (Studwell 2013, 152).

almost pure free-market approach. Japan and Korea employed more activist industrial policies, but there is little evidence demonstrating their precise contribution (positive or negative) to the country's development. Malaysia and Indonesia have weaker political institutions that do not keep industrial policy free from corruption and rent seeking. Yet, for the most part, all of these East Asian countries have enjoyed macroeconomic stability, relied on private enterprise and market competition, stressed investment in human capital, and adopted outward-oriented policies rather than import substitution. These are the common elements cutting across the countries' vast differences.

A tentative conclusion regarding government's role in trade is that it should facilitate private-sector development. Most developing countries that have shifted from the production of primary products to nontraditional activities have done so with the cooperation of the public sector. The government is not picking the sectors into which resources should move, but should clear obstacles and reduce uncertainties relating to investment—in general, facilitate private-sector activities. Whether one considers Chile's diversification away from copper into fruits and salmon, Costa Rica and ecotourism, Bangladesh and garments, Colombia and cut flowers, governments have almost invariably played an important supporting role.[58]

Unfortunately, governments in many developing countries do not facilitate or support the private sector but instead create obstacles for its growth. Even worse, in many countries, particularly but by no means exclusively in Africa, economic success is best achieved by political power and connections rather than by commercial ability or effort.[59] Corrupt regimes that provide no security to market transactions and throw obstacles in the way of business formation and commerce are perhaps the single greatest problem in promoting economic development.[60]

---

[58] Hausmann and Rodrik 2003.

[59] Robert Guest, *The Economist's* Africa correspondent, argues that personal advancement in Africa is easier to achieve through political success than commercial success. In his view, to become rich, or even minimally prosperous, one must either seek political power or cultivate and become a client of those in power. The more that African bureaucrats and politicians extort and expropriate, the less there is to extort and expropriate, which makes the competition for power even more desperate and violent (Guest 2004).

[60] Adam Smith stated the following in a lecture in 1755: "Little else is requisite to carry a state to the highest degree of opulence from the lowest barbarism but peace, easy taxes, and a tolerable administration of justice: all the rest being brought about by the natural

Recent experience has demonstrated that the economic status of developing countries is not immutably fixed by nature. Neither the geography nor the institutions of China or India or Korea changed when they embarked upon their policy reforms, and yet their economies have been utterly transformed by changes in government policy. Unfortunately, economic policies that stifle development are still pervasive around the world.

_____Sweatshops and Labor Standards

Foreign investment has played a big role in bringing China and other Asian countries into the world trading system. Multinational companies have invested in low-wage developing countries to produce inexpensive labor-intensive goods, such as clothing and shoes, and assemble consumer electronics, such as smart phones and laptops. So how do you feel about wearing an inexpensive shirt or carrying a phone that was probably produced by workers in China or Southeast Asia who toiled for long hours with low pay? Are Nike and Apple earning large profits by exploiting cheap labor in Asian sweatshops?

Many people feel uncomfortable when they think about the workers producing the goods they buy. Consequently, concerned citizens in developed countries have protested against low wages and poor working conditions in developing countries. The Worker Rights Consortium, established by students, unions, and human rights groups, accuses leading multinationals of employing workers in unsafe, sweatshop conditions while failing to pay a living wage. Working conditions in many developing countries are indeed horrible by the standards of developed countries—recent factory fires in Bangladesh have reminded us of this fact—and the world community wants to see those standards of living improve. The question is how best to accomplish that objective.

Do low wages reflect the exploitation of labor and thereby give developing countries an unfair advantage in trade? In general, the answer is no. Workers in developed countries enjoy high wages and benefits be-

course of things. All governments which thwart this natural course, which force things into another channel, or which endeavour to arrest the progress of society at a particular point, are unnatural, and to support themselves are obliged to be oppressive and tyrannical" (Smith 1980, 322). Unfortunately, all too many developing countries lack these three simple requirements.

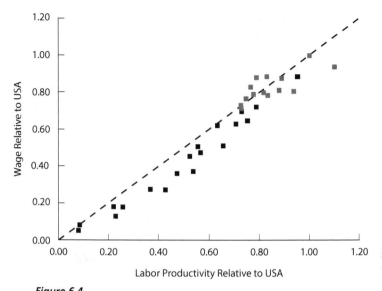

_____*Figure 6.4*

Labor Costs and Productivity in Manufacturing for Thirty-Three Countries, 2000
Source: Marshall 2012.

cause their labor productivity is high. By contrast, workers in developing countries get paid lower wages because labor productivity is lower. Figure 6.4 illustrates the strong relationship between wages and labor productivity (both relative to the United States) for a diverse group of thirty-three countries in 2000. The correlation is striking: the higher a country's overall labor productivity, the higher the country's average wages. In this case, productivity explains 97 percent of the variation in relative wages across countries.[61] Statistical analysis has regularly shown that labor productivity alone explains about 70–80 percent of the cross-country variation in average wages in manufacturing.[62]

Figure 6.4 simply confirms the thesis of a book published more than two centuries ago, Adam Smith's *Wealth of Nations*. Smith argued that

[61] Marshall 2012.

[62] After also accounting for differences in per capita GDP and in price levels across countries, over 90 percent of the variation in wages between countries can be explained. Even though these purely economic variables explain virtually all of the differences in wage rates across countries, Rodrik (1999) finds that indicators of political freedom also contribute some additional explanatory power.

labor productivity, through the division of labor and the extent of the market, determines a country's national income, and therefore differences in labor productivity across countries account for differences in incomes across countries. The implication is simple and straightforward: the way to increase a country's standard of living–as measured by its average wage—is to increase the productivity of its workforce. Not everyone thinks it works that way. Some observers have feared that countries such as China will adopt better technology and increase labor productivity but somehow keep wages low. The combination of highly productive workers and very low wages will give those countries a crushing cost advantage on world markets, putting downward pressure on the wages of workers in the developed world. But as Paul Krugman has noted, "Economic history offers no example of a country that experienced long-term productivity growth without a roughly equal rise in real wages. . . . The idea that somehow the old rules no longer apply, that new entrants on the world economic stage will always pay low wages even as their productivity rises to advanced-country levels, has no basis in actual experience."[63]

Indeed, the rapid increase in Chinese wages in recent years simply confirms this observation. As developing countries improve the productivity of their workers, through the accumulation of capital and the acquisition of better technology, they become more valuable and competitive pressure bids up the average wage. As a result, the growth in domestic wages tracks the growth in domestic productivity. In chapter 4, we saw that this is true in the United States (see figure 4.8) and it is true in other countries as well. As figure 6.5 shows, the acceleration of productivity in South Korea in the 1980s was accompanied by a dramatic rise in labor compensation. By contrast, the Philippines has been much less successful at increasing productivity and therefore has not seen a comparable rise in wages. The evidence is clear: countries that successfully increase productivity will experience a rise in wages, while countries whose productivity is stagnant will see little change in wages.

Still, the best and most direct way to raise wages and labor standards is to enhance the productivity of the workers through economic development. Trade and investment are important components of that devel-

[63] Krugman 1996, 56.

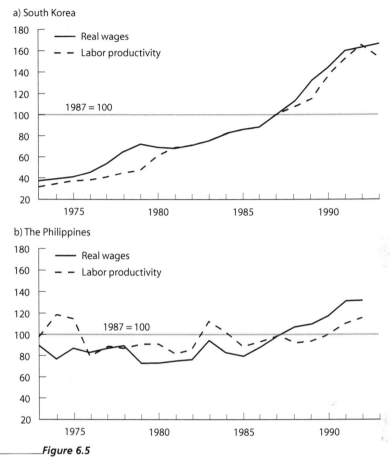

_____**Figure 6.5**
Real Wages and Labor Productivity in Manufacturing, South Korea and the Philippines, 1973–1993
   Sources: World Bank 1975 and updates from World Development Indicators.

opment, and therefore efforts to limit trade or to shut down factories are counterproductive. In fact, most foreign-owned firms pay substantially higher wages than comparable domestic firms.[64] And these wages are often many multiples of what the workers would have earned if they had stayed toiling in rural agricultural villages, which is where many urban

[64] See Aitken, Harrison, and Lipsey (1996) for a study of foreign firms in Mexico, Venezuela, and the United States. Lipsey and Sjöholm (2001) show that foreign-owned firms in Indonesia pay higher wages than locally owned firms.

factory workers come from. In Vietnam, for instance, while the general population (mainly employed in agriculture in rural areas) could afford per capita expenditures of $205 in 1998, people working in foreign-owned businesses spent $420 that year.[65] Poverty rates are much lower for those holding jobs with foreign-owned firms. While 37 percent of the Vietnamese workers were classified as poor in 1998, only 8 percent of those working in foreign-owned businesses were considered poor. And although 15 percent of all workers were classified as "very poor," none of the workers in foreign-owned textile and leather-goods businesses were in that category. In Cambodia, foreign-owned factories not only pay their workers more but also offer better working conditions than other factories.[66]

The fact that foreign-owned "sweatshops" in poorer countries pay above-average wages in the local labor market may explain the low turnover (or quit) rate of workers at such firms. It may also explain why these jobs are so desirable that, in some instances, workers must pay one month's salary as a bribe to employment officers at such firms in order to get hired. And even though the wages are low by Western standards, the savings rate of factory workers is much higher than that of workers elsewhere in the economy—an interesting fact in light of the accusation that such firms are not paying a living wage. In Vietnam and elsewhere, workers often request overtime because they are seeking to maximize their income. International codes and rules that limit hours of work may interfere with the desire of these individuals to earn more money.

Even if the wages and working conditions in developing countries are dismal by the standards of the present-day United States, these multinational firms are at least providing employment opportunities and incomes that might not otherwise exist, enabling the poor to support their families. Two reporters for the *New York Times* provide a vivid example. When they were first assigned to cover Asia, they, like most people, were outraged at the sweatshop conditions. They later changed their opinion:

> In time, though, we came to accept the view supported by most Asians: that the campaign against sweatshops risks harming the very people it

[65] Glewwe 2000.

[66] Warren and Robertson 2011.See also Robertson, Brown, Pierre, and Sanchez-Puerta 2009.

is intended to help. . . . Those sweatshops tended to generate the wealth to solve the problems they created. . . . It may sound silly to say that sweatshops offer a route to prosperity, when wages in the poorest countries are sometimes less than $1 per day. Still, for an impoverished Indonesian or Bangladeshi woman with a handful of kids who would otherwise drop out of school and risk dying of mundane diseases like diarrhea, $1 or $2 a day can be a lifetransforming wage."[67]

Most sweatshop workers are young women, many of whom have migrated from rural villages to industrial cities. By Western standards, they endure long hours, low pay, and poor conditions. And yet, despite the monotony of factory work, they found it a vast improvement over the back-breaking monotony of field work, according to a sociologist who lived with migrant factory workers in southern China. Many of these women earned seven to eight times what their fathers earned working in rural agriculture in their home villages, and could send money back to their families.[68] Yet the motivation for these young women leaving their home was much more than financial. They left behind a patriarchal order in which their father could marry them off to the village idiot without their say in the matter. With their factory work, they gained freedom and independence, as well as dignity and self-respect. It enabled them to spend their life and their money the way they wanted, such as shopping, going to see a movie, or taking English or computer classes at night—things that would have been impossible in their rural communities.

Activist groups have sometimes improved working conditions by putting companies in the spotlight of bad publicity if their contractors treat workers poorly in developing countries.[69] But the fundamental problem facing workers in developing countries is not the existence of sweatshops, but the lack of good alternative employment opportunities. Efforts to stop exports from low-wage countries, to prevent investment there by multinationals, or to impose high minimum wages or benefits beyond the productivity level of the domestic workforce will simply diminish the

---

[67] Kristof and WuDunn 2000, 70–71.

[68] Lee 1998.

[69] Harrison and Scorse 2010 find that real wages go up for workers in firms that are targeted, but firm investment sometimes falls. Elliott, Kar, and Richardson (2004) examine the views of activists in developed countries that are pressing for better treatment of labor in developing countries.

demand for labor in those countries and take away one of the few opportunities that workers have to better themselves and their families. Those who simply want to shut down sweatshops have failed to consider what alternative opportunities for employment can be created.[70] In fact, one immigrant from Cambodia told me that the term "sweatshop" is a complete misnomer. In comparison to the hot, humid conditions of agricultural work, where you stand exposed to the sun in muddy fields and have to rip leeches off your legs every few hours, a factory is one of the few places in Cambodia where a person doesn't sweat so much.

What about importing goods made with child labor? While the United States prohibits imports of goods made with forced or indentured child labor, it does not have a generic ban on imported goods made with underage workers. Some activists have suggested that developed countries should refuse to import any goods made with child labor. But just as trade policy is an inefficient instrument for achieving environmental objectives, as chapter 2 suggested, it is also an inefficient instrument for improving labor standards. An import ban on goods made with child labor might stop the use of children to produce goods for the U.S. market, but it would not put an end to child labor. Only about 5 percent of working children are employed in the export sector in developing countries. An import ban might simply shift them to other sectors of the domestic economy (about 80 percent are employed in the primary agricultural sector). At worst, an import ban could push them into less desirable or more hazardous work, or even leave them without work and thereby condemn them to starvation.[71] Import bans fail to address the root cause of child labor or offer any resolution to the underlying conditions that create it.

The most effective way of eliminating child labor is to attack the fundamental causes, which are poverty and the lack of affordable or adequate educational opportunities. As figure 6.6 indicates, the incidence of child labor is strongly related to per capita GDP. In fact, about 80 percent

---

[70] For a comprehensive discussion of sweatshops, see Powell 2014.

[71] "Caroline Lequesne of Oxfam, a British charity, has just returned from Bangladesh, where she visited factories to determine the impact of American retailers' human-rights policies. She reckons that between 1993 and 1994 around 30,000 of the 50,000 children working in textile firms in Bangladesh were thrown out of factories because suppliers feared losing their business if they kept the children on. But the majority of these children have, because of penury, been forced to turn to prostitution or other industries like welding, where conditions pose far greater risks to them." *The Economist*, June 3, 1995, 59.

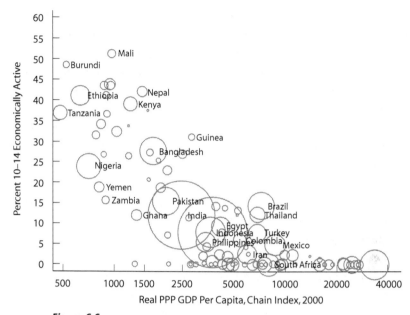

_____*Figure 6.6*
Child Labor and GDP per Capita, 2000
Source: Edmonds and Pavcnik 2005.

of the international variation in child labor is explained by this variable alone. Child labor virtually disappears once a country's annual per capita income reaches $5,000. Developing countries can help reduce child labor by raising rural incomes through agricultural price liberalization. Evidence from Vietnam suggests that when the domestic price of rice rose after the government permitted more rice exports, farmers responded by reducing the use of child labor.[72] Developed countries can help developing countries raise their income by allowing them to sell their products more easily in the markets of the richer economies. Compulsory education laws that mandate school attendance have also proven effective in reducing child labor and are more easily monitored than direct bans on imports.

Meanwhile, labor unions in developed countries have a different set of concerns. Organized labor has long maintained that countries with lower labor standards have an unfair competitive advantage in trade and that

[72] Edmonds and Pavcnik 2006.

they attract jobs and investment at the expense of countries with higher standards. In developed countries, labor unions and other NGOs have pressed for explicit and enforceable labor standards—including minimum wages, employment hours, occupational health and safety regulations, minimum age of employment, worker rights to organize, and so on—in trade agreements. Without these economic standards, they argue, workers in developing countries will be exploited and those countries will attract investment and gain jobs at the expense of developed countries, which will then face pressures to reduce labor standards, starting a race to the bottom.

There are several issues here. First, do poor labor standards enable a country to export more than it might otherwise? There is little empirical evidence that low labor standards, in themselves, exert an important influence on trade flows. Several studies have failed to find a strong relationship between measures of labor standards and international trade flows (such as export performance in labor-intensive goods) or direct investment flows (such as whether countries with low standards attract more foreign investment).[73] The OECD has concluded that "empirical findings confirm the analytical result that core labor standards do not play a significant role in shaping trade performance. The view which argues that lowstandard countries will enjoy gains in export market shares to the detriment of highstandard countries appears to lack solid empirical support."[74]

Second, would enforceable labor standards in trade agreements help workers in developing countries? In fact, the threat of trade sanctions to enforce labor standards in developing countries risks harming the very workers we are trying to help.[75] As Paul Krugman puts it, "Even if we

[73] See, for example, Rodrik 1996.

[74] OECD 1996, 33. The OECD (2000, 33) concluded that "this finding has not been challenged by the literature appearing since the 1996 study was completed."

[75] For example, insisting upon the right to form a union would not help many workers in developing countries. As Srinivasan (1998, 76) has noted, "For an overwhelming majority of poor workers in developing countries whose dominant mode of employment is selfemployment in rural agricultural activities or in the urban informal sector, unionization has little relevance. Even where relevant and where the freedom to form unions has been exercised to a significant extent, namely in the organized manufacturing and public sector in poor countries, labor unions have been promoting the interests of a small section of the labor force at the expense of many."

could assure the workers in Third World export industries of higher wages and better working conditions, this would do nothing for the peasants, day laborers, scavengers, and so on who make up the bulk of these countries' populations. At best, forcing developing countries to adhere to our labor standards would create a privileged labor aristocracy, leaving the poor majority no better off."[76] At worst, those export industries would be shut down, causing those workers to lose their jobs.

Furthermore, the threat of using trade sanctions to enforce labor standards is precisely why developing countries are so afraid of including them in the WTO. In the 1990s, the U.S. government fought to include labor standards in trade agreements. Developing countries strenuously objected to any linking of trade policy and labor standards. They feared that if developed countries are allowed to restrict imports from countries deemed not to have adequate labor standards, they will have yet another excuse for denying low-wage countries access to their markets, thereby preventing developing countries from taking advantage of their comparative advantage in labor-intensive goods. They also fear that that if labor standards are written into trade agreements, it will simply become another avenue by which developed countries can block their trade.

They have a point. In the past, American unions have opposed liberalization of trade even with countries that signed an agreement governing labor standards.[77] For example, unions such as UNITE, the Teamsters, and

[76] Krugman 1998a, 84. Economic development is the only known way to increase wages. The alternatives—massive foreign aid, stronger demands for social justice—are unrealistic or ineffective. As Krugman comments, "As long as you have no realistic alternative to industrialization based on low wages, to oppose [trade and industrialization] means that you are willing to deny desperately poor people the best chance they have of progress for the sake of what amounts to an aesthetic standard—that is, the fact that you don't like the idea of workers being paid a pittance to supply rich Westerners with fashion items."

[77] In January 1999, the United States signed an agreement with Cambodia that promised a 14 percent increase in Cambodia's annual quota for textile shipments if the country agreed to meet certain core labor standards. Although the Cambodian garment industry established high minimum wages and agreed to paid vacations, unionization rights, and a ban on child labor, the Union of Needletrades, Industrial and Textile Employees (UNITE) wrote to the U.S. Trade Representative (USTR) opposing any increase in the quota. Following this, and without consulting other views, USTR ruled in December 1999 that Cambodia was not in "substantial compliance" with the agreement and denied the quota increase. The Cambodian government and garment industry were shocked because they believed they had gone beyond the agreement in improving standards. Five months later, USTR agreed to a smaller increase, of 5 percent, after Cambodia and the ILO established a program to moni-

the AFL-CIO also opposed legislation that gave African countries the same tariff preferences that the United States had previously extended to Caribbean and other poor developing countries. The African Growth and Opportunity Act of 2000 aimed to help the continent by giving duty-free access to the U.S. market in selected goods. The proposal to allow African textile producers duty-free access to the U.S. market proved to be quite controversial even though Africa's share of U.S. apparel consumption was only 0.45 percent. Instead of being viewed as a small way of helping African countries improve their economies and improve their competitive position relative to China, laborbacked opponents dubbed the legislation as "NAFTA for Africa" and fought its passage through Congress.[78] Their staunch opposition to freer trade with Africa fueled suspicions that labor unions are not really interested in helping poor African workers deeply mired in poverty, but simply oppose any measure that might increase trade.

Because of strong developing country opposition, the WTO membership agreed that labor standards should not be a part of multilateral negotiations. Indeed, the membership agreed that the International Labor Organization (ILO) is the proper forum for international discussion of labor issues.

Experience has shown that it is all too easy to mask an antitrade agenda with labor and environmental concerns, as is evident by many anticommercial NGOs and antiimport labor unions. This is regrettable because there are deep and legitimate questions about using trade measures to enforce labor and environmental standards, and therefore the possibility of common ground gets lost in the advocacy of extreme positions. Yet there are inherent flaws in giving the WTO a non–trade related mission, such as enforcing environmental agreements or regulating labor standards. The risk is that these poorly targeted and indirect instruments for improving environmental and labor conditions will fail to achieve their objective yet at the same time will expand the allowable rationales

---

tor work conditions. Helene Cooper, "A Trade Deal Helps Cambodian Workers, But Payoff Is Withheld," *Wall Street Journal*, February 28, 2000.

[78] The U.S. International Trade Commission concluded that the impact of removing the quota on the U.S. apparel industry would be negligible and that, at most, only 676 U.S. jobs would be affected. U.S. International Trade Commission 1997, 3–12.

for trade barriers, thus undermining the liberal trading system without generating compensating benefits.

_____*Fair Trade*

While developing countries have yet to reach their full potential in large part because of their own policies, trade barriers and subsidies in the developed world have not helped matters. Development NGOs have excoriated the developed countries for keeping their markets closed to imports from developing countries. Oxfam's website says that "rich countries and powerful corporations have captured a disproportionate share of the benefits of trade, leaving developing countries and poor people worse off." The reason, they say, is that trade rules and trade policies are skewed against the world's poorest countries. As an Oxfam report cries out, "The harsh reality is that [developed country] policies are inflicting enormous suffering on the world's poor. When rich countries lock poor people out of their markets, they close the door to an escape route from poverty."[79]

This statement is exaggerated but contains some truth. Whether it is closed markets for agricultural goods, high barriers on the importation of labor-intensive manufactures, or efforts to require poor countries to adopt more stringent labor standards, many developed country policies are contrary to the interests of developing countries.

In terms of agriculture, the rich countries of the OECD maintain high trade barriers for agricultural products and heavily subsidize their farmers. For every dollar earned by OECD farmers, about 18 cents comes from government policies. In 2013, the OECD subsidized domestic farm producers by $257 billion, of which $114 billion came from high prices resulting from tariffs and export subsidies and $143 billion was transferred by taxpayers through government payments to farmers.[80] The value of transfers to OECD farmers is greater than the entire GDPs of many developing countries. Because these domestic subsidies and trade barriers have a huge impact on world agricultural markets, they in turn

[79] Oxfam 2002, 5.
[80] OECD 2014, 71.

affect low-income developing countries, where agriculture is a very large sector, employing about 60 percent of the labor force and producing about 25 percent of GDP.

Studies have shown that the reduction of agricultural tariffs and trade barriers by OECD and developing countries would produce substantial benefits for both sets of countries. If high-income countries alone opened their markets to imported agricultural goods, their welfare would rise by almost $32 billion and developing country welfare by $12 billion (2001 dollars).[81] Most of the benefits of trade liberalization accrue to the developed countries themselves because their consumers are footing most of the bill. (Similarly, if developing countries reduced their own agricultural trade barriers, which are often much higher than those in developed countries, they too would capture most of the benefits for themselves.)

However, the same mutual benefit does not hold true if industrial countries eliminated domestic and export subsidies to their agricultural producers. Many developing countries are net importers of agricultural goods and actually benefit from these subsidies. Because these subsidies reduce the prices of the goods that they buy on world markets, many developing countries would lose by their elimination. If high-income countries eliminated domestic and export subsidies without touching import barriers, then those countries would gain $3 billion in welfare, but developing countries as a whole would lose nearly $1 billion.[82] The gains from eliminating agricultural subsidies accrue mainly to the country that eliminates the subsidy.

Thus, from the perspective of developing countries, there is a strong stake in reducing barriers to agricultural trade in developed countries and in their own country as well. (As table 3.1 showed, developing countries impose very high tariffs on agricultural imports.) However, the impact of removing developed country export subsidies has more varied effects on developing countries depending upon whether one is a net importer or net exporter of those goods. If one cares about poor consumers in developing countries, then low prices for agricultural goods is desirable; if one

[81] Hertel and Keeney 2006.

[82] Hoekman, Ng, and Olarreaga (2004) similarly find that a 50 percent cut in tariffs improves welfare for industrial, developing, and least-developed countries alike, but a 50 percent cut in domestic subsidies helps industrial countries but harms developing and least-developed countries.

cares about poor farmers in developing countries, then high agricultural prices are desirable. (Developing countries seem to care more about producers, given the tight restrictions they impose on agricultural imports.)

However, an overall liberalization of all policy instruments by developed countries would increase household income among the poor in developing countries.[83] The greater market access to rich-country markets would compensate the poorer countries for the higher food prices they would have to pay on some products. Indeed, research has shown that eliminating border measures such as tariffs would produce changes in world prices that are many times greater than the benefits from eliminating domestic agricultural subsidies.[84] Thus, from the standpoint of agricultural-exporting developing countries, market access (lower import barriers) is much more valuable than domestic subsidy reduction in developed countries.

Still, subsidies to specific crops can impose tremendous hardship on poor farmers in particular developing countries. Cotton is a prime—if exceptional—example. In recent decades, the United States and European Union have heavily subsidized their domestic cotton growers. In the mid-2000s, the government lavished up to $4 billion per year on subsidies to America's 25,000 cotton farmers, with 80 percent of the subsidies going to the top 10 percent of all farmers. This was more than the entire GDP of the West African country of Burkina Faso. The European Union also subsidized cotton producers by almost $1 billion per year.

World cotton prices fell by more than half between 1997 and 2002, although they have rebounded since then. The United States accounts for about 20 percent of world cotton production, and so any expansion of U.S. production tends to reduce the world price. These subsidies inflicted great harm on cotton producers in Central and West Africa and elsewhere, intensifying poverty in already very poor countries. At the time, cotton exports accounted for 40 percent of exports in Burkina Faso and Benin and 30 percent of exports in Uzbekistan, Chad, and Mali. Cotton also accounts for over 5 percent of GDP in these countries.[85] Because cotton has been such an important source of foreign exchange earnings for these countries, any decline in the world market price—due to subsi-

[83] Hertel, Keeney, Ivanic, and Winters 2007.
[84] Hoekman, Ng, and Olarreaga 2004.
[85] Baffes 2005.

dies or other reasons—has had a tremendous negative ripple effect through their economies. During this particular period, the livelihood of more than 10 million poor farmers was at stake. The elimination of U.S. cotton subsidies was estimated to reduce U.S. production by more than 25 percent, reduce U.S. exports by nearly 40 percent, and increase world cotton prices by about 12 percent. This would translate into a gain of roughly $80 million in producer surplus for the four key cotton exporting nations in Africa.[86]

Brazil objected to the American subsidies and filed a case with the WTO in 2002, which two years later ruled that the U.S. subsidies violated the Agreement on Agriculture. The United States did not bring its policy into compliance with the ruling and, in 2010, the WTO authorized Brazil to retaliate against $830 million of U.S. exports. To prevent this from happening, the United States reached an agreement with Brazil whereby it would pay $147 million per year to the Brazilian cotton growers association. In essence, American taxpayers began paying both U.S. and Brazilian cotton farmers! Finally, in October 2014, they settled the dispute when the United States agreed to make a final, one-time payment of $300 million and Brazil agreed not to take countermeasures or bring another WTO case while the current U.S. farm bill is in effect (until 2018).

In the case of manufactured goods, developed countries have low tariffs on average but much higher tariffs on labor-intensive manufactures, particularly textiles and apparel. These are precisely the goods in which developing countries have a comparative advantage. Developing countries have long complained about the Multi-Fiber Arrangement, but even with its abolition they still face very high tariffs on these goods. In the United States, for example, the exports of Cambodia, Bangladesh, and Sri Lanka, among the poorest countries in the world, faced an average tariff of about 15 percent. Meanwhile, the exports of Norway, France, and Germany faced an average tariff of 1 percent. In 2012, Bangladesh paid $732 million in customs duties to get its goods into the United States; France paid $383 million. Yet Bangladesh exported just $5 billion worth of goods, while France exported over $40 billion.[87]

---

[86] Alston, Sumner, and Brunke 2007.

[87] http://progressive-economy.org/2015/02/13/fact-sheet-u-s-tariffs-by-country-2012/ (accessed January 21, 2015).

U.S. policy does not deliberately attempt to stifle the trade of developing countries in favor of richer countries, but it does so implicitly by virtue of the tariffs it levies on different goods. Industrial products generally face very low import duties, whereas labor-intensive manufactured goods, such as clothing and consumer products, face much higher tariffs. The developing countries could have much better success in world trade if they did not confront these higher barriers in OECD markets. Indeed, recent reductions in trade barriers in developed countries have been shown to have a pronounced positive impact on export performance and economic growth in developing countries.[88]

One way that concerned citizens have attempted to help the rural poor in developing countries is through an initiative called "Fair Trade," which is designed to overcome the "injustice" of low market prices for agricultural commodities. Fair Trade organizations buy coffee, tea, cocoa, cotton, and other developing country exports at above-market prices as a way of giving poor farmers extra income. They certify the goods with the fair trade label and sell them to Western consumers who are willing to pay a higher price to help lift those farmers out of poverty, provide them with a more stable source of income, and encourage them to engage in environmentally sustainable cultivation.

The Fair Trade movement, as a purely voluntary venture on the part of buyers and sellers, is well-meaning. The question is whether it is effective in achieving its goals. Studies have shown that Fair Trade–certified producers do receive higher prices for their goods than conventional farmers.[89] However, the gains to these farmers are much lower than they appear once one takes into account the costly administrative process of becoming and staying certified, which requires multiple reports and audits. Furthermore, while the farmers who sell their goods may reap some benefit from the higher prices, their workers may not. A study of farming in Uganda and Ethiopia by development economists at the University of London for the United Kingdom's Department for International Development was "unable to find any evidence that Fairtrade has made a positive difference to the wages and working conditions of those employed in the production of the commodities produced for Fairtrade certified export in

---

[88] Romalis 2007.
[89] Dragusanu, Giovannucci, and Nunn 2014; Dammert and Mohan 2015.

the areas where the research has been conducted. . . . In some cases, indeed, the data suggest that those employed in areas where there are Fairtrade producer organisations are significantly worse paid, and treated, than those employed for wages in the production of the same commodities in areas without any Fairtrade certified institutions (including in areas characterised by smallholder production)."[90] The jury is still out, but this unfortunate conclusion raises questions about the value of the Fair Trade label.

In conclusion, growing world trade has presented developing countries with a tremendous opportunity to improve their own condition. Yet trade restrictions are much more extensive in the developing world than elsewhere. Much of the blame for the lack of development falls not on the people of these countries, but on their governments and their poor policies that inhibit economic activity. As the examples of India and China dramatically demonstrate, it is usually their own misguided policies, not actions taken by the rest of the world, that have been holding them back from achieving higher rates of economic growth and greater poverty reduction.

---

[90] Cramer, Johnston, Oya, and Sender 2014, 15–16. "This is the case for 'smallholder' crops like coffee—where Fairtrade standards have been based on the erroneous assumption that the vast majority of production is based on family labour—and for 'hired labour organization' commodities like the cut flowers produced in factory-style greenhouse conditions in Ethiopia."

7

The World Trading System: The WTO, Trade Disputes, and Regional Agreements

For almost seventy years, the General Agreement on Tariffs and Trade (GATT) has provided a system of world trade rules under which international trade has flourished. In 1994, the Uruguay Round of trade negotiations produced sweeping agreements to liberalize trade in agriculture and apparel and to extend trade rules to new areas such as services, investment, and intellectual property. In addition, the World Trade Organization (WTO) was established as a formal multilateral institution with stronger procedures for resolving disputes than the GATT had. This chapter examines the WTO as an institution, the controversies surrounding its dispute settlement decisions, and the stalled Doha Round of trade negotiations. Because the WTO membership has had difficulty in reaching new agreements, regional trade agreements have proliferated in recent years. The two biggest prospective agreements are the Trans-Pacific Partnership (TPP), involving the United States and other Pacific Rim countries, and the Transatlantic Trade and Investment Partnership (TTIP) between the United States and the European Union. This chapter will assess the pros and cons of these regional agreements.

The Origins of the GATT System

The motivation to establish a formal system of world trade rules came from the terrible experience of the Great Depression in the 1930s. The Depression was a worldwide economic disaster. Between 1929 and 1932, the volume of world trade fell 26 percent, world industrial production fell

32 percent, and unemployment in many countries topped 20 percent. As the slump intensified, countries responded by raising tariffs and imposing import quotas in a desperate attempt to insulate themselves from the worldwide economic collapse and boost domestic employment. Widespread protectionism—in the form of tariffs, quotas, foreign exchange restrictions, and the like—materialized overnight. These "beggar thy neighbor" policies sought to bolster one's own economy at the expense of one's trading partners by switching spending from foreign goods to domestic goods. Yet reducing imports proved to be a futile way of combating the economic downturn, because one country's imports were another country's exports. The combined effect of this global turn toward protectionism was a collapse of every country's exports, which merely exacerbated the world's economic problems.[1]

The United States bears some responsibility for these developments. During the 1928 election campaign, prior to the Great Depression, President Herbert Hoover called for increased tariffs on agricultural imports to help U.S. farmers. Once Congress started considering higher duties, however, things began to spin out of control. Logrolling coalitions pushed tariff rates higher and higher, resulting in the infamous Smoot-Hawley tariff of 1930. Warning of the adverse economic consequences of the high tariffs, more than one thousand American economists signed a petition urging President Hoover not to sign the bill. The warning was not heeded, and the Smoot-Hawley tariff helped push up the average tariff on dutiable imports to nearly 50 percent. While economic historians do not believe that the Smoot-Hawley tariff caused the Depression, the high tariffs contributed to the downward spiral of trade as other countries retaliated against the United States. The U.S. action made it easier for other countries to follow suit, thereby contributing to the worldwide rise in trade barriers.[2]

Out of the ruins of the Depression came a new approach to U.S. trade policy. At the request of President Franklin Roosevelt, Congress enacted the Reciprocal Trade Agreements Act (RTAA) in 1934. The initial RTAA authorized the president to enter into tariff agreements with foreign countries and to reduce import duties by no more than 50 percent. Although

---

[1] See Irwin 2012.

[2] For details on the Smoot-Hawley tariff, see Irwin 2011.

the negotiating authority required regular renewal, Congress gave its approval prior to any trade agreement reached by the president. Congress also endorsed the unconditional mostfavored nation (MFN) clause, under which the lower U.S. tariffs negotiated with one country would be automatically extended to other countries.

The RTAA was "too little, too late" to have a big effect on protectionism in the 1930s, but it had a lasting impact as a political innovation. The RTAA fundamentally changed American trade politics by tipping the political balance of power in favor of lower tariffs in several ways.[3] First, Congress effectively gave up its ability to legislate duties on specific goods when it delegated tariff negotiating power to the executive branch. Prior to that, Congress had always been very responsive to domestic import-competing interests and did not give much thought to exporters, consumers, or the possibility of foreign retaliation. Congressional votes on trade now came to be framed in terms of whether or not, and under what circumstances, the RTAA should be continued, not how high the steel tariff and the wool tariff and the automobile tariff ought to be. Vote trading among interests that favored various tariffs was no longer feasible. Thus, the RTAA reduced access to legislative mechanisms that supported redistributive bargains and logrolling coalitions that had led to high tariffs.

Second, the RTAA delegated authority and agenda-setting power to the president, who represented a broad-based constituency and was therefore more likely than Congress to favor lower tariffs. The national electoral base of the president is thought to make the executive more apt to favor policies that benefit the nation as a whole, whereas the narrower geographic representative structure of Congress leads its members to have more parochial interests. Furthermore, the president is more likely than Congress to use trade negotiations to advance the nation's foreign policy goals.

Third, the RTAA reduced the threshold of political support needed for members of Congress to approve agreements that reduced tariffs. Prior to the RTAA, a minority could block foreign trade agreements because treaties had to be approved by a two-thirds majority in the Senate. Now, renewal of the RTAA required a simple majority in Congress. This shifted

---

[3] See the analysis of Bailey, Goldstein, and Weingast 1997 and Irwin and Kroszner 1999.

the threshold of political support needed to approve trade agreements and made them easier to enact. Whereas protectionist forces in the past had to muster only 34 percent of all senators to block a reciprocity treaty, now they needed 51 percent of senators to kill a renewal of the RTAA.

Finally, the RTAA helped to bolster the bargaining and lobbying position of exporters in the political process. Previously, the main trade-related special-interest groups on Capitol Hill were domestic producers facing import competition. Exporters were harmed by import restrictions, but only indirectly. The cost to exporters of any particular import duty was small, and therefore exporters failed to organize an effective political opposition. The RTAA explicitly linked foreign tariff reductions that were beneficial to exporters to lower tariff protection for producers competing against imports. This enabled exporters to organize and oppose high domestic tariffs because they wanted to secure lower foreign tariffs on their products. In addition, by expanding trade, the tariff reductions negotiated under the RTAA increased the size of export industries and decreased the size of industries competing with imports, and thereby increased the relative political clout of interests supporting renewals of the RTAA.

These features of the RTAA reduced the costs and increased the benefits of organization and lobbying by interests favoring freer trade.

The General Agreement on Tariffs and Trade

To officials at the time, the lesson of the 1930s was absolutely clear: like appeasement in the realm of diplomacy, protectionism was a serious economic policy mistake that helped make the decade a disaster. After World War II, world leaders agreed that cooperative actions should be taken to reduce barriers to international trade. Even as the war raged, American and British officials began exploring postwar trade arrangements. The United States aimed to convert the piecemeal, bilateral RTAA approach into a broader, multilateral system based on nondiscrimination and the reduction of trade barriers.[4]

After several preliminary meetings, representatives from twentythree countries met in Geneva in 1947 and agreed on tariff reductions and on the text of a General Agreement on Tariffs and Trade (GATT). The tariff

---

[4] On the origins of the GATT, see Irwin, Mavroidis, and Sykes 2008.

reductions were negotiated on a bilateral, product-by-product basis under the "reciprocal mutual advantage" principle, ensuring that no country would be forced to make unilateral concessions. If a bilateral agreement on specific commodity tariffs were reached, the lower negotiated rates would then be applied to all other members, through the mostfavored nation clause, and considered bound at those rates. The United States reduced its tariff by about 20 percent in the first GATT round.[5] Precise estimates of the degree to which other countries reduced their tariffs are unavailable, but major European countries reduced their import tariffs significantly between the early 1930s and the early 1950s, although quantitative restrictions and exchange controls persisted in many of these countries.

The text of General Agreement on Tariffs and Trade set out principles for the conduct of commercial policy. The main provisions are summarized in table 7.1.[6] First and foremost, Article 1 declares that all GATT signatories would extend unconditional most favored nation (MFN) treatment to all other contracting parties. The MFN clause forbids countries from using trade measures to discriminate against other GATT partners. Governments would have discretion in choosing the terms on which they permitted foreign goods into their country, but as a matter of principle (if not always practice) they would not be allowed to treat the goods of one signatory of the GATT differently from the same goods of another.[7]

Similarly, Article 3 requires that countries imposing domestic taxes and regulations adhere to the standard of "national treatment." National treatment is another form of nondiscrimination in which domestic and im-

---

[5] But as figure 1.4 illustrated, average U.S. tariffs dropped sharply from about 45 percent in 1933 to just over 10 percent in the early 1950s. Most of this reduction was not the result of negotiated reductions in tariff rates, but the result of the effect of inflation on specific duties. Because these duties were unchanged in terms of nominal amounts, inflation during and after World War II dramatically eroded the ad valorem equivalent of these duties. See Irwin 1998.

[6] Hoekman and Kostecki (2009) provide an excellent overview of world trade rules.

[7] The MFN clause in Article 1 simply reads, "With respect to customs duties and charges of any kind imposed on or in connection with importation or exportation . . . any advantage, favour, privilege or immunity granted by any contracting party to any product originating in or destined for any other country shall be accorded immediately and unconditionally to the like products . . . of all other contracting parties." But Article 24 permits countries to deviate from unconditional MFN in the case of free trade agreements and customs unions. The text of the GATT is available on the WTO website.

_____Table 7.1.

Major Provisions of the General Agreement on Tariffs and Trade

Provision	Description
Article 1	General Most Favored Nation Treatment
Article 2	Schedule of Tariff Concessions
Article 3	National Treatment on Internal Taxes and Regulation
Article 6	Antidumping and Countervailing Duties
Article 10	Transparency of Trade Regulations
Article 11	General Elimination of Quantitative Restrictions
Article 12	Restrictions to Safeguard the Balance of Payments
Article 14	Exceptions to Rule of Nondiscrimination
Article 16	Subsidies
Article 17	State Trading Enterprises
Article 19	Emergency Action on Imports of Particular Products (Safeguards)
Article 20	General Exceptions
Article 21	Security Exceptions
Article 23	Nullification and Impairment
Article 24	Customs Unions and Free Trade Areas

Source: World Trade Organization, http://www.wto.org/english/docs_e/legal_e/legal_e
.htm.

ported goods are supposed to face the same regulatory standards. This
provision prevents governments from setting one standard for domestic
products and then imposing a more stringent standard for similar imported products.

The other articles of the GATT deal with more specific trade policy
issues. Article 6 condemns dumping and allows countries to impose antidumping duties if the dumping causes or threatens to cause material
injury to an established industry. Article 16 indicates that countries should
avoid the use of subsidies for primary products and proposes that countries limit subsidies in general. Article 11 is a sweeping prohibition on the
use of quantitative restrictions, although Article 12 permits the imposition
of import quotas when countries have balance-of-payments difficulties.
Article 18 is a general exemption for developing countries from GATT
rules to give them flexibility to promote infant industries and protect their
balance of payments. Other articles of the GATT address mundane details
such as the valuation of merchandise for customs purposes, marks of origin, and the transparency of trade regulations.

Unlike the World Bank and International Monetary Fund (IMF), the
GATT was not a formal international institution. The countries signing the
GATT were "contracting parties" and not "members" because the GATT

was simply an agreement among governments and not officially an organization. The GATT as an institution consisted only of a small secretariat
in Geneva. The advantage of this situation was that the GATT remained
a small body–with relatively few participating countries–devoted to a
single mission: promoting further attempts to liberalize trade and establishing broad rules for commercial policy. In contrast to the World Bank
and IMF, both of which have large mandates, with the large budgets and
bureaucracies as well, the GATT had a rather narrow focus.

After the establishment of the GATT, the contracting parties met on a
regular basis to negotiate further reductions in trade barriers. Table 7.2
lists these negotiating "rounds," as they are called, and their major accomplishments. In the 1950s, more countries acceded to the GATT, but
further tariff reductions were negligible. In 1958, six European countries
agreed to eliminate all tariffs on each other's goods, thus forming a common market (the European Economic Community, a precursor to today's
European Union). U.S. exporters were concerned that their sales would
suffer because American goods would still be subject to import duties in
Europe. To reduce the tariff advantage given to intra-European trade,
Congress took a serious interest in reducing trade barriers between the
United States and Europe and authorized the president to undertake new
negotiations. The Kennedy Round, begun in 1964 and concluded in 1967,
resulted in a 35 percent reduction in tariffs, on average. These cuts were
generally across the board, with each country receiving exemptions for
sensitive sectors. The across-the-board approach proved to be more efficient and less cumbersome than the product-by-product negotiations
used in previous rounds, although this was not obvious from the length
of the negotiations.

The Tokyo Round negotiations in the 1970s sliced tariffs by another
third. By this time, however, tariffs on manufactured goods in the major
industrialized countries had generally fallen to low levels. As a result, the
Tokyo Round began the trend toward even more difficult negotiations
about nontariff barriers to trade. "The lowering of tariffs has, in effect,
been like draining a swamp," it was said at the time. "The lower water
level has revealed all the snags and stumps of non-tariff barriers that still
have to be cleared away."[8]

[8] Baldwin 1970, 2.

_____Table 7.2.
GATT Negotiating Rounds

Negotiating round	Dates	Major accomplishments
Geneva	1947	GATT established. About 20 percent tariff reduction negotiated.
Annecy	1949	Accession of 11 new contracting parties. Minor tariff reduction (about 2 percent).
Torquay	1950–51	Accession of 7 new contracting parties. Minor tariff reduction (about 3 percent).
Geneva	1955–56	Minor tariff reduction (about 2.5 percent).
Dillon Round	1960–61	Negotiations involving external tariff of European Community. Minor tariff reduction (4 percent).
Kennedy Round	1964–67	About 35 percent tariff reduction.
Tokyo Round	1973–79	About 33 percent tariff reduction. Six codes negotiated (e.g., subsidies, technical barriers.).
Uruguay Round	1986–94	WTO established. Additional tariff reductions. New agreements on dispute settlement, agriculture, clothing, services, investment, and intellectual property.
Doha Development Round	2001–	To be determined. Agreement on trade facilitation reached in December 2013.

Source: Compiled by the author.

The Tokyo Round resulted in several codes dealing with nontariff issues such as subsidies, technical barriers, import licenses, government procurement, customs valuation, and antidumping procedures. These codes substantially broadened the scope of trade rules in certain areas, but also contained wideranging exceptions. In addition, countries could pick and choose which, if any, of the codes it wished to adopt, an approach that became known as "GATT à la carte." A majority of GATT members, including most developing countries, chose not to sign the codes. Indeed, developing countries were given "special and differential" treatment, meaning that they were not required to cut their trade barriers and adhere to GATT rules to the same extent as the industrialized countries.

The Trade Act of 1974, which authorized U.S. participation in the Tokyo Round, also included a provision called "fast track," or what today is sometimes called "trade promotion authority." Because trade agreements now involve much more than just reducing tariff rates, such as dealing with nontariff barriers and government regulations, they require changes in domestic legislation. Rather than have Congress meddle with the outcome of the multilateral negotiations by amending the agreements, which would essentially bring the negotiating process to a halt, Congress agreed to give trade agreements expedited consideration and vote them up or down with no possibility of amendment. (The executive branch keeps Congress well informed about the substance of the negotiations to ensure that it will approve any deal that is reached.) If the president does not have such negotiating authority, it is more difficult—but not impossible—for U.S. negotiators to conclude international trade agreements. (President Barack Obama has asked Congress to renew presidential negotiating authority, which expired in 2007 under President George W. Bush.)

The Uruguay Round (1986–94) turned out to be the most important multilateral trade negotiation since the original formation of the GATT. For the first time, developing countries decided to be full participants in the talks, which changed the negotiating dynamic considerably. As in previous rounds, countries agreed to reduce tariffs on merchandise goods, although tariffs were already at relatively low levels for developed countries.[9] The participants also agreed to liberalize trade in areas that had eluded previous negotiators, particularly agriculture and clothing. And it extended rules to new areas such as services, investment, and intellectual property. Finally, the Uruguay Round brought about important institutional changes, both in creating the World Trade Organization (WTO) and strengthening the dispute settlement process.[10] At the same time, these far-reaching agreements produced controversy the likes of which the GATT had never seen.

The Uruguay Round also brought trade in textiles and apparel and in agricultural goods under GATT discipline, two very important accomplishments. In the case of textiles and apparel, the Multi-Fiber Arrangement (MFA), a complex web of bilateral export restraints and import

---

[9] Developed countries reduced tariffs on industrial products (excluding petroleum) by about 40 percent on a tradeweighted average basis. This brought average tariff levels in these countries down from 6.3 percent to 3.8 percent. Developing countries reduced their tariffs by 20 percent on average, bringing their average rates down from 15.3 percent to 12.3 percent (Preeg 1995, 191).

[10] See Hoekman and Kostecki (2009) for an overview of the accomplishments of the Uruguay Round and the substance of WTO agreements.

quotas that clogged trade in these goods, was completely abolished. For several decades, the MFA had allowed developed countries to put quantitative limits on their imports of apparel goods, product by product, country by country, in a way that GATT rules did not generally permit. The MFA was phased out over ten years, ending in January 2005, and the elimination of these quantitative restrictions has been a major step toward freer trade in clothing. Of course, the United States and other developed countries have continued to protect their textile and apparel producers with relatively high tariffs, but these tariffs are nondiscriminatory and the rigid and distortive country-specific quotas that had prevailed are no longer in place.

[handwritten margin note: just non-discriminatory protection]

Reform of agricultural trade has also eluded negotiators ever since the GATT's formation because of the political sensitivity of domestic support for farmers. The Uruguay Round was the first multilateral negotiation to even put agricultural policies on the table. A key problem facing the negotiators was that countries protected agricultural producers through a complex host of measures, including tariffs, import quotas, domestic price supports, and export subsidies. At the time, the policy distortions in agricultural markets were large and costly.[11]

The Uruguay Round's Agreement on Agriculture limited the use of export subsidies and internal price supports by capping and reducing these outlays from a given base period. The agreement also sought to ensure greater market access by requiring countries to convert all nontariff barriers (variable import levies, import quotas and prohibitions, voluntary export restraints, etc.) into a single import tariff. After this "tariffication" of existing restrictions, the tariffs were to be reduced over ten years by an average one-third for developed countries and by one-quarter for developing countries. The resulting tariffs, however, are incredibly high. Many countries used the process of converting the complex trade barriers into tariffs as an opportunity to cheat, raising tariffs above the existing combination of nontariff restrictions. This practice, known as "dirty tariffication," means that the actual liberalization in agriculture was slight.[12] Still, the agreement was an important first step in getting agricultural trade barriers on the negotiating table.

[handwritten margin note: countries cheat this attempt (-> tariffication)]

[11] Anderson 2009.
[12] Ingco 1996. See also Orden, Blanford, and Josling 2011.

Of course, although export subsidies are prohibited in principle, other domestic agricultural subsidies have persisted. In 2013, OECD countries provided $257 billion in support to agricultural producers, half of which was tied to commodity output.[13] The European Union's farm policy, called the Common Agricultural Policy, involves a bewildering array of subsidies and other programs that take up about 40 percent of the EU's budget. France and other countries with powerful farm lobbies have fiercely resisted efforts to change the policy.

Furthermore, government support for agricultural producers, and the distortions caused by those policies, has fallen significantly over the past decade. Some of this is due to policy changes. For example, government payments to farmers have shifted from price supports to income support. Price supports distorted markets because they gave farmers an incentive to overproduce; income support decouples the financial transfer from the decision to produce.[14] High commodity prices in recent years have also significantly reduced the need for government support for farmers. As a result, the "producer subsidy equivalent," a measure of how much U.S. farm income comes from government programs, fell from 22 percent in 1986–88 to 8 percent in 2010–12. In fact, the U.S. farm bill passed in early 2014 ended direct cash payments to farmers, although producers still have a substantial safety net in the form of crop insurance and disaster relief. Even the European Union reduced its producer subsidy equivalent from 39 percent in 1986–88 to 19 percent in 2010–12. And, by shifting from price supports to income transfers, its programs have become less market distorting. Countries that still have exceptionally high levels of government support for agriculture include Japan, South Korea, Norway, and Switzerland.

While high commodity prices have reduced the demand for subsidies by agricultural producers in importing countries, those same high prices have sometimes led exporting countries to impose export taxes on agricultural goods.[15] They have done so in an effort to keep domestic farm

---

[13] OECD 2014, 71.

[14] Swinnen, Olper, and Vandemoortele (2012) suggest that the WTO did not have an impact on the overall level of support given to agriculture, but can take some credit for shifting that support to less distortive policy instruments (cash payments and income support rather than measures linked to production, such as price supports).

[15] Mitra and Josling 2009 and Abbott 2012.

prices lower than they would otherwise be. By restricting export supply, these actions have increased the level and volatility of world agricultural prices and have generated serious concerns in importing countries about adequate access to supply. There are few WTO disciplines on agricultural export taxes, despite the fact that those policies can disrupt world markets just as much as import restrictions. Because of the difficult political interests involved, the reform of agricultural trade policies will be an objective for many years to come.

The Uruguay Round made little progress in regulating the use of antidumping laws, but countries did pledge not to "see, take or maintain any voluntary export restraints, orderly marketing arrangements or any other similar measures on the export or the import side."[16] Previously, the socalled gray measures had been used by countries to restrict trade without explicitly violating GATT rules. They are now eliminated, at least in principle. When countries seek to protect domestic industries from foreign competition, they are obligated to follow existing procedures and rules regarding safeguards and escape clauses. If adhered to, this provision also constitutes a major improvement in multilateral disciplines on trade policy.

The Uruguay Round also produced a General Agreement on Trade in Services (GATS) and established rules regarding trade-related investment measures (TRIMs) and trade-related intellectual property (TRIPs). Although these agreements are weak by the standards of the GATT treatment of goods, they constitute the first attempt to extend the principle of nondiscrimination to new areas of international commerce. The core obligations in the GATS center around three principles: most favored nation treatment, market access, and national treatment. The main sectors include telecommunications, financial services, air and maritime transport, and construction. Although the agreement contains specific commitments to liberalization, coverage is incomplete because the important provisions of the GATS apply only to the sectors specified by the member countries. In general, trade in services was freed only slightly, but a framework was established in which liberalization could be pursued in the future.

The TRIMs agreement was even more modest in making national treatment the standard for regulating foreign investment. The agreement aims

[16] Article 1:1(b) of the Agreement on Safeguards, in Word Trade Organization 1999, 280.

to eliminate quantitative restrictions on investment, including limits on the share of foreign ownership in certain industries. Because of opposition from developing countries, there was no attempt to consider such issues as the right of firms to establish enterprises in other countries, or the elimination of trade-related performance requirements on foreign investment.

The TRIPs agreement consolidates previous international accords protecting copyrights, trademarks, patents, and industrial designs, and provides for the enforcement of these agreements within the WTO. As a major producer of intellectual property, the United States has pushed for including these matters in trade negotiations. The pharmaceutical industry, the music and motion picture industry, and the software and high technology industries have a strong interest in protecting their inventions and innovations from copycats. The potential use of trade sanctions to enforce the intellectual property agreement is a major change in global policy.

The TRIPs agreement is one of the most controversial parts of the WTO. Many developing countries complained that, unlike tariff reductions that are mutually beneficial for countries, the TRIPs agreement merely transfers income from developing to developed countries by strengthening the ability of multinational corporations to charge higher prices in poorer countries.[17] The controversy is particularly intense regarding pharmaceuticals and whether protecting intellectual property prevents poor developing countries from producing or importing cheap, generic anti-malarial or anti-HIV drugs that are necessary to save lives. The WTO membership recognized this problem in 2001 and granted developing countries a waiver that extends the TRIPs implementation schedule from 2006 to 2016. It might have to be extended again, although the TRIPs agreement also permits "compulsory licensing" in which governments can force makers of patented drugs to permit local production under certain circumstances.[18] However, the controversy surrounding

---

[17] Maskus (2000) estimates that the full implementation of the TRIPS agreement would transfer $5.8 billion from developing countries to the United States, and another $2.5 billion to five other developed countries.

[18] See Maskus 2012 and Maskus 2014. Furthermore, Kyle and Qian (2014) find that patent protection in TRIPs increases the availability of new drugs in developing countries because generics are often absent from the market.

they ♡ now / they've developed

TRIPs has died down because now developing countries, such as China and India, have become innovative and take an increasing interest in protecting intellectual property.

Many economists believe that the protection of intellectual property is not a trade issue that should be under the purview of the WTO, especially given the existence of the World Intellectual Property Organization. In addition, some argue that it sets a bad precedent: using instruments of trade policy to protect intellectual property makes it harder to reject demands to use them to enforce other non–trade related objectives, such as environmental or labor standards. It opens the door to many interests who want to use the threat of trade sanctions to achieve their own non-trade objectives, and thus puts the WTO in the business of enforcing behavior in areas only tangentially related to trade. These potential outcomes of efforts to protect intellectual property dilute the institution's focus on the reduction of trade barriers.

Bold more to bring politics in

The Uruguay Round was a "single undertaking," meaning that all participants and future members of the WTO are bound to follow all of the agreements reached. The Uruguay Round was the first round of multilateral trade negotiations in which developing countries played an active role, and their participation helped shape the outcome. Developed countries agreed to abolish the MFA's clothing quotas and to reform agricultural trade, increasing trade in sectors where developing countries have a comparative advantage. In return, developing countries accepted rules in the new areas of trade where developed countries have a comparative advantage. This exchange of market access came to be known as the "grand bargain." As we shall see, developing countries soon came to view the grand bargain as a major disappointment.

Still didn't get quite what they wanted

Has the GATT Been a Success?

Before turning to the WTO, let us pause to consider whether the GATT been a success. The answer is clearly yes. The architects of the postwar world trading system desperately wanted to avoid a repeat of the interwar trade policies after World War II. They not only accomplished this goal but also succeeded in eliminating most of the high barriers that arose during the 1930s. The reduction in trade barriers and the stability of tariff policy in most countries in the decades after 1947 have permitted

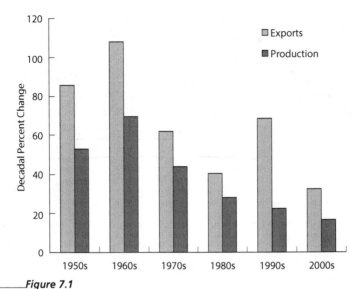

_____*Figure 7.1*

Growth in Volume of World Exports and World Production, by Decade, 1950–2010

Source: World Trade Organization, International Trade Statistics 2013, Table A1 (http://wto.org/english/res_e/statis_e/its2013_e/its13_toc_e.htm).

the expansion of world trade to proceed unchecked. As figure 7.1 indicates, the volume of world merchandise trade has grown much more rapidly than the volume of world merchandise output over the postwar period. This is particularly true in the 1990s, when there was an explosion of trade due to trade reforms in developing countries, particularly in China and India.[19]

This figure alone does not prove that the GATT was responsible for much or all of this expansion. But various studies indicate that the GATT can take a good deal of credit for the growth in postwar world trade. A detailed study of bilateral trade flows during the half century since 1946 reveals that countries that participated in the GATT enjoyed trade that is 43 percent larger than a pair of nonparticipating countries.[20] However,

[19] Figure 7.1 shows a marked slowdown in the growth of world trade in the 2000s. Research by Constantinescu, Mattoo, and Ruta (2015) has found a structural change in the relationship between trade and world GDP growth in recent years due to the slowing pace of vertical specialization (discussed in chapter 1) rather than increased protectionism or a change in the composition of trade or output.

[20] Goldstein, Rivers, and Tomz 2007.

this overall effect has not been constant over time. The stimulus to trade arising from participation in the GATT was greatest early on—at over 80 percent in the 1950s—but has diminished to only about 11 percent by the 2000s. This is partly because so few countries now remain outside of the GATT/WTO system.

more trade

Similarly, another study concluded that the GATT has had a strong and positive impact on world trade, finding that industrial-country bilateral imports are 65 percent greater as a result of the agreement.[21] However, GATT participation by developing countries did not increase their trade nearly as much, perhaps because they were given "special and differential" treatment for so long and were not required to liberalize their trade policies. Finally, this analysis shows that bilateral trade for GATT participants is not higher in the case of clothing, footwear, and agriculture, precisely the sectors of trade that have been largely exempt from liberalization.[22]

Why do we care abt each other

Granting that the GATT and WTO have succeeded in increasing world trade, another question is why multilateral trade agreements have been politically successful in liberalizing trade. From a strictly economic point of view, the GATT's system of reciprocity in tariff reductions and rules for commercial policy is unnecessary because countries are better off pursuing a policy of free trade regardless of the trade policies pursued by others. As set out in chapter 2, the case for free trade is a unilateral one: as economist Joan Robinson once put it, a country should not throw rocks in its harbors simply because other countries have rocks in theirs. The mercantilist language of international trade negotiations—that a reduction in one's own trade barriers is a "concession" to others—is wrong from an economic standpoint.

---

[21] Subramanian and Wei 2007.

[22] In fact, according to the study, imports by new developing-country members of the WTO are greater by virtue of their membership, but imports by old developing-country members of the GATT are not. This is because new members are required to liberalize their trade policies before joining the WTO, whereas long-standing members were protected from changing their policies because of special and differential treatment. Rose (2004) originally questioned whether the GATT had any significant impact on trade and, in his examination of the bilateral trade data, he failed to find much of an effect of GATT participation. However, in his table 1 benchmark regressions, when country fixed effects are included in the analysis (which is generally considered to be the most appropriate specification), GATT participation is indeed related to more trade. See also Tomz, Goldstein, and Rivers 2007.

The reason that reciprocity via multilateral trade agreements has worked well since 1947 is that such agreements have both economic and political value for governments seeking to contain protectionist pressures. When countries choose their tariffs alone, the outcome can be inefficient economically because governments are pressured by import-competing producers into maintaining trade restrictions.[23] Multilateral tariff cooperation is a way to avoid an economically inefficient result. Furthermore, the gains from trade are magnified if other countries also reduce their trade barriers. Trade agreements are also beneficial politically because they enhance domestic support for open trade. Such agreements make exporters more politically active, counterbalancing the power of interests opposed to imports and thus facilitating trade liberalization.[24] Although unilateral free trade is beneficial, not all unilateral policies are free trade, as our discussion of trade politics in chapter 3 described.

The GATT's economic and political value was demonstrated by the fact that countries adhered to its provisions even though the agreement had no direct mechanism to enforce them. Under Article 23, if any contracting party failed to carry out its obligation or undertakes an action that "nullifies or impairs" a benefit due to another party, other countries could ask the GATT to allow them to suspend their concessions or waive their obligations to the offending country. In other words, if one country fails to adhere to the rules, then other countries are not obligated to adhere to the rules with respect to that country. They can retaliate by raising tariffs against the rulebreaker's goods. In the "chicken war" of 1962, the United States imposed tariffs on $26 million in European goods because Europe violated GATT rules by imposing a high variable levy on poultry imports.

Thus, the countries that signed the GATT contract were responsible for enforcing the agreement; no independent power resides with the GATT itself, which essentially relies on the goodwill of the signatories. Countries were concerned about their reputation and wanted to adhere to the agreement. Reputation can be a powerful device for preventing the ero-

---

[23] If tariff policies are interdependent, such that an increase in one country's tariff leads to an increase in another country's tariff, then a noncooperative equilibrium will include relatively high tariffs and be inefficient. See Bagwell and Staiger 2010.

[24] Hillman and Moser (1996) provide a theoretical analysis of this point.

[handwritten margin note: prisoner's dilemma not really tho]

sion of agreements because a country that fails to abide by the rules forfeits the right to insist that other countries do so, and thus risks discrimination against its exports.[25] Evidence suggests that countries try to cultivate good reputations and fear retaliation for noncompliance with the agreed-upon rules.[26]

[handwritten margin note: GATT punishment bit more than WTO]

For all of these reasons, most countries that were not a part of the GATT have wanted to become members of the WTO. Although the obligations are extensive, they are less than the costs of remaining outside the agreement and losing the benefits of MFN treatment by other countries. As a result, membership in the WTO has become increasingly attractive. At the start of the Uruguay Round in 1986, the GATT consisted of ninety-one contracting parties. The WTO was established in 1995 with nearly 130 members, and by early 2015 the membership had risen to 160 nations, accounting for over 90 percent of world trade. As of 2015, a handful of small countries, ranging from Afghanistan to Uzbekistan, are negotiating to join the organization.

Despite its success, the GATT legal framework has several notable defects. The agreement is written broadly, often with several exceptions for every rule. These exceptions give countries the flexibility to deal with unexpected contingencies and to maneuver through politically difficult decisions on policy. But they also provide loopholes and excuses for evading the basic principles of the agreement. For example, Article 1 contains the MFN clause, but Article 14 is entitled "Exceptions to the Rule of Nondiscrimination," and Article 24 permits countries to form customs unions and free trade areas, which are inherently discriminatory. Article 11 generally forbids the use of import quotas and quantitative restrictions, but Article 13 states that when they are imposed, they should be administered in a nondiscriminatory way, a provision that would be unnecessary if Article 11 were fully effective.

[handwritten margin note: so yes some disc'tion]

---

[25] In Hudec's view, "other governments interested in maintaining the integrity of legal commitments are willing to go to considerable lengths to expose the defendant government to criticism for not keeping its word. . . . To be caught not performing one's own obligation is to lose the right to enforce the obligations on others, thereby losing specific trade opportunities as well as imperiling the entire liberal trading system. Rarely, if ever, does the gain from a violation of GATT obligations make it worth jeopardizing the benefits of the existing trade order" (1998, 36).

[26] Bown 2004b.

Despite these deficiencies, over the past half century the multilateral trading system has achieved many of its original goals. Countries that are party to the GATT have generally adhered to the rules. Nondiscrimination has been established as a benchmark for commercial policy, and tariff barriers have been significantly reduced in successive negotiating rounds. In addition, world trade relations have been generally good: specific disputes have been contained and policies have been stable, providing an environment in which international commerce has flourished. To be sure, discriminatory policies remain, nontariff barriers exist, antidumping measures are used, and disputes still arise and sometimes fester. But on the whole, the postwar system of world trade must be judged a great success.

One reason for the general decline in protectionism is that world economic growth over the past half century has been relatively smooth, punctuated by only a few recessions but free of major depressions. This expansion has muted protectionist demands and pressures on governments to deviate from GATT rules. Economic growth and rising incomes have mitigated the pain associated with structural shifts, due to international trade or other factors, by creating new opportunities for those displaced. In short, the economic shocks confronting the trading system have not been strong enough to bring about a move back toward closed markets.[27]

The world trading system was tested during the global financial crisis in 2008. The subsequent recession, one of the most severe since the Great Depression, prompted fears that governments would employ protectionist policies to insulate their economies from the downturn, just as they had in the 1930s. For example, about half of the 25 percent decline in the volume of world trade between 1929 and 1932 was due to higher trade barriers.[28] Many observers worried that the temptation to respond to the Great Recession with "beggar-thy-neighbor" trade policies would lead to a wholesale abandonment of WTO rules and disciplines.

Fortunately, leading central banks quickly and aggressively eased monetary policies to address the financial crisis and economic downturn.

[27] Irwin and O'Rourke 2014.
[28] Madsen 2001.

in essence, Central Banks did a good enough job so no protech was called for (not compl)

The contrast with the 1930s was stark: during the Great Depression, central banks could not respond this way because they had to adhere to the rules of the gold standard. As a result, economic conditions were allowed to deteriorate and governments were forced to use trade policy measures to address the crisis.[29] By contrast, in the early stages of the Great Recession, the quick response of monetary authorities stopped the free-fall in economic activity and countries generally refrained from imposing beggar-thy-neighbor policies.[30] As a result, although the volume of world trade fell 12 percent in 2009, only 2 percent (0.2 percentage points) of that decline was due to higher trade barriers.[31]

How much did the WTO help the world to avoid a nasty outbreak of protectionism during the recent crisis? If the WTO rules had not been in place, might countries have been tempted to raise tariffs and other barriers to trade? It is very hard to answer these questions. Many developing countries have applied tariffs that are well below their bound tariffs. The applied tariffs are those that they actually choose to levy on imports; the bound tariffs are the maximum those tariffs can be as negotiated in the Uruguay Round. (This means that these countries could, if they wanted, raise their tariffs up to the bound level without violating any international agreements.)

The applied and bound tariff averages are shown in table 7.3. Developing countries could have increased their import tariffs without violating any international agreements, and thus without fear of retaliation. And yet, in general, they did not raise them. One factor preventing an outbreak of protectionism has been the rise of "global value chains," that is, *intra trade by final good is finished* trade in intermediate goods and components, which make trade barriers more disruptive to production.[32]

On the other hand, many countries quietly used "murky protectionism" in the form of subsidies, government procurement rules, health and safety regulations, and other discriminatory practices to limit imports during this period.[33] It remains to be seen whether these measures were a temporary response to the crisis, or will remain in place for some time to come.

other ways to limit imports

[29] Eichengreen and Irwin 2010, Irwin 2012.
[30] Bown and Crowley 2013.
[31] See Kee, Neagu, and Nicita 2013 and Henn and McDonald 2014.
[32] Baldwin and Evenett 2012 and Gawande, Hoekman, and Cui 2015.
[33] Evenett and Vines 2012.

_____Table 7.3.
Applied and Bound Tariffs, 2010

	Applied rates	Bound rates
Total		
All countries	3.7	9.9
High-income countries	2.5	5.2
Developing—non-LDC	6.9	21.8
Less-developed countries	11.1	n.a.
Agricultural goods		
All countries	14.5	40.3
High-income countries	15.0	31.9
Developing—non-LDC	13.4	53.9
Less-developed countries	12.5	94.1
Nonagricultural goods		
All countries	2.9	7.8
High-income countries	1.7	3.5
Developing—non-LDC	6.4	19.1
Less-developed countries	10.9	n.a.

Source: Martin and Mattoo 2011.

_____**The World Trade Organization**

Established in 1995, the WTO was initially a much more visible and controversial organization than the GATT had ever been. The controversy stemmed from fears that the WTO would have extensive powers to strike down domestic environmental, health, and safety regulations that might conflict with world trade rules, and thereby undermine national sovereignty and lead to a "race to the bottom." Because these fears have not been realized, and because the WTO membership has failed to reach any significant, new trade agreements, the WTO is not today the target of intense criticism. Yet the WTO remains a key international institution, so it is important to get a sense of what the organization is all about, particularly its dispute settlement mechanism.[34]

The World Trade Organization is something more, but not much more, than the GATT. While the GATT was simply an intergovernmental agreement overseen by a small secretariat, the WTO is an official international organization. The scope of the WTO is broader than that of the GATT

[34] For a general overview of the WTO, see Hoekman and Kostecki 2009.

, more than goods

because it oversees multilateral agreements relating not just to goods, but also to services, investment, and intellectual property.

The WTO remains a relatively small institution. Located in Geneva, Switzerland, the WTO secretariat consists of just 639 employees, about a quarter of whom are translators. In 2013, the WTO's budget was about $224 million.[35] The support staff and budget are small in comparison to other international organizations, such as the World Bank, the International Monetary Fund (IMF), and the Food and Agriculture Organization (FAO), and even some nongovernmental organizations. For example, in 2013, the World Bank had a staff of about seven thousand and an administrative budget of about $1.9 billion, and the IMF had a staff of about twenty-three hundred and a budget of $997 million. (That said, unlike the World Bank or IMF, the WTO does not have any money to lend to developing countries.) Yet these figures do not reflect the WTO's true importance as the cornerstone of the world trading system: its mission—to keep the international trading system functioning smoothly—is more clearly focused and perhaps even more important than the World Bank's vaguely defined goal of promoting economic development.

very imp.

The WTO is simply a forum for the member countries to consult with one another over trade policy matters, and possibly negotiate trade agreements and adjudicate trade disputes. The WTO does conduct factfinding surveillance reviews of members' policies. But, ultimately, the WTO has very little power in itself. It cannot force countries to negotiate with one another. It cannot make them obey the agreements that they had previously reached or agreed to adhere to. And it cannot require the countries to comply with its findings in the dispute settlement cases.

The WTO has virtually no independent power and strives to be a neutral party among all the member countries. The directorgeneral of the WTO has no policymaking authority and cannot comment directly on members' policies. The power to make trade policy and to write the rules governing it resides specifically with the member governments, not with the WTO. For this reason, the WTO is often called a "member-driven" organization: it accomplishes what the members collectively agree to do, and the institution itself cannot force that process.

can't actually really do anything

---

[35] World Trade Organization 2013, 139–41.

good for IR essay

The two major activities of the WTO are trade negotiations and dispute settlement. In its nearly twenty-year existence, the WTO membership has been remarkably unsuccessful in terms of reaching new trade agreements. As mentioned earlier, developing countries came to view the grand bargain of the Uruguay Round as a major disappointment: they took on many new obligations in services, investment, and intellectual property, but did not reap major benefits in terms of market access in agriculture and clothing. (In agriculture, developed-country subsidies remained in place, and in clothing, China came along in the 1990s and almost completely took over the market.) Developing countries, particularly India, Brazil, and China, have become more assertive in international trade negotiations, blocking any deals that do not deal adequately with their concerns.

why grand bargain failed

more of a voice

The first stumble came at a WTO ministerial meeting in Seattle in 1999. The meeting aimed to address the concerns of developing countries, but the United States brought up the sensitive issue of labor standards. Developing countries reject any inclusion of labor standards in trade agreements for fear the provisions could be used to block their exports. The meeting was also disrupted by violent protests by anti-globalization groups fearful of the new WTO. This came to be called "the Battle of Seattle" and was even made into a low-budget Hollywood movie.

In November 2001, however, in a meeting at Qatar, a new round of trade negotiations was launched. The Doha Development Round, as it is called, has the specific goal of using trade to further the development goals of the poorest countries. The formal agenda originally included six broad areas: agriculture, nonagricultural market access, services, the so-called Singapore issues (transparency in government procurement, trade facilitation, investment, and competition policy) and rules (trade remedies), TRIPs, and development-related issues. The Doha Round negotiations have been extremely problematic—agricultural policy reform is a political challenge in the United States and European Union, developing countries have objected to negotiations on investment and competition (which were then dropped), and the TRIPs agreement remains contentious.

wow so it too failed

As a result, the Doha Round has languished amid recriminations and finger pointing. Every side thinks the other should be making more concessions.

↳ THE AGE Old CLASSIC

cessions. A mini-ministerial meeting in 2008 managed to narrow differences on many issues, but ended in failure when India and China insisted upon special safeguards that would allow them to raise tariffs on agricultural imports.[36] A ministerial meeting in Bali in 2013 led to a WTO agreement on one part of the Doha agenda, trade facilitation, but even this minor success later collapsed.

The Doha Round was supposed to have been completed by 2005. Of course, past trade negotiations rarely met such deadlines, which is why the GATT was sometimes referred to as the "General Agreement to Talk and Talk." But the GATT consisted of a small number of like-minded developed countries among whom it was relatively easy to reach a consensus. The WTO has a much larger membership that includes many developing countries that are suspicious of trade liberalization. Like the GATT, the WTO operates on the basis of a consensus among its members. Of course, reaching any consensus is extremely difficult, and very easy to block. A former director-general has likened the WTO to a car with one accelerator and 150 handbrakes.[37]

The failure of the Doha Round after many years of negotiation has led many to question the usefulness of the WTO as a negotiating forum. Stating that the round would be for "development" gave developing countries a sense that they were entitled to unreciprocated trade concessions, that is, that developed countries would open their markets completely to developing countries, which would not have to do anything in return. Unfortunately for them, this is not the way multilateral trade negotiations work. Yet, despite many gloomy prognostications about the fate of the negotiations, there is still hope that the Doha Round will be completed at some point, even if the results are meager. Unlike the WTO meeting in Seattle in 1999, which attracted a large number of protesters from around the world, few groups bother to protest at its meetings anymore. This is

---

[36] See Blustein 2009.

[37] Moore 2003, 110. On gridlock at the WTO, see Collier 2005 and Wolfe 2015; on the difficulties of reaching an agreement at the WTO, see Martin and Messerlin 2007. As noted earlier, the membership included 160 countries as of mid-2014. Of course, not all members have equal input on the negotiations. The United States and European Union carry the most weight, but China, India, and Brazil are important players as well. Many small developing countries cannot afford representation in Geneva and hence designate a country, such as India, to represent its interests. For an inside look at how negotiations are conducted, see Blustein 2009.

a sad commentary on how the WTO is no longer perceived to be important. The organization itself is not nearly as powerful as its early critics
feared, and nobody expects the membership to reach any ground-
breaking agreements anytime soon.

What might be the economic effects of a Doha agreement? Several
studies have forecast the possible consequences of the Doha package that
was on the table when talks broke down in 2008.[38] The package includes
tariff reductions on manufactured goods, reduction in agricultural support
and increased market access, and further trade facilitation. The consensus
is that such a package would increase world welfare anywhere from 0.2
to 1.4 percent of world GDP, or $150 billion to $900 billion. The benefits
would be broadly shared among countries. Although the numbers are not
enormous, they are understated because they do not take into account
the productivity and other benefits of trade described in chapter 2. Furthermore, the figures do not include any potential gains from increased
trade in services because, as of that date, current service "offers" at the
WTO would not liberalize actual policies. And the "insurance" value of
an agreement, which would reduce developing countries' tariff bindings
down to applied levels, preventing them from going up in the future,
would be significant.

_____The WTO and Dispute Settlement

What most distinguishes the WTO from the GATT, aside from the new
agreements, is the dispute settlement process. The original GATT made
little provision for settling disputes between member countries. When
conflicts arose, the Secretariat began an informal and ad hoc process to
help resolve disputes through negotiation. The Uruguay Round agreement established a dispute settlement mechanism that largely formalized
existing practices. But it also strengthened the process by providing for
specific time tables to expedite cases and, perhaps most important, by
preventing countries from blocking the establishment of a panel or the
adoption of a panel report.[39]

---

[38] Martin and Mattoo 2011 and International Monetary Fund 2011.

[39] The dispute settlement process was strengthened in the Uruguay Round mainly because the U.S. Congress insisted on it. Frustrated with the GATT system, Congress wanted
to improve the speed and effectiveness of the dispute settlement mechanisms and proce-

How does the new dispute settlement mechanism work? Countries may file "violation" complaints, alleging that a specific rule (such as non-discrimination) has been broken, or "nonviolation" complaints, alleging that a government action "nullifies or impairs" a previous concession even if no specific rule has been broken. If initial consultations to resolve the dispute are not successful, a three-member panel is appointed to determine whether WTO rules have been violated. If it establishes a violation, the panel suggests that the disputed policy be brought into conformity with the rules, but generally leaves to the parties themselves the task of working out a solution. The panel decision can be appealed to an Appellate Body, which rules on matters of law and legal interpretation in the panel report.

As under the GATT, if the policy in question is found to violate the rules, the country can bring its policy into conformity with the rules, or keep the policy in place and offer compensation (lower tariffs) on other goods exported from the complaining country, which then has the option of accepting or rejecting the compensation offer. If neither alternative has been implemented, the complaining country can seek authorization to "suspend the application to the Member concerned of concessions or other obligations in the covered agreements." In other words, the complainant can get WTO permission retaliate by raising tariffs—or, in WTO lingo, withdrawing previous tariff "concessions"—against to the country that has chosen not to comply with the finding. Such retaliations occur infrequently because most disputes are settled through negotiations. Some recent high-profile cases in which countries were authorized to retaliate include a U.S. case against the European Union's ban on hormone-treated beef, an EU-led case against the Bush administration's steel safeguard tariffs, and a Brazilian case against U.S. cotton subsidies.

---

dures. In 1988, Congress instructed negotiators to seek the opening of foreign markets, the elimination of trade-distorting policies, and the establishment of "a more effective system of international trading disciplines and procedures." U.S. House of Representatives 2003, 230. As a U.S. Trade Representative (2000, 41) report noted, "Under the GATT, panel proceedings took years, the defending party could simply block any unfavorable judgment, and the GATT panel process did not cover some of the agreements. Under the WTO, there are strict timetables for panel proceedings, the defending party cannot block findings unfavorable to it, and there is one comprehensive dispute settlement process covering all of the Uruguay Round Agreements." When members of Congress now complain that the strong dispute settlement system impinges on U.S. sovereignty, it is helpful to remember that it was the Congress itself that demanded that it be strengthened because of its previous weaknesses.

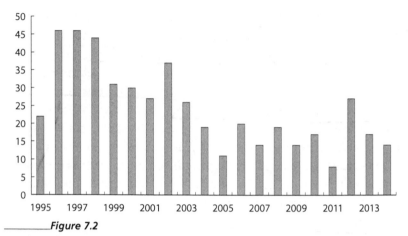

_____**Figure 7.2**

Number of Disputes at the WTO, 1995–2014

Source: World Trade Organization (http://wto.org/english/tratop_e/dispu_e/dispu_status_e.htm).

In the first twenty years of the WTO, from 1995 through 2014, a total of 488 disputes have been brought to the dispute settlement system, about twenty-three cases per year. Figure 7.2 shows the annual number of requests for consultations received by the WTO's dispute settlement body since its formation in 1995. The number of requests was fairly high when the WTO was first established, but the number has settled down to a lower level in recent years. It should be noted that many conflicts be- *usually* *not to serious* tween countries do not become formal disputes, but are resolved in various WTO negotiating committees. For example, the WTO committees on Sanitary and Phytosanitary Measures (SPS) and Technical Barriers to Trade (TBT) provide a forum for countries to discuss differences about the rules and their application in particular cases and, in fact, very few conflicts become formal dispute cases.[40] In addition, the WTO played a role in resolving a long-standing disagreement between the European Union and Latin American countries over the EU's discriminatory policy regarding banana imports, a quarrel that was finally resolved in 2011.[41]

What are the disputes about? Most of the cases involve a country's trade policy practice regarding a specific good or goods. For example, in 2013, the United States and New Zealand challenged Indonesia's impos-

[40] See Horn, Mavroidis, and Wijkstrom 2013.
[41] Guth 2012.

example of complaint

ing a reference-price import ban (meaning that imports were banned unless the domestic price reached a certain level) on agricultural goods such as California flowers and New Mexico chile peppers. China challenged the method by which the United States imposed antidumping duties on its products, while South Korea complained specifically about a U.S. antidumping case on washing machines. The EU complained about Russia's import restrictions on pork and live pigs, and in another case the EU and Japan charged that Russia imposed discriminatory taxes on automobiles under the guise of "recycling fees." Panama contested Colombia's clothing policy, while Indonesia complained about Pakistan's antidumping case regarding paper products. And the list goes on.

The stakes in the disputes vary widely. In some cases, the stakes are small and the concerns are very narrow. For example, a fish fight broke out within the European Union when the EU banned herring and mackerel from the Faroe Islands (controlled by Denmark) after a squabble about fishing quota allotments. Denmark raised a stink and, in early 2014, requested that a panel be established to look into the legality of the EU ban.

In other cases, the stakes are enormous and the implications are large. The United States and European Union have had cases against one another regarding financial support for large commercial aircraft, namely, government subsidies for Airbus (in the case of the EU) and Boeing (in the case of the United States). The United States has long accused the EU of subsidizing Airbus aircraft (such as the super-jumbo A-380) to the detriment of Boeing (which produces the 747). The EU accuses the United States of providing indirect subsidies to Boeing. *they both do it.* Although the Appellate Body has ruled mainly in favor of the United States, the dispute is so large and complex, involving tens of billions of dollars, and the stakes are so large and political in nature, that the WTO dispute settlement system is ill equipped to provide a definitive resolution to this longstanding conflict. Instead, a diplomatic solution would be more appropriate. *Sometimes can't solve completely*

In the first five years of the dispute settlement system, the United States brought many more cases against other countries than were brought against it. Since then, however, many more cases have been brought against the United States. In the first seventeen years of the WTO (1995–2012), the United States filed ninety-nine complaints about foreign trade measures and was the subject of one hundred forty complaints. Of *turned tables* the ninety-nine complaints, sixty-one had been resolved by mid-2012. Of these cases, twenty-nine were resolved to U.S. satisfaction without litigation, thirty-eight received favorable rulings by WTO panels, and in four the United States lost on core issues at the WTO. Of the one hundred forty complaints brought against the United States, eighty-eight had been resolved by mid-2012. Of these cases, twenty-one were resolved without litigation, the United States won seventeen, and in fifty some aspect of U.S. policy was found inconsistent with WTO rules.[42] This is because any country that brings a case to the WTO tends to win, and any country that is a defendant tends to lose. This reflects the fact that countries usually bring only strong cases to the WTO because it is costly, in terms of time and effort, to do so.

How has the dispute settlement process worked? In a report to Congress in 2000, the independent General Accountability Office concluded that the dispute settlement process has worked well for the United States. Examining the cases considered by the WTO up to that time, the GAO found that most led to beneficial changes in foreign regulations and practices and that "none of the changes the United States has made in response to WTO disputes have had major policy or commercial impact to date, though the stakes in several were important."[43]

Sometimes politicians in Washington judge the dispute settlement mechanism only on the basis of whether the United States "wins" the cases it files and those brought against it. Clearly the mechanism is more important than that. It was established simply to ensure that the rules that countries agreed upon together and pledged to abide by actually mean something. Sometimes the United States is on the wrong side. For example, in 1995 Costa Rica won a complaint against the United States concerning restrictions on imports of underwear. The fact that small countries can receive fair treatment under the rule of law is a strength of the world trading system.[44] The alternative is that more powerful countries simply dictate outcomes to others.

But even when the United States loses a case, the WTO cannot force change in U.S. laws, regulations, or policies. The WTO cannot strike

---

[42] Data from USTR website, www.ustr.gov.

[43] U.S. General Accounting Office 2000b, 2–3.

[44] Bown (2009) discusses how developing countries have generally received fair treatment under the WTO dispute settlement system.

down any U.S. law, as an American court can. As the General Accountability Office puts it, "The United States maintains that it has the right not
to comply with WTO rulings. However, the United States recognizes that
it may bear a penalty for not complying with WTO rulings, both in the
form of retaliatory duties on U.S. exports and in terms of its reputation as
a key player in the world trading system."[45] WTO panels merely determine whether disputed policies conflict with WTO rules and, if they do,
recommend that members bring those policies into conformity. The dis-
puting countries must still resolve the matter themselves, often through a
negotiated settlement.[46]

The dispute settlement process is not without controversy. Some legal
experts have raised the concern that WTO panels and the Appellate Body
have exceeded their mandate to interpret the agreements and have created new rights and imposed new obligations on members. Has the WTO
overreached its authority by failing to give sufficient deference to policymakers in member countries? While most legal scholars believe that it has
not overreached, with the possible exception of trade remedies, others
are concerned that judicial legislation does occur.[47]

For example, trade remedies, such as antidumping and safeguard measures, discussed in chapter 5, have come under WTO scrutiny, and these
reviews have often found problems with the imposition of remedies by
domestic authorities. With regard to safeguards, the WTO has found fault
with just about every escape clause action undertaken by any member.

---

[45] U.S. General Accounting Office 2000b, 16.

[46] Some nonparticipants are disturbed by the closed proceedings during disputes and
ask whose interests get represented in the panels. Many NGOs, particularly environmental
groups, have complained that the WTO is secretive and antidemocratic in its procedures.
Although they are now allowed to file amicus (friends of the court) briefs, NGOs are generally barred from the dispute settlement process. This is because the WTO agreements are
strictly governmenttogovernment agreements that deal with governmental policy, and not
the behavior of private firms. The appropriate way for commercial and noncommercial
domestic interests, which are not parties to the negotiated agreements, to influence the
WTO is through their member governments. The GATT and WTO have typically operated
under a diplomatic veil rather than as an open forum in the past, because commercial negotiations involved reducing tariffs in one sector to secure lower foreign tariffs for another
sector, thus trading off various domestic interests. The United States wants the institution to
become more open and transparent, but other members have strongly resisted. Because the
WTO is a consensual body, the issue is not one to decide unilaterally and against the wishes
of the other members.

[47] Davey 2001; McRae 2004.

The WTO decisions sometimes have been unclear and often difficult to implement, creating formidable legal obstacles to using safeguards even though, as chapter 5 indicated, they may be superior to antidumping duties as a form of trade intervention.[48] Furthermore, the Appellate Body has sometimes offered up questionable, sometimes contradictory, often idiosyncratic, legal reasoning and final decisions that bring into doubt the credibility of the dispute settlement system.[49]

At the same time, the panels and Appellate Body have a difficult time with many of the cases before them. They have to apply broadly written agreements to specific factual cases that are often politically charged. Reflecting the fact that many diplomatic compromises are necessary to conclude an agreement, the WTO legal texts are filled with what lawyers call "constructive ambiguity" or what economists call "incomplete contracts." Because the agreements are often so vague, it is little wonder that the WTO panelists and Appellate Body are sometimes criticized for their decisions in specific cases. *hard to answer cases*

Another worry for the WTO is the decline in the number of cases brought to it. If trade negotiations are stalled and there are no disputes to adjudicate, then what should the WTO be doing?

Environmental Regulations and WTO Rules

Several WTO rulings have also raised questions about whether trade rules take precedence over domestic environmental, health, and safety regulations, thereby impinging on a country's sovereignty. Critics, such as Global Trade Watch, which is part of Ralph Nader's Public Citizen organization, charge that the WTO has undermined every environmental regulation it has reviewed. For example, Global Trade Watch charges that "in the WTO forum, global commerce takes precedence over everything—democracy, public health, equity, access to essential services, the environment, food safety and more . . . years of experience under the WTO have confirmed environmentalists' fears: the WTO is undermining existing local, national, and international environmental and conservation policies."[50]

[48] Irwin 2003.
[49] Cartland, Depayre, and Woznowski 2012.
[50] Wallach and Woodall 2004, 13, 20.

Unfortunately, the passionate opposition to certain rulings has given rise to much exaggeration and distortion. The General Accounting Office points out that "WTO rulings to date against U.S. environmental measures have not weakened U.S. environmental protections."[51] Most trade disputes are quite banal, and as of mid-2014, only about two dozen of the 481 disputes brought before the WTO have dealt with environmental or health issues. And these few environmental cases have mainly focused on whether the regulation in question has been implemented in a nondiscriminatory way, not whether that regulation is justifiable. At the same time, however, some cases illustrate the difficult issues and potential conflicts that can arise when trade and environmental policy intersect.

What precisely are the trade rules that affect environmental measures? The most relevant provision of the GATT is Article 20, entitled "General Exceptions:"

> Subject to the requirement that such measures are not applied in a manner which would constitute a means of arbitrary or unjustifiable discrimination between countries where the same conditions prevail, or a disguised restriction on international trade, nothing in this Agreement shall be construed to prevent the adoption or enforcement by any contracting party of measures . . .
>
> (b) necessary to protect human, animal or plant life or health . . .
>
> [or]
>
> (g) relating to the conservation of exhaustible natural resources if such measures are made effective in conjunction with restrictions on domestic production or consumption.[52]

The key element of Article 20 is the introductory paragraph. This provision allows countries to enact and enforce various measures that may restrict trade in order to achieve various objectives, provided that the measure is nondiscriminatory, does not constitute a disguised restriction

---

[51] U.S. General Accounting Office 2000b, 14.

[52] World Trade Organization 1999, 455. The remaining provisions relate to the protection of public morals, protection of national treasures of artistic, historic, or archaeological value, to trade in gold and silver, and to products of prison labor, and they include other measures such as intergovernmental commodity agreements and customs enforcement.

on international trade, and is necessary to achieve the stated objective. The subsections of Article 20 specify objectives that would justify measures to restrict trade. The most important subsections, (b) and (g), permit regulatory measures to protect human and animal health and to conserve natural resources.[53]

For example, throughout history, global commerce has been linked to the spread of disease.[54] This means that government should sometimes, ⟨—now⟩ with good reason, impose quarantines and mandate sanitary regulations on imports to protect the public health. For this reason, members of the World Trade Organization came up with the Sanitary and Phytosanitary (SPS) agreement that sets out rules for how governments can restrict imports in applying food safety and animal and plant health measures.

GATT and WTO decisions affirm that Article 20 allows countries to maintain consistent and nondiscriminatory environmental regulations.[55] Article 20 has been the focus of disputes when environmental trade measure have been implemented in a discriminatory fashion, not so much because of the exceptions specified in subsections (b) and (g). The United States has long insisted that nondiscrimination be the basis of international trade relations, which is why the most favored nation clause is instituted as Article 1, and national treatment is instituted as Article 3, of the GATT. The United States would be understandably upset if foreign regulations discriminated against American exports. If the United States insists upon receiving fair treatment abroad, it cannot be surprised that other countries demand nondiscriminatory treatment from the United States. ⟨Golden Rule⟩

[53] Wallach and Woodall (2004, 21) complain that the Article 20 exceptions apply only in certain narrowly defined circumstances and that in many cases the "exceptions were so narrowly interpreted as to render them moot." But if this is really the problem, then the members of the WTO should simply amend the Article 20 exceptions to reflect a broader view. After all, those rules are not made up by the WTO as some independent entity, but were agreed upon by the member countries of the WTO, among them the United States and European Union.

[54] Harrison 2013.

[55] For example, in 1994, a GATT panel affirmed that the corporate average fuel economy (CAFE) standards, regulating the fuel efficiency of automobiles sold in the United States, were a perfectly acceptable form of product regulation to protect public health and environment, as long as those standards did not explicitly discriminate on the basis of country of origin. Similarly, a WTO panel in 2000 upheld France's ban on asbestos imports, on the grounds that they were hazardous materials, after Canada had challenged the embargo.

This appears to be a noncontroversial proposition. Surprisingly, Public Citizen's most widely trumpeted example of the WTO's weakening of U.S. environmental regulations involves precisely this issue.

The Public Citizen book *Whose Trade Organization?* opens by accusing the WTO of forcing the Environmental Protection Agency (EPA) to weaken its environmental standards on imported gasoline. This case "was the first concrete evidence of the WTO's threat to environmental policy" and "an example of how the WTO could be used to skirt a country's democratic policymaking and judicial systems," bringing "credibility to critics' concerns that the WTO could threaten national sovereignty to set and effectively enforce important policies."[56]

Yet the case did not involve the stringency of the EPA's regulation, but simply the nondiscriminatory implementation of the regulation as required by the introductory paragraph of Article 20. Simply put, the U.S. regulation discriminated against imported gasoline to the benefit of domestically refined gasoline. The EPA was free to demand any standard of cleanliness it chose, but was obligated under Article 20 to apply the same standard to domestic and foreign producers.

In December 1993, the EPA issued a regulation to reduce the amount of contaminants in domestic and imported gasoline. Its purpose was to limit harmful emissions from automobile exhaust. Each domestic refiner was required to meet a new, more stringent standard based on its own 1990 benchmark quality level. This individual standard was permitted because a single industrywide baseline would make compliance very costly for certain domestic oil refiners, which vary in cleanliness. Imported gasoline, however, was subject to a uniform baseline, and foreign refiners were not offered the option of establishing an individual benchmark. And though this was partly for ease of administration, a less publicized reason was deliberate discrimination. As an EPA administrator later testified before Congress, the agency thought "that it was appropriate, if we had a choice, to lean in the direction of doing something that would favor their competitive position [i.e., that of domestic refiners] visàvis the [foreign producers]."[57] In other words, the EPA built in discrimination to help domestic oil refiners compete against foreign refiners.

[56] Wallach and Woodall 2004, 25.
[57] Quoted in Palmeter 1999.

In 1995, Venezuela and Brazil brought a complaint to the WTO, charging that the United States was applying a more stringent standard on imported gasoline. The panel ruled against the United States, which then appealed to the Appellate Body. The Appellate Body determined that while such regulations were permitted under Article 20, this regulation involved discrimination and therefore violated the introductory provision of the article. The Appellate Body recommended that the regulation be brought into conformity with WTO obligations, but left it to the United States to determine how it would comply.

At this point, the United States had three options: it could ignore the Appellate Body finding, let the regulation stand but offer compensation to Venezuela and Brazil in the form of lower tariffs on other products, or bring the regulation into conformity with the WTO obligation.[58] It is useful to consider the implications of each option.

If the United States chose to ignore the ruling, Venezuela and Brazil could have—after obtaining the permission of the WTO—retaliated against the United States. That is, they could withdraw previous tariff concessions extended to U.S. goods, equivalent in value to their lost gasoline exports. In practice, Venezuela and Brazil might choose not to retaliate against the United States, realizing that such actions would probably fail to accomplish anything. But they might choose this option, which would be permissible under WTO rules.

Alternatively, the United States could keep the existing regulation in place, but compensate Venezuela and Brazil by lowering tariffs against other goods. If this compensation were acceptable to Venezuela and Brazil, the case would be over. But this response requires lowering U.S. tariffs on another industry, an unlikely outcome. One trade lawyer pointed out, "Imagine the U.S. Trade Representative explaining to an industry why the United States had agreed to lower tariffs on its products in order to keep in place a discriminatory rule that favored the oil industry."[59]

[58] Public Citizen makes the options appear more draconian, saying that the "WTO's ruling forced the U.S. to make a 'no-win' choice: repeal the regulation and permit imports of gasoline with higher contamination levels . . . or keep the policy and face $150 million in trade sanctions each year the U.S. failed to comply" (Wallach and Woodall, 2004, 28). The EPA regulation would not have to be "repealed," just modified to eliminate the discrimination. The regulation would not make imports dirtier as long as the domestic regulation was made as stringent as that on imports.

[59] Palmeter 1999, 86.

In the end, the United States brought the EPA's regulation into conformity with the WTO nondiscrimination requirement. This could have been accomplished by requiring domestic refiners to meet the same statutory baseline that applied to imports, but the domestic industry did not want this option. Instead, in August 1997 the EPA allowed foreign refiners to use individual baselines, as domestic producers were allowed to do. To ensure that imports of "dirty" gas did not increase, the EPA established a benchmark for imported gasoline quality based on the volumeweighted average of individual benchmarks for domestic refiners. The EPA monitors imported gasoline closely and imposes remedies if imports do not meet that benchmark.[60]

Note that compliance with the WTO rules and resolution of this dispute had nothing to do with whether a more or less stringent standard was applied. It only required that the *same* standard be applied to domestic and foreign sources of gasoline. The EPA could have resolved the case by raising the domestic standard, rather than lowering the standard applied to imports. Thus, the case is far from one in which the WTO "undermines" domestic environmental regulation, as Global Trade Watch and others have made it out to be. In fact, Public Citizen, which decries corporate influence on government policy, put itself in the position of defending a rule that worked to the advantage of the domestic petroleum industry, one of the nation's most politically powerful special interest groups. (It is also important to understand the small stakes in this case: most of the gasoline consumed in the United States is refined in the United States from imported crude petroleum; the United States imports only a small amount of finished motor gasoline, usually less than 5 percent of the total U.S. supply.)

Some observers have also questioned whether WTO rules stand in the way of a country ensuring that its food supply is safe. In fact, those rules do not prevent a country from regulating or even temporarily banning imports when there is evidence of a risk to the public health. When the United States banned imports of livestock and meats from Europe in 2001 because of fears of mad cow and foot-and-mouth disease, the action was allowed under WTO rules. In 2007, the United States banned imports of

---

[60] For a full description, see the EPA's notice in the August 28, 1997, issue of the *Federal Register* (45544–68), available online at http://www.access.gpo.gov.

five types of farm-raised fish and shrimp from China because they had been found to contain unsafe drugs. Other countries also sometimes block U.S. agricultural exports on grounds of safety, such as the recent European ban on American apples that have a chemical preservative that could break down and become carcinogenic.

At the same time, public health is sometimes used as a justification for regulations intended only to protect special interests. Negotiators have attempted to allow health and safety regulations even if they restrict trade, while trying to discourage regulatory protectionism, that is, trade barriers designed to protect domestic producers but cloaked under a health or safety rationale. Distinguishing these two cases, however, can be extremely difficult.

The use of public health as an excuse for protectionist regulations is not a new problem.[61] Today, the United States and other countries maintain trade barriers that are ostensibly designed to protect the public health, but upon further examination are actually maintained for the benefit of producers. The Department of Agriculture estimated that questionable foreign regulations cost the United States about $5 billion in agricultural, forestry, and fishery exports in 1996.[62]

For example, the long-running dispute between the United States and European Union over hormone-treated beef is a classic example of the extreme difficulty in drawing the line between regulations to protect consumers and regulations to protect producers. The conflict began in 1985, when Europe restricted the use of natural hormones for therapeutic purposes and banned the use of synthetic hormones for growth purposes in cattle and meat sold in the EU. At the same time, the EU prohibited the importation of animals or meat from animals that had been treated with

[61] In the late 1880s, for example, many European countries banned the sale of American pork after rumors spread that it was tainted with trichinosis. Even though there proved to be no evidence of such a problem, the ban was enormously beneficial to European pork farmers, who had well-known difficulties competing against low-priced American pork. According to one historian of the incident, "The general fear of trichinosis was a godsend for European protectionists." The American consulate in Le Havre reported that French inspectors were instructed to find trichinae in at least 25 percent of American pork that they examined. The Foreign Minister of Austria-Hungary publicly admitted that protection to domestic producers was a determining factor in the exclusion, though it was ostensibly imposed for sanitary reasons. See Gignilliat 1961.

[62] Roberts and DeRemer 1997.

such hormones. Thus, the regulation seemed to be nondiscriminatory because the same standard was applied to domestic and imported meat. In such cases, the regulation cannot be held in violation of Article 1 or Article 20 of the GATT.

Implemented in 1989, the measure wiped out about $100 million in American beef exports to Europe. The United States strenuously objected, arguing that the EU ban was unjustifiable because the hormones had been found safe when used in accordance with good practices of animal husbandry. The safety of the hormones had been accepted not just by the U.S. Food and Drug Administration, but by numerous international scientific panels. Efforts to resolve the dispute under the Tokyo Round's Agreement on Technical Barriers failed because it dealt only with endproduct characteristics, and naturally occurring hormones cannot be distinguished from cattle and beef treated with supplemental hormones. As a result, the United States retaliated in 1989 by imposing 100 percent tariffs on $100 million of agricultural imports from Europe.

The United States sought to clarify international rules on health and safety regulations during the Uruguay Round, and the result was the Agreement on the Application of Sanitary and Phytosanitary Measures (SPS). The SPS agreement provides that trade-related sanitary measures should be based on scientific principles and maintained with sufficient scientific evidence (Article 2.2) or be based on international standards (if they exist). Sanitary measures should be nondiscriminatory and not be more traderestrictive than required to achieve the appropriate level of sanitary protection. In addition, Article 5.5 of the SPS states that governments should strive to achieve consistency in the protection of health risks and "shall avoid arbitrary or unjustifiable distinctions in the levels it considers to be appropriate in different situations, if such distinctions result in discrimination or a disguised restriction on international trade."[63]

The United States (supported by Australia, Canada, and New Zealand) used the SPS to challenge the EU ban on beef imports, arguing that the ban failed to meet any of these requirements. The WTO panel convened experts, two chosen by the United States, two chosen by the European Union, and another by those four, to evaluate the scientific evidence re-

---

[63] World Trade Organization 1999, 62. For an evaluation of the SPS Agreement, see Josling, Roberts, and Orden 2004.

garding the hormones. The five scientists unanimously concluded that there was no public health risk. In 1995 the United Nations Codex Alimentarius Commission and a scientific panel convened by the EU declared that there is no human health risk from the hormones when used in accordance with proper animal husbandry, confirming what other international science bodies had stated.

The record also showed that high levels of several of the hormones occurred naturally in other products, and yet they were not regulated. For example, of the six hormones at issue, the one identified as most dangerous by the EU is found from ten times to hundreds of times more concentrated in such products as eggs, cabbage, broccoli, and soybean oil than in hormone-treated beef. If the objective was to protect the public from exposure to specific hormones, then why was the sale of eggs not banned, since there are seventy-five times more naturally occurring hormones in a single egg than in a kilogram of beef? In the view of the U.S. government, these facts made the ban arbitrary and inconsistent. According to the United States, the real motivation for the measure was to protect domestic beef producers from foreign competition and to reduce surplus beef supplies in the EU. If consumer health were the true motivation, then the EU should not have continued to allow the use of growth additives by its competitive pork producers instead of disallowing it just in its less competitive beef industry.[64]

The EU countered by arguing that the ban was justified under Article 20(b) of the GATT and claimed that the United States was simply attacking the "level" of protection provided. The EU maintained that the WTO could not rule on the appropriate level of protection provided by any regulation, but merely whether the measure itself was in conformity with the SPS. The EU argued that the ban was based on the "precautionary" principle, which took the view that if scientific evidence did not establish

---

[64] The United States noted that Europe introduced milk quotas in 1984 to reduce the oversupply of dairy products, and this resulted in an increase in cattle slaughter, which more than doubled the stock of surplus beef (World Trade Organization 1997, 20). As Roberts (1998, 394) points out, "It was no coincidence, the United States argued, that EC officials were willing to allow the use of productivity-enhancing inputs in the internationally competitive pork sector, but substantially more conservative about allowing the use of such inputs in a sector which relied on costly domestic price support measures, import protection, and export subsidies to maintain producer profitability."

beyond a doubt that the hormone residues were safe for humans, then a ban was appropriate.[65] The EU stressed that it did not ban all meat imports, and that hormonefree beef could be sold in Europe.

In 1997, the WTO panel ruled that the hormone ban was not based on scientific evidence or a risk assessment and therefore was inconsistent with the EU's obligations under the SPS agreement. The Appellate Body reaffirmed that decision in 1998. In 1999, after the EU failed to implement any changes in policy, the United States imposed 100 percent tariffs on European imports valued at nearly $120 million, the estimated annual amount of lost U.S. beef exports. Proposals to resolve the impasse by replacing the import ban with a labeling requirement, allowing consumers to make the choice about whether to purchase hormone-treated beef, ran into difficulties. As of 2008, a negotiated settlement had yet to be reached and the tariffs remain in place.

[handwritten margin note: not been solved yet formally]

As already noted, Article 20 allows trade restrictions with the proviso that they be imposed in a nondiscriminatory fashion, but also that they are not "a disguised restriction on international trade." Discrimination was never an issue in this case because the use of hormones was forbidden in domestic as well as imported meat. The question is whether the measure was a "disguised restriction" on trade. The problem is that this standard is virtually impossible to determine because it gets to the unobserved motives behind a trade action. If the intention was not disguised, it would be obvious. The head of the European Alliance for Safe Meat, and a member of the European parliament, admitted that "the decision to ban these substances was made for political and commercial reasons and not, as the public was led to believe, for consumer protection."[66] Such admissions only fuel the suspicion that there is no compelling health or safety reason for the ban, but that it was designed to help special interests, namely European beef producers.

The challenge confronting trade policymakers is to distinguish health and safety protection from regulatory protectionism enacted under the

[65] Article 5.7 of the SPS states, "In cases where relevant scientific evidence is insufficient, a Member may provisionally adopt sanitary or phytosanitary measures on the basis of available pertinent information." The EU did not formally invoke this provision because its ban was permanent, and as the record made clear there was abundant scientific evidence that judicious use of hormones was not harmful.

[66] Quoted in Aaronson 2001, 153.

name of health and safety. As it turns out, there are tangible benefits to giving many of the existing regulations a hard look. As a result of the SPS agreement, the United States lifted a controversial eighty-three-year ban on Mexican avocados and allowed the importation of uncooked Argentine beef for the first time in eighty years (from regions of Argentina recognized as free of foot-and-mouth disease). In addition, Japan removed its forty-six-year ban on U.S. tomatoes, New Zealand citizens are now able to purchase Canadian salmon, and Australians are now able to buy cooked poultry meat. In each case, the restriction's public health rationale was questionable.

And yet merely writing rules (such as SPS) is not going to end such trade disputes. Negotiated rules are a useful way of finding common ground, but countries are bound to have different assessments of the risk tradeoffs involved in any given regulation. For example, the United States and European Union have different assessments of the risks of genetically modified foods, such as corn and other agricultural crops. In Europe, the food is under suspicion until proven safe, whereas in the United States, the food is acceptable until proven harmful. There is little scientific evidence that such foods are harmful, but Europe invokes the precautionary principle to justify restrictions on its use. These different principles cannot be easily bridged simply by writing down rules. The question is how far WTO members want to go in limiting the ability of governments to adopt trade restrictions when scientific evidence does not exist or is ambiguous about a particular rationale. One approach is to allow countries complete freedom in choosing their own product safety standards because they benefit the most from proper regulation and bear the cost of regulatory protectionism. Governments and the business community, however, appear to benefit from having some common ground, some rules that provide a transparent and stable system for distinguishing appropriate from inappropriate standards.

The WTO may have a limited role in such conflicts. Some trade disputes are not a matter for litigation and a legal solution, but negotiation and a diplomatic solution. As one observer of the WTO has put it, "Too much policy in the WTO is now formulated on the basis of finding legal 'solutions' to problems, often through legal interpretations of the GATT and WTO agreements, instead of through decisions taken by all members after a fullfledged policy debate. Today's WTO is moving toward being a

'House of Litigation,' lost in the intricacies of legal rulings, rather than an institution based on widely accepted principles that have produced tim-etested policies."[67] This is a critical issue that the WTO membership will have to confront in coming years.

What are some of the lessons to be learned from these and other trade and environment cases? One lesson is that unilateral trade sanctions are a poor instrument for achieving environmental objectives. Simply keeping foreign goods out of the U.S. market may be viscerally satisfying, but it does not solve the problem. The refusal of the United States to buy fish that have been caught in ways that harm other animals does nothing directly to help those other animals. Sanctions do not prevent a country from diverting tuna and shrimp caught with harmful methods away from the U.S. market toward other markets that would accept it. In the end, international agreements on standards are clearly preferable to trade embargoes, and a global approach must be taken in those negotiations, because the lack of cooperation by a few key countries can undermine the goal.

While the threat of sanctions can sometimes provide the incentive for countries to join negotiations, it is also true that countries are apt to resent and resist the imposition of U.S. standards. When other nations are reluctant to negotiate about a problem, the carrot of subsidies rather than the stick of sanctions can be used to promote the adoption of safer production methods. For example, in the 1990s Mexico clashed with the United States in GATT and WTO disputes about American restrictions on imported tuna caught in nets that could harm dolphins and turtles.[68] Instead of disrupting trade and generating a controversial, high-profile trade dispute, a straightforward solution to the problem would have been to subsidize the purchase of dolphin-safe nets and turtle excluder devices for use around the world. These technologies are not expensive. Rather than spending millions of dollars on legal fees over many years in an effort to solve the problem through compulsion, a combination of foreign aid,

[67] Sampson 2000, 7. Sampson has also noted that "perhaps [legal] rulings such as this have some short-term political merit in finding immediate 'solutions' to politically sensitive matters, but in the long term, policy choices as important as the legitimacy of the unilateral application of trade measures to enforce domestic societal preferences extraterritoriality should not be left to litigation of this nature, with confusing and uncertain outcomes" (111).

[68] For a review of the dispute, see Kelly 2014.

World Bank assistance, and NGO financial resources should have been pooled to give these dolphin and turtlesaving technologies to fishermen in developing countries.

_____Regional Trade Agreements

Although multilateral trade agreements such as the GATT have been an integral part of the international trade landscape since World War II, they have not been the only—or even the most important—method of liberalizing trade policy. Unilateral trade policy changes, rooted in domestic reforms, have been very important throughout history. As discussed in chapter 6, many developing countries have decided to make big changes in their trade regime by themselves, such as China in 1979, India in 1991, among many others. In fact, the World Bank reports that two-thirds of the tariff reductions in developing countries during the period 1983 to 2003 were due to unilateral reforms; just 25 percent were due to multilateral agreements (the Uruguay Round) and 10 percent due to regional agreements.[69]

Aside from multilateral agreements in the WTO or unilateral reforms taken on one's own, another method of reducing trade barriers is through bilateral or regional trade initiatives. Under this approach, which has proven popular in recent years, a distinction should be made between free trade agreements and customs unions. In a free trade agreement (FTA), such as NAFTA, two or more countries agree to eliminate tariffs on each other's goods, but maintain their own tariffs against imports from nonmember countries. In a customs union, such as the European Union, the member countries eliminate tariffs on each other's goods and impose a common external tariff on imports from nonmembers.

These bilateral and regional agreements come in various shapes and sizes. Some of them are substantial, such as the European Union, NAFTA, and the Common Market of the South (MERCOSUR, for Mercado Común del Sur in South America). Others are of modest importance, such as the EU-Mexico or Japan-Mexico free trade agreements. Many are trivial, such as the Taiwan-Guatemala agreement or the Singapore-Jordan accord.

Handwritten margin notes: "Domestic changes = HUGE" and "Regional trade"

[69] World Bank 2005b, 42. Also see Bhagwati 2002 for a series of case studies on the importance of unilateral trade liberalization.

Some make sense as regional partnerships, such as the Southern Africa Customs Unions (which includes South Africa, Botswana, Lesotho, Swaziland, and Namibia), whereas other link quite different countries (the Trans-Pacific Strategic Economic Partnership of Chile, New Zealand, Brunei, and Singapore).

The motivations for these agreements vary. In many instances, they are pursued as much for their political importance as for their economic effects. The formation of the European Economic Community in 1958, the precursor to the present-day European Union, was driven by a desire to solidify political and economic ties among Western European countries. When Mexico signaled that it was interested in joining the U.S.-Canada FTA to promote closer political ties and economic integration, it would have been nearly impossible for any U.S. administration to reject the opportunity to improve relations. In others cases, countries might want to obtain more secure market access to major markets, to make binding commitments for domestic policy as a signal to foreign investors, or to integrate markets more deeply than is possible through WTO agreements (such as more detailed agreements on trade in services). In particular, developing countries use trade agreements as an opportunity to implement and lock-in domestic reforms which face domestic opposition, particularly in democracies.[70]

Such trade arrangements have proliferated in recent years (see figure 7.3). The World Trade Organization reports that, whereas the GATT was notified of 124 such agreements between 1948 and 1994, the WTO has been notified of 402 agreements (in effect) from 1995 to 2014. Yet simply counting the number of bilateral and regional agreements is misleading because many of them are inconsequential. The main reason for the rapid increase in the number of RTAs during the 1990s was the proliferation of bilateral and plurilateral free trade agreements among countries of the former East bloc in Eastern Europe and the former Soviet Union: "the increased number of RTAs in the 1990s and early 2000s was largely driven by a decline in regionalism and shift toward multilateralism on the part of two dozen formerly centrally planned economies."[71] The breakup of the former Soviet Union, Yugoslavia, and Czechoslovakia has resulted in

---

[70] Baccini and Urpelainen 2014.
[71] Pomfret 2007, 928.

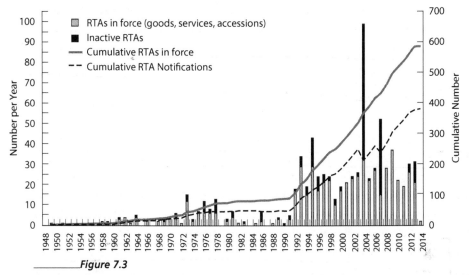

_____**Figure 7.3**

Number of Regional Trade Arrangements in Force, 1948–2014

Source: World Trade Organization, Regional Trade Agreements Information System (http://rtais.wto.org/UI/PublicMaintainRTAHome.aspx).

a huge number of free trade agreements between places that were formally tied together within one nation or through the Eastern bloc's Council of Mutual Economic Assistance.[72] This is the response to regional disintegration and the dissolution of a larger region bloc rather than an increase in regionalism, and most of the new countries embrace the multilateral system.

Still, the spread of more significant bilateral and regional trade arrangements presents difficulties for the multilateral trading system of the GATT and WTO. Such agreements depart from the nondiscriminatory, most favored nation treatment set out in Article 1 of the GATT, even though they are permitted under Article 24 of the same agreement. There is a tension between the nondiscriminatory, multilateral approach to trade liberalization and the discriminatory, preferential approach taken in bilateral and regional deals. For this reason, they are sometimes referred to as "preferential" trade agreements.

[72] For example, in 2005, Moldova formalized free trade agreements with Bulgaria, Macedonia, Serbia and Monetenegro, Bosnia and Herzegovina, Croatia, and others.

more discrim.

Indeed, many economists have viewed these preferential trade arrangements with skepticism, if not dismay, particularly in comparison to unilateral or multilateral approaches to trade liberalization.[73] The classic analysis of preferential trade arrangements distinguishes two effects: trade creation and trade diversion. When the United States and Mexico eliminated tariffs on each other's goods, for example, prices to consumers fell and trade was created. Indeed, most such agreements substantially increase trade. One study finds that free trade agreements roughly doubled trade between a pair of countries within a decade.[74]

they help w/ amnt of trade

might decline over-all

But just because more trade is generated does not mean it is all for the good. U.S. and Mexican exporters, to continue with this example, are also given preference over other countries in each other's markets. This possibly diverts existing trade away from nonmember countries. In other words, trade may grow between partners but decline between the partners and nonpartners. Trade is stimulated not on the basis of economic efficiency, but because preferential tax treatment that gives an incentive to trade with certain countries and not with others. In the worst case, the tax preference may induce countries to obtain their imports from less efficient but preferred suppliers. This raises the possibility that economic welfare is actually reduced.

In practice, the precise magnitudes of trade creation and trade diversion are hard to determine. In the case of NAFTA, for example, it is extremely difficult to distinguish the effects of the slowly phased-in tariff preferences on U.S.-Mexico trade from those of the peso crisis in December 1994 and the ongoing rise of the maquiladoras. One recent study found that NAFTA not only succeeded in expanding intra-bloc trade, but it also improved Mexico's welfare by 1.3 percent and U.S. welfare by 0.1 percent, although Canada's welfare fell by 0.06 percent.[75] In fact, the welfare effects of the preference trade agreements are not always easy to gauge. Assessment hinges on whether (pre-tariff) import prices were actually higher than they would have been in the absence of the preferential treatment. There is precious little empirical evidence on this crucial point: some research suggests that, in the case of the MERCUSOR trade

[73] See Bhagwati 2008 for a spirited attack on preferential trade agreements.
[74] Baier and Bergstrand 2007.
[75] Caliendo and Perro 2014.

[handwritten: Interesting & makes sense]

agreement in South America, preferences harmed the welfare of non-members by forcing them to reduce their export prices.[76]

Furthermore, preferential trade arrangements detract from two key components of the multilateral trading system: nondiscrimination and transparency. Nondiscrimination is desirable not only because it promotes economic efficiency, but also because it levels the playing field in terms of power relationships: tiny Jamaica or St. Kitts get the same access to the U.S. market as Canada or the EU. The adverse effect of trade preferences on nonparticipants is damaging to the world trading system. Some small, poorer countries that do not have the clout to merit an FTA agreement with the United States or EU, such as African countries or smaller Caribbean or Asian countries, are excluded and discriminated against in the larger markets.

[handwritten: present agreements hurts small guys]

While the United States and EU sometimes offer these poor developing countries special trade preferences, these preferences have problems as well.[77] Usually they are granted on just a select group of goods, not all goods like an FTA, and thus reinforce the specialization of the developing countries in certain commodities. The preferences also require frequent renewal, meaning that foreign investors face uncertainty about whether market access will continue. Finally, once given preferences, developing countries want to preserve them, even resisting any multilateral liberalization that might reduce overall trade barriers but would erode their preferential access. For example, in the 1990s the EU restricted banana imports from Central American countries so that it could import bananas from former colonies in Africa and the Caribbean, even though the latter suppliers were much less efficient. The latter suppliers, particularly small islands in the Caribbean, fiercely resisted Central American efforts to open up the EU banana market on a nondiscriminatory basis.

[handwritten: keep them special.]

[handwritten: Small guys won't let go. they get preferenti agreement]

And preferential trade arrangements undermine transparency by creating complex and conflicting policies governing imports of the same goods from different countries. This fragments the world trading system and increases the cost and uncertainty of trade. One potentially serious distortion to trade that arises in preferential agreements is rules of origin.

---

[76] Winters and Chang 2000.

[77] In the U.S. case, the Caribbean Basin Initiative, the African Growth and Opportunity Act (AGOA), and the Andean Trade Preferences Act, all give selective preferences to developing country imports.

trans-shipment

In an FTA, each member country retains its own tariff schedule that it applies to imports from nonmember countries.[78] This gives rise to trans-shipment: the incentive to bring imports into the low-tariff country and then ship them into the high-tariff country to avoid paying the higher duties. To stop transshipment, NAFTA mandates that duty-free treatment extend only to goods with sufficient "North American" content.

About two hundred pages of the two-thousand-page NAFTA text are devoted to rules of origin, which are stricter than those in the U.S.-Canada Free Trade Agreement. In the Canadian agreement, automobiles must have 50 percent North American content to receive duty-free treatment, but this was raised to 62.5 percent in NAFTA. In the original agreement with Canada, textile and apparel goods must be made from North American fabric to be eligible, but under NAFTA the yarn from which the fabric is woven must also be of North American content. Thus, Mexican garments receive duty-free treatment in the United States only if the yarn is made, the cloth woven, and the cutting and sewing done primarily in North America. Rules of origin can distort trade when exporters strive to raise artificially the North American content so that the goods can qualify for duty-free treatment in the United States.[79]

One of the key issues concerning regional trade arrangements is whether they are stepping stones toward the multilateral liberalization of trade, or stumbling blocks that impede multilateralism and simply create trade blocs that distort commerce into artificial regional patterns. One hope is for "open regionalism" that allows any country that wishes to join an agreement the freedom to do so, or that eventually leads to the merging of the various agreements at a broader level. It is difficult to know, a priori, whether regional and multilateral trade arrangements are complements or substitutes. In practice, open regionalism does not appear to work: the various agreements are not easily harmonized, and accession for interested parties is not easy because insiders often want to continue to discriminate against outsiders. The empirical evidence on stepping stones versus stumbling blocks is mixed. Some studies show that the United States and European Union reduced their tariffs less in the Uruguay Round on goods heavily traded in its existing FTAs, implying that

doth? working against itself

---

[78] In a customs union such as the EU, all member countries have a common external tariff.

[79] Krueger 1999.

[handwritten: Don't appear to help multi-lateralism]

the preferential agreements were stumbling blocks to multilateral reforms.[80] In contrast, for Latin American countries, FTAs appear to be linked to faster declines in external tariffs, but not in the case of customs unions.[81]

After the formation of the GATT, the United States signed very few free trade agreements (with Israel in 1985, Canada in 1989, and NAFTA in 1993). However, in the early 2000s, the Bush administration made such trade agreements a central part of its trade strategy. Robert Zoellick, the U.S. trade representative under President George W. Bush, argued that bilateral agreements were a part of a "competitive liberalization" strategy that would jump-start the WTO process in which the most reluctant reformers could slow progress toward dismantling trade barriers. In Zoellick's view, the United States would bypass the WTO and pursue bilateral and regional trade agreements as a way of putting pressure on those reluctant reformers. As he argued,

[handwritten: bilateral to fuel competit- liberalization]

> If some regions are too slow to open their markets, the United States should move on to others. America should spur a competitive dynamic for openness and transparency. Competition can work wonders: when the United States pursued NAFTA and APEC, the EU finally felt the pressure to complete the global Uruguay Round trade negotiations. If others hold back in the new WTO round, the United States should repeat this strategy of regionalism with a global goal in order to break the logjam.[82]

As a result, the United States significantly increased the number of bilateral trade negotiations for a few years after from 2001. As indicated in table 7.4, the United States concluded agreements with Jordan, Australia, Chile, Singapore, Peru, Morocco, Bahrain, South Korea, Colombia, Panama, and five Central American countries (Costa Rica, El Salvador, Guatemala, Honduras, and Nicaragua) and the Dominican Republic (CAFTA-DR, which stands for "Central American Free Trade Agreement and the Dominican Republic").

Despite the hopes that bilateral agreements would fuel "competitive liberalization," it seemed to trigger more bilateral agreements rather than

[80] Limão 2006 and Karacaovali and Limão 2008.
[81] Estevadeordal, Freund, and Ornelas 2008.
[82] Zoellick 2000.

_____Table 7.4.
U.S. Regional and Bilateral Trade Agreements

Country or region	Status (as of June 2014)
Israel	In effect since 1985
North American Free Trade Agreement (NAFTA)—Canada and Mexico	In effect since 1994
Jordan	In effect since 2001
Singapore	In effect since 2004
Chile	In effect since 2004
Australia	In effect since 2005
Morocco	In effect since 2005
Central American Free Trade Agreement & Dominican Republic (CAFTA-DR)—Costa Rica, El Salvador, Guatemala, Honduras, Nicaragua	In effect since 2006
Bahrain	In effect since 2006
Peru	In effect since 2009
Oman	In effect since 2009
Colombia	In effect since 2012
Panama	In effect since 2012
Republic of Korea	In effect since 2012
Southern African Customs Union (Botswana, Lesotho, Namibia, South Africa, Swaziland)	Negotiations launched June 2003
Trans-Pacific Partnership (TPP)	Negotiations launched in December 2010
Transatlantic Trade and Investment Partnership (TTIP)	U.S.-EU negotiations launched in July 2013

Source: Office of the U.S. Trade Representative.

Note: TPP involves the United States, Japan, Australia, Brunei, Canada, Chile, Malaysia, Mexico, New Zealand, Peru, Singapore, and Vietnam. South Korea and Taiwan have expressed an interest in joining the negotiations.

accelerate the completion of the Doha Round.[83] For example, shortly after the United States signed NAFTA with Mexico, the European Union sought a similar trade agreement with Mexico to keep its exports competitive in the country. Indeed, the United States has not been alone in negotiating bilateral and regional trade deals. The EU has actively pursued them, and they have spread throughout Asia and Latin America as well. Some have argued that this takes attention away from the multilateral discussions at the WTO, the only forum where agricultural subsidies and trade barriers

[83] Evenett and Meier 2008.

can be effectively discussed and where the interests of small countries stand a chance for representation.

We have already mentioned the idea that such trade agreements are a credible way of introducing economic reforms that come with openness to trade. For example, such agreements could serve as a commitment device to destroy rents generated by protectionist policies. By reducing such rents through increased competition, FTAs make political power less financially attractive to antidemocratic groups, such as oligarchs. Therefore, governments in unstable democracies may want to pursue FTAs to more firmly establish the rule of law and consolidate the institution of democracy. In fact, recent research has confirmed a link between the simultaneous rapid growth of regional trade agreements and worldwide democratization since the late 1980s.[84] Furthermore, countries signing free trade agreements, particularly those that yield large economic gains, are less likely to go to war with one another.[85]

At the same time, the formation of competing trade blocs could fuel great power rivalries. For example, China and the Association of South East Asian Nations (ASEAN) reached an FTA that came into force in 2010. This had been a worrisome development for Korea, which was not included, but not as much for Japan, which had an FTA with ASEAN. And American commercial interests could be compromised if China secures preferential access to raw materials and important markets in Asia and elsewhere, putting the United States at a competitive disadvantage.

The Democrats' capture of the Congress in the 2006 midterm elections spelled the end of the Bush trade agenda.[86] Then the Obama administration stopped pursuing FTAs in deference to the Democratic

---

[84] Liu and Ornelas 2014.

[85] Martin, Mayer, and Thoenig 2012.

[86] The Bush administration's push for bilateral FTAs created some problems in Congress. Some agreements were uncontroversial and passed the Congress easily, such as those with Australia, Singapore, Morocco, and Bahrain. Others encountered stiff opposition and required much arm twisting to ensure their passage, such as CAFTA-DR and Oman. The close, partisan nature of these trade votes gave individual members of Congress an incentive to keep their position ambiguous until they obtained a political favor from the president in exchange for their vote. Because of skepticism about the political value (to members of Congress) of trade agreements, Congress became increasingly reluctant to endorse more and more new FTAs. Simply put, Congress does not want to deal with the issue on a frequent basis.

Party's opposition to trade agreements, particularly with developing countries. Many Democrats believe that such trade agreements should include stronger labor and environmental provisions, but others do not want them pursued at all. After several years of delay, and with great reluctance, the Obama administration finally submitted to Congress two FTAs negotiated by the Bush administration, one with Columbia and another with Korea. Congress passed them in 2011, largely with Republican support.

The fear of FTAs among Democrats is largely related to the opposition of labor unions to these agreements. The unions complain that these agreements will lead to more imports and a loss of American jobs. In fact, because U.S. barriers to imports are already so low, these agreements more often open up foreign markets for American exports. For example, in its investigation of the U.S.-Colombia FTA, the International Trade Commission concluded that the agreement would have a small, positive impact on U.S. exports, which face tariffs in the 10–20 percent range in Colombia, and almost no impact on U.S. imports because more than 90 percent of Colombia's goods (which account for just 0.5 percent of total U.S. imports) already entered the U.S. market duty-free.[87] Thus, the agreement would have been a "tax cut on exports" with virtually no impact on American jobs, but nonetheless the whole deal was politically controversial.

While trade agreements have long sparked opposition from labor unions and environmental groups, they have also generated controversy over their provisions regarding investor-state relations. These provisions allow foreign investors to sue host governments in third-party arbitration tribunals when a government fails to treat investors fairly under an investment agreement. The goal is to provide extra security to foreign investors and hence attract investment. The special dispute settlement process avoids domestic courts for fear that they will favor the host government over foreign investors. Critics charge that such provisions allow corporations to contest government regulations in a nontransparent, antidemocratic setting (the tribunals), while proponents point out that governments sign such agreements to commit to treating foreign investment

[87] U.S. International Trade Commission 2006.

fairly. Chapter 11 of NAFTA, which deals with investor-state dispute settlement, has led to several controversial cases.[88]

Because investor-state dispute settlement provisions are now being included in trade agreements, new opposition to those agreements has arisen. Yet the investor-state relations are most appropriately dealt with in bilateral investment treaties rather than trade agreements. Some of the political opposition to trade agreements would go away if those provisions were not included in the agreements. As one American proponent of trade liberalization argues, it is "unnecessary, unreasonable, and unwise" to include investor protection provisions in trade agreements because they are "a significant reason why trade agreements engender so much antipathy" and yet they are "not even essential to the task of freeing trade."[89]

In its second term, the Obama administration began to push two major trade initiatives, the Trans-Pacific Partnership (TPP) and the Transatlantic Trade and Investment Partnership (TTIP). TPP involves the United States and about a dozen Pacific Rim countries, while TTIP is a U.S.-EU venture. The goal of both negotiations is to conclude agreements that will increase market access among the participants by reducing tariff and especially nontariff barriers to trade. As of early-2015, TPP was supposedly close to being concluded. However, many complex issues were still under discussion. There were negotiating groups on competition policy, cross-border services, customs issues, e-commerce, environment, financial services, government procurement, intellectual property, investment, labor, market access for goods, rules of origin, sanitary and phytosanitary standards, technical barriers to trade, telecommunications, textiles and apparel, and trade remedies. It is difficult to know whether rules in these areas, such as regulatory coherence, will expand trade. For example, it is harder to

[88] For example, in 2009 a NAFTA panel awarded Cargill, a multinational company specializing in agricultural products, $77 million from the government of Mexico for violating the agreement after the country raised its tariff on imported drinks made with high-fructose corn syrup but not the tariff on drinks made with cane sugar.

[89] Ikenson 2014, 1. He gives eight reasons for why investor-state provisions should not be included in trade agreements, including that they socialize the risk of foreign direct investment, exceed "national treatment" obligations, expose an increasing number of U.S. laws and regulations to challenges, reinforce the idea that trade primarily benefits large corporations, and are ripe for exploitation by creative lawyers.

measure, say, the impact of technical barriers through government regulations on trade than it is to estimate the impact of tariff changes on trade. One estimate suggested that the TPP could generate a global annual benefit of $295 billion by 2025.[90] However, freer trade in agricultural goods, for example, may be difficult to achieve because Japan and other Asian countries are sensitive about protecting local rice farmers.

The TPP involves major Pacific Rim countries—with the notable exception of China.[91] The exclusion of China was not an accident; the goal of U.S. negotiators was to conclude an agreement to their liking and then invite China to join on those terms, rather than having the difficult time of negotiating directly with China. The Obama administration wanted to ensure that the United States, and not just China, would have a major role in shaping trade in Asia in the decades to come. That is because China has been seeking its own free trade agreements with Asian countries and is actively supporting a Regional Comprehensive Economic Partnership (RCEP) with the ten members of the Association of Southeast Asian Nations (ASEAN) and with Japan, Korea, Australia, India, and New Zealand. The creation of such a trade bloc would constitute a threat to U.S. trade interests in the region, which is why the United States has viewed the TPP as a strategic priority.

By contrast, there is no such urgency with the TTIP negotiations between the United States and the European Union. These negotiations began in 2013 and probably have a long way to go. The broad agenda is similar to that of the TPP. Because tariff barriers are already fairly low between the two partners, the negotiations will focus mainly on rules and harmonizing regulatory barriers. But even though the United States and EU share a desire to promote trade, the negotiations will be particularly complex and will likely be more problematic than many anticipate.

Although regional trade agreements have been subject to many valid criticisms, such agreements have some countervailing benefits. The concerns about trade creation and trade diversion take a purely static view of trade, ignoring the beneficial effects on productivity as a result of greater competition. Trade diversion may not be a serious concern if tariff levels are already low and rules of origin are liberal. Developing countries

[90] Petri and Plummer 2012.

[91] Other major countries, such as Korea, Taiwan, and Indonesia, are also not yet part of the negotiations.

may be able to lock in greater access to richer, developed markets, although they also may take on burdensome requirements in intellectual property and other areas. And sometimes regional trade agreements might be able to provide templates that later can be adopted at the multilateral level, as was the case with the U.S.-Canada agreement on services trade.

Despite these benefits, one serious concern is that these trade agreements tend to exclude smaller, poorer countries in South Asia, Latin America, and Africa. This could make it harder for those countries, which already suffer from high trade costs, from participating fully in world trade. It also risks a serious fragmentation of the world trading system into high-income countries that have the capacity to participate in these complex negotiations and low-income countries that cannot. The idea of "open regionalism," with any country being able to join any agreement that it likes, might solve this problem but has yet to become a reality.

[margin note: increases global trade disparity]

One final matter concerns the scope of the regional trade agreements that the United States continues to pursue under both Democratic and Republican administrations. As we have seen, formal tariff and quota barriers to trade (i.e., those imposed at the border when foreign goods enter a market) have generally fallen to low levels. Consequently, trade agreements have increasingly focused on "behind the border" regulatory measures that affect trade. This makes the agreements potentially more invasive and controversial. And it raises a fundamental question: what is the objective of such agreements and how is free trade to be defined? Does free trade mean "no protection" for domestic producers (nondiscrimination) or does it mean a "single market" (open access)?[92]

For example, if the European Union bans all genetically modified food, is that a trade barrier? If free trade is defined as nondiscrimination, then the regulation is not a problem since it applies equally to domestic and foreign food producers. If free trade is defined as a single market, then the ban is a problem because most farmers around the world will not be able to sell their goods in the EU market. Which conception of free trade is most desirable and attainable? The WTO agreements attempt to balance these two conceptions by giving governments space for their own regula-

---

[92] Simon Lester, "America's Free Trade Conundrum." January 8, 2015. http://national interest.org/feature/americas-free-trade-conundrum-11993 (accessed February 4, 2015).

tory policies but also trying to limit the protectionist effects of such policies. Finding such a balance is difficult, but future regional agreements may attempt to achieve a degree of integration that goes beyond that in the WTO. Looking forward, future trade agreements will increasingly have to confront these difficult issues.

Given the obstacles to reaching multilateral trade agreements with the WTO membership, the trend toward more bilateral and regional agreements is likely to continue. Because of their overlapping nature, to say nothing of their complexity, regional trade agreements detract from the simplicity that was part of the multilateral system's design. At the same time, some of the regional agreements could serve as templates for multilateral negotiations. And the hope remains that regional agreements can, at some point in the future, be "multilateralized," that is, harmonized and folded into the WTO. While the nondiscriminatory multilateral approach to trade liberalization may be closer to the economist's ideal, many countries are unwilling to wait for a WTO consensus to undertake efforts to further expand trade.

Conclusion

No nation was ever ruined by trade, even seemingly the most
disadvantageous.

—George Whaley, 1774

Speaking at Dartmouth College several years ago, former senator George Mitchell said that he had drawn two conclusions from his role as mediator in the conflict in Northern Ireland: that economic opportunity is a prerequisite for peace, and that America's vision of that economic opportunity is the basis of its influence in the world.

These simple observations have some connection to trade policy. For nearly three-quarters of a century, the United States has nurtured a rules-based world trading system centered on the principle of nondiscrimination and the goal of gradually reducing trade barriers. The United States is admired around the world as a place of economic opportunity, where individuals are given a chance to succeed regardless of their background. (The election of Barack Obama as president of the United States has underscored this fact.) America's free and competitive markets, and its willingness to accept goods and services from all over the world, is one reason it is so highly regarded. If the United States weakens its commitment to a system of open world trade, other countries will inevitably follow. The United States is expected to set an example for the world, and people everywhere look to it for leadership. The trade policy choices that it makes have ramifications far beyond America's shores and have implications well beyond economics.

The open world trading system has faced many challenges in the past and will continue to face challenges in the future. In the 1970s and 1980s, the major threat to open trade was protectionism in developed countries. Protectionist pressures are always present because, as this book has noted many times, some economic interests will always be adversely affected by imports and will seek to limit them. In those two decades, painful recessions and structural changes led to an increase in the demand for trade barriers. In the United States and elsewhere, industry after industry, from footwear and apparel to automobiles and steel to semiconductors and consumer electronics, received protection from foreign competition through antidumping duties, import quotas, voluntary export restraints, orderly market arrangements, and other trade barriers.[1] Fortunately, these import restrictions proved temporary and most of them had lapsed by the early 1990s.

During the 1990s and 2000s, the main challenge facing the world trading system was not protectionism driven by interest groups, but the anti-globalization movement. This new challenge came from nongovernmental organizations (NGOs) often called "civil society." These "public interest" groups did not represent economic interests, but stood for particular causes and included "consumer associations, conservation and environmental groups, societies concerned with development in poor countries, human rights groups, movements for social justice, humanitarian societies, organizations representing indigenous people, and church groups from all denominations."[2] In many instances, these groups were hostile to the existing system of world trade, and even the idea of a market economy.[3] Although these anti-globalization groups have not been represented in the corridors of power, they have been able to achieve broad appeal by focusing on human rights, corporate responsibility, and sus-

---

[1] See Krueger (1996) for a collection of industry case studies on U.S. trade policy during this period.

[2] Henderson 2001, 19. See also Robertson 2000.

[3] "With some exceptions, they are hostile to, or highly critical of, capitalism, multinational corporations, freedom of cross-border trade and capital flows, and the idea of a market economy," notes David Henderson (2001, 20), the former chief economist of the OECD. "They are a force on the side of interventionism." Despite differences of interest and emphasis among these groups, the more radical elements "share a vision of the world in which past history and present-day market-based economic systems are portrayed in terms of patterns of oppression and abuses of power. Free markets and capitalism are seen as embodying and furthering environmental destruction, male dominance, class oppression, racial intolerance, imperialist coercion and colonial exploitation." As *The Economist* once put it, "It is no coincidence that the keenest economic reformers among the developing and ex-communist countries are the new champions of free trade. It is also no coincidence that those in the industrial countries who are most fearful about the future seek to lessen the rich world's reliance on the market economy, and have made it their first goal to smash the GATT and the other institutions of liberal trade. Both sides, in their different ways, are right. Each has recognized that the market economy is ultimately inseparable from a liberal order of international trade. See "Battle Lines," *The Economist*, December 24, 1994, 14.

tainable development, all of which are agreeable in principle but behind which are very different views of policy.[4]

The recent books of the prominent Canadian journalist Naomi Klein are extreme examples of this view. Klein's 2000 book *No Logo* was a spirited attack on multinational corporations and the policies of the WTO.[5] In her 2007 book *The Shock Doctrine: The Rise of Disaster Capitalism*, Klein argues that natural disasters, wars, and coups are welcomed (if not organized by) by those who favor neoliberal economic policies because they provide an opportunity to impose privatization and free trade on an unwilling citizenry. These policies, she maintains, have produced catastrophic results, including economic depressions and mass poverty. She likens free-market shock therapy to electroshock torture.

The wide-ranging charges made by Klein and the anti-globalization groups were impressive in their scope and received a great deal of attention. At the time, these groups seemed poised to become an influential part of the debate for bringing into serious question the benefits of globalization. "If the critics were right," Martin Wolf, the chief economics commentator of the *Financial Times,* pointed out, "supporters of the global market economy would be in favour of mass poverty, grotesque inequality, destruction of state-provided welfare, infringement of national sovereignty, subversion of democracy, unbridled corporate power, environmental degradation, human rights abuses and much more."[6] These claims prompted Wolf to write *How Globalization Works* and the eminent economist Jagdish Bhagwati to write *In Defense of Globalization*, both published in 2004, to counter the growing skepticism.

But, of course, the critics were not right. Time and experience demonstrated that globalization did not lead to an intensification of poverty. Instead, expanding world trade proved to be an escalator for bringing poor people out of poverty. Between 1990 and 2011, the portion of the world's population living in extreme poverty fell from 36 to 15 percent, according to the World Bank. The International Labor Office reported that

---

[4] "All three appear, and are presented, as proof against doubt and objections: who could want to oppose, deny or restrict human rights, to prefer that corporations should act non-responsibly, or to advocate development that was unsustainable? Yet all these virtuous-seeming notions, as now interpreted, bear a collectivist message" (Henderson 2001, 31).

[5] See Segerstrom 2003 for a level-headed critique.

[6] Wolf 2004, 23.

the number of workers in the world earning less than $1.25 a day has fallen to 375 million in 2013 from 811 million in 1991.[7] The past two decades have seen extraordinary progress in poverty reduction in the developing world. Who should get the credit, the Millennium Development Goals of the United Nations and other international aid agencies? Not quite. As *The Economist* put it, "The MDGs may have helped marginally, by creating a yardstick for measuring progress, and by focusing minds on the evil of poverty. Most of the credit, however, must go to capitalism and free trade, for they enable economies to growth—and it was growth, principally, that has eased destitution."[8]

The evidence for this has been so overwhelming that, as noted in chapter 6, even U2's Bono grudgingly conceded the benefits of global commerce. And, as chapter 2 pointed out, trade can check corporate power through greater competition, can improve the environment by allowing the spread of new, cleaner technologies, and may even unleash a process of change that promotes democracy, as we have seen in Chile, Mexico, South Korea, Taiwan, and elsewhere. The alternative of economic nationalism, on the other hand, has exacerbated rather than ameliorated many of the problems that the critics identify. In retrospect, the anti-globalization NGOs and other groups have not posed as strong a threat to the open trading system as many had anticipated because their view of globalization as a race to the bottom was erroneous.

The most recent challenge to the system of open trade arose during the world's financial crisis and Great Recession of 2008–9. Marked by plummeting stock markets, sharply rising unemployment rates, a deep slump in output, and the threat of deflation, the crisis prompted many comparisons to the Great Depression of the 1930s. Many commentators feared a resurgence of protectionism and beggar-thy-neighbor policies, as seen in the 1930s. Although trade barriers did increase during the crisis, trade interventions were much more tempered than just about anyone expected.

There are many reasons why 1930s-style protectionism did not repeat itself. First, countries today have many more policy instruments for addressing economic crises than they did in the 1930s. Governments then

[7] Douglas Irwin, "The Ultimate Global Antipoverty Program," *Wall Street Journal*, November 3, 2014.

[8] "Toward the End of Poverty," *The Economist*, June 1, 2013, 11.

took no responsibility for supporting financial institutions and were unable to pursue reflationary monetary policies because of fixed exchange rates under the gold standard. Countries resorted to draconian import restrictions in the 1930s because they lacked other macroeconomic policy instruments, mainly monetary policy, to stabilize the financial system and improve economic conditions. Today, central banks can act swiftly to provide liquidity and shore up the financial system, preventing a wholesale economic collapse.   ⌐better prepared

Second, in the 1930s, countries could impose higher trade barriers without violating any international agreements or expecting much of a foreign reaction. Today, WTO agreements restrict the use of such discretionary trade policy. Countries that are tempted to violate WTO agreements can have no illusion that they will avoid swift foreign retaliation if they choose that path. When a country is certain that its exports will be hit by other countries if it chooses to impose WTO-inconsistent import barriers, it will think twice about doing so.   *too much protect ain't allowed*

Third, foreign investment has transformed the world economy. Leading firms around the world have become so multinational in their production operations and supply chains that they have a vested interest in resisting protectionism. Many domestic industries no longer have a strong incentive to demand import restrictions because foreign rivals now produce in the domestic market, thereby erasing any gain from trade barriers for domestic firms. For example, unlike in the early 1980s, U.S. automakers did not ask for trade protection because it would not solve any of their problems; they are diversified into other markets with equity stakes in foreign producers, and foreign firms operate large production facilities in the United States.

All of these factors have sustained political support for an open trading system and have prevented a trade policy retreat toward closed markets in the face of a painful crisis period and a slow global recovery from the recession.

What are the future threats to the system of open trade? It is very difficult to predict what concerns will arise about international trade over the next decade. Public attention has turned to the issue of rising inequality, exemplified by the global critical acclaim that greeted Thomas Piketty's book *Capital in the Twenty-First Century*, published in 2014. While Piketty worried about capital accumulation, not globalization, as the key driver of income inequality within countries, many others still worry about trade as a factor. The fear that trade with low-wage countries has undermined the middle class in high-wage countries remains widespread. Yet at the same time, it should be recognized that globalization has actually *reduced* world-wide income inequality among individuals, largely because of rising incomes in China and India.[9]

Another looming issue is the relationship between trade and climate change. In an effort to reduce carbon emissions, countries might start imposing tariffs on the carbon content of imports to compensate for taxes on domestic producers. Unless this issue is handled well, it could lead to "green protectionism" that would severely disrupt world trade.

Carbon emissions have been linked to global climate change and constitute a negative externality that call for an international response. While U.S. greenhouse gas emissions, predominantly CO_2, fell 10 percent between 2005 and 2012, albeit from high levels, such emissions continue to increase in the developing world.[10] For example, China has vastly expanded its use of coal-burning furnaces to produce electricity and fuel its industry, leading to horrific levels of pollution in its major cities. Not only does this have serious adverse health consequences for the Chinese people, there is evidence that pollution from China is coming across the Pacific Ocean and affecting the environment in the United States, as well as its link to global warming. Since the problem of greenhouse gas emissions is global, the best solution to this negative externality would be a global tax on CO_2 emissions, regardless of the source country. Companies, farmers, and consumers would be charged a fee for every ton of CO_2 that they emit in production or that cause emissions in their use (such as gasoline). However, to date, international action to reduce emissions has failed, as evidenced by the collapse of the 2009 Copenhagen summit.

Individual countries could reduce their own carbon emissions by imposing their own carbon tax. This would increase the cost of producing steel, chemicals, farm goods, and other products whose production involves the emissions of CO_2. Because this tax on domestic producers would affect their competitive position relative to foreign producers, a border tax adjustment that imposes a similar levy on the carbon content

[9] Milanovic 2013.

[10] http://www.epa.gov/climatechange/ghgemissions/usinventoryreport.html.

of imports could be used to level the playing field with foreign producers of those goods. This would prevent "carbon leakage," or the substitution of dirty imports for cleaner domestic production.

This raises the problem of calculating the "carbon-content" of foreign goods. For example, if an automobile manufactured in the United States generates ten tons of carbon dioxide, which is then taxed at $60 per ton, the additional cost per car is $600. Should cars imported from Korea be taxed at that rate as well, or should a calculation be made about the carbon tonnage associated with producing the car in Korea? Should the United States investigate how many tons of carbon dioxide are associated with different goods produced by different firms in different countries and levy the tax accordingly? This sounds much like an antidumping investigation, but involves an even more complicated set of factors. In fact, it is likely that making border tax adjustments based on carbon emissions consistent with WTO rules "will have such onerous informational needs that importing countries will find implementation nearly impossible."[11] Furthermore, would the process of determining the carbon tariff be fair and free of political influence?

Even worse, some countries, such as the United States, seem more inclined to adopt a system of "cap and trade" rather than a straightforward carbon tax. This less-efficient alternative makes the border tax adjustment even more complicated. Under "cap and trade," the government sets a total allowable national emission of CO_2 per year and producers are required to have a permit specifying how much they are allowed to emit. If the government auctions off the permits, or the permits are tradable on an exchange, the price of the permit would be roughly equivalent to a carbon tax. But then countries would have different permit prices, which might fluctuate month to month and which would then have to be reconciled by complex border tax adjustments.

The problem is compounded when politics enters the equation, as it inevitably would. Article 3.5 of the United Nations Framework Convention on Climate Change states that the following: "Measures taken to combat climate change, including unilateral ones, should not constitute a means of arbitrary or unjustifiable discrimination or a disguised restriction on international trade." Yet domestic firms would be tempted to complain

[11] Moore 2011, 1681.

about foreign pollution as a way of getting carbon tariffs imposed on their foreign rivals. Such a situation could lead to absolute chaos in the world trading system. Even Ralph Nader has warned that "runaway environmental protectionism—which Washington's K Street lobbyists would be only too happy to grease—would almost certainly lead to a collapse of the multilateral trading system."[12]

In a worse-case scenario, one country's complaint about another country's carbon tariff would lead to a cycle of retaliatory and counter-retaliatory import restrictions, as each country tries to impose its environmental standards on others, shutting down world trade. Arriving at an impartial view of what deserves to be taxed could be impossible. For example, the United States might want to impose penalties on imports of Chinese goods produced using "dirty" manufacturing methods. But China might respond by saying that the overall U.S. production process releases more carbon because, although the U.S factory might be cleaner, American workers drive to and from work and live in large homes and therefore have a much bigger carbon footprint than their Chinese counterparts. Then they could justify imposing green taxes on imports from the United States.

Should the world community begin to get serious about limiting carbon emissions, the challenge of integrating new environmental rules into the world trading system and avoiding "green protectionism" will be critical. Some WTO rules may have to be changed to ensure this. For example, the WTO subsidies agreement may be an obstacle to government support for renewal energy sources.[13]

As noted earlier, perhaps the best solution would be an international agreement on a global tax on CO_2 emissions. Such an agreement, although difficult to reach and to implement, would address the root source of greenhouse gas emissions, provide for a uniform treatment of producers across different countries, and thereby preserve the open world trading system and all the benefits that it creates.

---

[12] Ralph Nader and Toby Heaps, "We Need a Global Carbon Tax," *Wall Street Journal*, December 3, 2008, A17.

[13] Hufbauer, Charnovitz, and Kim 2009. For example, are government subsidies or tax breaks for wind, solar, and hydro energy development permissible under the subsidies code of the WTO? Maybe not, as Rubini (2014) argues.

Such a tax would reduce trade, but more trade is not always the goal. Effective environmental and safety regulations should not be avoided simply because they reduce international trade. The notion that all trade must be kept free at all costs is simply wrong. As Thomas Babington Macaulay put it in a parliamentary speech in 1845,

> I am, I believe, as strongly attached as any member of this House to the principle of free trade, rightly understood. Trade, considered merely as trade, considered merely with reference to the pecuniary interest of the contracting parties, can hardly be too free. But there is a great deal of trade which cannot be considered merely as trade, and which affects higher than pecuniary interests. And to say that government never ought to regulate such trade is a monstrous proposition, a proposition at which Adam Smith would have stood aghast.[14]

In any event, the difficult policy choices at the intersection of trade policy and climate change policy could be where the key battles over the world trading system are fought in coming years.

To conclude, trade policy has always been one of the most contentious areas of economic policy and is therefore the subject of a never-ending debate. Though the post–World War II period has been marked by a concerted reduction in trade barriers, the matter is not settled because the pressures to weaken the commitment to open markets never abate. The world trading system is far from perfect, and many reforms and changes in rules should be under discussion. Yet, in so doing, we should always keep in mind the manifold benefits of world trade and the contribution of trade to the welfare and prosperity of billions of people around the world.

[14] Macaulay 1900, 102.

References

Aaronson, Susan A. 2001. *Taking Trade to the Streets: The Lost History of Public Efforts to Shape Globalization*. Ann Arbor: University of Michigan Press.

Abbott, Philip C. 2012. "Export Restrictions as Stabilization Responses to Food Crisis." *American Journal of Agricultural Economics* 94: 428–34.

Acemoğlu, Daron, David Autor, David Dorn, Gordon Hanson, and Brendan Price. 2015. "Import Competition and the Great US Employment Sag of the 2000s." *Journal of Labor Economics*.

Acharya, Ram C., and Wolfgang Keller. 2009. "Technology Transfer through Imports." *Canadian Journal of Economics* 42: 1411–48.

Addison, John T., Douglas A. Fox, and Christopher J. Ruhm. 1995. "Trade and Displacement in Manufacturing." *Monthly Labor Review* 118: 58–67.

Ades, Alberto, and Rafael Di Tella. 1999. "Rents, Competition, and Corruption." *American Economic Review* 89: 982–93.

Ahn, Dukgeun, and Patrick Messerlin. 2014. "United States—Antidumping Measures on Certain Shrimp and Diamond Sawblades from China: Never-Ending Zeroing in the WTO." *World Trade Review* 13: 267–79.

Aitken, Brian, Ann Harrison, and Robert E. Lipsey. 1996. "Wages and Foreign Ownership: A Comparative Study of Mexico, Venezuela, and the United States." *Journal of International Economics* 40: 345–71.

Alston, Julian, M., Daniel A. Sumner, and Henrich Brunke. 2007. "Impacts of Reductions in U.S. Cotton Subsidies on West African Cotton Producers." Oxfam Research Paper, June.

Amiti, Mary, and Josef Konings. 2007. "Trade Liberalization, Intermediate Inputs, and Productivity: Evidence from Indonesia." *American Economic Review* 97: 1611–38.

Amiti, Mary, and Shang-Jin Wei. 2009. "Offshoring of Services and Productivity: Evidence from the US." *World Economy* 32: 203–20.

Anderson, James, and Eric van Wincoop. 2003. "Gravity with Gravitas: A Solution to the Border Puzzle." *American Economic Review* 93: 170–92.

———. 2004. "Trade Costs." *Journal of Economic Literature* 42: 691–751.

Anderson, Kym. 1992. "Effects on the Environment and Welfare of Liberalizing World Trade: The Cases of Coal and Food." In Kym Anderson and Richard Blackhurst (eds.), *The Greening of World Trade Issues*. Ann Arbor: University of Michigan Press.

———. 1998. "Agricultural Trade Reforms, Research Initiatives, and the Environment." In E. Lutz (ed.), *Agriculture and the Environment: Perspectives on Sustainable Rural Development*. Washington, D.C.: World Bank.

———. 2009. *Distortions to Agricultural Incentives: A Global Perspective, 1955–2007*. Washington, D.C.: World Bank.

Anderson, Kym, Will Martin, and Dominic van der Mensbrugghe. 2006. "Doha Merchandise Trade Reform: What is at Stake for Developing Countries?" *World Bank Economic Review* 20: 169–95.

Anderson, Thomas. 2012. "U.S. Affiliates of Foreign Companies: Activities in 2010." *Survey of Current Business* 92: 213–28.

Antweiler, Werner, Brian R. Copeland, and M. Scott Taylor. 2001. "Is Free Trade Good for the Environment?" *American Economic Review* 91: 877–908.

Asian Productivity Organization. 2013. *APO Productivity Databook*. Tokyo: APO.

Audley, John J. 1997. *Green Politics and Global Trade: NAFTA and the Future of Environmental Politics*. Washington, D.C.: Georgetown University Press.

Audley, John J., Demetrios G. Papademetriou, Sandra Polaski, and Scott Vaughan. 2004. *NAFTA's Promise and Reality: Lessons from Mexico for the Hemisphere*. Washington, D.C.: Carnegie Endowment for International Peace.

Autor, David, David Dorn, and Gordon Hanson. 2013a. "The China Syndrome: Local Labor Market Effects of Import Competition in the United States." *American Economic Review* 103: 2121–68.

———. 2013b. "The Geography of Trade and Technology Shocks in the United States." *American Economic Review* 103: 220–25.

Autor, David H., David Dorn, Gordon H. Hanson, and Jae Song. 2014. "Trade Adjustment: Worker-Level Evidence." *Quarterly Journal of Economics* 129: 1799–860.

Autor, David H., Lawrence F. Katz, and Melissa S. Kearney. 2008. "Trends in U.S. Wage Inequality: Revising the Revisionists." *Review of Economics and Statistics* 90: 300–323.

Baccini, Leonardo, and Johannes Urpelainen. 2014. "International Institutions and Domestic Politics: Can Preferential Trading Agreements Help Leaders Promote Economic Reform?" *Journal of Politics* 76: 195–214.

Baffes, John. 2005. "The Cotton Problem." *World Bank Research Observer* 20: 109–44.

Bagwell, Kyle, and Robert W. Staiger. 2010. "The World Trade Organization: Theory and Practice." *Annual Review of Economics* 2: 223–56.

Baier, Scott L., and Jeffrey H. Bergstrand. 2001. "The Growth of World Trade: Tariffs, Transport Costs, and Income Similarity." *Journal of International Economics* 53, 1–27.

———. 2007. "Do Free Trade Agreements Actually Increase Members' International Trade?" *Journal of International Economics* 71: 72–95.

Bailey, Michael, Judith Goldstein, and Barry Weingast. 1997. "The Institutional Roots of American Trade Policy: Politics, Coalitions, and International Trade." *World Politics* 49: 309–38.

Baily, Martin Neil, and Barry P. Bosworth. 2014. "U.S. Manufacturing: Understanding Its Past and Its Potential Future." *Journal of Economic Perspectives* 28: 3–26.

Baily, Martin Neil, and Robert Z. Lawrence. 2004. "What Happened to the Great U.S. Job Machine? The Role of Trade and Electronic Offshoring." *Brookings Papers on Economic Activity* 2: 211–70.

Baldwin, Richard E., and Simon J. Evenett. 2012. "Beggar-thy-Neighbor Policies during the Crisis Era: Causes, Constraints, and Lessons for Maintaining Open Borders." *Oxford Review of Economic Policy* 28: 211–34.

Baldwin, Robert E. 1970. *Nontariff Distortions to International Trade.* Washington, D.C.: Brookings Institution.

———. 1988. "The Inefficacy of Trade Policy." In *Trade Policy in a Changing World Economy.* Chicago: University of Chicago Press.

Balke, Norman, and Robert J. Gordon. 1989. "The Estimation of Prewar Gross National Product: Methodology and New Evidence." *Journal of Political Economy* 97: 38–92.

Banister, Judith, and George Cook. 2011. "China's Employment and Compensation Cost in Manufacturing Through 2008." *Monthly Labor Review* 134: 39–52.

Barbier, Edward B., Nancy Bockstael, Joanne C. Burgess, and Ivar Strand. 1995. "The Linkage between the Timber Trade and Tropical Deforestation—Indonesia." *World Economy* 20: 411–42.

Barefoot, Kevin B. 2012. "U.S. Multinational Companies: Operations of U.S. Parents and Their Foreign Affiliates in 2010." *Survey of Current Business* 91: 51–74.

Barringer, William H., and Kenneth J. Pierce. 2000. *Paying the Price for Big Steel: $100 Billion in Trade Restraints and Corporate Welfare.* Washington, D.C.: American Institute for International Steel.

Baughman, Laura M., and Joseph F. François. 2013. "Imports Work for America." Working Paper, Trade Partnership Worldwide, Washington, D.C., May.

Beason, Richard, and David Weinstein. 1996. "Growth, Economies of Scale, and Targeting in Japan (1955–1990)." *Review of Economics and Statistics* 78: 286–95.

Beghin, John C., et al. 2003. "The Cost of the U.S. Sugar Program Revisited." *Contemporary Economic Policy* 21: 106–16.

Beghin, John C., and Amani Elobeid. 2013. "The Impact of the U.S. Sugar Program Redux." Working Paper, Center for Agriculture and Rural Development, Iowa State University, May.

Bems, Rudolfs, Robert C. Johnson, and Kei-Mu Yi. 2013. "The Great Trade Collapse." *Annual Review of Economics* 5: 375–400

Berman, Eli, John Bound, and Zvi Griliches. 1994. "Changes in the Demand for Skilled Labor within U.S. Manufacturing: Evidence from the Annual Survey of Manufacturers." *Quarterly Journal of Economics* 109: 367–97.

Bernard, Andrew B., and J. Bradford Jensen. 1999. "Exceptional Exporter Performance: Cause, Effect, or Both?" *Journal of International Economics* 47: 1–26.

Bernard, Andrew, J. Bradford Jensen, Stephen Redding, and Peter Schott. 2007. "Firms in International Trade." *Journal of Economic Perspectives* 21: 105–30.

Bernard, Andrew, Brad Jensen, and Peter Schott. 2006. "Survival of the Best Fit: Exposure to Low-Wage Countries and the (Uneven) Growth of U.S. Manufacturing Plants." *Journal of International Economics* 68, 219–37.

Bernhofen, Daniel M., and John C. Brown. 2005. "Estimating the Comparative Advantage Gains from Trade: Evidence from Japan." *American Economic Review* 95: 208–25.

Bernhofen, Daniel M., Zouheir El-Sahli, and Richard Kneller. 2013. "Estimating the Effects of the Container Revolution on World Trade." CESifo Working Paper Series 4136, CESifo Group Munich.

Bhagwati, Jagdish (ed.). 2002. *Going Alone: The Case for Relaxed Reciprocity in Freeing Trade*. Cambridge: MIT Press.

———. 2004. *In Defense of Globalization*. New York: Oxford University Press.

———. 2008. *Termites in the Trading System: How Preferential Agreements Undermine Free Trade*. New York: Oxford University Press.

Bhagwati, Jagdish, and Alan Blinder. 2009. *Offshoring of American Jobs: What Response from U.S. Economic Policy?* Cambridge: MIT Press.

Bhagwati, Jagdish, and Arvind Panagariya. 1996. "Preferential Trading Areas and Multilateralism: Strangers, Friends, or Foes?" In J. Bhagwati and A. Panagariya (eds.), *The Economics of Preferential Trading Areas*. Washington, D.C.: AEI Press.

———. 2013. *Why Growth Matters: How Economic Growth in India Reduced Poverty and the Lessons for Other Developing Countries*. New York: Oxford University Press.

Bhagwati, Jagdish, and T. N. Srinivasan. 2002. "Trade and Poverty in Poor Countries." *American Economic Review* 92:180–83.

Billmeier, Andreas, and Tommaso Nannicini. 2013. "Assessing Economic Liberalization Episodes: A Synthetic Control Approach." *Review of Economics and Statistics* 95: 983–1001.

Blinder, Alan. 2006. "Offshoring: The Next Industrial Revolution?" *Foreign Affairs* 85:113–28.

Blonigen, Bruce A. 2006. "Evolving Discretionary Practices of U.S. Antidumping Activity." *Canadian Journal of Economics* 39: 874–900.

———. 2011. "Revisiting the Evidence on Trade Policy Preferences." *Journal of International Economics* 85: 129–35.

Blonigen, Bruce A., and Thomas J. Prusa. 2003. "Antidumping." In E. Kwan Choi and James Harrigan (eds.), *Handbook of International Trade*. Oxford: Blackwell.

———. 2015. "Dumping and Antidumping Duties." In Kyle W. Bagwell and Robert W. Staiger (eds.), *Handbook of Commercial Policy*. Amsterdam: Elsevier.

Blustein, Paul. 2009. *Misadventures of the Most Favored Nations*. New York: Public Affairs.

Borjas, George J., Richard B. Freeman, and Lawrence F. Katz. 1997. "How Much Do Immigration and Trade Affect Labor Market Outcomes?" *Brookings Papers on Economic Activity* 1: 1–67.

Bovard, James. 1991. *The Fair Trade Fraud*. New York: St. Martin's Press.

Bown, Chad P. 2004a. "Developing Countries as Plaintiffs and Defendants in GATT/WTO Trade Disputes." *World Economy* 27, 59–80.

———. 2004b. "Trade Disputes and the Implementation of Protection under the GATT: An Empirical Assessment." *Journal of International Economics* 62, 263–94.

———. 2009. *Self-Enforcing Trade: Developing Countries and WTO Dispute Settlement*. Washington, D.C.: Brookings Institution.

Bown, Chad P., and Meredith A. Crowley. 2013. "Import Protection, Business Cycle, and Exchange Rates: Evidence from the Great Recession." *Journal of International Economics* 90: 50–64.

Bown, Chad P., and Thomas J. Prusa. 2011. "U.S. Antidumping: Much Ado about Zeroing." In Aaditya Mattoo and William J. Martin (eds.), *Waiting on Doha*. Washington, D.C.: World Bank.

Brander, James A. 1995. "Strategic Trade Policy." In Gene M. Grossman and Kenneth Rogoff (eds.), *Handbook of International Economics*, Vol. 3. New York: Elsevier.

Branstetter, Lee G. 2001. "Are Knowledge Spillovers International or Intranational in Scope? Microeconometric Evidence from the U.S. and Japan." *Journal of International Economics* 53: 53–80.

Broda, Christian, and David Weinstein. 2006. "Globalization and the Gains from Variety." *Quarterly Journal of Economics* 121: 541–85.

Brown, Andrew G., and Robert M. Stern. 2008. "What Are the Issues in Using Trade Agreements for Improving International Labor Standards?" *World Trade Review* 7: 331–58.

Brown, Sherrod. 2006. *Myths of Free Trade: Why American Trade Policy Has Failed*. New York: New Press.

Buchanan, Patrick. 1998. *The Great Betrayal: How American Sovereignty and Social Justice Are Being Sacrificed to the Gods of the Global Economy*. Boston: Little, Brown.

Bureau of Labor Statistics. 2004. "Extended Mass Layoffs Associated with Domestic and Overseas Relocations, First Quarter 2004, Summary." June 10.

Burtless, Gary, and Robert Z. Lawrence, Robert E. Litan, and Robert J. Shapiro.

1998. *Globaphobia: Confronting Fears about Open Trade.* Washington, D.C.: Brookings Institution, Progressive Policy Institute, and Twentieth Century Fund.

Caliendo, Lorenzo, and Fernando Perro. 2015. "Estimates of the Trade and Welfare Effects of NAFTA." *Review of Economic Studies* 82: 1–44.

Card, David, Jochen Kluve, and Andrea Weber. 2010. "Active Labour Market Policy Evaluations: A Meta-Analysis." *Economic Journal* 120: F452–77.

Cartland, Michel, Gerard Depayre, and Jan Woznowski. 2012. "Is Something Going Wrong in the WTO Dispute Settlement?" *Journal of World Trade* 46: 979–1016.

Cavallo, Michele, and Anthony Landry. 2010. "The Quantitative Role of Capital Goods Imports in U.S. Growth." *American Economic Review* 100: 78–82.

Ceglowski, Janet, and Stephen Golub. 2012. "Does China Still Have a Labor Cost Advantage?" *Global Economic Journal* 12: 1–28.

Collard-Wexler, Allan, and Jan de Loecker. 2015. "Reallocation and Technology: Evidence from the U.S. Steel Industry." *American Economic Review* 105: 131–71.

Collier, Paul. 2005. "Why the WTO Is Deadlocked: And What Can Be Done about It." *World Economy* 29: 1423–49.

Collins, Benjamin. 2012. "Trade Adjustment Assistance for Workers." Congressional Research Service, Library of Congress. July 11, R42012.

Collins, Susan (ed.). 1998. *Exports, Imports, and the American Worker.* Washington, D.C.: Brookings Institution.

Congressional Budget Office. 1994. "How the GATT Affects U.S. Antidumping and Countervailing Duty Policy." Washington, D.C., September.

———. 1998. "Antidumping Action in the United States and Around the World: An Analysis of International Data." Washington, D.C., June.

———. 2004. "Economic Analysis of the Countervailing Duty and Subsidy Offset Act of 2000." Washington, D.C., March 2.

———. 2008. "How Changes in the Value of the Chinese Currency Affect U.S. Imports." Washington, D.C., July.

Connolly, Michelle, and Kei-Mu Yi. 2015. "How Much of South Korea's Growth Miracle Can Be Explained by Trade Policy?" *American Economic Journal: Macroeconomics*, forthcoming.

Constantinescu, Cristina, Aaditya Mattoo, and Michele Ruta. 2015. "The Global Trade Slowdown: Cyclical or Structural?" World Bank Policy Research Working Paper No. 7158, Washington, D.C., January.

Corden, W. Max. 1974. *Trade Policy and Economic Welfare.* Oxford: Clarendon Press.

Council of Economic Advisers. 2014. *Economic Report of the President.* Washington, D.C.: GPO.

Cramer, Christopher, Deborah Johnston, Carlos Oya, and John Sender. 2014. "Fair Trade, Employment, and Poverty Reduction in Ethiopia and Uganda." School of Oriental and African Studies, University of London, Report to the Department for International Development, United Kingdom, April.

Dai, Xiudian, Alan Cawson, and Peter Holmes. 1996. "The Rise and Fall of High-Definition Television: The Impact of European Technology Policy." *Journal of Common Market Studies* 34: 149–66.

Dammert, Ana C., and Sarah Mohan. 2015. "A Survey of the Economics of Fair Trade." *Journal of Economic Surveys*, forthcoming.

Das, Gurcharan. 2001. *India Unbound*. New York: Knopf.

Dasgupta, Susmita, Benoit Laplante, Hua Wang, and David Wheeler. 2002. "Confronting the Environmental Kuznets Curve." *Journal of Economic Perspectives* 16: 147–68.

Davey, William J. 2001. "Has the WTO Dispute Settlement System Exceeded Its Authority?" *Journal of International Economic Law* 4: 79–110.

Davis, Lucas W., and Matthew E. Kahn. 2010. "International Trade in Used Vehicles: The Environmental Consequences of NAFTA." *American Economic Journal: Economic Policy* 2: 58–82.

Davis, Steven J., John C. Haltiwanger, and Scott Schuh. 1995. *Job Creation and Destruction*. Cambridge: MIT Press.

de La Cruz, Justino, Robert B. Koopman, Zhi Wang, and Shang-Jin Wei. 2011. "Estimating Foreign Value-added in Mexico's Manufacturing Exports." Office of Economics Working Paper No. 2011–04A, U.S. International Trade Commission, Washington, D.C.

de Melo, Jaime, and David Tarr. 1992. *A General Equilibrium Analysis of U.S. Foreign Trade Policy*. Cambridge: MIT Press.

———. 1993. "Industrial Policy in the Presence of Wage Distortions: The Case of the U.S. Auto and Steel Industries." *International Economic Review* 34: 833–51.

Dean, Judith, and Mary E. Lovely, 2010. "Trade Growth, Production Fragmentation, and China's Environment." In Robert C. Feenstra and Shang-Jin Wei (eds.), *China's Growing Role in World Trade*. Chicago: University of Chicago Press.

Dean, Judith M., Mary E. Lovely, and Hua Wang. 2009. "Are Foreign Investors Attracted to Weak Environmental Regulations? Evaluating the Evidence from China." *Journal of Development Economics* 90: 1–13.

Decker, Paul T., and Walter Corson. 1995. "International Trade and Worker Displacement: Evaluation of the Trade Adjustment Assistance Program." *Industrial and Labor Relations Review* 48: 758–74.

Deng, Paul D., and Gary H. Jefferson. 2011. "Explaining Spatial Convergence of China's Industrial Productivity." *Oxford Bulletin of Economics and Statistics* 73: 818–32.

Dew-Becker, Ian, and Robert J. Gordon. 2005. "Where Did the Productivity Growth Go? Inflation Dynamics and the Distribution of Income." *Brookings Papers on Economic Activity* 2: 67–150.

Dickens, William T. 1995. "Do Labor Rents Justify Strategic Trade and Industrial Policy?" NBER Working Paper No. 5137, May.

Dietzenbacher, Erik, Jiansuo Pei, and Cuhong Yang. 2012. "Trade, Production Fragmentation, and China's Carbon Dioxide Emissions." *Journal of Environmental Economics and Management* 64: 88–101.

Djankov, Simeon, Caroline Freund, and Cong S. Pham. 2010. "Trading on Time." *Review of Economics and Statistics* 92: 166–73.

Dolfin, Sarah, and Peter Z. Schochet. 2012. "The Benefits and Costs of the Trade Adjustment Assistance (TAA) Program under the 2002 Amendments." Document No. PR12–85, Mathematica Policy Research, Princeton, N.J., December.

Dollar, David, and Aart Kraay. 2004. "Trade, Growth, and Poverty." *Economic Journal* 114: F22–F49.

Dollar, David, and Borje Ljunggren. 1997. "Vietnam." In Padma Desai (ed.), *Going Global: Transition from Plan to Market in the World Economy.* Cambridge: MIT Press.

Dollar, David, and Kenneth Sokoloff. 1990. "Patterns of Productivity Growth in South Korean Manufacturing Industries, 1963–1979." *Journal of Development Economics* 303: 309–27.

Dragusanu, Raluca, Daniele Giovannucci, and Nathan Nunn. 2014. "The Economics of Fair Trade." *Journal of Economic Perspectives* 28: 217–36.

Dutt, Pushan. 2009. "Trade Protection and Bureaucratic Corruption: An Empirical Investigation." *Canadian Journal of Economics* 42: 155–83.

Eaton, Jonathan, and Samuel Kortum. 2001. "Trade in Capital Goods." *European Economic Review* 45: 1195–235.

Ebenstein, Avraham, Ann Harrison, Margaret McMillan, and Shannon Phillips. 2014. "Estimating the Impact of Trade and Offshoring on American Workers." *Review of Economics and Statistics* 96: 581–95.

Edmonds, Eric, and Nina Pavcnik. 2005. "Child Labor in the Global Economy." *Journal of Economic Perspectives* 18: 199–220.

———. 2006. "International Trade and Child Labor: Cross-Country Evidence." *Journal of International Economics* 68:115–40.

Edwards, Lawrence, and Robert Z. Lawrence. 2013. *Rising Tide: Is Growth in Emerging Economies Good for the United States?* Washington, D.C.: Peterson Institute for International Economics.

Edwards, Sebastian, and Daniel Lederman. 2002. "The Political Economy of Unilateral Trade Liberalization: The Case of Chile." In Jagdish Bhagwati (ed.), *Going Alone: The Case for Relaxed Reciprocity in Freeing Trade.* Cambridge: MIT Press.

Eichengreen, Barry, and Douglas A. Irwin. 2010. "The Slide to Protectionism in the Great Depression: Who Succumbed and Why?" *Journal of Economic History* 70: 873–98.

Eichengreen, Barry, and David Leblang. 2008. "Democracy and Globalization." *Economics and Politics* 20: 289–334.

Elliott, Kimberly Ann, and Richard Freeman. 2004. "White Hats or Don Quixotes? Human Rights Vigilantes in the Global Economy." In Richard B. Freeman, Joni Hersch, and Lawrence Mishel (eds.), *Emerging Labor Market Institutions for the Twenty-First Century*. Chicago: University of Chicago Press for the NBER.

Elliott, Kimberly Ann, Debayani Kar, and J. David Richardson. 2004. "Assessing Globalization's Critics: 'Talkers Are No Good Doers?'" In Robert E. Baldwin and L. Alan Winters (eds.), *Challenges to Globalization: Analyzing the Economics*. Chicago: University of Chicago Press for NBER.

Elsby, Michael W. L., Bart Hobijn, and Aysegul Sahin. 2014. "The Decline of the U.S. Labor Share." *Brookings Papers on Economic Activity* 2: 1–52.

Estevadeordal, Antoni, Brian Frantz, and Alan M. Taylor. 2003. "The Rise and Fall of World Trade, 1870–1939." *Quarterly Journal of Economics* 118: 359–407.

Estevadeordal, Antoni, Caroline Freund, and Emanuel Ornelas. 2008. "Does Regionalism Affect Trade Liberalization towards Non-members?" Centre for Economic Performance Working Paper No. 868, London School of Economics.

Estevadeordal, Antoni, and Alan M. Taylor. 2013. "Is the Washington Consensus Dead? Growth, Openness, and the Great Liberalization 1970s–2000s." *Review of Economics and Statistics* 95: 1669–90.

Etkes, Haggay, and Asaf Zimring. 2015. "When Trade Stops: Lessons from the Gaza Blockade, 2007–2010." *Journal of International Economics* 95: 16–27.

Evenett, Simon J., and Michael Meier. 2008. "An Interim Assessment of the US Trade Policy of 'Competitive Liberalization.'" *World Economy* 31: 31–66.

Evenett, Simon J., and David Vines. 2012. "Crisis Era Protectionism and the Multilateral Governance of Trade: An Assessment." *Oxford Review of Economic Policy* 28: 195–210.

Feenstra, Robert C. 1984. "Voluntary Export Restraint in U.S. Autos, 1980–81." In Robert Baldwin and Anne Krueger (eds.), *The Structure and Evolution of Recent U.S. Trade Policy*. Chicago: University of Chicago Press.

———, (ed.). 2000. *The Impact of International Trade on Wages*. Chicago: University of Chicago Press.

———. 2006. "New Evidence on the Gains from Trade." *Review of World Economics* 142: 617–41.

Feenstra, Robert C., and Gordon H. Hanson. 2003. "Global Production and Rising Inequality: A Survey of Trade and Wages." In E. Kwan Choi and James Harrigan (eds.), *Handbook of International Trade*. New York: Basil Blackwell.

Feenstra, Robert C., James R. Markusen, and William Zeile. 1992. "Accounting for Growth with New Inputs." *American Economic Review* 82: 415–21.

Feinberg, Robert A., and Kara Reynolds. 2008. "Friendly Fire: The Impact of U.S. Antidumping Enforcement on U.S. Exporters." *Review of World Economics* 144: 366–78.

Feldstein, Martin. 2006. "The Case for a Competitive Dollar." Remarks at the Annual SIEPR Summit, Stanford University, March 3. http://www.nber.org/feldstein/su030306.html.

Feldstein, Martin. 2008. "Did Wages Reflect Productivity Growth?" *Journal of Policy Modeling* 30: 591–94.

Fernandes, Ana M. 2007. "Trade Policy, Trade Volumes and Plant-level Productivity in Colombian Manufacturing Industries." *Journal of International Economics* 71: 52–71.

Fernandez, Raquel, and Dani Rodrik. 1991. "Resistance to Reform: Status Quo Bias in the Presence of Individual–Specific Uncertainty." *American Economic Review* 81: 1146–55.

Ferreira, Francisco H. G., Julian Messina, Jamele Rigolini, Luis-Felipe López-Calva, Maria Ana Lugo, and Renos Vakis. 2013. *Economic Mobility and the Rise of the Latin American Middle Class*. Washington, D.C.: World Bank.

Ferreira, Pedro C., and Jose L. Rossi. 2003. "New Evidence from Brazil on Trade Liberalization and Productivity Growth." *International Economic Review* 44: 1383–405.

Ferreira, Susana. 2004. "Deforestation, Property Rights, and International Trade." *Land Economics* 80: 174–93.

Feyrer, James. 2008. "Trade and Income—Exploiting Time Series in Geography." Unpublished working paper, Dartmouth College.

Field, Alfred J., and Edward M. Graham. 1997. "Is There a Special Case for Import Protection for the Textile and Apparel Sectors Base on Labour Adjustment?" *World Economy* 20: 137–57.

Finger, J. Michael (ed.). 1993. *Antidumping: How It Works and Who Gets Hurt*. Ann Arbor: University of Michigan Press.

———. 1996. "Legalized Backsliding: Safeguard Provisions in GATT." In Will Martin and L. Alan Winters (eds.), *The Uruguay Round and Developing Countries*. New York: Cambridge University Press.

Finger, J. Michael, Merlinda D. Ingco, and Ulrich Reincke. 1996. *The Uruguay Round: Statistics on Tariff Concessions Given and Received*. Washington, D.C.: World Bank.

Fitzgerald, Terry J. 2008. "Where Has All the Income Gone?" Federal Reserve Bank of Minneapolis Region, September, 24–29.

Flam, Harry. 1985. "A Heckscher-Ohlin Analysis of the Law of Declining International Trade." *Canadian Journal of Economics* 18: 602–15.

Flamm, Kenneth. 1996. *Mismanaged Trade? Strategic Policy and the Semiconductor Industry*. Washington, D.C.: Brookings Institution.

Food and Agriculture Organization. 2002. *FAO Annual Yearbook: Fertilizer 1999*. Rome: FAO, 2002.

François Joseph F., and Laura M. Baughman. 2001. "Estimated Economic Effects of Proposed Import Relief Remedies for Steel." The Trade Partnership, Washington, D.C., December.

François, Joesph F., and Bernard M. Hoekman. 2010. "Services Trade and Policy." *Journal of Economic Literature* 48: 642–92.

Frank, Charles R., Jr., Kwang S. Kim, and Larry E. Westphal. 1975. *Foreign Trade*

Regimes and Economic Development: South Korea. New York: National Bureau of Economic Research.

Frankel, Jeffrey. 2000. "Globalization of the Economy." In Joseph Nye and John Donahue (eds.), *Governance in a Globalizing World*. Washington, D.C.: Brookings Institution.

Frankel, Jeffrey A., and David Romer. 1999. "Does Trade Cause Growth?" *American Economic Review* 89: 379–99.

Frankel, Jeffrey A., and Andrew K. Rose. 2002. "An Estimate of the Effect of Currency Unions on Trade and Income." *Quarterly Journal of Economics* 117: 437–66.

———. 2005. "Is Trade Good or Bad for the Environment? Sorting out the Causality." *Review of Economics and Statistics* 87: 85–91.

Freeman, Richard B., and Morris M. Kleiner. 2005. "The Last American Shoe Manufacturers: Changing the Method of Pay to Survive Foreign Competition." *Industrial Relations* 44: 307–30.

Freund, Caroline, and Bineswaree Bolaky. 2008. "Trade, Regulations, and Income." *Journal of Development Economics* 87: 309–21.

Freund, Caroline, and Emanuel Ornelas. 2010. "Regional Trade Agreements." *Annual Review of Economics* 2: 139–66.

Gallaway, Michael P., Bruce A. Blonigen, and Joseph E. Flynn. 1999. "Welfare Costs of the U.S. Antidumping and Countervailing Duty Laws." *Journal of International Economics* 49: 211–44.

Gartzke, Erik, and Yanatan Lupu. 2012. "Trading on Perceptions: Why World War I Was Not a Failure of Economic Interdependence." *International Security* 36: 115–50.

Gawande, Kishore, Bernard Hoekman, and Yue Cui. 2015. "Global Supply Chains and Trade Policy Responses to the 2008 Crisis." *World Bank Economic Review* 29: 102-28.

Gawande, Kishore, and Pravin Krishna. 2003. "The Political Economy of Trade Policy: Empirical Approaches." In E. Kwan Choi and James Harrigan (eds.), *Handbook of International Trade*. Oxford: Blackwell.

Gignilliat, John L. 1961. "Pigs, Politics, and Protection: The European Boycott of American Pork." *Agricultural History* 35: 3–24.

Glewwe, Paul. 2000. "Are Foreign-Owned Businesses in Vietnam Really Sweatshops?" Agricultural Economist Newsletter, University of Minnesota Extension Service, No. 701. Summer.

Goldberg, Penny, and Nina Pavcnik. 2007. "Distributional Effects of Globalization in Developing Countries." *Journal of Economic Literature* 45: 39–82.

Goldberg, Pinelopi K., Amit Khandelwal, Nina Pavcnik, and Petia B. Topalova. 2010. "Imported Intermediate Inputs and Domestic Product Growth: Evidence from India." *Quarterly Journal of Economics* 125: 1727–67.

Goldstein, Judith L., Douglas Rivers, and Michael Tomz. 2007. "Institutions in International Relations: Understanding the Effects of the GATT and WTO on World Trade." *International Organization* 61: 37–67.

Goldstein, Morris, and Nicholas Lardy. 2008. *Debating China's Exchange Rate Policy*. Washington, D.C.: Peterson Institute for International Economics.

Golub, Stephen S. 1999. *Labor Costs and International Trade*. Washington, D.C.: AEI Press.

Goos, Maarten, Alan Manning, and Anna Salomons. 2014. "Explaining Job Polarization: Routine-Biased Technical Change and Offshoring." *American Economic Review* 104: 2509–26.

Gopinath, Gita, and Brent Neiman. 2014. "Trade Adjustment and Productivity in Large Crises." *American Economic Review* 104: 793–831.

Gresser, Edward. 2002a. "America's Hidden Tax on the Poor: The Case for Reforming U.S. Tariff Policy." Progressive Policy Institute Policy Report, March.

———. 2002b. "Toughest on the Poor: America's Flawed Tariff System." *Foreign Affairs* 81: 9–14.

———. 2007. *Freedom from Want: American Liberalism and the Global Economy*. Brooklyn, N.Y.: Soft Skull.

Groombridge, Mark A. 2001. "America's Bittersweet Sugar Policy." Trade Briefing Paper. Center for Trade Policy Studies, Cato Institute, Washington, D.C., December.

Groshen, Erica L., Bart Hobijn, and Margaret M. McConnell. 2005. "U.S. Jobs Gained and Lost through Trade: A Net Measure." Current Issues in Economics and Finance, Federal Reserve Bank of New York, August.

Grossman, Gene M., and Alan B. Krueger. 1993. "Environmental Impacts of a North American Free Trade Agreement." In Peter Garber (ed.), *The Mexico-U.S. Free Trade Agreement*. Cambridge: MIT Press.

Grossman, Gene M., and Giovanni Maggi. 1998. "Free Trade vs. Strategic Trade: A Peak into Pandora's Box." In R. Sato, R. V. Ramachandran, and K. Mino (eds.), *Global Competition and Integration*. Boston: Kluwer Academic Publishers.

Guest, Robert. 2004. *The Shackled Continent: Power, Corruption, and African Lives*. London: Macmillan.

Guth, Eckart. 2012. "The End of the Bananas Saga." *Journal of World Trade* 46: 1–32.

Haggard, Stephan, Andrew MacIntyre, and Lydia Tiede. 2008. "The Rule of Law and Economic Development." *Annual Review of Political Science* 11: 205–34.

Hale, Galina, and Bart Hobjin. 2011. "The U.S. Content of 'Made in China.'" Federal Reserve Bank of San Francisco Economic Letter. August 8.

Hansen, Wendy L., and Thomas J. Prusa. 1996. "Cumulation and ITC Decision-Making: The Sum of the Parts Is Greater Than the Whole." *Economic Inquiry* 34: 746–69.

Harrison, Ann E. 1994. "Productivity, Imperfect Competition and Trade Reform: Theory and Evidence." *Journal of International Economics* 36: 53–73.

Harrison, Ann, John McLaren, and Margaret McMillan. 2011. "Recent Perspectives on Trade and Inequality." *Annual Review of Economics* 3: 261–89.

Harrison, Ann E., and Jason Scorse. 2010. "Multinationals and Anti-Sweatshop Activism." *American Economic Review* 100: 247–73.

Harrison, Mark. 2013. *Contagion: How Commerce Has Spread Disease.* New Haven: Yale University Press.

Hart, Jeffrey A. 1993. "The Antidumping Petition of the Advanced Display Manufacturers of America: Origin and Consequences." *World Economy* 16: 85–109.

———. 1994. "The Politics of HDTV in the United States." *Policy Studies Journal* 22: 213–28.

Haskel, Jonathan, Robert Z. Lawrence, Edward E. Leamer, and Matthew J. Slaughter. 2012. "Globalization and U.S. Wages: Modifying Classic Theory to Explain Recent Facts." *Journal of Economic Perspectives* 26: 119–40.

Hausmann Ricardo, and Dani Rodrik. 2003. "Economic Development as Self-Discovery." *Journal of Economic Development* 72: 603–33.

Hegre, Havard, John R. Oneal, and Bruce Russett. 2010. "Trade Does Promote Peace: New Simultaneous Estimates of the Reciprocal Effects of Trade and Conflict." *Journal of Peace Research* 47: 763–74.

Henderson, David. 2001. *Anti-Liberalism 2000: The Rise of New Millennium Collectivism.* London: Institute of Economic Affairs.

Henn, Christian, and Brad McDonald. 2014. "Crisis Protectionism: The Observed Trade Impact." *IMF Economic Review* 62: 77–118.

Hertel, Thomas W., and Roman Keeney. 2006. "What Is at Stake: The Relative Importance of Import Barriers, Export Subsidies, and Domestic Support." In Kym Anderson and Will Martin (eds.), *Agricultural Trade Reform and the Doha Development Agenda.* Washington, D.C.: World Bank.

Hertel, Thomas W., Roman Keeney, Maros Ivanic, and L. Alan Winters. 2007. "Distributional Effects of WTO Agricultural Reform in Rich and Poor Countries." *Economic Policy* 50: 1–49.

Hillman, Arye, and Peter Moser. 1996. "Trade Liberalization as Politically Optimal Exchange of Market Access." In Matthew Canzoneri, Wilfred Ethier, and Vittorio Grilli (eds.), *The New Transatlantic Economy.* New York: Cambridge University Press.

Hiscox, Michael. 2007. "Through a Glass and Darkly: Framing Effects and Individuals' Attitudes Towards International Trade." *International Organization* 60: 755–80.

Hoekman, Bernard, and Michel Kostecki. 2009. *The Political Economy of the World Trading System: From GATT to WTO.* 3rd ed. New York: Oxford University Press.

Hoekman, Bernard, and Alessandro Nicita. 2011. "Trade Policy, Trade Costs, and Developing Country Trade." *World Development* 39: 2069–79.

Hoekman, Bernard, Francis Ng, and M. Olarreaga. 2004. "Reducing Agricultural

Tariffs versus Domestic Support: What Is More Important for Developing Countries?" *World Bank Economic Review* 18: 175–204.

Holmes, Thomas J., and James A. Schmitz, Jr. 2010. "Competition and Productivity: A Review of the Evidence." *Annual Reviews in Economics* 2: 619–42.

Horn, Henrik, Louise Johannesson, and Petros C. Mavroidis. 2011. "The WTO Dispute Settlement System, 1995–2010: Some Descriptive Statistics." *Journal of World Trade* 45: 1107–38.

Horn, Henrik, Petros C. Mavroidis, and Erik Wijkstrom. 2013. "In the Shadow of the DSU: Addressing Specific Trade Concerns in the WTO SPS and TBT Committees." *Journal of World Trade* 47: 729–59.

Houser, Trevor, et al. 2008. *Leveling the Carbon Playing Field: International Competition and US Climate Policy Design*. Washington, D.C.: Peterson Institute for International Economics.

Hudec, Robert. 1990. *The GATT Legal System and World Trade Diplomacy*. 2nd ed. Salem, N.H.: Butterworth Legal Publishers.

———. 1998. "Does the Agreement on Agriculture Work? Agricultural Disputes after the Uruguay Round." International Agricultural Trade Research Consortium Working Paper No. 98–2, April. http://www.umn.edu/iatrc.

———. 2000. "The Product-Process Doctrine in GATT/WTO Jurisprudence." In Marco Bronckers and Reinhard Quick (eds.), *New Directions in International Economic Law: Essays in Honour of John H. Jackson*. Boston: Kluwer Law International.

Hufbauer, Gary C., Steve Charnovitz, and Jisun Kim. 2009. *Global Warming and the World Trading System*. Washington, D.C.: Peterson Institute for International Economics.

Hufbauer, Gary C., Cathleen Cimino, and Tyler Moran. 2014. "NAFTA at 20: Misleading Charges and Positive Achievements." Peterson Institute for International Economics, Policy Brief PB14–13, May.

Hufbauer, Gary C., and Kimberly A. Elliott. 1994. *Measuring the Costs of Protection in the United States*. Washington, D.C.: Institute for International Economics.

Hufbauer, Gary C., and Sean Lowry. 2012. "U.S. Tire Tariffs: Saving Few Jobs at High Cost," Peterson Institute for International Economics Policy Brief No. PB12–9, April.

Hufbauer, Gary C., and Jeffrey J. Schott. 2005. *NAFTA Revisited: Achievements and Challenges*. Washington, D.C.: Institute for International Economics.

———. 2009. "Buy American: Bad for Jobs, Worse for Reputation." Peterson Institute for International Economics Policy Brief 09–02, February.

Hummels, David. 2007. "Transportation Costs and International Trade in the Second Era of Globalization." *Journal of Economic Perspectives* 21: 131–54.

Hummels, David, Jun Ishii, and Kei Mu Yi. 2001. "The Nature and Growth of Vertical Specialization in World Trade." *Journal of International Economics* 54: 75–96.

Hummels, David, and Peter Klenow. 2005. "The Variety and Quality of a Nation's Exports." *American Economic Review* 95: 704–23.

Hummels, David, Dana Rapoport, and Kei-Mu Yi. 1998. "Vertical Specialization and the Changing Nature of World Trade." *Federal Reserve Bank of New York Economic Policy Review* 79–99.

Hummels, David, and Georg Schaur. 2013. "Time as a Trade Barrier." *American Economic Review* 103: 2935–59.

Ianchovichina, Elena, and Will Martin. 2004. "Impacts of China's Accession to the World Trade Organization." *World Bank Economic Review* 18: 3–37.

Ikenson, Dan. 2004. "Zeroing In: Antidumping's Flawed Methodology under Fire." Center for Trade Policy Studies, Free Trade Bulletin No. 11. Cato Institute, Washington, D.C., April 27.

Ikenson, Dan. 2010. "Protection Made to Order: Domestic Industry's Capture and Reconfiguration of U.S. Antidumping Law." Trade Policy Analysis No. 44. Cato Institute, Washington, D.C.

———. 2011. "Economic Self-Flagellation: How U.S. Antidumping Policy Subverts the National Export Initiative." Trade Policy Analysis No. 46. Cato Institute, Washington, D.C.

———. 2014. "A Compromise to Advance the Trade Agenda: Purge Negotiations of Investor State Dispute Settlement." Free Trade Bulletin No. 41. Cato Institute, Washington, D.C.

Ingco, Merlinda D. 1996. "Tariffication in the Uruguay Round: How Much Liberalization?" *World Economy* 19: 425–46.

Inglehart, Ronald, and Christian Welzel. 2009. "How Development Leads to Democracy: What We Know about Modernization." *Foreign Affairs* 88: 33–48.

International Monetary Fund. 2011. "The WTO Doha Trade Round—Unlocking the Negotiations and Beyond." Strategy, Policy, and Review Department, November 16.

Irwin, Douglas A. 1996a. *Against the Tide: An Intellectual History of Free Trade.* Princeton: Princeton University Press.

———. 1996b. "Trade Politics and the Semiconductor Industry." In Anne O. Krueger (ed.), *The Political Economy of American Trade Policy.* Chicago: University of Chicago Press.

———. 1998. "Changes in U.S. Tariffs: The Role of Import Prices and Commercial Policies." *American Economic Review* 88: 1015–26.

———. 2003. "Causing Problems? The WTO Review of Causation and Injury Attribution in U.S. Section 201 Cases." *World Trade Review* 2: 297–325.

———. 2005a. "The Rise of U.S. Antidumping Actions in Historical Perspective." *World Economy* 28: 651–68.

———. 2005b. "Welfare Effects of Autarky: Evidence from the Jeffersonian Embargo of 1807–1809." *Review of International Economics* 13: 631–45.

———. 2011. *Peddling Protectionism: Smoot-Hawley and the Great Depression.* Princeton: Princeton University Press.

Irwin, Douglas A. 2012. *Trade Policy Disaster: Lessons from the 1930s*. Cambridge: MIT Press.

Irwin, Douglas A., and Peter J. Klenow. 1994. "Learning-by-Doing Spillovers in the Semiconductor Industry." *Journal of Political Economy* 102: 1200–27.

Irwin, Douglas A., and Randall S. Kroszner. 1999. "Interests, Institutions, and Ideology in Securing Policy Change: The Republican Conversion to Trade Liberalization after Smoot-Hawley." *Journal of Law and Economics* 42: 643–73.

Irwin, Douglas A., Petros C. Mavroidis, and Alan O. Sykes. 2008. *The Genesis of the GATT*. New York: Cambridge University Press.

Irwin, Douglas A., and Kevin H. O'Rourke. 2014. "Free Trade and Multilateralism in Historical Perspective." In Robert C. Feenstra and Alan M. Taylor (eds.), *Globalization in an Age of Crisis: Multilateral Economic Cooperation in the Twenty-First Century*. Chicago: University of Chicago Press.

Irwin, Douglas A., and Nina Pavcnik. 2004. "Airbus versus Boeing Revisited: International Competition in the Aircraft Market." *Journal of International Economics* 64: 223–45.

Jacobson, Louis. 1998. "Compensation Programs." In Susan Collins (ed.), *Imports, Exports, and the American Worker*. Washington, D.C.: Brookings Institution.

Jacobson, Louis, Robert J. Lalonde, and Daniel Sullivan. 2011. "Policies to Reduce High-Tenured Workers Earnings Losses through Job Retraining." Hamilton Project Discussion Paper 2011–11. Brookings Institution, Washington, D.C.

Jaffe, Adam B., et al. 1995. "Environmental Regulation and the Competitiveness of U.S. Manufacturing: What Does the Evidence Tell Us?" *Journal of Economic Literature* 33: 132–63.

Jefferson, Gary H., Albert G. Z. Hu, and Jian Su. 2006. "The Sources and Sustainability of China's Economic Growth." *Brookings Papers on Economic Activity* 1: 1–60.

Jensen, J. Bradford, and Lori G. Kletzer. 2008. "'Fear' and Offshoring: The Scope and Potential Impact of Imports and Exports of Services." Peterson Institute for International Economics Policy Brief No. 08–1. Washington, D.C., January.

Johnson, Martin, and Chris Rasmussen. 2014. "Jobs Supported by Exports 2013: An Update." International Trade Administration, U.S. Department of Commerce, February.

Johnson, Robert C. 2014. "Five Facts about Valued-Added Exports and Implications for Macroeconomics and Trade Research." *Journal of Economic Perspectives* 28: 119–42.

Johnson, Robert C., and Guillermo Noguera. 2012. "Accounting for Intermediates: Production Sharing and Trade in Value Added." *Journal of International Economics* 86: 224–36.

Jones, Charles I. 2001. "Comment on Rodríguez and Rodrik." In Ben S. Bernanke and Kenneth Rogoff (eds.), *NBER Macroeconomics Annual, 2000*. Cambridge: MIT Press.

Jones, Kent. 2004. *Who's Afraid of the WTO?* New York: Cambridge University Press.

Josling, Timothy, Donna Roberts, and David Orden. 2004. *Food Regulation and Trade: Toward a Safe and Open Global System.* Washington, D.C.: Institute for International Economics.

Kahn, Matthew. 2003. "The Geography of U.S. Pollution Intensive Trade: Evidence from 1958 to 1994." *Regional Science and Urban Economics* 33: 383–400.

Kaivanto, Kim. 2007. "Trade-Related Job Loss, Wage Insurance and Externalities: An Ex Ante Efficiency Rationale for Wage Insurance." *World Economy* 30: 962–71.

Karabarbounis, Loukas, and Brent Nieman. 2014. "The Global Decline in the Labor Share." *Quarterly Journal of Economics* 129: 61–103.

Karacaovali, Baybars, and Nuno Limão. 2008. "The Clash of Liberalizations: Preferential vs. Multilateral Trade Liberalization in the European Union." *Journal of International Economics* 74: 299–327.

Karp, Larry. 2011. "The Environment and Trade." *Annual Review of Resource Economics* 3: 397–41.

Kasahara, Hiroyuki, and Joel Rodrigue. 2008. "Does the Use of Imported Intermediates Increase Productivity? Plant-level Evidence." *Journal of Development Economics* 87: 106–18.

Kee, Hiau Looi, Cristina Neagu, and Alessandro Nicita. 2013. "Is Protectionism on the Rise? Assessing National Trade Policies during the Crisis of 2008." *Review of Economics and Statistics* 95: 342–46.

Kee, Hiau Looi, Alessandro Nicita, and Marcelo Olarreaga. 2009. "Estimating Trade Restrictiveness Indices." *Economic Journal* 119: 172–99.

———. 2008. "Import Demand Elasticities and Trade Distortions." *Review of Economics and Statistics* 90: 666–82.

Kehoe, Timothy J., and Kim J. Ruhl, 2010. "Why Have Economic Reforms in Mexico Not Generated Growth?" *Journal of Economic Literature* 48: 1005–27.

Keller, Wolfgang. 2004. "International Technology Diffusion." *Journal of Economic Literature* 42: 752–83.

———. 2010. "International Trade, Foreign Direct Investment, and Technology Spillovers." In B. Hall, N. Rosenberg (eds.), *Handbook of the Economics of Innovation.* Amsterdam: Elsevier North-Holland.

Kelly, Trish. 2014. "Tuna-Dolphin Revisited." *Journal of World Trade* 48: 501–24.

Kim, Euysung. 2000. "Trade Liberalization and Productivity Growth in Korean Manufacturing Industries: Price Protection, Market Power, and Scale Efficiency." *Journal of Development Economics* 62: 55–83.

Kitano, Taiju. 2013. "Did Temporary Protection Induce Technology Adoption? A Study of the U.S. Motorcycle Industry." Unpublished working paper, Hitotsubashi University.

Kitano, Taiju, and Hiroshi Ohashi. 2009. "Did U.S. Safeguard Resuscitate Harley Davidson in the 1980s?" *Journal of International Economics* 79: 186–97.

Klenow, Peter, and Andrés Rodríguez-Claire. 1997. "Quantifying Variety Gains from Trade Liberalization." Working Paper, University of Chicago, September.

Kletzer, Lori G. 1998a. "Job Displacement." *Journal of Economic Perspectives* 12: 115–36.

———. 1998b. "Trade and Job Displacement in U.S. Manufacturing: 1979–1991." In Susan Collins (ed.), *Imports, Exports, and the American Worker*. Washington, D.C.: Brookings Institution.

———. 2000. "Trade and Job Loss in U.S. Manufacturing, 1979–1994." In Robert Feenstra (ed.), *The Impact of International Trade on Wages*. Chicago: University of Chicago Press for the NBER.

———. 2001. *Job Loss from Imports: Measuring the Costs*. Washington, D.C.: Institute for International Economics.

———. 2004. "Trade-related Job Loss and Wage Insurance: A Synthetic Review." *Review of International Economics* 12: 724–48.

Koopman, Robert, Zhi Wang, and Shang-Jin Wei. 2014. "Tracing Value-Added and Double Counting in Gross Exports." *American Economic Review*, 104: 459–94.

Kose, M. Ayhan, Guy Meredith, and Christopher Towe. 2004. "How Has NAFTA Affected the Mexican Economy? Review and Evidence." IMF Working Paper 94/59.

Krishna, Pravin, and Devashish Mitra. 1998. "Trade Liberalization, Market Discipline and Productivity Growth: New Evidence from India." *Journal of Development Economics* 56: 447–62.

Kristof, Nicholas D., and Sheryl WuDunn. 2000. "Two Cheers for Sweatshops." *New York Times Magazine*, September 24, pp. 70–71.

Krueger, Anne O. 1974. "The Political Economy of a Rent Seeking Society." *American Economic Review* 64: 291–303.

———. 1990. "Free Trade is the Best Policy." In Robert Z. Lawrence and Charles L. Schultze (eds.), *An American Trade Strategy: Options for the 1990s*. Washington, D.C.: Brookings Institution.

——— (ed.). 1996. *The Political Economy of American Trade Policy*. Chicago: University of Chicago Press.

———. 1997. "Trade Policy and Economic Development: How We Learn." *American Economic Review* 87: 1–22.

———. 1999. "Free Trade Agreements as Protectionist Devices: Rules of Origin." In James R. Melvin, James C. Moore, and Raymond Reizman (eds.), *Trade, Theory and Econometrics: Essays in Honor of John S. Chipman*. New York: Routledge.

Krugman, Paul R. 1990. *The Age of Diminished Expectations*. Cambridge: MIT Press.

———. 1994. "Competitiveness: A Dangerous Obsession." *Foreign Affairs* 73: 28–44.

———. 1995. "Dutch Tulips and Emerging Markets." *Foreign Affairs* 74: 28–44.

———. 1996. *Pop Internationalism*. Cambridge: MIT Press.

———. 1998a. "Ricardo's Difficult Idea: Why Intellectuals Don't Understand Comparative Advantage." In Gary Cook (ed.), *The Economics and Politics of International Trade*. London: Routledge.

———. 1998b. *The Accidental Theorist*. New York: Norton.

———. 2008. "Trade and Wages, Reconsidered." *Brookings Papers on Economic Activity* 1: 103–54.

Kull, Steven. 2000. *Americans on Globalization*. Program on International Policy Attitudes, University of Maryland, March 28.

———. 2004. *Americans on Globalization, Trade, and Farm Subsidies*. Program on International Policy Attitudes, University of Maryland, January 22.

Kyle, Margaret, and Yi Qian. 2014. "Intellectual Property Rights and Access to Innovation: Evidence from TRIPS." NBER Working Paper No. 20799.

Lardy, Nicholas. 1992. *Foreign Trade and Economic Reform in China, 1978–1990*. New York: Cambridge University Press.

Lawrence, Robert Z. 2008. *Blue Collar Blues: Is Trade to Blame for Rising U.S. Income Inequality?* Washington, D.C.: Peterson Institute for International Economics.

———. 2014. "Adjustment Challenges for U.S. Workers." In C. Fred Bergsten, Gary C. Hufbauer, and Sean Miner (eds.), *Bridging the Pacific: Toward Free Trade and Investment between China and the United States*. Washington, D.C.: Peterson Institute for International Economics.

Lawrence, Robert Z., and Lawrence Edwards. 2013. "U.S. Employment Deindustrialization: Insights from History and the International Experience." Peterson Institute for International Economics Policy Brief No. 13–27. Washington, D.C., October.

Lawrence, Robert Z., and Robert E. Litan. 1986. *Saving Free Trade: A Pragmatic Approach*. Washington, D.C.: Brookings Institution.

Lee, Ching Kwan. 1998. *Gender and the South China Miracle: Two Worlds of Factory Women*. Berkeley: University of California Press.

Lee, Jaymin. 2011. "The Performance of Industrial Policy: Evidence from Korea." *International Economic Journal* 25: 1–27.

Lee, Jong-Wha. 1995. "Capital Goods Imports and Long-Run Growth." *Journal of Development Economics* 48: 91–110.

———. 1996. "Government Interventions and Productivity Growth." *Journal of Economic Growth* 1: 391–414.

Lemieux, Thomas. 2010. "What Do We Really Know about Changes in Wage Inequality?" In Katharine G. Abraham, James R. Spletzer, and Michael Harper (eds.), *Labor in the New Economy*. Chicago: University of Chicago Press for the NBER.

Lerner, Abba P. 1936. "The Symmetry between Import and Export Taxes." *Economica* 3: 306–13.

Levinsohn, James. 1993. "Testing the Imports-as-Market-Discipline Hypothesis." *Journal of International Economics* 35; 1–22.

———. 1999. "Employment Responses to International Liberalization in Chile." *Journal of International Economics* 47: 321–44.

Levinsohn, James, and Wendy Petropoulos. 2001. "Creative Destruction or Just Plain Destruction? The U.S. Textile and Apparel Industries since 1972." NBER Working Paper No. 8348.

Levinson, Arik. 2009. "Technology, International Trade, and Pollution from U.S. Manufacturing." *American Economic Review* 99: 2177–92.

———. 2010. "Offshoring Pollution: Is the United States Increasingly Importing Polluting Goods?" *Review of Environmental Economic Policy* 4: 63–83.

Levy, Frank, and Ari Goelman. 2005. "Offshoring and Radiology." *Brookings Trade Forum* 1: 411–23.

Lewis, William W. 2004. *The Power of Productivity: Wealth, Poverty, and the Threat to Global Stability*. Chicago: University of Chicago Press.

Lileeva, Alla, and Daniel Trefler. 2010. "Improved Access to Foreign Markets Raises Plant-level Productivity . . . For Some Plants." *Quarterly Journal of Economics* 125: 1051–99.

Limão, Nuno. 2006. "Preferential Trade Agreements as Stumbling Blocks for Multilateral Trade Liberalization: Evidence for the U.S." *American Economic Review* 96: 896–914.

Limão, Nuno, and Anthony Venables. 2001. "Infrastructure, Geographical Disadvantage, Transport Costs and Trade." *World Bank Economic Review* 15: 451–79.

Linden, Greg, Kenneth L. Kraemer, and Jason Dedrick. 2007. "Who Captures the Value in a Global Innovation System? The Case of Apple's iPod." Personal Computing Center, University of California at Irvine.

Lindsay, Brink. 2001. "Poor Choice: Why Globalization Didn't Create 9/11." *New Republic*, November 12.

———. 2004. "Job Losses and Trade: A Reality Check." Trade Policy Briefing Paper No. 19, Center for Trade Policy Studies. Cato Institute, Washington, D.C., March 17.

Lindsey, Brink, Daniel T. Griswold, and Aaron Lukas. 1999. "The Steel 'Crisis' and the Costs of Protectionism." Trade Policy Briefing Paper No. 4. Center for Trade Policy Studies, Cato Institute, Washington, D.C., April 16.

Lindsey, Brink, and Dan Ikenson. 2003. *Antidumping Exposed: The Devilish Details of Unfair Trade Law*. Washington, D.C.: Cato Institute.

Lipsey, Robert E., and Fredrik Sjöholm. 2001. "Foreign Direct Investment and Wages in Indonesian Manufacturing." NBER Working Paper No. 8299, May.

Liu, Runjuan, and Daniel Trefler. 2011. "A Sorted Tale of Globalization: White Collar Jobs and the Rise of Service Offshoring." NBER Working Paper No. 17559, November.

Liu, Xuepeng, and Emanuel Ornelas. 2014. "Free Trade Agreements and the Consolidation of Democracy." *American Economic Journal: Macroeconomics* 6: 29–70.

Lopez-Cordova, J. Ernesto, and Christopher Meissner. 2004. "Globalization and Democracy, 1870–2000." Working Paper, Cambridge University, United Kingdom.

Low, Patrick. 1993. *Trading Free: The GATT and U.S. Trade Policy.* New York: Twentieth Century Fund.

Lu, Yi, Zhigang Tao, and Yan Zhang. 2013. "How Do Exporters Respond to Antidumping Investigations?" *Journal of International Economics* 91: 290–300.

Macaulay, Thomas Babington. 1900. *The Complete Writings of Lord Macaulay.* Volume 18: *Speeches and Legal Studies.* Boston: Houghton, Mifflin.

MacDonald, Patrick J. 2009. *Invisible Hand of Peace: Capitalism, the War Machine, and International Relations Theory.* New York: Cambridge University Press.

Madsen, Jakob B. 2001. "Trade Barriers and the Collapse of World Trade during the Great Depression." *Southern Economic Journal* 67: 848–68.

———. 2007. "Technology Spillover through Trade and TFP Convergence: 135 Years of Evidence for the OECD Countries." *Journal of International Economics* 72: 464–80.

Mansfield, Edward D., Helen Milner, and Peter Rosendorf. 2000. "Free to Trade: Democracies, Autocracies, and International Trade." *American Political Science Review* 94: 305–321.

Mansfield, Edward, D., and Brian M. Pollins. 2003. *Economic Interdependence and International Conflict: New Perspectives on an Enduring Debate.* Ann Arbor: University of Michigan Press.

Margalit, Yotam. 2011. "Costly Jobs: Trade-Related Layoffs, Government Compensation, and Voting in U.S. Elections." *American Political Science Review* 105: 166–88.

Marshall, Kathryn G. 2012. "International Productivity and Factor Price Comparisons." *Journal of International Economics* 87: 386–90.

Martin, Philippe, Thierry Mayer, and Mathias Thoenig. 2008. "Make Trade Not War?" *Review of Economic Studies* 75: 865–900.

———. 2012. "The Geography of Conflicts and Regional Trade Agreements." *American Economic Journal: Macroeconomics* 4: 1–35.

Martin, Will, and Elena Ianchovichina. 2001. "Trade Liberalization in China's Accession to the World Trade Organization." World Bank Policy Research Working Paper No. 2623. Washington, D.C., June.

Martin, Will, and Aaditya Mattoo. 2011. *Unfinished Business: The WTO's Doha Agenda.* Washington, D.C.: World Bank.

Marin, Will, and Patrick Messerlin. 2007. "Why Is It So Difficult? Trade Liberalization under the Doha Agenda." *Oxford Review of Economic Policy* 23: 347–66.

Maruyama, Warren H. 2011. "Climate Change and the WTO: Cap and Trade versus Carbon Tax?" *Journal of World Trade* 45: 679–726.

Maskus, Keith. 1997. "Should Core Labor Standards Be Imposed Through International Trade Policy?" World Bank Policy Research Paper No. 1817, August.

——. 2000. *Intellectual Property Rights in the Global Economy.* Washington, D.C.: Institute for International Economics.

——. 2012. *Private Rights and Public Problems: The Global Economics of Intellectual Property in the 21st Century.* Washington, D.C.: Peterson Institute for International Economics.

——. 2014. "The New Globalization of Intellectual Property Rights: What's New This Time?" *Australian Economic History Review* 54: 262–84.

Mattoo, Aaditya, Arvind Subramanian, Dominique van der Mensbrugghe, and Jianwu He. 2009. "Reconciling Climate Change and Trade Policy." Peterson Institute for International Economics Working Paper No. 09–15.

Maurer, Noel. 2006. "Was NAFTA Necessary? Trade Policy and Relative Economic Failure since 1982." Harvard Business School Working Paper, No. 06–043. Boston, Mass.

Mayer, Wolfgang. 1984. "Endogenous Tariff Formation." *American Economic Review* 74: 970–85.

Mazumdar, Joy. 2001. "Imported Machinery and Growth in LDCs." *Journal of Development Economics* 65: 209–24.

McCaig, Brian. 2011. "Exporting Out of Poverty: Provincial Poverty in Vietnam and U.S. Market Access." *Journal of International Economics* 85: 102–13.

McKinsey Global Institute. 1993. *Manufacturing Productivity.* Washington, D.C.: McKinsey and Co.

McLean, Ian, and Kris Mitchener. 1999. "U.S. Economic Growth and Convergence, 1880–1980." *Journal of Economic History* 59: 1016–42.

McRae, Donald. 2004. "What is the Future of WTO Dispute Settlement?" *Journal of International Economics Law* 7: 3–21.

Messerlin, Patrick A. 2001. *Measuring the Costs of Protection in Europe.* Washington, D.C.: Institute for International Economics.

Michaels, Guy, Ashwini Natraj, and John Van Reenen. 2014. "Has ICT Polarized Skill Demand? Evidence from Eleven Countries over 25 Years." *Review of Economics and Statistics* 96: 60–77.

Milanovic, Branko. 2013. "Inequality by the Numbers: In History and Now." *Global Policy* 4: 198–208.

Milazzo, Matteo. 1998. *Subsidies in World Fisheries: A Reexamination.* World Bank Technical Paper No. 406. Washington, D.C.

Mill, John Stuart. [1848] 1909. *Principles of Political Economy.* London: Longmans.

——. [1859] 1982. *On Liberty.* New York: Penguin.

Milner, Chris, 2013. "Declining Protection in Developing Countries: Fact or Fiction?" *World Economy* 36: 689–700.

Milner, Helen, and Bumba Mukherjee. 2009. "Democratization and Economic Globalization." *Annual Review of Political Science* 12: 163–81.

Mitra, Siddhartha, and Timothy Josling. 2009. "Agricultural Export Restrictions: Welfare Implications and Trade Disciplines." International Food and Agricultural Trade Policy Council.

Mohammad, Sharif, and John Whalley. 1984. "Rent Seeking in India: Its Costs and Policy Significance." *Kyklos* 37: 387–413.

Montesquieu. [1748] 1989. *The Spirit of the Laws*. Translated by A. M. Cohler, B. C. Miller, and H. S. Stone. New York: Cambridge University Press.

Montgomery, Mark. 1995. "Reassessing the Waste Trade Crisis: What Do We Really Know?" *Journal of Environment and Development* 4: 1–28.

Moore, Michael O. 1996. "Steel Protection in the 1980s: The Waning Influence of Big Steel?" In Anne O. Krueger (ed.), *The Political Economy of American Trade Policy*. Chicago: University of Chicago Press.

———. 1999. "Antidumping Reform in the United States: A Faded Sunset." *Journal of World Trade* 33: 1–17.

———. 2005. "VERs vs. Price Undertakings under the WTO." *Review of International Economics* 13: 298–310.

———. 2007. "Antidumping Reform in the Doha Round: A Pessimistic Assessment." *Pacific Economic Review* 12: 335–79.

———. 2011. "Implementing Carbon Tariffs: A Fool's Errand?" *World Economy* 34: 1679–702.

Moore, Mike. 2003. *A World without Walls: Freedom, Development, Free Trade, and Global Governance*. New York: Cambridge University Press.

Morris, Julian. 2000. "International Environmental Agreements: Developing Another Path." In Terry L. Anderson and Henry I. Miller (eds.), *The Greening of U.S. Foreign Policy*. Stanford: Hoover Institution Press.

Murthy, N. R. Narayana. 2001. "Reflections of an Entrepreneur." Commencement address at the Wharton School of Business, University of Pennsylvania, May 20. http://knowledge.wharton.upenn.edu/india/article.cfm?articleid=4004/.

Nader, Ralph (ed.). 1993. *The Case Against Free Trade: GATT, NAFTA, and the Globalization of Corporate Power*. San Francisco: Earth Island Press.

Nelson, Douglas. 2006. "The Political Economy of Antidumping." *European Journal of Political Economy* 22: 554–90.

Nicita, Alessandro, Marcelo Olarreaga, and Peri Silva. 2014. "Cooperation in WTO's Tariff Waters." Working paper, UNCTAD and University of Geneva.

Ohashi, Hiroshi. 2005. "Learning by Doing, Export Subsidies, and Industry Growth: Japanese Steel in the 1950s and 60s." *Journal of International Economics* 66: 297–323.

Orden, David, David Blanford, and Tim Josling. 2011. *WTO Disciplines in Agricultural Support: Seeking a Fair Basis for Trade*. New York: Cambridge University Press.

Organization for Economic Cooperation and Development [OECD]. 1994. *The OECD Jobs Study: Facts, Analysis, Strategy*. Paris: OECD.

Organization for Economic Cooperation and Development [OECD]. 1996. *Trade, Employment, and Labour Standards: A Study of Core Workers' Rights and International Trade.* Paris: OECD.

———. 2000. *International Trade and Core Labour Standards.* Paris: OECD.

———. 2014. *Agricultural Policy: Monitoring and Evaluation 2014: OECD Countries and Emerging Markets.* Paris: OECD.

Orme, William A., Jr. 1996. *Understanding NAFTA: Mexico, Free Trade, and the New North America.* Austin: University of Texas Press.

Ottaviano, Gianmarco I. P., Giovanni Peri, and Greg C. Wright. 2013. "Immigration, Offshoring, and American Jobs." *American Economic Review* 103: 1925–59.

Oxfam. 2002. *Rigged Rules and Double Standards: Trade, Globalisation, and the Fight against Poverty.* London: Oxfam.

Pack, Howard, and Kamal Saggi. 2006. "Is There a Case for Industrial Policy? A Critical Survey." *World Bank Research Observer* 21: 267–97.

Palmeter, N. David. 1999. "National Sovereignty and the World Trade Organization." *Journal of World Intellectual Property* 2: 77–91.

Panagariya, Arvind. 2004. "Miracles and Debacles: In Defense of Trade Openness." *World Economy* 27: 1149–72.

———. 2005. "Agricultural Liberalisation and the Least Developed Countries: Six Fallacies." *World Economy* 28: 1277–99.

Panagariya, Arvind, Shekhar Shah, and Deepak Mishra. 2001. "Demand Elasticities in International Trade: Are They Really Low?" *Journal of Development Economics* 64: 313–42.

Pareto, Vilfredo. 1971. *Manual of Political Economy.* Translated by Ann S. Schwier. New York: Augustus M. Kelley.

Pastor, Robert. 1983. "The Cry-and-Sigh Syndrome: Congress and Trade Policy." In Allen Shick (ed.), *Making Economic Policy in Congress.* Washington, D.C.: American Enterprise Institute.

Pavcnik, Nina. 2002. "Trade Liberalization, Exit, and Productivity Improvements: Evidence from Chilean Plants." *Review of Economic Studies* 69: 245–76.

Pessoa, Joao P., and John Van Reenen. 2013. "Decoupling of Wage Growth and Productivity Growth: Myth and Reality." Centre for Economic Performance, London School of Economics, Discussion Paper 1246.

Petri, Peter A., and Michael G. Plummer. 2012. "The Trans-Pacific Partnership and Asia-Pacific Integration: Policy Implications." Peterson Institute for International Economics Policy Brief PB12–16, June.

Petri, Peter A., Michael G. Plummer, and Fan Zhai. 2012. *The Trans-Pacific Partnership and Asian-Pacific Integration: A Quantitative Assessment.* Policy Analyses in International Economics No. 98. Washington, D.C.: Peterson Institute for International Economics

Pierce, Justin R. 2011. "Plant-level Responses to Antidumping Duties: Evidence from U.S. Manufacturers." *Journal of International Economics* 85: 222–33.

Pierce, Justin R, and Peter K. Schott. 2012. "The Surprisingly Swift Decline of U.S. Manufacturing Employment." NBER Working Paper No. 18655.

Pierce, Richard J. 2000. "Antidumping Law as a Means of Facilitating Cartelization." *Antitrust Law Journal* 67: 725–43.

Pomfret, Richard. 2007. "Is Regionalism an Increasing Feature of the World Economy?" *World Economy* 30: 923–47.

Powell, Benjamin. 2014. *Out of Poverty: Sweatshops in the Global Economy.* New York: Cambridge University Press.

Prasad, Eswar S. 2014. *The Dollar Trap: How the U.S. Dollar Tightened its Grip on Global Finance.* Princeton: Princeton University Press.

Prasad, Kislaya. 2012. "Economic Liberalization and Violent Crime." *Journal of Law and Economics* 55: 925–48.

Preeg, Ernest H. 1995. *Traders in a Brave New World: The Uruguay Round and the Future of the International Trading System.* Chicago: University of Chicago Press.

Prusa, Thomas J. 1998. "Cumulation and Antidumping: A Challenge to Competition." *World Economy* 21: 1021–33.

———. 2001. "On the Spread and Impact of Antidumping Duties." *Canadian Journal of Economics* 34: 591–611.

Ravallion, Martin, and Shoahua Chen. 2007. "China's (Uneven) Progress against Poverty." *Journal of Development Economics* 82: 1–42

Read, Robert. 2005. "The Political Economy of Trade Protection: The Determinants and Welfare Impact of the 2002 US Emergency Steel Safeguard Measures." *World Economy* 28: 1119–37.

Reid, Peter C. 1990. *Made Well in America: Lessons From Harley-Davidson on Being the Best.* New York: McGraw-Hill.

Revenga, Ana L. 1992. "Exporting Jobs? The Impact of Import Competition on Employment and Wages in U.S. Manufacturing." *Quarterly Journal of Economics* 107: 255–84.

Reynolds, Kara. 2006. "Subsidizing Rent-Seeking: Antidumping Protection and the Byrd Amendment." *Journal of International Economics* 70: 490–502.

Reynolds, Kara M. 2013. "Under the Cover of Antidumping: Does Administered Protection Facilitate Domestic Collusion?" *Review of Industrial Organization* 42: 415–34.

Reynolds, Kara M., and John S. Palatucci. 2012. "Does Trade Adjustment Assistance Make a Difference?" *Contemporary Policy Issues* 30: 43–59.

Roberts, Donna. 1998. "Preliminary Assessment of the Effects of the WTO Agreement on Sanitary and Phytosanitary Measures Trade Regulations." *Journal of International Economic Law* 2: 377–405.

Roberts, Donna, and Kate DeRemer. 1997. *An Overview of Technical Barriers to U.S. Agricultural Exports.* Economic Research Service, U.S. Department of Agriculture, Staff Paper AGES-9705, Washington, D.C., March.

Roberts, Mark J., and James R. Tybout. 1996. *Industrial Evolution in Developing*

Countries: Micro Patterns of Turnover, Productivity, and Market Structure. New York: Oxford University Press for the World Bank.

Robertson, David. 2000. "Civil Society and the WTO." *World Economy* 23: 1119–34.

Robertson, Raymond, Drusilla Brown, Gaëlle Pierre, and Laura Sanchez-Puerta (eds.). 2009 *Globalization, Wages, and the Quality of Jobs Five Country Studies.* Washington, D.C.: World Bank.

Rodríguez, Francisco, and Dani Rodrik. 2001. "Trade Policy and Economic Growth: A Skeptic's Guide to Cross-National Evidence." In Ben S. Bernanke and Kenneth Rogoff (eds.), *NBER Macroeconomics Annual, 2000.* Cambridge: MIT Press.

Rodrik, Dani. 1989. "Optimal Trade Taxes for a Large Country with Non-atomistic Firms." *Journal of International Economics* 26: 157–67.

———. 1995. "Political Economy of Trade." In Gene M. Grossman and Kenneth Rogoff (eds.), *The Handbook of International Economics*, Vol. 3. Amsterdam: Elsevier.

———. 1996. "Labor Standards in International Trade: Do They Matter and What Do We Do About Them?" In Robert Lawrence et al. (eds.), *Emerging Agenda for Global Trade: High Stakes for Developing Countries.* Washington, D.C.: Overseas Development Council.

———. 1999. "Democracies Pay Higher Wages." *Quarterly Journal of Economics* 114: 707–38.

Romalis, John. 2007. "Market Access, Openness and Growth." NBER Working Paper No. 13048, April.

Romer, Paul. 1994. "New Goods, Old Theory, and the Welfare Costs of Trade Restrictions." *Journal of Development Economics* 43: 5–38.

Rose, Andrew K. 2004. "Do We Really Know that the WTO Increases Trade?" *American Economic Review* 94: 98–114.

Rubini, Luca. 2014. "'The Good, the Bad, and the Ugly.' Lessons on Methodology in Legal Analysis from the Recent WTO Litigation on Renewable Energy Subsidies." *Journal of World Trade* 48: 895–938.

Ruffin, Roy J. 2002. "David Ricardo's Discovery of Comparative Advantage." *History of Political Economy* 34: 727–48.

Rutherford, Thomas F., and David G. Tarr. 2002. "Trade Liberalization, Product Variety, and Growth in a Small Open Economy: A Quantitative Assessment." *Journal of International Economics* 56: 247–72.

Rutkowski, Aleksander. 2006. "Withdrawals of Anti-dumping Complaints in the EU: A Sign of Collusion." *World Economy* 30: 470–503.

Sampson, Gary P. 2000. *Trade, Environment, and the WTO: The Post-Seattle Agenda.* Washington, D.C.: Overseas Development Council.

Samuelson, Paul A. 1972. *The Collected Scientific Papers of Paul A. Samuelson.* Vol. 3. Cambridge: MIT Press.

Sanchez, Julian. 2003. "Lou's Blues: Lou Dobbs and the New Mercantilism." October 30. http://www.reason.com.

Saunders, Caroline, Andrew Barber, and Greg Taylor. 2006. "Food Miles: Comparative Energy/Emissions Performance of New Zealand's Agricultural Industries." Research Report No. 285. Christchurch, New Zealand: Lincoln University.

Sazanami, Yoko, Shujiro Urata, and Hiroki Kawai. 1995. *Measuring the Costs of Protection in Japan.* Washington, D.C.: Institute for International Economics, January.

Schatz, Howard J., and David G. Tarr. 2002. "Exchange Rate Overvaluation and Trade Protection." In Bernard Hoekman, Aaditya Mattoo, and Philip English (eds.), *Development, Trade, and the WTO: A Handbook.* Washington, D.C.: World Bank.

Scheve, Kenneth R., and Matthew J. Slaughter. 2001. "What Determines Individual Trade Policy Preferences?" *Journal of International Economics* 54: 267–292.

Schoepfle, Gregory K. 2000. "U.S. Trade Adjustment Assistance Policies for Workers." In Alan V. Deardorff and Robert M. Stern (eds.), *Social Dimensions of U.S. Trade Policies.* Ann Arbor: University of Michigan Press.

Schott, Peter K. 2008. "The Relative Sophistication of China's Exports." *Economic Policy* 23: 5–49.

Scott, Robert E. 1999. "NAFTA's Pain Deepens: Job Destruction Accelerates in 1999 with Losses in Every State." Economic Policy Institute Briefing Paper No. 88. Washington, D.C., November.

Scott, Robert E., and Will Kimball. 2014. "China Trade, Outsourcing and Jobs." Economic Policy Institute Briefing Paper No. 385, Washington, D.C., December.

Segerstrom, Paul. 2003. "Naomi Klein and the Anti-Globalization Movement." In Mats Lundahl (ed.), *Globalization and Its Enemies.* Stockholm: Economic Research Institute.

Sharpe, Andrew, Jean-François Arsenault, and Peter Harrison. 2008. "The Relationship between Labour Productivity and Real Wage Growth in Canada and OECD Economies." Centre for the Study of Living Standards, Report 2008–08. Ottawa, December.

Shen, Guobing, and Xiaolan Fu. 2014. "The Trade Effects of U.S. Antidumping Actions against China Post WTO Entry." *World Economy* 37: 86–104.

Sheu, Gloria. 2014. "Price, Quality, and Variety: Measuring the Gains from Trade in Differentiated Products." *American Economic Journal: Applied Economics* 6: 66–89.

Shin, Hyun Ja. 1998. "Possible Instances of Predatory Pricing in Recent U.S. Antidumping Cases." In Robert Z. Lawrence (ed.), *Brookings Trade Forum, 1998.* Washington, D.C.: Brookings Institution.

Shirk, Susan L. 1994. *How China Opened Its Door: The Political Success of the PRC's Foreign Trade and Investment Reforms.* Washington, D.C.: Brookings Institution.

Sivadasan, Jagadeesh. 2009. "Barriers to Entry and Productivity: Evidence from India." *B.E. Journal of Economic Analysis & Policy* 9, Article 42.

Smeltz, Dina S., and Craig Kafura. 2014. "A NAFTA's Platinum Anniversary, American Attitudes toward Cross-Border Ties." Chicago Council on Foreign Affairs, March.

Smith, Adam. [1776] 1976. *An Inquiry into the Nature and Causes of the Wealth of Nations*. Oxford: Clarendon Press.

———. 1977. *Correspondence of Adam Smith*. Oxford: Clarendon Press.

———. [1763] 1978. *Lectures on Jurisprudence*. Oxford: Clarendon Press.

———. 1980. *Essays on Philosophical Subjects*. Oxford: Clarendon Press.

Specter, Michael. 2008. "Big Foot." *New Yorker*. February 25.

Srinivasan, T. N. 1998. *Developing Countries and the Multilateral Trading System*. Boulder, Colo.: Westview Press.

Srinivasan, T. N., and Suresh Tendulkar. 2003. *Reintegrating India with the World Economy*. Washington, D.C.: Institute for International Economics.

Stolper, Wolfgang F., and Paul A. Samuelson. 1941. "Protection and Real Wages." *Review of Economic Studies* 9: 58–73.

Studwell, Joe. 2013. *How Asia Works: Success and Failure in the World's Most Dynamic Region*. New York: Grove Press.

Subramanian, Arvind, and Shang-Jin Wei. 2007. "The WTO Promotes Trade, Strongly but Unevenly." *Journal of International Economics* 72:151–75.

Sumaila, U. Rashid, Vicky Lam, Frédéric Le Manach, Wilf Swartz, and Daniel Pauly. 2013. "Global Fisheries Subsidies." European Parliament, Directorate-General for Internal Policies, Policy Department B: Structural and Cohesion Policies.

Sumner, Daniel A. 2006. "Reducing Cotton Subsidies: The DDA Initiative." In Kym Anderson and Will Martin (eds.), *Agricultural Trade Reform and the Doha Development Agenda*. Washington, D.C.: World Bank.

Suomela, John W. 1993. *Free Trade versus Fair Trade: The Making of American Trade Policy in a Political Environment*. Turku, Finland: Institute for European Studies.

Swinnen, Johan, Alessandro Olper, and Tjijs Vandemoortele. 2012. "Impact of the WTO on Agricultural and Food Policies." *World Economy* 35: 1089–101.

Sykes, Alan O. 1998. "Antidumping and Antitrust: What Problems Does Each Address?" In Robert Z. Lawrence (ed.), *Brookings Trade Forum, 1998*. Washington, D.C.: Brookings Institution.

———. 2003. "The Safeguards Mess: A Critique of WTO Jurisprudence." *World Trade Review* 2: 261–96.

Syverson, Chad. 2011. "What Determines Productivity?" *Journal of Economic Literature* 49: 326–65.

Taylor, Christopher T. 2004. "The Economic Effects of Withdrawn Antidumping Investigations: Is There Evidence of Collusive Settlements?" *Journal of International Economics* 62: 295–312.

Thorton, John L. 2008. "Long Time Coming: The Prospects for Democracy in China." *Foreign Affairs* 87: 17–26.

Tomz, Michael, Judith L. Goldstein, and Douglas Rivers. 2007. "Do We Really Know that the WTO Increases Trade? Comment." *American Economic Review* 97: 2005–18.

Tonelson, Alan. 1994. "Beating Back Predatory Trade." *Foreign Affairs* 73: 123–35.

Topalova, Petia, and Anit Khandelwal. 2011. "Trade Liberalization and Firm Productivity: The Case of India." *Review of Economics and Statistics* 93: 995–1009.

Tornell, Aaron. 1991. "Time Inconsistency of Protectionist Programs." *Quarterly Journal of Economics* 106: 963–74.

Tornell, Aaron, Frank Westermann, and Lorenza Martinez. 2004. "NAFTA and Mexico's Less-than-Stellar Performance." NBER Working Paper No. 10289, February.

Trefler, Daniel. 1993. "Trade Liberalization and the Theory of Endogenous Protection: An Econometric Study of U.S. Import Policy." *Journal of Political Economy* 101: 138–60.

———. 2004. "The Long and Short of the Canada-U.S. Free Trade Agreement." *American Economic Review* 94: 870–95.

Tullock, Gordon. 1975. "The Transitional Gains Trap." *Bell Journal of Economics* 6: 671–78.

Tybout, James R. 2003. "Plant and Firm Level Evidence on 'New' Trade Theories." In E. Kwan Choi and James Harrigan (eds.), *Handbook of International Trade*. New York: Basil Blackwell.

Tybout, James R., and M. Daniel Westbrook. 1995. "Trade Liberalization and the Dimensions of Efficiency Change in Mexican Manufacturing Industries." *Journal of International Economics* 39: 53–78.

United Nations. 1962. *Yearbook of International Trade Statistics 1960.* New York: United Nations.

United Nations Development Program. 2002. *Arab Human Development Report, 2002: Creating Opportunities for Future Generations.* New York: United Nations.

U.S. Bureau of the Census. 1975. *Historical Statistics of the United States, From Colonial Times to 1970.* Washington, D.C.: GPO.

———. 2008. *Statistical Abstract of the United States, 2008.* Washington, D.C.: GPO.

U.S. Department of Commerce. International Trade Administration. 2006. "Employment Changes in U.S. Sugar Manufacturing: The Impact of Sugar Prices." March. http://www.ita.doc.gov/media/Publications/pdf/sugar06.pdf.

U.S. Department of Commerce. Office of Inspector General. 1993. "Import Administration's Investigations of Steel Industry Petitions," Report No. TTD-5541-4-0001, December.

U.S. General Accounting Office. 1993. "Sugar Program: Changing Domestic and

International Conditions Require Program Changes." RCED/93/84. Washington, D.C.

———2000a. "Sugar Program: Supporting Sugar Prices Has Increased Users' Costs While Benefiting Producers." RCED/00/126. Washington, D.C., June.

———2000b. "World Trade Organization: Issues in Dispute Settlement." NSIAD-00–210. Washington, D.C..

———. 2003. "World Trade Organization: Standard of Review and Impact of Trade Remedy Rulings." GAO-03–824. Washington, D.C..

U.S. House of Representatives, Committee on Ways and Means. 1994. *Hearings: North American Free Trade Agreement (NAFTA) and Supplemental Agreements to the NAFTA.* Washington, D.C.: GPO.

———. 2003. *Greenbook.* Washington, D.C.: GPO.

———. 2013. *Compilation of U.S. Trade Statutes: 2013 Edition.* Committee Print 113–2. Washington, D.C.: GPO.

U.S. International Trade Commission. 1995. "The Economic Effects of Antidumping and Countervailing Duty Orders and Suspension Agreements." Investigation No. 332–344. Publication 2900. Washington, D.C., June.

———. 1997. "Likely Impact of Providing Quota-Free and Duty-Free Entry to Textiles and Apparel from Sub-Saharan Africa." Investigation 332–379. Publication 3056. Washington, D.C., September.

———. 1999. "Production Sharing: Use of U.S. Components and Materials in Foreign Assembly, Operations 1995–1999." USITC Publication 3265. Washington, D.C., December.

———. 2003. Steel Consuming Industries: Competitive Conditions with Respect to Steel Safeguard Measures. Volume III: Executive Summaries. Investigation No. 332–452. Publication 3632. Washington, D.C., September.

———. 2006. U.S.-Colombia Trade Promotion Agreement: Potential Economy-wide and Selected Sectoral Effects. Publication 3896. Washington, D.C., December.

———. 2007. "Steel Wire Garment Hangers from China." Investigation No. 731–TA–1123 (Preliminary). Publication 3951. Washington, D.C.

———. 2013. "The Economic Effects of Significant U.S. Import Restraints. Eighth Update 2013." Investigation No. 332–325. Publication 4440. Washington, D.C.

U.S. Trade Representative. 2000. "2000 Trade Policy Agenda and 1999 Annual Report." Washington, D.C.

Vandenbussche, Hylke, and Maurizio Zanardi. 2008. "What Explains the Proliferation of Antidumping Laws?" *Economic Policy* 23: 93–138.

Vandenbussche, Hylke, and Maurizio Zanardi, 2010. "The Chilling Trade Effects of Antidumping Proliferation." *European Economic Review* 54: 760–77.

Wacziarg, Romain. 2001. "Measuring the Dynamic Gains from Trade." *World Bank Economic Review* 15: 393–429.

Wacziarg, Romain, and Karen H. Welch. 2008. "Trade Liberalization and Growth: New Evidence." *World Bank Economic Review* 22: 187–231.

Wade, Robert. 2004. *Governing the Market: Economic Theory and the Role of Government in East Asian Industrialization*. Princeton: Princeton University Press.

Wallach, Lori, and Patrick Woodall. 2004. *Whose Trade Organization?* New York: New Press.

Warren, Cael, and Raymond Robertson. 2011. "Globalization, Wages, and Working Conditions: A Case Study of Cambodian Garment Factories." Center for Global Development Working Paper No. 257, June.

Watkins, Kevin. 2002. "Cultivating Poverty: The Impact of US Cotton Subsidies on Africa." Oxfam Briefing Paper No. 30, September.

Watson, James L. 1997. *Golden Arches East: McDonald's in East Asia*. Stanford: Stanford University Press.

Webb, J., Adrian G. Williams, Emma Hope, David Evans, and Ed Moorhouse. 2013. "Do Foods Imported into the UK Have Greater Environmental Impact than the Same Foods Produced within the UK?" *International Journal of Life Cycle Assessment* 18: 1325–43.

Wei, Shang-Jin, and Yi Wu. 2003. "The Life-and-Death Consequences of Globalization." International Monetary Fund Working Paper, June.

Westphal, Larry E. 1990. "Industrial Policy in an Export Propelled Economy: Lessons from South Korea's Experience." *Journal of Economic Perspectives* 4: 41–59.

Winters, L. Alan, and Won Chang. 2000. "Regional Integration and Import Prices: An Empirical Investigation." *Journal of International Economics* 51: 363–78.

Winters, L. Alan, Neil McCulloch, and Andrew McKay. 2004. "Trade Liberalization and Poverty: The Evidence So Far." *Journal of Economic Literature* 42: 72–115.

Wolf, Martin. 2004. *Why Globalization Works*. New Haven: Yale University Press.

Wolfe, Robert. 2015. "First Diagnose, Then Treat: What Ails the Doha Round?" *World Trade Review* 14: 7–28.

World Bank. 1975. *World Tables*. Baltimore: Johns Hopkins University Press.

———. 1993. *The East Asian Miracle: Economic Growth and Public Policy*. New York: Oxford University Press.

———. 1995. *World Tables*. Baltimore: Johns Hopkins University Press.

———. 2000. *World Development Indicators, 2000*. Washington, D.C.: World Bank.

———. 2001. *Global Economic Prospects and the Developing Countries*. Washington, D.C.: World Bank.

———. 2004. *Doing Business in 2004: Understanding Regulation*. Washington, D.C.: World Bank.

———. 2005a. *Economic Growth in the 1990s: Learning from a Decade of Reform*. Washington, D.C.: World Bank.

———. 2005b. *Global Economic Prospects: Trade, Regionalism, and Development*. Washington, D.C.: World Bank.

———. 2007. *Doing Business, 2008*. Washington, D.C.: World Bank.

World Bank. 2008a. *World Trade Indicators 2008: Benchmarking Policy and Performance.* Washington, D.C.: World Bank.

———. 2008b. *International Trade and Climate Change: Economic, Legal, and Institutional Perspectives.* Washington D.C.: World Bank.

———. 2011. *Perspectives on Poverty in India: Stylized Facts from Survey Data.* Washington D.C.: World Bank.

———. 2012. *Well Begun, Not Yet Done: Vietnam's Remarkable Progress on Poverty Reduction and the Emerging Challenges.* Hanoi: World Bank.

World Resources Institute. 1999. *World Resources.* Washington, D.C.: World Resources Institute.

World Trade Organization. 1997. "Report of the Panel: EC Measures Concerning Meat and Meat Products (Hormones), Complaint by the United States." WT/DS26/R/US. Geneva, August 18.

———. 1998. *Annual Report, 1998.* Geneva: WTO.

———. 1999. *The Legal Texts: The Results of the Uruguay Round of Multilateral Trade Negotiations.* New York: Cambridge University Press.

———. 2003. "International Trade Statistics, 2003." Geneva.

———. 2004. "Annual Report, 2004." Geneva, June.

———. 2012. "Trade Policy Review: United States." WT/TPR/S/275. Geneva, November.

———. 2013. *Annual Report, 2013.* Geneva: WTO.

———. 2014. "Trade Policy Review: United States." WT/TPR/S/307. Geneva, November.

Wu, Harry X. 2001. "China's Comparative Labour Productivity Performance in Manufacturing, 1952–1997 Catching Up or Falling Behind?" *China Economic Review* 12: 162–89.

Xing, Yuqing, and Neal Detert. 2010. "How the iPhone Widens the U.S. Trade Deficit with PRC." National Graduate Institute for Policy Studies Discussion Paper 10–21. Tokyo.

Yi, Kei-Mu. 2003. "Can Vertical Specialization Explain the Growth of World Trade?" *Journal of Political Economy* 112: 52–102.

Zanardi, Maurizio. 2006. "Antidumping: A Problem in International Trade." *European Journal of Political Economy* 22: 591–617.

Zoellick, Robert B. 2000. "A Republican Foreign Policy." *Foreign Affairs* 79: 63–78.

Index

141–145, 142n52, 144n57; the plight of workers displaced as a result of imports, 147–149; and the rise in average wages, 140–141; trade and the distribution of wages, 139–142, 142n50; and the wage gap between college and high school graduates (the "college premium"), 143, 143n54, 144; wage losses among tenured workers, 148; and the wages/productivity relationship, 137–139

Wallach, Lori, 2, 271n53
Watson, James L., 60n58
Wealth of Nations, The (Smith), 32–34, 33n2, 77–79, 79n5, 223–224
Western Europe, reliance on chemicals to boost agricultural yields, 70n79
Whaley, George, 295
Whose Trade Organization? (Public Citizen), 272
Williams, Adrian, 71
Wisconsin, 151
Wolf, Martin, 297
women: displacement of women in the workforce, 147, 147n65; income gains for, 198; women workers in sweatshops, 227
Woodall, Patrick, 271n53
Worker Rights Consortium, 222
workers. *See* labor/workers
World Bank, 211, 260, 281; and benchmark indicators of trade policy across the world, 58n50; on the high costs of business regulation in developing countries, 213n42; on the results of trade reform, 212–213; report on the East Asian economic miracle, 217
World Trade Organization (WTO), 165, 177, 214, 232, 236, 256, 259–263, 268n46, 282, 294; Agreement of on Antidumping, 170; Agreement on Safeguards, 187; and agricultural export taxes, 250; Appellate Body of, 176, 269, 273, 278; bashing of, 2; budget of (2013), 260; comparisons of to GATT, 259–260; and the controversial nature of the TRIPs agreement, 251–252; Doha Development Round of, 261–263; entry of China into (2001), 131, 184–185n44,

202; establishment of, 239, 247; and government subsidies for wind, solar, or hydro power, 302; as a "House of Litigation," 279–280; membership of, 262, 262n37; multilateral discussions at, 288–289; positive impact of on world trade, 254–255, 254n22; primary activities of, 261; protests in Seattle against (1999), 1, 261; size of, 260; staff of, 260; success of in stopping protectionism during the Great Recession, 258; and support for agricultural producers, 249n14; Technical Barriers to Trade (TBT) committee of, 265. *See also* World Trade Organization (WTO), dispute settlement process of; World Trade Organization (WTO), and environmental regulations
World Trade Organization (WTO), dispute settlement process of, 263–269, 263–264n39; cases brought by the United States against other countries, 266–267; complaints concerning the process, 268–269, 268n46; decisions of concerning safeguards, 268–269; limited role of the WTO in trade conflicts, 279–280, 280n67; number of dispute cases brought before the WTO (1995–2014), 265; types of disputes brought before, 266; and U.S. law, 267–268
World Trade Organization (WTO), and environmental regulations, 269–281, 270n52; and the EPA's ruling on contaminants in imported and domestic gasoline, 272–274, 273n58; and France's ban on asbestos imports, 271n55; and the relevance of GATT Article 20 ("General Exceptions"), 270–273, 271n55; and safe food supplies, 274–276
World War I, 61n60

Yale University, Singapore campus of, 16
Yamaha, 193–194
Yang, Cuhong, 68n76
Yi Qian, 251n18
Yugoslavia, 282

Zambia, 199
"zeroing," 169–170
Zoellick, Robert, 287